# MANUAL OF BUSIN  ·  FRENCH

The *Manual of Business French* is the essential companion for all who use French for business communication.

The *Manual* is divided into five sections covering all the requirements for business communication, whether written or spoken. Fully bilingual, the *Manual* is of equal value to the relative beginner or the fluent speaker.

Features include:
- 40 spoken situations, from booking a ticket to making a sales pitch
- 80 written communications covering memos, letters, faxes and résumés
- Facts and figures on the countries that use the language
- A handy summary of the main grammar points
- A 5000-word two-way glossary of the most common business terms

Written by an experienced native and non-native speaker team working in business language education, this unique *Manual of Business French* is an essential one-stop reference for all students and professionals studying or working in business and management where French is used.

**Stuart Williams** is Principal Lecturer at the School of Languages and European Studies of the University of Wolverhampton. **Nathalie McAndrew-Cazorla** works in corporate communications for an international bank.

In the same series

*French Business Situations**
Stuart Williams and Nathalie McAndrew-Cazorla

*German Business Situations**
Paul Hartley and Gertrud Robins

*Italian Business Situations**
Vincent Edwards and Gianfranca Gessa Shepheard

*Spanish Business Situations**
Michael Gorman and María-Luisa Henson

*Manual of Business German*
Paul Hartley and Gertrud Robins

*Manual of Business Italian*
Vincent Edwards and Gianfranca Gessa Shepheard

*Manual of Business Spanish*
Michael Gorman and María-Luisa Henson

*Accompanying cassettes available

# MANUAL OF BUSINESS FRENCH

## A comprehensive language guide

**Stuart Williams
and
Nathalie McAndrew-Cazorla**

**London and New York**

In the preparation of the Business Situations and Business Correspondence sections of this handbook every effort was made to avoid the use of actual company names or trade names. If any has been used inadvertently, the publishers will change it in any future reprint if they are notified.

First published 1996
by Routledge
11 New Fetter Lane, London EC4P 4EE

Simultaneously published in the USA and Canada
by Routledge
29 West 35th Street, New York, NY 10001

Reprinted 2002

*Routledge is an imprint of the Taylor & Francis Group*

© Stuart Williams and Nathalie McAndrew-Cazorla 1996

Typeset in Rockwell and Univers by Solidus (Bristol) Ltd
Printed in Great Britain by St Edmundsbury Press Ltd, Bury St Edmunds, Suffolk

*British Library Cataloguing in Publication Data*
A catalogue record for this book is available from the British Library

*Library of Congress Cataloging in Publication Data*
A catalogue record for this book has been requested

ISBN 0–415–09267–1 (hardback)
ISBN 0–415–12901–X (pbk)

# Contents

# Business Situations

# How to use the Business Situations

The spoken situations which follow are intended to cover a wide range of business interactions, from the brief and informal through to the more formal and prolonged exchange typical of the negotiating or interview situation. The user is encouraged not simply to read the situations together with their parallel English version, but to attempt, individually or in group work, with the help of the recording if applicable, the following exploitation exercises:

- using the original situations as models, construct dialogues on similar lines with the available vocabulary
- use the situations, or sections of them, as the basis for role-play exercises
- interpreting practice French/English, English/French
- practice in oral summary (i.e. listen to the recorded French version, and then summarize the content, in English or in French)
- oral paraphrase: listen to one version, then recount it using different expressions, but attempting to keep the same meaning
- transcription/dictation practice from the recording
- translation practice French/English, English/French

The material in the situations is intended as a basis for further expansion and exploitation, and is ideal for use in in-house training programmes, or in open learning centres, as well as for individual use.

# Première partie
## Section I

# Au téléphone
## On the telephone

# 1  Making an enquiry

## (a) Can I visit?

| | |
|---|---|
| *Maureen Simmons* | Good morning. Robinson's Motors. |
| *Mr Lewis* | Hello, my name is Lewis. I've just seen your advert for the Riva 25s available on fleet terms. We've been looking for half a dozen vehicles at the right price for a while and your offer interests us. |
| *Maureen Simmons* | Fine. Would you like me to send you more information? |
| *Mr Lewis* | No, thanks. I'd rather come down to your salesroom this afternoon with a colleague to discuss the matter with you. |
| *Maureen Simmons* | No problem, sir. My name is Maureen Simmons and I'll be available from 2.30. Can you give me your name again and your company, please? |
| *Mr Lewis* | Of course. It's Alan Lewis, from Stafford Electronics. I know where you are, so I'll be there for 2.30. See you then, goodbye. |
| *Maureen Simmons* | Thanks, see you later. |

## (b) Do you sell . . . ?

| | |
|---|---|
| *Telephonist* | Preece and Pritchard. Good morning. |
| *James Davies* | Good morning. Could you put me through to Sales? |
| *Telephonist* | Certainly. Just a moment. |
| *Assistant* | Sales, good morning. |
| *James Davies* | My name is James Davies, from Goodright Inc. I'm ringing to enquire if you sell water pumps? |
| *Assistant* | Yes, we do. Industrial and domestic. |
| *James Davies* | Can you send me a copy of your catalog and price list? |
| *Assistant* | Certainly, just give me your details. I'll get it off to you later today. |

# 1  Comment se renseigner

## (a) Puis-je venir vous rendre visite?

| | |
|---|---|
| *Marie Simon* | Bonjour. Automobiles Robinson. |
| *Alain Leroi* | Bonjour Madame, Monsieur Leroi à l'appareil. Je viens juste de voir votre annonce concernant la Riva 25 et plus particulièrement l'achat en nombre pour les entreprises. Cela fait déjà un certain temps que nous cherchions six véhicules à un prix intéressant et votre offre pourrait nous intéresser. |
| *Marie Simon* | Oui, très bien. Voudriez-vous que je vous fasse parvenir de plus amples informations concernant cette offre? |
| *Alain Leroi* | Non, merci. J'aurais préféré venir vous rendre visite avec un collègue dans vos locaux cet après-midi afin d'en discuter. |
| *Marie Simon* | Bien sûr, aucun problème. Je suis Marie Simon et je serai disponible à partir de 14h30. Pourriez-vous me redonner votre nom s'il vous plaît, ainsi que le nom de votre entreprise? |
| *Alain Leroi* | Bien sûr. Je suis Alain Leroi et il s'agit de l'entreprise Saumon Electronique SA. Je sais où vous vous situez et serai dans vos locaux à 14h30. A tout à l'heure. Merci. |
| *Marie Simon* | Je vous en prie,[1] au revoir. |

1   The usual rejoinder to *merci*; cf. 'You're welcome.'

## (b) Vendez-vous des . . . ?

| | |
|---|---|
| *Téléphoniste* | Perrault et Richard. Bonjour. |
| *Jean David* | Bonjour. Pourriez-vous me passer quelqu'un du service commercial s'il vous plaît? |
| *Téléphoniste* | Oui, bien sûr; veuillez patienter quelques instants. |
| *Employé* | Service commercial, bonjour. |
| *Jean David* | Jean David à l'appareil, de l'entreprise Bonne Voie SA. Je vous appelle pour savoir si vous vendez des pompes à eaux. |
| *Employé* | Oui, bien sûr. A utilisation industrielle et individuelle. |
| *Jean David* | Vous serait-il possible de m'envoyer un exemplaire de votre catalogue et vos tarifs? |
| *Employé* | Bien sûr. Si vous me donnez vos coordonnées, je vous les envoie aujourd'hui même. |

# 2  Ordering

## (a) Placing an order

| | |
|---|---|
| *Tracy* | DIY Stores, Tracy speaking. How can I help you? |
| *Customer* | I should like to order some plywood please. |
| *Tracy* | Certainly sir, please wait a moment while I put you through. |
| *Wood department* | Wood department. |
| *Customer* | I would like to order quite a large quantity of plywood. |
| *Wood department* | Certainly sir. Do you know what quality or can you tell me what it is for? |
| *Customer* | The purpose is to make shelving and the quality should be good enough to hold books. |
| *Wood department* | Right, then I would suggest three-ply 1½ cm thickness. How many metres do you want to order? |
| *Customer* | I need 150 metres. Is there a discount for quantity? |
| *Wood department* | There are progressive discounts from 50 metres. |
| *Customer* | Very good. I will give you my address and perhaps you can tell me when I can expect delivery and what invoicing procedure you operate. |

## (b) Changing an order

| | |
|---|---|
| *Colin Pine* | Please put me through to Steve Jones in Sales. . . . Hello, Steve. Colin here. I've had a think about what you suggested yesterday regarding the photocopier we ordered. We've decided to change our order from the CF202 to the FC302. I think that will meet our requirements better. Shall I send you a new order? |
| *Steve Jones* | That would be a good idea. And can you send it with a note cancelling the initial order? |
| *Colin Pine* | Yes, thanks. Bye. |

# 2  Commander

## (a)  Faire une commande

| | |
|---|---|
| *Tina* | Magasins Bricolage,[1] Tina à l'appareil. Puis-je vous aider? |
| *Client* | Je voudrais commander du contreplaqué s'il vous plaît. |
| *Tina* | Oui, veuillez patienter quelques instants s'il vous plaît, je vous passe la personne qui s'en occupe. |
| *Rayon bois*[2] | Rayon bois. |
| *Client* | J'aimerais commander une quantité relativement importante de contreplaqué. |
| *Rayon bois* | Oui, vous en connaissez la qualité , ou pouvez-vous me dire à quelle utilisation vous le destinez? |
| *Client* | C'est pour faire des étagères et la qualité doit pouvoir être assez bonne pour supporter des livres. |
| *Rayon bois* | Oui, alors je vous suggérerais de prendre du contreplaqué à trois couches et d'un centimètre et demi d'épaisseur. Combien de mètres en voulez-vous? |
| *Client* | J'aurai besoin de 150 mètres. Y a-t-il une remise pour les grandes quantités? |
| *Rayon bois* | Il y a des remises progressives à partir de 50 mètres. |
| *Client* | Très bien. Je vais vous donner mon adresse et peut-être pourrez-vous me dire quand je peux espérer la livraison et quelles sont vos modes de facturation. |

1  French for DIY is taken from the verb *bricoler* 'to make and mend'.
2  *Rayon* is the word for 'department' of a department store.

## (b)  Modifier une commande

| | |
|---|---|
| *Charles Prince* | Pourriez-vous me passer Sasha Jarre du service commercial. . . . Bonjour Sasha, Charles à l'appareil. J'ai repensé à ce que vous m'avez suggéré hier au sujet de la photocopieuse que nous avons commandée. Nous avons décidé de modifier notre commande et voudrions le modèle FC302 au lieu du CF202. Je pense qu'il sera plus approprié à nos besoins. Voulez-vous que je vous envoie un nouveau bon de commande? |
| *Sasha Jarre* | Cela serait une bonne idée. Pourriez-vous également m'envoyer une notification écrite de l'annulation de votre première commande? |
| *Charles Prince* | Entendu. Merci. Au revoir. |

# (c) Cancelling an order

| | |
|---|---|
| *Store manageress* | Hello, Sandhu's Wholesale. |
| *Client* | Morning. It's Mrs Wilson here, of Lomas Supermarket. I'm ever so sorry, but my brother has got our order wrong this week. Do you mind if we change it over the phone? |
| *Store manageress* | No, madam, as long as there's nothing perishable that we've had to order specially. Can you give me the order number? |
| *Client* | Yes, it's SCC231. We only put it in three days ago and it's all packaged catering goods. All we want to do is cancel the soft drinks and the cereals, and have instead another 15 large boxes of Mercury. Do you think that's possible? |
| *Store manageress* | I've found the order and the invoice. We can change that before you call tomorrow and I'll make you out another bill. Will you pay on the spot? |
| *Client* | Yes, by cheque as usual. Thanks for your help. Goodbye. |

# (d) Confirming receipt of an order

| | |
|---|---|
| *Telephonist* | Klapp and Weaver. Good morning. |
| *Julie Little* | Morning. Can I speak to Mr Preece, please? |
| *Telephonist* | Yes, putting you through now. Thank you. |
| *George Preece* | Hello, Preece here. |
| *Julie Little* | Morning Mr Preece. Julie Little here. I'm ringing to confirm receipt of our order number B/397/386. |
| *George Preece* | The radial tyres? |
| *Julie Little* | Yes, that's the one. They arrived today. You asked me to confirm receipt as soon as possible. |
| *George Preece* | Well, thanks for getting back to me. |
| *Julie Little* | We'll settle your invoice in the next few days. |
| *George Preece* | Fine. Thanks for ringing. Goodbye. |
| *Julie Little* | Goodbye. |

# (c) Annuler une commande

| | |
|---|---|
| *Gérante du magasin* | Bonjour, Vente en gros Sagan. |
| *Cliente* | Bonjour. Mme Villeneuve à l'appareil, Supermarché Lamartine. Je suis vraiment désolée mais mon frère a fait une erreur cette semaine en passant notre commande. Cela vous ennuierait-il de faire la modification par téléphone? |
| *Gérante du magasin* | Non madame, à partir du moment où il ne s'agit pas de produits périssables qu'il nous fallait commander spécialement. Pourriez-vous me donner le numéro de votre commande? |
| *Cliente* | Oui, bien sûr, c'est le SCC231. Il y a seulement trois jours que nous avons passé cette commande et il ne s'agit que de produits alimentaires conditionnés. Tout ce que nous voulons, c'est annuler les boissons non alcoolisées et les céréales et recevoir en échange 15 grandes boîtes de Mercure. Est-ce que vous pensez que ce sera possible? |
| *Gérante du magasin* | J'ai trouvé la commande et la facture. Nous pouvons changer tout cela avant que vous veniez demain et je vous ferai une nouvelle facture. Pourrez-vous payer tout de suite? |
| *Cliente* | Oui, par chèque comme d'habitude. Merci beaucoup. Au revoir. |

# (d) Confirmer une commande

| | |
|---|---|
| *Téléphoniste* | Claude et Tisserand. Bonjour. |
| *Juliette Legrand* | Bonjour. Puis-je parler à M. Perle s'il vous plaît? |
| *Téléphoniste* | Oui, ne quittez pas[1] s'il vous plaît, merci. |
| *Georges Perle* | Bonjour, M. Perle à l'appareil. |
| *Juliette Legrand* | Bonjour M. Perle. Juliette Legrand à l'appareil. Je vous appelle pour vous dire que nous avons bien reçu notre commande n° B/397/386. |
| *Georges Perle* | Les pneus à carcasse radiale? |
| *Juliette Legrand* | Oui, c'est cela. Ils sont arrivés aujourd'hui. Vous m'aviez demandé de vous appeler dès que je les aurais. |
| *Georges Perle* | Merci beaucoup de m'avoir appelé. |
| *Juliette Legrand* | Nous réglerons votre facture[2] d'ici quelques jours. |
| *Georges Perle* | Très bien. Merci. Au revoir. |
| *Juliette Legrand* | Au revoir. |

1 Literally, 'do not leave', i.e. 'hold the line'.
2 'We will settle your invoice.'

# (e) Clarifying details of an order

| | |
|---|---|
| *Edward* | Good afternoon, DIY Stores, Edward speaking. |
| *Customer* | Hello, I am ringing about an order I made on the 27th. My name is Jones. |
| *Edward* | Just a moment . . . Mr B. Jones, 24 litres of paint to be delivered on the 4th? |
| *Customer* | Yes, that's the order but I would like to change one or two details if I may. |
| *Edward* | Certainly sir. Go ahead. |
| *Customer* | I originally ordered 6 litres of eggshell blue matt, I would like to change that to sky blue vinyl silk. Is that OK? |
| *Edward* | Yes that is all right. We have it in stock. Anything else? |
| *Customer* | Just the delivery address. Could you deliver the paint to the site, 34 Western Way, on the 4th as agreed? |
| *Edward* | No problem, sir. |

# (e) Clarifier certains éléments d'une commande

*Edouard*     Magasins Bricolage, bonjour, M. Edouard à l'appareil.

*Client*      Bonjour, j'appelle au sujet d'une commande que j'ai faite le 27. Je suis M. Joffe.

*Edouard*     Attendez une seconde ... M. B. Joffe, 24 litres de peinture devant être livrés le 4?

*Client*      Oui, c'est bien la commande mais j'aimerais changer un ou deux détails si je le peux.

*Edouard*     Mais bien sûr. Allez-y, je vous écoute.

*Client*      J'ai tout d'abord commandé 6 litres de peinture, coquille d'œuf bleu mat, et j'aimerais les remplacer par une peinture vinylique bleu ciel. Est-ce que c'est possible?

*Edouard*     Oui, bien sûr, c'est tout à fait possible. Nous en avons en stock. Y a-t-il autre chose?

*Client*      Simplement l'adresse à laquelle la commande doit être livrée. Vous serait-il possible de livrer la peinture sur le chantier,[1] 34 Western Way, le 4 comme convenu?

*Edouard*     Aucun problème, Monsieur.

1   *Chantier* can be used for any work site, building site, etc.

# 3  Making an appointment

| | |
|---|---|
| *Receptionist* | Good morning, Chiltern International. Can I help you? |
| *Paul Wignall* | Good morning, I would like to speak to Mrs Mills's secretary. |
| *Receptionist* | One moment, please. |
| *Secretary* | Sue Jones. |
| *Paul Wignall* | Good morning, Ms Jones. My name is Wignall, from Whitnash Industries. I shall be in your area next week and would like to discuss product developments with Mrs Mills. Tuesday or Wednesday would suit me best. |
| *Secretary* | Please hold on and I'll check Mrs Mills's diary. She could see you Wednesday morning at 10. |
| *Paul Wignall* | That would be fine. Thank you very much. |
| *Secretary* | You're welcome. |
| *Paul Wignall* | Goodbye. |
| *Secretary* | Goodbye. |

# 3 Prendre rendez-vous

| | |
|---|---|
| *Réceptionniste* | Chartres International, bonjour. Puis-je vous aider?[1] |
| *Paul Vincent* | Bonjour, j'aimerais parler à la secrétaire de Mme Millais s'il vous plaît. |
| *Réceptionniste* | Oui, un instant s'il vous plaît. |
| *Secrétaire* | Suzanne Gérard à l'appareil. |
| *Paul Vincent* | Bonjour Mme Gérard. Je suis M. Vincent de Villefranche SA. Je serai dans votre région la semaine prochaine et j'aimerais discuter du développement des produits avec Mme Millais. Mardi ou mercredi me conviendraient le mieux. |
| *Secrétaire* | Attendez un instant s'il vous plaît. Je vérifie dans l'agenda de Mme Millais. Elle pourrait vous voir mercredi matin à 10h00. |
| *Paul Vincent* | Ce sera parfait. Merci beaucoup. |
| *Secrétaire* | Je vous en prie. |
| *Paul Vincent* | Au revoir. |
| *Secrétaire* | Au revoir. |

1 Alternative: 'Que puis-je faire pour vous?'

# 4 Invitation to attend a meeting

| | |
|---|---|
| *Secretary* | Hello, Mr Anguita? |
| *Director* | Yes, speaking. |
| *Secretary* | Julia Clemente here. I'm secretary to Lucía Ordóñez, public relations manager at Agencia Rosell, Barcelona. |
| *Director* | Oh, yes. We met last month at the trade fair in Tarragona. She mentioned that your agency could perhaps assist my company. |
| *Secretary* | That's right. Well, since then she has been in touch with a number of local firms who wish to set up joint projects elsewhere in Europe. A meeting is scheduled for Tuesday, 6 October, at our offices here in Barcelona. She has written to invite you. I'm ringing now to give you advance warning. |
| *Director* | That's very kind. I'll check my diary and either way I'll get my secretary to ring you before the weekend. Will you thank Ms Ordóñez and tell her I hope I will be able to make it on the 6th? |
| *Secretary* | I will. Thank you, Mr Anguita. By the way, our number is 3516784. |
| *Director* | Sorry, I nearly forgot to ask you! Right. Send her my regards, and thanks again. Goodbye. |
| *Secretary* | Good afternoon. |

# 4 Invitation à participer à une réunion

| | |
|---|---|
| *Secrétaire* | Bonjour, Monsieur Anguita? |
| *Directeur* | Oui, moi-même. |
| *Secrétaire* | Julia Clémente à l'appareil. Je suis la secrétaire de Lucía Ordóñez, directrice des relations publiques à Agencia Rosell à Barcelone. |
| *Directeur* | Ah, oui. Nous nous sommes rencontrés le mois dernier lors du salon professionnel à Tarragone. Elle m'a fait savoir que votre agence pourrait peut-être aider mon entreprise. |
| *Secrétaire* | Oui, c'est bien cela. Eh bien depuis, elle est entrée en contact avec plusieurs entreprises de la région qui désirent entreprendre des démarches communes dans d'autres pays européens. Une réunion devrait avoir lieu mardi 6 octobre ici, dans nos bureaux de Barcelone. Elle vous a écrit pour vous inviter à y participer et je vous téléphone pour vous en prévenir à l'avance. |
| *Directeur* | C'est très gentil. Je vais vérifier mon agenda et quelle que soit ma réponse, je demanderai à ma secrétaire de vous téléphoner avant le week-end prochain. Remerciez Madame Ordóñez et dites-lui[1] que j'espère vraiment pouvoir venir le 6. |
| *Secrétaire* | Je le lui dirai. Merci, Monsieur Anguita. Je vous donne notre numéro de téléphone ici, c'est le 35 17 784. |
| *Directeur* | Ah oui, j'aurais presque oublié de vous le demander. Bon, transmettez-lui mes meilleurs salutations et merci encore. Au revoir. |
| *Secrétaire* | Je vous en prie. Au revoir. |

1 *Lui* – 'to her' as well as 'to him'.

# 5  Apologizing for non-attendance

## (a) At a future meeting

| | |
|---|---|
| *Nancy Richards* | Nancy Richards. |
| *Bill Perkins* | Morning, Nancy. Bill Perkins here. |
| *Nancy Richards* | Hello, Bill, how are you? |
| *Bill Perkins* | Fine thanks. Look, I've just received notice of the meeting for the Sales Department next Tuesday. |
| *Nancy Richards* | Yes, is there a problem? |
| *Bill Perkins* | Afraid so. I'll have to send my apologies. I'm already committed to a trade fair trip. |
| *Nancy Richards* | OK. I'll pass on your apologies. Can you send someone else? |
| *Bill Perkins* | I've a colleague who can probably come. Her name is Susie Rogerson. She'll contact you later today. |
| *Nancy Richards* | Fine. Well, have a nice trip. I'll see you when you get back. |

# 5   Se faire excuser de ne pas pouvoir assister

## (a) A une réunion ultérieure

| | |
|---|---|
| *Nadine Richard* | Allô, Nadine Richard à l'appareil. |
| *Bernard Péguy* | Bonjour Nadine. C'est Bernard Péguy. |
| *Nadine Richard* | Bonjour Bernard, comment allez-vous? |
| *Bernard Péguy* | Très bien, merci. Je viens juste d'apprendre qu'il y aura une réunion pour le service commercial mardi. |
| *Nadine Richard* | Oui. Y-a-t-il un problème? |
| *Bernard Péguy* | Oui, j'en ai peur. Il faudra que vous m'excusiez mais je me suis déjà engagé et dois me rendre à un salon professionnel. |
| *Nadine Richard* | D'accord. Je transmettrai. Quelqu'un d'autre pourrait-il vous représenter? |
| *Bernard Péguy* | J'ai une collègue qui pourrait probablement venir. Il s'agit de Suzanne Roger. Elle vous contactera plus tard aujourd'hui. |
| *Nadine Richard* | Très bien. Bon, faites bon voyage. Je vous verrai lors de votre retour. |

# (b) At a meeting that has already been held

| | |
|---|---|
| *George Parsons* | Could you put me through to the Managing Director please. |
| *Secretary* | Certainly, sir. One moment please. |
| *Henry Sachs* | Hello, George. We missed you yesterday. |
| *George Parsons* | I am calling to apologize. I didn't write because I intended to come and was prevented at the last moment. |
| *Henry Sachs* | I gather there's a spot of bother in the Gulf. |
| *George Parsons* | Oh, you've heard. Bad news travels fast. Yes, we have a container ship on its way and rumours of war at its destination. |
| *Henry Sachs* | What will you do? Send it somewhere else pro tem? |
| *George Parsons* | Yes, but don't worry – I'll sort it out. Meanwhile how did your 'do' go? |
| *Henry Sachs* | Very well. All the important people came. Barry Clerkenwell from the BOTB was asking for you. I said you'd give him a bell. |
| *George Parsons* | Will do. I'm really sorry that I couldn't make it. |

# (b) A une réunion qui a déjà eu lieu

| | |
|---|---|
| *Georges Poisson* | Pourriez-vous me passer le directeur général s'il vous plaît? |
| *Secrétaire* | Bien sûr, Monsieur. Veuillez patienter quelques instants s'il vous plaît. |
| *Henri Sachs* | Bonjour Georges. Tu nous as manqué[1] hier. |
| *Georges Poisson* | Je te demande de m'excuser. Je n'ai pas écrit car je pensais vraiment pouvoir venir mais j'ai eu un empêchement de dernière minute. |
| *Henri Sachs* | J'ai cru comprendre que le Golfe est à la source de quelques soucis. |
| *Georges Poisson* | Ah, tu es au courant.[2] Les mauvaises nouvelles se répandent vite. Oui, nous avons un porte-conteneurs en route, et il y a rumeur de guerre à destination. |
| *Henri Sachs* | Que vas-tu faire? L'envoyer ailleurs temporairement? |
| *Georges Poisson* | Oui mais ne t'inquiète pas. Je résoudrai ce problème. Et pour toi, comment s'est passée ta soirée? |
| *Henri Sachs* | Très bien. Toutes les personnes importantes étaient présentes. Thierry Maréchal du Ministère m'a demandé de tes nouvelles. Je lui ai dit que tu lui passerais un coup de fil.[3] |
| *Georges Poisson* | Je le ferai. Je suis vraiment désolé de ne pas avoir pu venir. |

1  Literally, *you were lacking to us.*
2  To be *au courant* (*de quelque chose*) means 'to be informed'. The familiar *tu* forms are being used by these friends.
3  Colloquial language (*langage parlé*). Cf. 'give him a bell'.

# 6  Making a complaint

| | |
|---|---|
| *Max Russell* | May I speak to the Service Department, please. |
| *Assistant* | Hello, Service Department. |
| *Max Russell* | Hello, my name's Russell, from Littleborough Plant & Equipment. Item IP/234 was ordered by us two weeks ago and has still not been delivered. I rang on Wednesday and was promised delivery by 5 p.m. yesterday. We still haven't received the part. |
| *Assistant* | I'm sorry, Mr Russell, let me check . . . I'm afraid the part still hasn't come in to us. It's still on order from the manufacturer. |
| *Max Russell* | Look, I'm not interested in all that. I just want to know when we'll get the part. I stand to lose a good customer if I don't repair his machinery. If I don't get the part today, I'll go to another supplier. |
| *Assistant* | I'll chase up the manufacturer and see what I can do. I'll get back to you by 1 o'clock and let you know what the situation is. |

# 6  Se plaindre[1]

| | |
|---|---|
| *Max Roussel* | Pourrais-je parler au service clientèle s'il vous plaît? |
| *Assistant* | Service clientèle, bonjour. |
| *Max Roussel* | Bonjour. Je suis M. Roussel de Equipement et Matériel Longchamps. Nous avons commandé, voici deux semaines l'article IP/234 et il n'a toujours pas été livré. J'ai téléphoné mercredi et on m'a promis une livraison hier à 17h00 au plus tard. Nous n'avons toujours pas reçu cette pièce. |
| *Assistant* | Je suis désolé, M. Roussel, attendez, je vérifie . . . Je suis désolé mais nous n'avons nous-mêmes toujours pas reçu cette pièce. Elle est toujours en commande chez le fabricant. |
| *Max Roussel* | Ecoutez, cela ne m'intéresse pas. Tout ce que je veux savoir c'est quand j'aurai cette pièce. Je risque de perdre un très bon client si je ne répare pas sa machine. Si je n'ai pas reçu ce qui me manque cet après-midi, j'irai le chercher chez un autre fournisseur! |
| *Assistant* | Je vais rappeler le fabricant et voir ce que je peux faire. Je vous rappelle avant 13h00 pour vous faire connaître la situation. |

1  Note this is a reflexive verb – *je me plains*, and so on.

# 7  Reminder for payment

| | |
|---|---|
| *Tardy customer* | Good day. Des Morrison speaking. |
| *Supplier* | Hello, Mr Morrison. It's Bankstown Mouldings here. Did you receive a letter from us last week reminding you about the outstanding account you have with us? |
| *Tardy customer* | No, can't say I've seen it. Mind you, that's no surprise when you see the state of this office. We've just moved from the middle of town. |
| *Supplier* | Oh. I didn't know that. Well, it's an invoice for $2,356 which we sent out on 17 April; it probably arrived on 19 or 20 April. |
| *Tardy customer* | Can you remind me what it was for? |
| *Supplier* | Of course. We supplied you in March with several hundred wood and plastic ceiling fittings for the houses you were working on at the time. The invoice code is QZ163P. |
| *Tardy customer* | OK. I'll ask my wife to have a good look for it. In the meantime, could you send me a copy so that we can pay up at the end of the month even if we can't trace the original? |
| *Supplier* | That's no problem. I'll fax it to you this afternoon if you have a machine. |
| *Tardy customer* | No way. I haven't seen ours since we moved! Send it by post to this address: Unit 12, Trading Estate, Pacific Highway. We'll settle up as soon as we get it. Sorry for the hassle. |
| *Supplier* | I'll post a copy today, and rely on you to keep your word. |

# 7  Rappel de règlement dû

| | |
|---|---|
| *Client en retard de paiement* | Bonjour. Daniel Montand à l'appareil. |
| *Fournisseur* | Bonjour, M. Montand. Société Moulages Lebrun à l'appareil. Avez-vous reçu notre lettre la semaine dernière vous rappelant que votre compte chez nous est arriéré? |
| *Client* | Non, je ne peux pas dire que je l'aie vue. Remarquez, il n'y a rien de surprenant quand on regarde l'état de ce bureau. Nous venons juste de déménager du centre ville. |
| *Fournisseur* | Ah, je ne le savais pas. C'est une facture d'un montant de 2 356 dollars que nous vous avons envoyée le 17 avril; elle vous est probablement parvenue le 19 ou le 20. |
| *Client* | Pouvez-vous me rappeler ce qu'elle représentait? |
| *Fournisseur* | Bien sûr. Nous vous avons fourni en mars plusieurs centaines d'installations en bois et en plastique pour les plafonds des maisons sur lesquelles vous travailliez à l'époque. Le numéro de la facture est QZ163P. |
| *Client* | Entendu, je vais demander à ma femme de la chercher. En attendant, pourriez-vous m'en envoyer une copie afin que je puisse vous payer à la fin du mois au cas où je ne retrouve pas l'original? |
| *Fournisseur* | Mais tout à fait. Je vous la télécopierai cet après midi. Vous avez un télécopieur? |
| *Client* | Non, ce n'est pas une bonne idée. Je n'ai pas revu notre machine depuis que nous avons déménagé. Envoyez-la à cette adresse: Atelier numéro 12, Zone Industrielle de la Loire, 44 000 Nantes. Nous vous réglerons dès réception. Désolé de vous avoir causé du tracas. |
| *Fournisseur* | Bon, je vous envoie une copie maintenant et espère pouvoir vous faire confiance.[1] |

1  *Faire confiance à quelqu'un* – literally, 'to trust someone'.

# 8  Enquiry about hotel accommodation

| | |
|---|---|
| *Telephonist* | Good morning, Hotel Brennan. Can I help you? |
| *Customer* | Hello. Can you put me through to Reservations? |
| *Telephonist* | Certainly. Putting you through now. |
| *Reservations desk* | Reservations. |
| *Customer* | Morning. Could you tell me if you have a double room free from 14 to 16 May, or from 18 to 20 May? |
| *Reservations desk* | Just a moment. I'll check for you. Yes, we do. On both dates. |
| *Customer* | Could you tell me the price? |
| *Reservations desk* | The price per night, with bath and including breakfast, is £160. That includes service and VAT. Do you want to make a reservation? |
| *Customer* | I'll get back to you on it. Thank you. Goodbye. |
| *Reservations desk* | Goodbye. |

# 8  Demande de renseignements au sujet de chambres d'hôtel

| | |
|---|---|
| *Téléphoniste* | Hôtel Brennan. Bonjour. Puis-je vous aider? |
| *Client* | Bonjour. Pouvez-vous me passer le service réservations s'il vous plaît? |
| *Téléphoniste* | Bien sûr. Patientez quelques instants s'il vous plaît. |
| *Service des réservations* | Service des réservations. |
| *Client* | Bonjour. Pouvez-vous me dire si vous avez une chambre double disponible du 14 au 16 mai ou du 18 au 20? |
| *Service des réservations* | Patientez une seconde s'il vous plaît. Je vérifie. Oui, c'est bon dans les deux cas. |
| *Client* | Pouvez vous m'indiquer vos prix? |
| *Service des réservations* | C'est 1 312 francs par nuit avec salle de bains, petit déjeuner compris. Service et TVA[1] sont également compris. Voulez-vous faire une réservation? |
| *Client* | Je vous rappelle. Merci beaucoup. Au revoir. |
| *Service des réservations* | Au revoir. |

1   Short for *taxe à la valeur ajoutée*.

# 9  Changing an appointment

| | |
|---|---|
| *Susana López* | Hello. May I speak to Elena Aznar? |
| *Elena Aznar* | Yes, that's me. How can I help you? |
| *Susana López* | This is Susana López. I rang yesterday to see if I could visit the Ministry on Friday to discuss with your staff the new plans for tax reforms in the recent Budget. Unfortunately, my boss has just told me that the time we fixed is no good as I have to attend an urgent meeting with him. Could we possibly change our appointment? |
| *Elena Aznar* | I'm sorry that's happened, but don't worry. When do you think you can come? |
| *Susana López* | Any chance of the following week, maybe Tuesday afternoon? |
| *Elena Aznar* | It is not possible, I'm afraid. How about Thursday at about 10.30? All the key staff should be here then. |
| *Susana López* | If you can give me a moment, I'll check. . . . Yes, that's fine as long as you don't mind me leaving by 1 p.m. – my boss has to fly to the States in the afternoon. |
| *Elena Aznar* | That will suit us. When you arrive, please inform the security staff and they will direct you to the relevant department, which is on the fourth floor. OK? |
| *Susana López* | Many thanks for being so helpful. Looking forward to seeing you on the 8th. |
| *Elena Aznar* | Me too. Goodbye. |

# 9  Reporter[1] un rendez-vous

| | |
|---|---|
| *Susana López* | Bonjour. Puis-je parler à Elena Aznar s'il vous plaît? |
| *Elena Aznar* | Oui, elle-même. Que puis-je faire pour vous? |
| *Susana López* | Je suis Susana López. J'ai téléphoné hier pour voir si je pouvais me rendre[2] au Ministère vendredi afin de discuter avec votre personnel des nouveaux projets de réforme fiscale annoncés dans le dernier budget. Malheureusement, mon directeur vient juste de me dire que le rendez-vous que j'ai pris ne convient pas car je dois assister à une importante réunion avec lui. Pourrions-nous changer l'heure de ce rendez-vous?[3] |
| *Elena Aznar* | Je suis désolée que vous ayez cet empêchement, mais ne vous inquiétez pas. Quand pensez-vous pouvoir venir? |
| *Susana López* | Y a-t-il une possibilité pour la semaine prochaine? Peut-être mardi après-midi? |
| *Elena Aznar* | Je ne crois pas, non ce n'est pas possible. Et jeudi à 10h30? Tout le personnel-clé devrait alors être disponible. |
| *Susana López* | Patientez un instant s'il vous plaît. Je vais vérifier. . . . Oui, c'est bon à partir du moment où vous n'avez pas d'objection à ce que je parte à 13h00 – mon directeur doit partir pour les États-Unis l'après-midi même. |
| *Elena Aznar* | Ce n'est pas grave du tout. Lorsque vous arriverez, veuillez en informer la sécurité et ils vous dirigeront vers le bon service qui se trouve au quatrième étage, d'accord? |
| *Susana López* | Très bien. Merci beaucoup. Au plaisir de vous revoir le 8. |
| *Elena Aznar* | Je vous en prie. Au revoir. |

1  Literally, 'to postpone'.
2  *Se rendre à* – literally, 'to go to'.
3  Note the clear distinction, as in English, between *rendez-vous* 'appointment' and *réunion* 'meeting'.

# 10  Informing of a late arrival

| | |
|---|---|
| *James Kennon* | James Kennon. |
| *Paul Alexander* | Morning James, Paul here. |
| *James Kennon* | Hi, Paul. How are things? |
| *Paul Alexander* | Not too good. I'm still at Heathrow – the flight has been delayed. |
| *James Kennon* | So you'll be late for the meeting. |
| *Paul Alexander* | Afraid so! I'm now due to arrive at Düsseldorf at 11.15. I should be with you about 12. |
| *James Kennon* | Don't worry. We'll push the start of the meeting back to 11.30 and take the less important agenda items first. |
| *Paul Alexander* | Fine. Thanks for that. Look, I have to go – they've just called the flight. |
| *James Kennon* | OK. See you later. Bye. |
| *Paul Alexander* | Bye. |

# 11  Ordering a taxi

| | |
|---|---|
| *Taxi firm* | Hello. |
| *Client* | Hello, is that A & B Taxis? |
| *Taxi firm* | Yes, sir. What can I do for you? |
| *Client* | I would like a cab straightaway to take our Sales Manager to the airport. |
| *Taxi firm* | Birmingham Airport? |
| *Client* | Yes, the new Eurohub. It's quite urgent. He has to check in in 35 minutes. |
| *Taxi firm* | Don't worry we'll get him there. Give me your address and a cab will be with you in 5 minutes. |

# 10  Prévenir d'une arrivée tardive

| | |
|---|---|
| *Jean Cardin* | Allô? Jean Cardin à l'appareil. |
| *Paul Alexandre* | Bonjour Jean. C'est Paul à l'appareil. |
| *Jean Cardin* | Salut Paul. Comment vas-tu? |
| *Paul Alexandre* | Cela pourrait aller mieux. Je suis toujours à Toulouse – le vol a du retard. |
| *Jean Cardin* | Alors tu seras en retard à la réunion? |
| *Paul Alexandre* | J'en ai bien peur! Je devrais maintenant arriver à Paris à 11h15 et être à ton bureau aux environs de midi. |
| *Jean Cardin* | Ne t'inquiète pas. Nous allons retarder le début de la réunion. Nous commencerons vers 11h30 et les points les moins importants de l'ordre du jour seront traités d'abord. |
| *Paul Alexandre* | OK. Merci beaucoup. Bon, il faut que j'y aille.[1] Ils viennent juste d'annoncer le vol. |
| *Jean Cardin* | OK. A tout à l'heure. Au revoir. |
| *Paul Alexandre* | Au revoir. |

1  Subjunctive after *il faut que* and *y* for 'to there' – 'I have to go'.

# 11  Demander un taxi

| | |
|---|---|
| *Taxis* | Bonjour. |
| *Client* | Bonjour. Je suis bien chez les Taxis A et B? |
| *Taxis* | Oui, Monsieur. Que puis-je faire pour vous? |
| *Client* | Je voudrais un taxi tout de suite pour emmener notre directeur des ventes à l'aéroport, s'il vous plaît. |
| *Taxis* | L'aéroport de Paris? |
| *Client* | Oui, Charles de Gaulle. C'est très urgent car il doit s'y présenter dans 35 minutes. |
| *Taxis* | Ne vous inquiétez pas. Nous ferons en sorte qu'il y soit.[1] Donnez-moi votre adresse et un taxi sera chez vous dans 5 minutes. |

1  *En sorte que* means 'in such a way that' (he gets there).

# 12  Checking flight information

| | |
|---|---|
| *Travel agent* | Russell's Travel, good morning. |
| *Customer* | Could you confirm my travel details for me, please? |
| *Travel agent* | Certainly sir. Do you have your ticket? Can you give me the date of departure and the flight number? |
| *Customer* | I am travelling on flight EA739 to Prague next Wednesday and then on to Bratislava the next day. |
| *Travel agent* | Flight EA739 leaves Heathrow at 11.35 a.m. and arrives in Prague at 15.05. Flight CZ417 leaves Prague at 16.30 and gets to Bratislava at 17.20. Is it an open ticket? |
| *Customer* | No, it's an Apex ticket. |
| *Travel agent* | That's fine, then. You must check in one hour before departure. |
| *Customer* | Thank you very much for your help. |
| *Travel agent* | Don't mention it. |

# 12  Vérifier l'horaire d'un vol

| | |
|---|---|
| *Agence de voyage* | Agence Roland, bonjour. |
| *Client* | Bonjour. Pourriez-vous vérifier la réservation de mon vol, s'il vous plaît? |
| *Agence de voyage* | Oui, bien sûr Monsieur. Avez-vous votre billet? Pouvez-vous me dire quand vous partez et le numéro de votre vol? |
| *Client* | Je dois prendre le vol EA739 pour Prague mercredi prochain et le lendemain je dois aller à Bratislava. |
| *Agence de voyage* | Le vol EA739 part de Heathrow à 11h35 et arrive à Prague à 15h05. Le vol CZ417 quitte Prague à 16h30 et arrive à Bratislava à 17h20. Est-ce un vol open? |
| *Client* | Non c'est un billet Apex. |
| *Agence de voyage* | Alors c'est bon. Vous devrez faire enregistrer vos bagages une heure avant le départ. |
| *Client* | Merci beaucoup. |
| *Agence de voyage* | Je vous en prie. |

# 13 Booking a flight

| | |
|---|---|
| *Customer* | Hello. Sunline Air Services? |
| *Airline clerk* | Yes, madam. This is Everton Frith. Can I help you? |
| *Customer* | Thank you. My name is Robertson. I'd like to book a direct flight to Antigua. How many times a week do you offer Luxury Class travel on your flights? |
| *Airline clerk* | There are departures from London each Monday afternoon and Thursday morning. Obviously, there are flights on other days with different airlines, but our tariffs are very competitive. |
| *Customer* | Yes, that's what they told me at the travel agency, but I wanted to check for myself. Could you quote me for two return tickets leaving on Thursday, 7 May? |
| *Airline clerk* | Can we first check flight availability and then look again at prices? |
| *Customer* | Yes, fine. So how does the 7th look? |
| *Airline clerk* | On the 9.30 departure there are several pairs of seats available still; for your return journey you can make arrangements at the other end. Shall I pass you over to my colleague, Janet, who can deal with everything else, including your personal details, form of payment and delivery of tickets to you. |
| *Customer* | Thank you for your help. |
| *Airline clerk* | My pleasure. Hold on and I'll put you through to her. Goodbye. |

# 13  Réserver un vol

| | |
|---|---|
| *Cliente* | Allô. Suis-je bien chez Avions du Soleil? |
| *Compagnie aérienne* | Oui, Madame. Je suis Etienne Falaise. Puis-je vous aider? |
| *Cliente* | Oui, s'il vous plaît. Mon nom est Rocard. J'aimerais réserver un vol direct pour Antigua. Combien de fois par semaine pouvez-vous offrir la Classe de Luxe sur vos vols? |
| *Compagnie aérienne* | Il y a des départs de Paris chaque lundi après-midi et jeudi matin. Il y a bien sûr d'autres vols mais sur d'autres compagnies aériennes. Ceci dit, nos tarifs sont très concurrentiels. |
| *Cliente* | Oui, c'est ce que l'agence de voyage m'a dit mais je voulais quand même vérifier par moi-même. Pourriez-vous m'indiquer le prix de deux billets aller-retour, s'il vous plaît. Le départ se fera le jeudi 7 mai. |
| *Compagnie aérienne* | Nous allons d'abord vérifier la disponibilité des vols et nous verrons les prix ensuite. |
| *Cliente* | Très bien. Qu'en est-il pour le 7? |
| *Compagnie aérienne* | Il y a plusieurs places de libre sur le vol de 9h30; pour le retour, vous pourrez réserver de là-bas si vous le voulez. Voulez-vous que je vous passe à ma collègue Jeannette pour ce qui est de[1] tout le reste – vos coordonnées, le règlement et la remise du billet. |
| *Cliente* | Merci beaucoup, Monsieur. |
| *Compagnie aérienne* | Je vous en prie. Ne quittez pas, je vous la passe. Au revoir. |

1  *Pour ce qui est de* 'in regard to'.

# 14  Thanking for hospitality

| | |
|---|---|
| *Jennie Denning* | Jennie Denning. |
| *Rachel Green* | Hello, Ms Denning. Rachel Green here, from Galway plc. |
| *Jennie Denning* | Hello, Mrs Green. Did you have a good flight back? |
| *Rachel Green* | Yes, very good thanks. I'm ringing to thank you for your hospitality last night. It was a very enjoyable evening, and it was very kind of you to ask us all round – particularly at such short notice! |
| *Jennie Denning* | I'm pleased you had an enjoyable evening. It was very interesting for me to meet you all. |
| *Rachel Green* | It really was kind of you. So thanks once again. If you ever come over here with James, you must visit us. |
| *Jennie Denning* | Yes, I'll do that. Thanks for ringing. |
| *Rachel Green* | And thank you. Goodbye. |
| *Jennie Denning* | Bye. |

# 14  Remercier quelqu'un de son hospitalité

| | |
|---|---|
| *Jacqueline Denis* | Jacqueline Denis à l'appareil. |
| *Régine Gras* | Bonjour Madame Denis. Régine Gras à l'appareil, de chez Granville SA. |
| *Jacqueline Denis* | Bonjour Madame Gras. Avez-vous fait un bon voyage? |
| *Régine Gras* | Oui, très bon, merci. Je vous appelle pour vous remercier de votre hospitalité hier soir. J'ai passé une très agréable soirée et c'était très gentil à vous de tous nous inviter chez vous, surtout en étant prévenue si tard! |
| *Jacqueline Denis* | Je suis heureuse que vous ayez passé une bonne soirée. C'était très intéressant pour moi de tous vous rencontrer. |
| *Régine Gras* | C'est très gentil à vous. Merci encore. S'il vous arrive de venir ici avec Jacques, il faudra que vous veniez nous rendre visite. |
| *Jacqueline Denis* | Bien sûr. Je le ferai. Merci d'avoir appelé. |
| *Régine Gras* | Merci. Au revoir. |
| *Jacqueline Denis* | Au revoir. |

# 15  Invitations

## (a) Accepting

| | |
|---|---|
| *John Brown* | Hello, this is John Brown of International Tool & Die. I am calling to accept your invitation to the lunch in honour of Mr Aspley. |
| *Chamber of Commerce employee* | You are only just in time Mr Brown. I am fixing the final number at 12 noon today. |
| *John Brown* | I'm sorry I did not reply sooner and in writing. I have just come back from a business trip. I'm so glad not to miss this occasion. |
| *Chamber of Commerce employee* | A lot of people think highly of our Euro MP. There's going to be a good turnout. |
| *John Brown* | I am pleased to hear it. Mr Aspley has certainly helped my business to get into the EC market. Are any VIPs coming? |
| *Chamber of Commerce employee* | The Lord Mayor is coming and so is the president of the European Parliament. I don't know about our local MPs. |
| *John Brown* | Anyway you've got me on your list? |
| *Chamber of Commerce employee* | Yes Mr Brown. You are on the list. |

# 15  Invitations

## (a) Accepter

| | |
|---|---|
| *Joseph Bergerac* | Bonjour, Joseph Bergerac d'Outils Internationaux à l'appareil. J'appelle pour vous annoncer que j'accepte votre invitation au déjeuner organisé en l'honneur de Monsieur Armand. |
| *Employé de la Chambre de Commerce* | Vous me prévenez juste à temps, Monsieur Bergerac. J'allais communiquer le nombre définitif à midi aujourd'hui. |
| *Joseph Bergerac* | Je suis désolé de ne pas vous avoir averti plus tôt et de ne pas l'avoir fait par écrit. Je viens juste de revenir d'un voyage d'affaires. Je suis très content de ne pas avoir raté cet événement. |
| *Employé de la Chambre de Commerce* | Beaucoup de gens estiment vraiment notre eurodéputé. Je crois qu'il y aura beaucoup de monde. |
| *Joseph Bergerac* | Je m'en réjouis. Je dois dire que Monsieur Armand a, sans aucun doute, beaucoup aidé mon entreprise à pénétrer le marché européen. Y aura-t-il des personnages de marque?[1] |
| *Employé de la Chambre de Commerce* | Oui, le maire sera présent ainsi que le président du Parlement européen. Je ne sais pas si nos élus locaux seront présents. |
| *Joseph Bergerac* | Bon, de toute façon, vous m'avez bien ajouté sur votre liste? |
| *Employé de la Chambre de Commerce* | Oui, Monsieur Bergerac, vous êtes bien sur ma liste. |

1  VIP is also used in French.

# (b) Declining

| | |
|---|---|
| *John Gregory* | Hello, Michael. This is John Gregory from Car Products International. We've organized a trip to the Indycar road race at Long Beach for our most valued clients. It's the last weekend of April. Would you be able to come? |
| *Michael Daniels* | Let me check my schedule. I'm sorry, John, but I'm down to go to a company sales conference in Malta that weekend. I'm afraid there's no way I can get out of that. |
| *John Gregory* | That's a pity. It would have been great to get together again. If you would like to send one of your staff, just let me know. |
| *Michael Daniels* | Will do. Goodbye. |
| *John Gregory* | So long. |

# (b) Décliner

*Jean Grégoire*   Allô, Michel? Jean Grégoire à l'appareil, de chez Produits
Automobiles International. Nous avons organisé un voyage à
Monaco pour nos clients les plus dévoués afin de leur
permettre d'assister au Grand Prix. Cela se passe le dernier
week-end d'avril. Aimerais-tu venir?

*Michel Daniel*   Attends une seconde, je vais vérifier dans mon agenda. Je suis
désolé Jean, mais je dois me rendre à Malte ce week-end-là
pour assister à notre conférence de dynamique des ventes. Je
suis désolé, mais il n'y a aucune chance que je puisse
l'annuler.

*Jean Grégoire*   C'est vraiment dommage. J'aurais bien aimé que nous nous
revoyions à cette occasion. Si tu veux envoyer l'un de tes
employés, fais-le-moi savoir.

*Michel Daniel*   Oui, je n'y manquerai pas. Merci. Au revoir.

*Jean Grégoire*   Au revoir.

# 16  Travel enquiry

## (a) Rail

| | |
|---|---|
| *Passenger* | Good afternoon. Could you tell me if there is a train out of Seville in the early afternoon going to Madrid? |
| *Booking clerk* | Do you mind how long the journey takes? |
| *Passenger* | Well, I have to be at a conference in the capital by 6 o'clock in the evening. |
| *Booking clerk* | There's a high-speed train which leaves every day at 12 midday. You'll be there by mid-afternoon. |
| *Passenger* | That sounds fine. Can I purchase my tickets by phone? |
| *Booking clerk* | No, I'm afraid you have to come and pay in person. |
| *Passenger* | Surely it's possible for a colleague or my personal assistant to make the purchase for me? |
| *Booking clerk* | Yes, sir, of course. |
| *Passenger* | Very well. I shall be travelling on Friday of this week and will require two singles. How much is that? |
| *Booking clerk* | 34,000 pesetas in first class or 21,000 in second. |
| *Passenger* | Fine. Thanks for your assistance. |

# 16   Renseignements concernant un voyage

## (a) En train

| | |
|---|---|
| *Passager* | Bonsoir. Pourriez-vous me dire s'il y a un train de Lyon à Madrid en début d'après-midi? |
| *Employé du service réservation* | La longueur du trajet vous importe-t-elle? |
| *Passager* | Eh bien, je dois assister à une conférence qui a lieu dans la capitale à 18h00. |
| *Employé du service réservation* | Tous les jours, il y a un train à grande vitesse qui part à midi, ce qui fait que vous arriveriez là-bas en milieu d'après-midi. |
| *Passager* | Ceci m'a l'air tout à fait bien. Puis-je acheter mes billets par téléphone? |
| *Employé du service réservation* | Non, j'ai bien peur qu'il faille que vous veniez payer personnellement. |
| *Passager* | Quand même, je suis sûr qu'il devrait être possible qu'un collègue ou mon assistante vienne les prendre pour moi, non? |
| *Employé du service réservation* | Oui, bien sûr, Monsieur. |
| *Passager* | Très bien. Je dois voyager vendredi prochain et il me faudra deux allers. Combien cela me coûtera-t-il? |
| *Employé du service réservation* | 1 314 francs en première classe ou 811 francs en deuxième classe. |
| *Passager* | Très bien. Merci beaucoup. |

# (b) Ferry

| | |
|---|---|
| *Booking clerk* | Speedline Ferries. Can I help you? |
| *Customer* | Yes, I'm taking my car over to France next week, from Dover to Calais. Can you give me the times of the crossings? |
| *Booking clerk* | Well, they're very frequent. About what time do you want to leave? |
| *Customer* | About 8 a.m. |
| *Booking clerk* | Well, there's one at 8.45, and another at 10.45. |
| *Customer* | Is there an earlier one? |
| *Booking clerk* | Yes, but that one goes at 6 a.m. |
| *Customer* | And what's the return fare? |
| *Booking clerk* | Your vehicle and how many passengers? |
| *Customer* | Just my car and me. |
| *Booking clerk* | The fare is £185. |
| *Customer* | That's fine. Can I book by phone using my credit card? |
| *Booking clerk* | Certainly sir. |
| *Customer* | Thanks for your help. Goodbye. |
| *Booking clerk* | You're welcome. Goodbye. |

# (b) En bateau

| | |
|---|---|
| *Employé du service* | Bateaux de France Rapides. Que puis-je faire pour vous? |
| *Passager* | J'ai l'intention d'aller en Angleterre en voiture la semaine prochaine. J'aimerais faire la traversée de Calais à Douvres. Pourriez-vous me donner les horaires de bateau s'il vous plaît? |
| *Employé du service* | Eh bien, les départs sont très fréquents. A environ quelle heure aimeriez-vous partir? |
| *Passager* | Vers les 8h00 du matin. |
| *Employé du service* | Eh bien, il y en a un vers 8h45 et un autre à 10h45. |
| *Passager* | Y en a-t-il un petit peu plus tôt? |
| *Employé du service* | Oui, mais il part à 6h00. |
| *Passager* | Et quel est le tarif pour un aller-retour? |
| *Employé du service* | Il y a votre véhicule et combien de passagers? |
| *Passager* | Seulement moi-même. |
| *Employé du service* | Le prix sera de 1 480 francs. |
| *Passager* | Très bien. Puis-je faire ma réservation par téléphone et vous payer par carte bancaire?[1] |
| *Employé du service* | Bien sûr, Monsieur. |
| *Passager* | Merci beaucoup. Au revoir. |
| *Employé du service* | Je vous en prie. Au revoir, Monsieur. |

1  Alternative: *carte bleue.*

# 17 Arranging delivery of goods

*Customer*    Hello, Mr James? You wanted me to ring you back.

*Supplier*    Thanks for calling. I wanted directions for the delivery of the parts that we have made to your factory on Monday.

*Customer*    Ah right, this will be your first delivery. Well, take the motorway north. Come off at exit 27 and head towards Northam.

*Supplier*    How do you spell that? N-O-R-T-H-A-M?

*Customer*    That's it. After five miles you'll come to the Eastfield road.

*Supplier*    E-A-S-T-F-I-E-L-D?

*Customer*    Yes. After two miles you meet the Eastfield ringroad, clearly indicated, at a traffic light. Go straight ahead and go through the next two traffic lights.

*Supplier*    So, that's two miles and three traffic lights . . .

*Customer*    At the fourth traffic light you turn left and then second right. This is Alverton Road and our premises are 150 yards down on the left.

*Supplier*    Thanks very much; our lorry will be there on Monday.

# 17   Organiser la livraison de marchandises

*Client*         Allô? Monsieur Jordan? Vous vouliez que je vous rappelle?

*Fournisseur*    Oui, merci de votre appel. Je voulais que vous m'indiquiez le chemin pour vous livrer les pièces détachées que nous avons fabriquées. Elles seront prêtes lundi.

*Client*         Ah, oui. Ce sera votre première livraison. Alors, il faut prendre l'autoroute Nord. Prenez la sortie 27 et dirigez-vous vers Nérac.

*Fournisseur*    Comment épelez-vous cela? N-É-R-A-C?

*Client*         Oui, c'est cela. Après avoir parcouru cinq kilomètres, vous arriverez à un grand rond-point. Prenez la route en direction d'Essonne.

*Fournisseur*    E-S-S-O-N-N-E?

*Client*         Exact. Environ deux kilomètres plus loin, vous arriverez sur le boulevard de ceinture d'Essonne, qui est très bien indiqué aux feux.[1] Allez tout droit et passez les deux autres feux.

*Fournisseur*    Alors, un rond-point, deux kilomètres et trois feux ...

*Client*         Au quatrième feu, tournez à gauche et ensuite deuxième rue à droite. Vous vous trouverez alors dans la rue de l'Auberge et nos locaux sont sur la gauche, à environ 150 mètres.

*Fournisseur*    Merci beaucoup. Notre camion y sera lundi.

1   Short for *feux tricolores* – 'traffic lights'.

# Deuxième partie
## Section II

# Face à face
## Face to face

# 18  Arriving for an appointment

| | |
|---|---|
| *Receptionist* | Good morning, can I help you? |
| *Frances Jones* | Good morning, my name is Frances Jones. I have an appointment with Mrs Jenkins at 10. |
| *Receptionist* | One moment, please, I'll just check. . . . Mrs Jenkins' secretary will come down to meet you. Please take a seat. |
| *Frances Jones* | Thank you. |
| *Receptionist* | Would you like a coffee while you are waiting? |
| *Frances Jones* | Yes, thank you. |
| *Receptionist* | Please help yourself, the coffee machine and the cups are on your left. |

# 18  Arriver pour un rendez-vous

| | |
|---|---|
| *Réceptionniste* | Bonjour Madame, que puis-je faire pour vous? |
| *Françoise Jacquard* | Bonjour, je suis Françoise Jacquard. J'ai rendez-vous avec Mme Gérard à 10h00. |
| *Réceptionniste* | Patientez quelques instants, s'il vous plaît, je vais me renseigner. . . . La secrétaire de Mme Gérard va venir vous chercher. Veuillez vous asseoir en attendant. |
| *Françoise Jacquard* | Merci. |
| *Réceptionniste* | Aimeriez-vous prendre un café en attendant? |
| *Françoise Jacquard* | Oui, avec plaisir. |
| *Réceptionniste* | Servez-vous, la machine à café et les tasses sont sur votre gauche. |

# 19 Arranging further contacts with a company

| | |
|---|---|
| *Mr Collins* | Thank you very much for your help this morning, Mr Vine. I think we've made a lot of progress on the matter of financing the deal. |
| *Mr Vine* | Yes, I agree. It's been useful to clear the air after the initial difficulties we experienced. Presumably, this will not be our last meeting as we must await the final decision and then act quickly. |
| *Mr Collins* | Indeed. Do you have any idea of when that will be? |
| *Mr Vine* | I've been promised an answer by the end of June, so if we say early July there will still be a couple of weeks before we close for the summer vacation. |
| *Mr Collins* | Fine. How about Monday the 3rd? |
| *Mr Vine* | I can't make the morning, but I shall be free all afternoon. More importantly, the main people involved will be able to work on the final proposals that week. If we need to develop our plans further, bringing in other companies or arranging further contacts, there should be time enough to do that. |
| *Mr Collins* | Shall we say 2 p.m. here? In the meantime we can still explore the possibilities or value of involving other parties both within and outside our companies. |
| *Mr Vine* | Very well. I'll get that organized. I'll give you a ring by the 14th to confirm everything we might know by then. |
| *Mr Collins* | Right. Thanks again. . . . Can I get to the carpark by going straight down in the elevator? |
| *Mr Vine* | Yes. First floor, first door on the left. See you in July if not before. |

# 19   Organiser un rendez-vous avec une entreprise avec laquelle il y a déjà eu des contacts

| | |
|---|---|
| *M. Colbert* | Je tenais à vous remercier de l'aide que vous nous avez apportée ce matin, M. Vigny. Il semble que nous ayons fait beaucoup de progrès au niveau des moyens de financement du projet. |
| *M. Vigny* | Oui, je suis tout à fait d'accord. Il était utile de clarifier les choses après les difficultés que nous avons eues au début. Ce n'est vraisemblablement pas la dernière réunion que nous ferons car nous devons attendre la décision finale, après quoi nous devrons agir très vite. |
| *M. Colbert* | Tout à fait. Sauriez-vous quand cela pourrait être? |
| *M. Vigny* | On m'a promis une réponse d'ici fin juin. Si nous disons début juillet, ça nous laissera toujours deux semaines avant la fermeture pour les vacances d'été. |
| *M. Colbert* | Que pensez vous du lundi 3? |
| *M. Vigny* | Je ne peux pas le matin, mais l'après-midi serait tout à fait possible. De plus, les principaux membres impliqués dans ce projet pourront travailler sur les dernières propositions cette même semaine. Si nous avons besoin d'adopter de nouvelles stratégies en invitant d'autres entreprises ou d'établir de nouveaux contacts, cela devrait nous laisser le temps de le faire. |
| *M. Colbert* | Que diriez-vous de 14h00? En attendant, nous pouvons toujours évaluer les possibilités ou l'utilité d'inviter d'autres membres à participer, qu'ils soient des nôtres ou de l'extérieur. |
| *M. Vigny* | Très bien. Je vais organiser tout cela. Je vous appellerai le 14 pour vous communiquer toute autre information que nous aurons pu recueillir d'ici là. |
| *M. Colbert* | Bon. Merci encore. . . . Puis-je retourner au parking en descendant par l'ascenseur? |
| *M. Vigny* | Oui, bien sûr. Rez de chaussée, première porte à gauche. Je vous dis au mois de juillet[1] si nous n'avons pas l'occasion de nous recontacter d'ici là. |

1   Literally, 'So I am saying till July . . .'.

# 20  Presenting a proposal

*Helen*  Morning, John. Do come in and take a seat.

*John*  Morning, Helen. Thanks.

*Helen*  You wanted to see me about our new product launch?

*John*  Yes, I think we should try to bring it forward to December.

*Helen*  That might be a bit tight. Any particular reason?

*John*  Well, we'd catch the important Christmas business, and we'd be ahead of the opposition.

*Helen*  I'm not sure our production people could handle it.

*John*  Not a major problem. Our plant in Wellington can take on more of the production. We have spare capacity there.

*Helen*  Have you discussed this with your people there?

*John*  Yes, and they're convinced they can deal with it.

*Helen*  We can't risk any slip-up on this – the launch is very important. And what about the advertising schedule?

*John*  That's OK. The advertising copy is virtually ready. The ads could be pulled forward to December.

*Helen*  Look, there's some advantage in doing this, but I'd like to talk about it with the board before giving you the go-ahead. There's a meeting tomorrow at 2. Can you make it?

*John*  I've got one or two things on, but I can reshuffle them.

*Helen*  Fine. Look, I've another meeting now, but I'll catch up with you later.

*John*  OK. See you later.

# 20 Présentation d'une proposition

| | |
|---|---|
| *Hélène* | Bonjour Jean. Je t'en prie, entre et assieds-toi. |
| *Jean* | Bonjour Hélène. Merci. |
| *Hélène* | Tu voulais me voir au sujet du lancement d'un nouveau produit? |
| *Jean* | Oui, je pense que nous devrions avancer le lancement au mois de décembre. |
| *Hélène* | Cela risque d'être juste. As-tu une raison précise? |
| *Jean* | Eh bien nous profiterions de l'activité commerciale des périodes de Noël et nous prendrions les devants sur la concurrence. |
| *Hélène* | Je ne suis pas sûre que l'équipe de production puisse y arriver. |
| *Jean* | Ce n'est pas un problème insurmontable. Notre usine de Nantes peut prendre une plus grande part de la production. Nous avons de la capacité de production disponible là-bas. |
| *Hélène* | En as-tu parlé avec le personnel là-bas? |
| *Jean* | Oui, et ils sont convaincus qu'ils peuvent y arriver. |
| *Hélène* | Nous ne pouvons nous permettre aucun cafouillage.[1] Le lancement est extrêmement important. Et au niveau du programme de publicité? |
| *Jean* | C'est bon. Les textes publicitaires sont pratiquement prêts. Les pubs[2] pourraient être avancées à décembre. |
| *Hélène* | Ecoute, il y a des avantages certains à réaliser un tel but, mais je dois soumettre ce projet au conseil d'administration avant de te donner une réponse. Il y a une réunion demain à 14h00. Pourras-tu y assister? |
| *Jean* | J'avais prévu deux ou trois choses mais je peux toujours remanier mon emploi du temps. |
| *Hélène* | Très bien. Ecoute, il faut que je te laisse, j'ai une autre réunion maintenant. On se reparle plus tard. |
| *Jean* | OK. A plus tard. |

1 Alternative: *déboire* (m).
2 Short for *publicité*.

# 21  Exploring business collaboration

| | |
|---|---|
| *Mr Berryman (visitor)* | Pleased to meet you, Monsieur Maurois, and thank you for arranging my hotel. |
| *M. Maurois (local businessman)* | The pleasure is mine, Mr Berryman. You wanted to discuss possible joint ventures with us. |
| *Mr Berryman* | Yes we are both in building and civil engineering. We want to expand into Europe. You might find us useful partners. |
| *M. Maurois* | It's a pity we didn't begin these discussions three months ago; we recently wanted to bid for a stretch of motorway in this region but we did not quite have the resources. |
| *Mr Berryman* | Was there no local company you could combine with? |
| *M. Maurois* | Unfortunately we are the only firm in the region with the necessary expertise. You would have been a good partner – we have made a study of your past projects. |
| *Mr Berryman* | And we have studied you, of course. We were thinking of the proposed port development just down the road. |
| *M. Maurois* | You are really on the ball Mr Berryman. We have just received the detailed specifications and were contemplating a tender. |
| *Mr Berryman* | And I have the spec in English in my briefcase! Shall we roll our sleeves up and work out a joint tender? |

# 21  Explorer la possibilité d'une collaboration en affaires

| | |
|---|---|
| *Mr Berryman (visiteur)* | Enchanté de faire votre connaissance, Monsieur Maurois, et merci d'avoir organisé mon hôtel. |
| *M. Maurois (entrepreneur local)* | Tout le plaisir était pour moi, Monsieur Berryman. Vous vouliez parler de la possibilité de créer une joint venture[1] avec nous. |
| *Mr Berryman* | Oui, nous sommes tous les deux dans le bâtiment et les travaux publics. Nous aimerions nous implanter en Europe. Vous pourriez trouver que nous sommes des partenaires intéressants. |
| *M. Maurois* | Il est vraiment dommage que nous n'ayons pas eu cette conversation il y a trois mois. Nous voulions faire une offre pour une section d'autoroute dans la région mais nous n'avions pas assez de ressources. |
| *Mr Berryman* | N'y avait-il pas d'entreprise locale avec laquelle vous auriez pu combiner vos efforts? |
| *M. Maurois* | Nous sommes malheureusement la seule entreprise locale ayant l'expertise nécessaire. Vous auriez été un bon associé. Nous avons étudié les projets que vous avez réalisés. |
| *Mr Berryman* | Nous avons fait les mêmes études vous concernant, bien sûr. Nous pensions au projet de développement du port qui se trouve près d'ici. |
| *M. Maurois* | Au moins, vous ouvrez l'œil et le bon,[2] Monsieur Berryman. Nous venons juste de recevoir les spécifications détaillées et nous pensions faire une offre. |
| *Mr Berryman* | Et j'ai les spécifications en anglais dans ma serviette! Et si nous nous attelions à la tâche pour préparer une offre jointe? |

1  Alternative: *une opération conjointe.*
2  Literally, 'You've got your eye open, and the right one, too.'

# 22  At the travel agent's

## (a) Enquiry/booking

| | |
|---|---|
| *Traveller* | Could you give me details of flights to Wellington, New Zealand, please? |
| *Assistant* | When do you wish to fly? |
| *Traveller* | The first week of June. |
| *Assistant* | Let me see. Which day do you want to depart? |
| *Traveller* | Tuesday, if possible. |
| *Assistant* | There's a flight leaving Sydney at 8 a.m. which gets into Wellington at 1 p.m. Do you want to make a booking? |
| *Traveller* | How much is the flight? |
| *Assistant* | It's 725 Australian dollars return. |
| *Traveller* | OK. Go ahead. |

## (b) Changing a booking

| | |
|---|---|
| *Client* | I'd like to change a flight reservation for Mr David Street. |
| *Assistant* | Could you give me the flight details please? |
| *Client* | BY567 to Rome on 21 March. Would it be possible to change it to 23 March? |
| *Assistant* | I'll just check. That's OK. The flight leaves at the same time. I'll issue a new ticket and send it to you later today. |
| *Client* | Thank you. |

# 22  A l'agence de voyages

## (a)  Demande d'information/réservation

*Passager*   Pourriez-vous me donner les horaires des vols à destination de Wellington, s'il vous plaît?

*Conseiller*   Oui, quand désirez-vous partir?

*Passager*   La première semaine de juin.

*Conseiller*   Quel jour de la semaine voudriez-vous partir?

*Passager*   Le mardi, si possible.

*Conseiller*   Il y a un vol au départ de Sydney à 8h00 qui arrive à Wellington à 13h00. Voulez-vous faire une réservation?

*Passager*   Quel est le prix du vol?

*Conseiller*   725 dollars australiens pour l'aller-retour.

*Passager*   OK. Allez-y. Faites la réservation.


## (b)  Modifier une réservation

*Cliente*   J'aimerais faire un changement de réservation pour le vol de M. David Sales, s'il vous plaît.

*Conseiller*   Oui, pouvez-vous me donner tous les renseignements que vous possédez concernant le vol?

*Cliente*   Oui, il s'agit du vol BY567 à destination de Rome qui part le 21 mars. Serait-il possible de repousser la réservation au 23 mars?

*Conseiller*   Attendez, je vérifie. C'est bon, le vol est à la même heure. Je vais vous faire un nouveau billet et je vous l'envoie dans le courant de la journée.

*Cliente*   Merci.

## (c) Flight cancellation

| | |
|---|---|
| *Client* | I'm ringing on behalf of Mrs Mary Thomas. She was due to fly to Capetown next Thursday, but she has unfortunately fallen ill. |
| *Assistant* | I see. |
| *Client* | Can she get a refund? |
| *Assistant* | How did she pay? |
| *Client* | By cheque, I think. |
| *Assistant* | If she took out travel insurance she will be able to get her money back, if her doctor signs a certificate. |
| *Client* | I'd better ask her. I'll get back to you when I know. |

# 23  Checking in at the airport

| | |
|---|---|
| *Assistant* | Good evening, sir. Can I have your ticket and passport? |
| *Passenger* | Certainly. |
| *Assistant* | Are you travelling alone? |
| *Passenger* | Yes, that's right. |
| *Assistant* | How many items of luggage are you checking in? |
| *Passenger* | Just this case. |
| *Assistant* | Can you put it on the belt, please? Did you pack it yourself? |
| *Passenger* | Yes. |
| *Assistant* | Are there any electrical items in it? |
| *Passenger* | No, they're in my hand baggage. |
| *Assistant* | What are they? |
| *Passenger* | An electric shaver and a lap-top computer. |
| *Assistant* | That's fine. Do you want smoking or non-smoking? |
| *Passenger* | Non-smoking please. |

## (c) Annulation d'un vol

| | |
|---|---|
| *Cliente* | Je vous appelle de la part de Madame Thomas. Elle devait prendre l'avion pour le Cap jeudi prochain, mais elle est malheureusement tombée malade. |
| *Conseiller* | Je vois. |
| *Cliente* | Pourra-t-elle être remboursée? |
| *Conseiller* | Comment a-t-elle payé? |
| *Cliente* | Par chèque je pense. |
| *Conseiller* | Si elle a pris une assurance de voyage, elle récupérera son argent si son docteur lui signe un certificat. |
| *Cliente* | Il vaut mieux que je lui demande. Je vous rappelle dès que j'ai une réponse. |

# 23 Faire les enregistrements à l'aéroport

| | |
|---|---|
| *Hôtesse* | Bonsoir Monsieur. Puis-je avoir votre ticket et votre passeport s'il vous plaît? |
| *Passager* | Bien sûr. |
| *Hôtesse* | Vous voyagez seul? |
| *Passager* | Oui, tout à fait.[1] |
| *Hôtesse* | Combien de bagages avez-vous pour la soute?[2] |
| *Passager* | Seulement cette valise. |
| *Hôtesse* | Pouvez-vous la mettre sur le tapis roulant, s'il vous plaît? L'avez-vous faite vous-même? |
| *Passager* | Oui. |
| *Hôtesse* | Y a-t-il des appareils électriques à l'intérieur? |
| *Passager* | Non, ils sont dans mes bagages à main. |
| *Hôtesse* | Qu'est-ce que c'est exactement? |
| *Passager* | Un rasoir électrique et un ordinateur portable. |
| *Hôtesse* | C'est bon. Vous voulez un siège fumeurs ou non fumeurs? |
| *Passager* | Non fumeurs, s'il vous plaît. |

1  Literally, 'entirely (so)'.
2  Literally, 'to be put in the hold'.

# 24  Checking in at a hotel

| | |
|---|---|
| *Receptionist* | Good afternoon, madam. |
| *Guest* | Good afternoon. I have a reservation in the name of Battersby. |
| *Receptionist* | A single room for two nights? |
| *Guest* | Surely that was changed to a double room? My husband is due to join me later this evening. |
| *Receptionist* | I'll just check. Oh, yes, there is a note to that effect. Will you be having dinner at the hotel? |
| *Guest* | Yes, dinner for one. Can I also order an early call tomorrow morning and can we have a newspaper? |
| *Receptionist* | 6 o'clock or 6.30? |
| *Guest* | That's too early. Say 7 o'clock. And could we have a copy of *The Times*? |
| *Receptionist* | I am sorry but we will not have the London *Times* until tomorrow afternoon. Would you like the *Herald Tribune* or perhaps a French newspaper? |
| *Guest* | No, thank you. I'll leave it. Can you call me a taxi for half an hour from now? And what time is dinner by the way? |

## 24  Arriver dans un hôtel où une réservation a été faite

| | |
|---|---|
| *Réceptionniste* | Bonsoir Madame. |
| *Cliente* | Bonsoir. J'ai fait une réservation au nom de Barrault. |
| *Réceptionniste* | Une chambre pour une personne pour deux nuits? |
| *Cliente* | Il s'agit d'une chambre pour deux personnes. J'ai prévenu que mon mari me rejoignait plus tard ce soir. |
| *Réceptionniste* | Je vérifie. Ah oui, il y a une note à ce sujet. Dînerez-vous à l'hôtel? |
| *Cliente* | Oui. Une table pour une personne seulement. Puis-je également me faire réveiller de bonne heure demain matin? J'aimerais également avoir le journal. |
| *Réceptionniste* | 6h00 ou 6h30? |
| *Cliente* | C'est un peu trop tôt. Disons 7h00. Pourrions-nous avoir un exemplaire du *Times*? |
| *Réceptionniste* | Je suis désolée mais nous ne recevons pas l'édition de Londres avant demain après-midi. Peut-être aimeriez-vous lire le *Herald Tribune* ou un journal français? |
| *Cliente* | Non merci. Ça ne fait rien. Pourriez-vous me commander un taxi pour dans une demi-heure? Au fait, à quelle heure le dîner est-il servi? |

# 25  Checking out of a hotel

*Guest*          I would like to check out now.

*Receptionist*   Certainly, sir. What is your room number?

*Guest*          Three two four (324).

*Receptionist*   Mr Lawrence? Did you make any phone calls this morning? Have you used the mini-bar?

*Guest*          No, I haven't made any calls since yesterday evening. Here is my mini-bar slip.

*Receptionist*   Thank you. Would you be so kind as to fill in the hotel questionnaire while I total your bill? How do you wish to pay?

*Guest*          By credit card.

*Receptionist*   Fine. I'll just be a minute. There you are, Mr Lawrence. Thank you very much.

# 25  Quitter un hôtel

| | |
|---|---|
| *Client* | J'aimerais vous régler.[1] |
| *Réceptionniste* | Oui Monsieur. Quel est votre numéro de chambre? |
| *Client* | Trois cent vingt-quatre (324). |
| *Réceptionniste* | M. Laurent? Avez-vous passé des appels téléphoniques ce matin? Avez vous utilisé le mini-bar? |
| *Client* | Non, je n'ai passé aucun coup de fil depuis hier soir. Voilà le rapport du mini-bar. |
| *Réceptionniste* | Merci. Voudriez-vous remplir le questionnaire de l'hôtel pendant que je fais votre note? Comment désirez-vous payer? |
| *Client* | Par carte bancaire. |
| *Réceptionniste* | Très bien. Je n'en ai que pour une minute. Voilà, M. Laurent. Merci beaucoup. |

1  Literally, 'I would like to settle you'.

# 26  Ordering a meal in a restaurant

| | |
|---|---|
| *Waitress* | Good afternoon, madam. Would you like the menu? |
| *Client 1* | Yes, thank you. And may we have a dry white wine and a pint of lager whilst we are choosing our meal? |
| *Waitress* | Certainly. Here is the menu; we also have a chef's special set meal at 15 dollars. |

\* \* \*

| | |
|---|---|
| *Client 1* | Would you like to have a look first? |
| *Client 2* | No: I'll have what you recommend as you know the local cuisine far better than I do. But I'm looking forward to my lager. |
| *Client 1* | Fine. Here come the drinks, anyway. May we have two salads as starters, please? Then for main course two pepper steaks with vegetables and jacket potatoes. I think we'll also have a bottle of house red with the steak. |
| *Waitress* | A bottle of red, two hors d'oeuvres and two pepper steaks; how would you like the steaks cooked? |
| *Client 2* | Well done for me, please. |
| *Client 1* | Medium for me. |

\* \* \*

| | |
|---|---|
| *Waitress* | Have you enjoyed your meal? |
| *Client 1* | Yes, it was fine, thank you. I don't think we'll have a dessert as we are running a bit late. Just two black coffees and the bill, please. |

\* \* \*

| | |
|---|---|
| *Waitress* | Your coffee and the bill, madam. Could you pay at the till when you leave? |
| *Client 1* | Of course. And this is to thank you for having looked after us so well. |
| *Waitress* | Thank you, madam. Please come again. |

# 26  Commander un repas dans un restaurant

| | |
|---|---|
| *Serveuse* | Bonsoir Madame. Voulez-vous la carte? |
| *Cliente 1* | Oui, merci. Pourriez-vous nous servir un verre de vin blanc sec et une grande bière blonde pendant que nous choisissons notre menu? |
| *Serveuse* | Très certainement. Voici le menu à la carte. Nous avons également un menu Spécial Chef[1] à 75 francs. |

\* \* \*

| | |
|---|---|
| *Cliente 1* | Aimerais-tu jeter un coup d'œil d'abord? |
| *Client 2* | Non, je suivrai tes bons conseils. Tu connais bien mieux la cuisine régionale que moi. Mais ma bière ne me ferait pas de mal![2] |
| *Cliente 1* | OK. Tiens, voilà les boissons. Nous voudrions deux salades en entrée, s'il vous plaît. Ensuite nous aimerions comme plat principal deux steaks au poivre avec légumes et pommes de terre en robe des champs. Je pense que nous prendrons également une bouteille de vin rouge de la maison pour le steak. |
| *Serveuse* | Une bouteille de vin rouge, deux salades et deux steaks au poivre; quelle cuisson[3] voulez-vous pour les steaks? |
| *Client 2* | Bien cuit pour moi s'il vous plaît. |
| *Cliente 1* | A point pour moi. |

\* \* \*

| | |
|---|---|
| *Serveuse* | Avez-vous apprécié votre repas? |
| *Cliente 1* | Oui, c'était très bien. Merci. Je ne crois pas que nous prendrons de dessert car nous sommes un peu en retard maintenant. Deux cafés noirs, s'il vous plaît, et la note. |

\* \* \*

| | |
|---|---|
| *Serveuse* | Votre café et la note, Madame. Vous paierez à la caisse en sortant. |
| *Cliente 1* | Très bien. Et voici pour vous remercier de vous être si bien occupée de nous. |
| *Serveuse* | Merci beaucoup, Madame. Revenez nous voir. |

1  French distinguishes between *le menu 'du jour'* or *'spécial'* – a set meal, and *le menu 'à la carte'* (also called *'la carte'*) – the list of all dishes.
2  Literally, 'would do me no harm'.
3  Literally, 'what (degree of) cooking?' Well done (*bien cuit*), medium (*à point*), rare (*saignant*).

# 27  Verifying a bill

| | |
|---|---|
| *Waiter* | Yes sir? Did you enjoy your meal? |
| *Customer* | Yes, but can I check the bill with you? |
| *Waiter* | Certainly – is there a problem? |
| *Customer* | I think there might be a mistake – we had four set menus at £15 a head and also the aperitifs and the wine. |
| *Waiter* | Yes? |
| *Customer* | But what's this item here? |
| *Waiter* | Four whiskies, sir. £10. |
| *Customer* | But we didn't have any! |
| *Waiter* | Just a moment sir, I'll go and check it for you. . . . I'm sorry, my mistake. I'll get you an amended bill at once. |
| *Customer* | Thank you. |

# 27  Vérification d'une facture

| | |
|---|---|
| *Serveur* | Oui Monsieur? Avez vous apprécié votre repas? |
| *Client* | Oui, mais puis-je vérifier la note avec vous? |
| *Serveur* | Très certainement. Y a-t-il un problème? |
| *Client* | Je pense qu'il y a une erreur. Nous avons pris quatre menus à 125 francs, les apéritifs et du vin. |
| *Serveur* | Oui? |
| *Client* | Mais à quoi correspond cela? |
| *Serveur* | Quatre whiskies, Monsieur. 80 francs. |
| *Client* | Mais nous n'en avons pas commandé! |
| *Serveur* | Attendez, Monsieur, je vais aller vérifier. . . . Je suis désolé, j'ai fait une erreur. Je vais vous faire rectifier cela[1] tout de suite. |
| *Client* | Merci. |

1  Literally, 'get that rectified for you'.

# 28  Drawing up a schedule of visits for reps

| | |
|---|---|
| *Senior representative* | Thanks for coming to this meeting. I thought it would be useful to discuss areas for the autumn quarter. |
| *Representative 2* | In fact, as it happens, the schedule of leads and follow-up visits shows a roughly equal split between the northwest, northeast and southwest regions. |
| *Representative 3* | We need to consider what to do about the lack of interest in our products in the south-east. |
| *Senior representative* | There is also a scattering of trade fairs that one or other of us should attend, including one in Marseilles in mid-September. |
| *Representative 2* | Perhaps we should all be there to work out a strategy for the southeast. And we could all be at the Paris Arts Ménagers Salon in early November. |
| *Representative 3* | Good idea. I have some contacts that might help. Shall we operate as originally suggested? Me in Bordeaux, George in Lille and Alf in Strasbourg? |
| *Senior representative* | That all seems fine to me. Are you happy Alf? Apart from the Marseilles and Paris fairs we can each do our regional fairs individually. |
| *Representative 2* | I am happy with that. Will we have the same budget as last year? |
| *Senior representative* | Good question. The operating budget has been increased by a meagre 5 per cent. Any requests for increased staffing need to be justified by increased business. |
| *Representative 3* | So what else is new? Let's get those dates in our diaries. |

# 28  Etablir un programme de visites pour des représentants

| | |
|---|---|
| *Représentant principal* | Je vous remercie d'être venu assister à cette réunion. J'ai pensé qu'il serait utile de discuter des régions pour le trimestre d'automne. |
| *Représentant 2* | En fait, et ce qui n'est pas si mal, le programme des visites de suivi indique une répartition à peu près égale entre les régions nord-ouest, nord-est et sud-ouest. |
| *Représentante 3* | Nous devons penser à ce que nous allons faire au sujet du sud-est où il y a un manque d'intérêt certain pour nos produits. |
| *Représentant principal* | Il y a également un certain nombre de salons professionnels auxquels certains d'entre nous devraient assister, y compris celui de Marseille qui a lieu à la mi-septembre. |
| *Représentant 2* | Peut-être devrions-nous tous y aller afin de définir une stratégie pour le sud-est. Et nous pourrions également tous être au Salon des Arts Ménagers à Paris début novembre. |
| *Représentante 3* | Très bonne idée. J'ai des contacts qui pourraient nous aider. Allons-nous procéder comme convenu au départ? Moi à Bordeaux, Georges à Lille et Alphonse à Strasbourg? |
| *Représentant principal* | Tout cela m'a l'air très bien. Ça vous convient, Alphonse? A l'exception de ceux de Marseille et Paris, les salons régionaux seront couverts par chacun d'entre nous individuellement. |
| *Représentant 2* | Je suis tout à fait d'accord avec ce principe. Disposons-nous du même budget que l'année dernière? |
| *Représentant principal* | Très bonne question. Le budget de fonctionnement a été augmenté d'un maigre 5%. Toute demande d'augmentation de personnel devra être justifiée par une augmentation du volume d'affaires. |
| *Représentante 3* | Comme d'habitude[1] ... Inscrivons ces dates dans nos agendas. |

1  Literally, 'As usual'.

# 29  Conducted visit of a department

| | |
|---|---|
| *Guide* | Before I show you round the department, come and meet my deputy, Frederick Fallon. |
| *Miss Smith* | Pleased to meet you, Mr Fallon. |
| *Frederick Fallon* | Welcome to the department, Miss Smith. |
| *Guide* | Frederick is responsible for the day-to-day running of the department. Now we'll start our tour. This is the general office, with Mrs Jones looking after reception, typing and word processing. |
| *Miss Smith* | How many secretaries work for Mrs Jones? |
| *Guide* | Normally five. One is currently on sick leave and one on holiday. . . . This is the overseas sales office. They have their own fax machines. We deal directly with our agents in Europe. . . . And this is the design section. Most of their work is now done by CAD/CAM. They've got some of the most sophisticated computer equipment in the company. David, can I introduce Miss Smith. |
| *David Hall* | Pleased to meet you, Miss Smith. |
| *Guide* | David has four designers working for him. And finally, this is Ted Stolzfuss, who is over here from our American parent company. Ted, meet Miss Smith. Ted is with us to look at the way we operate in Europe. |

# 29  Visite accompagnée d'un service

| | |
|---|---|
| *Guide* | Avant de vous faire faire le tour du service, je vais vous présenter mon adjoint, Frédéric Fallon. |
| *Mlle Siffert* | Enchantée de faire votre connaissance, M. Fallon. |
| *Frédéric Fallon* | Bienvenue dans notre service, Mlle Siffert. |
| *Guide* | Frédéric est responsable du fonctionnement journalier du service. Nous allons maintenant commencer la visite. Voici le bureau général avec Mme Joliot qui s'occupe de l'accueil et de la dactylographie et du traitement de texte. |
| *Mlle Siffert* | Combien de secrétaires travaillent avec Mme Joliot? |
| *Guide* | Normalement cinq. L'une d'entre elles est actuellement en congé de maladie et une autre est en vacances. . . . Ici, c'est le bureau des ventes à l'étranger. Ils possèdent leurs propres télécopieurs. Nous traitons directement avec nos agents en Europe. . . . Ici, c'est le service qui s'occupe de la conception. La plupart de leurs travaux sont réalisés par CAO/FAO.[1] Ils possèdent les équipements informatiques les plus sophistiqués. David, puis-je vous présenter Mlle Siffert? |
| *David Harpon* | Enchanté de faire votre connaissance, Mademoiselle. |
| *Guide* | Quatre designers travaillent pour David. Voilà, et pour finir voici Ted Stolzfuss, qui nous vient de notre maison-mère en Amérique.[2] Ted, voici Mlle Siffert. Ted est ici pour analyser notre mode de fonctionnement européen. |

1  Abbreviation for *conception/fabrication assistée par ordinateur.*
2  Or *aux États-Unis* (*d'Amérique*).

# 30  Informal job interview

| | |
|---|---|
| *Personnel manager* | Good morning, Ms Jiménez, and welcome. I hope you had no trouble getting here. |
| *Gloria Jiménez* | Good morning. Thank you, it was nice of you to invite me in for a chat. |
| *Personnel manager* | First, let me introduce you to Pepe Romero, who is in charge of advertising. As you can see, he's always snowed under with work, eh Pepe? Gloria Jiménez, Pepe Romero. |
| *Pepe Romero* | Pleased to meet you. Don't take her too seriously. You'll see for yourself when you start next week. |
| *Gloria Jiménez* | How many staff do you have in this department? |
| *Pepe Romero* | Seven full-timers and a couple of freelancers who help out when we have special projects on. |
| *Gloria Jiménez* | It looks a friendly set-up, anyway. |
| *Personnel manager* | Yes, you're right, they are one of our most efficient and successful departments. Would you like to meet Fernando, with whom you will be working most closely? He is our art director. |
| *Gloria Jiménez* | Fine. Has he been with the company for a long time? |
| *Personnel manager* | No, he was brought in recently when the company merged. Oh, it looks as if he's in a meeting, so we'll wait here and talk a bit more about you. How did you get into commercial design? |
| *Gloria Jiménez* | After university I realized that there were good prospects for young people with ideas in the field of design and advertising, so I took a course in advertising in Seville not long before the World Fair was awarded to the city. |
| *Personnel manager* | Did you actually work on the World Fair project? |
| *Gloria Jiménez* | Yes, my first job was with a Japanese agency that was promoting its high-tech industries, and I carried on until the Fair closed last year. |
| *Personnel manager* | That sounds just the sort of experience we are looking for. Ah, here comes Fernando. |

# 30  Entretien informel

| | |
|---|---|
| *Chef du personnel* | Bonjour Mlle Jiménez. J'espère que vous êtes arrivée sans trop de problèmes. |
| *Gloria Jiménez* | Bonjour. Non, merci. C'est très gentil à vous de m'avoir invitée à passer[1] aujourd'hui. |
| *Chef du personnel* | Tout d'abord, laissez-moi vous présenter Pepe Romero qui s'occupe de la publicité. Comme vous pouvez vous en rendre compte, il est toujours débordé[2] de travail, n'est-ce pas Pepe? Gloria Jiménez, Pepe Romero. |
| *Pepe Romero* | Enchanté de faire votre connaissance. Ne prenez pas ce qu'elle dit trop au sérieux. Vous pourrez en juger par vous-même lorsque vous commencerez la semaine prochaine. |
| *Gloria Jiménez* | Combien d'employés avez-vous dans ce service? |
| *Pepe Romero* | Sept à temps complet[3] et deux freelances[4] qui nous aident lorsque nous avons des projets plus particuliers. |
| *Gloria Jiménez* | Il semble y avoir une ambiance très sympathique. |
| *Chef du personnel* | Oui, vous avez raison. Ce service est l'un des plus efficaces et il a beaucoup de succès. Voulez-vous rencontrer Fernando avec qui vous travaillerez plus particulièrement? C'est notre directeur artistique. |
| *Gloria Jiménez* | Oui, bien sûr. Cela fait-il longtemps qu'il travaille dans cette entreprise? |
| *Chef du personnel* | Non, on l'a fait venir récemment, lorsque l'entreprise a fusionné. Ah, j'ai l'impression qu'il est en réunion. Nous allons rester ici et parler un peu plus de vous en attendant. Comment vous êtes-vous orientée vers le design commercial? |
| *Gloria Jiménez* | Après l'université, j'ai réalisé qu'il y avait de bons débouchés pour les jeunes qui ont des idées dans le domaine du design et de la publicité, alors j'ai suivi un cours à Séville peu avant l'attribution à cette ville de l'exposition universelle. |
| *Chef du personnel* | Avez-vous été amenée à travailler sur ce projet? |
| *Gloria Jiménez* | Oui, mon premier emploi était au sein d'une agence japonaise qui faisait la promotion des industries de haute technologie du pays. J'ai occupé mon poste jusqu'à la clôture de l'exposition, l'an dernier. |
| *Chef du personnel* | Cela m'a tout l'air du genre d'expérience que nous recherchons. Ah, voici Fernando. |

1 Literally, 'to call in', 'to come by'. 2 Literally, 'overflowed'. 3 Alternative: *plein temps*.
4 Alternative: *travailleurs indépendants*.

# 31  Formal job interview

## Part 1

| | |
|---|---|
| *Interviewer* | Do come in, Ms Hellington, and take a seat. |
| *Jane Hellington* | Thank you. |
| *Interviewer* | Well, if I can make a start, can you tell us why you want this particular post? |
| *Jane Hellington* | As I said in my application, I'm working with quite a small company at the moment. My promotion prospects are limited because of that. |
| *Interviewer* | So that is your main reason? |
| *Jane Hellington* | Not just that. I've been with the company for five years now, and although I found the work interesting at first, I now feel that I want a more varied post which is more challenging. |
| *Interviewer* | Do you think this job would be what you are looking for? |
| *Jane Hellington* | Yes, I do. You're a big company in the process of expansion, and the department I'd be working in would give me much more variety. |
| *Interviewer* | Do you think that moving from a small department to a much larger one would be a problem? |
| *Jane Hellington* | It would be rather new at first, but I worked with a big company before my present job, and I do integrate well. I'm confident that I am ready to make a change. |

# 31 Entrevue officielle

## Première partie

| | |
|---|---|
| *Sous-directeur*[1] | Entrez, Mlle Hinault, asseyez-vous. |
| *Janine Hinault* | Merci. |
| *Sous-directeur* | Je vous en prie. Bon, eh bien, nous allons commencer. Pouvez-vous nous dire pourquoi vous désirez occuper le poste que nous proposons? |
| *Janine Hinault* | Comme je l'ai dit dans ma lettre de candidature, je travaille actuellement dans une entreprise relativement petite. De ce fait, mes perspectives de promotion sont très limitées. |
| *Sous-directeur* | Est-ce votre raison principale? |
| *Janine Hinault* | Pas seulement. Cela fait cinq ans que je travaille pour cette entreprise et, bien que j'aie trouvé le travail intéressant au début, j'aimerais occuper un poste offrant davantage de possibilités , qui soit plus motivant. |
| *Sous-directeur* | Et vous pensez que ce que nous offrons répondrait à ce que vous cherchez? |
| *Janine Hinault* | Oui, je le pense. Vous êtes une grosse entreprise en plein développement, et le service dans lequel je travaillerais offre des tâches bien plus variées. |
| *Sous-directeur* | Pensez-vous que de quitter un petit service pour vous installer dans un bien plus grand pourrait présenter un problème? |
| *Janine Hinault* | Cela paraîtra sûrement bien différent au début, mais j'ai déjà travaillé dans une grande société avant d'occuper mon poste actuel, et je m'adapte très facilement. Je sais que je suis prête à faire ce changement. |

1 There is no single-word equivalent in French for 'interviewer' used in this context. The exact equivalent would be *Personne faisant passer l'entrevue*.

# Part 2

| | |
|---|---|
| *Interviewer* | As you know, we're a multinational organization, and that means that one of the things we're looking for in this post is a competence in languages. |
| *Jane Hellington* | Yes, well, as you'll see from my CV I studied German and Spanish at school, and I've lived and worked in France for several years. |
| *Interviewer* | How would you describe your language competence? |
| *Jane Hellington* | My French is fluent, and I can still remember the basics in German and Spanish. |
| *Interviewer* | What if we asked you to take further language training? |
| *Jane Hellington* | I'd welcome that. I feel that it's important to get them to as high a level as possible. |
| *Interviewer* | Fine. On another issue: if we were to offer you the post, when could you take it up? |
| *Jane Hellington* | In two months. I'm working on a project in my current post, and I'd like to see that through first. Would that be a problem? |
| *Interviewer* | I don't think so, but I'd have to check with the department before confirming, of course. Well now, are there any questions you want to ask us? |
| *Jane Hellington* | Just two: you mention your management training programme in your particulars. Can you tell me more about it? |
| *Interviewer* | Yes, we expect all our middle managers to try to reach their full potential through self-development. We help them in that by running a series of in-house residential training courses. |
| *Jane Hellington* | How often? |
| *Interviewer* | Three or four times a year, and we expect everyone to attend them, as far as possible. |
| *Jane Hellington* | That's fine. One other question, if I may? |
| *Interviewer* | Certainly. |
| *Jane Hellington* | When will you let me have your decision? |
| *Interviewer* | We'll be contacting the successful candidate by phone this evening, and we'll be writing to the others. |
| *Jane Hellington* | Thanks very much. |
| *Interviewer* | Well, thank you for coming to interview, Ms Hellington. Goodbye. |
| *Jane Hellington* | Goodbye. |

# Deuxième partie

| | |
|---|---|
| *Sous-directeur* | Comme vous le savez, nous sommes un organisme multinational, ce qui veut dire que l'un de nos principaux critères de choix pour ce poste réside dans la compétence en matière de langues. |
| *Janine Hinault* | Eh bien, vous pourrez le voir dans mon curriculum vitae, j'ai étudié l'allemand et l'espagnol à l'école, et j'ai vécu et travaillé en Angleterre pendant plusieurs années. |
| *Sous-directeur* | Comment décririez-vous vos aptitudes en langues? |
| *Janine Hinault* | Je parle l'anglais couramment, et je possède des bases solides en allemand et en espagnol. |
| *Sous-directeur* | Et si nous vous demandions de faire à nouveau des stages de langue? |
| *Janine Hinault* | J'en serais heureuse. Je trouve qu'il est très important de parvenir au meilleur niveau possible. |
| *Sous-directeur* | Très bien. Un autre point: si nous devions vous offrir le poste, quand pourriez-vous commencer? |
| *Janine Hinault* | Dans deux mois. Je travaille actuellement sur un projet et j'aimerais le finir avant de partir. Cela poserait-il un problème? |
| *Sous-directeur* | Je ne pense pas, mais il faudra quand même que je vérifie auprès du service avant de pouvoir confirmer. Très bien, avez-vous des questions à nous poser? |
| *Janine Hinault* | Seulement deux. Vous mentionnez le programme de formation dans la description. Pouvez vous m'en dire plus à ce sujet? |
| *Sous-directeur* | Nous voudrions que tous nos cadres moyens essaient d'exploiter leur potentiel au maximum par le biais de l'auto-développement. Nous les aidons en organisant une série de stages internes de formation. |
| *Janine Hinault* | Quand ont-ils lieu? |
| *Sous-directeur* | Trois à quatre fois par an, et nous tenons à ce que tout le monde y assiste, autant que possible. |
| *Janine Hinault* | Très bien. Une autre question si je peux me permettre. |
| *Sous-directeur* | Tout à fait. |
| *Janine Hinault* | Quand me ferez-vous connaître votre décision? |
| *Sous-directeur* | Nous contacterons par téléphone la personne choisie ce soir, et nous écrirons aux autres. |
| *Janine Hinault* | Très bien. Merci. |
| *Sous-directeur* | Merci d'avoir assisté à cette entrevue, Mlle Hinault. Au revoir. |
| *Janine Hinault* | Au revoir. |

# Part 3

| | |
|---|---|
| *Jane Hellington* | Hello. Jane Hellington. |
| *Brendan Carter* | Good evening, Ms Hellington. Brendan Carter here, from Keystone Engineering. I'm ringing to offer you the post here. |
| *Jane Hellington* | Really? Well, thank you very much! |
| *Brendan Carter* | I suppose my first question has to be whether or not you wish to accept the post. |
| *Jane Hellington* | Yes, I do. Thank you. |
| *Brendan Carter* | The starting salary would be as agreed, with a salary review after your first six months. |
| *Jane Hellington* | Yes, that's fine. |
| *Brendan Carter* | When could you start? |
| *Jane Hellington* | As I explained at interview, there is a project I'm working on at the moment that I'd like to see through. So if possible I'd like to start in two months. |
| *Brendan Carter* | Shall we say 1 June, then? Will that suit you? |
| *Jane Hellington* | Probably. I'll just need to discuss things with my present employer first. I'll do that after I get your offer in writing, and then ring you. |
| *Brendan Carter* | You'll need to get down here a few times before, of course, to meet one or two people and get the feel of the place. |
| *Jane Hellington* | Yes, certainly. I'd like to do that. |
| *Brendan Carter* | Well then, I'll just get our personnel people to send the formal written offer to you. That should be with you in a couple of days. |
| *Jane Hellington* | Thank you for offering me the post. |
| *Brendan Carter* | I look forward to working with you. Goodbye and see you soon. |
| *Jane Hellington* | Yes, goodbye. |

# Troisième partie

| | |
|---|---|
| *Janine Hinault* | Bonjour. Janine Hinault à l'appareil. |
| *Bernard Cartier* | Bonsoir Mlle Hinault. Bernard Cartier à l'appareil, de chez Ingénierie Pierrefitte. Je vous appelle pour vous offrir le poste. |
| *Janine Hinault* | Vraiment? Merci beaucoup! |
| *Bernard Cartier* | Je suppose que ma première question devrait être de vous demander si vous voulez accepter le poste ou non. |
| *Janine Hinault* | Oui, je l'accepte. Merci. |
| *Bernard Cartier* | Le salaire de départ sera comme convenu, et il sera revu après six mois. |
| *Janine Hinault* | Oui, c'est très bien. |
| *Bernard Cartier* | Quand pouvez-vous commencer? |
| *Janine Hinault* | Comme je l'ai dit lors de l'entrevue, il y a un projet sur lequel je travaille en ce moment que j'aimerais conduire à terme.[1] Ainsi, si cela est possible, j'aimerais commencer dans deux mois. |
| *Bernard Cartier* | Le 1er juin, donc? Cela vous conviendrait-il? |
| *Janine Hinault* | Probablement. Il faut simplement que j'en discute avec mon employeur actuel. Je le ferai dès que j'aurai la confirmation écrite de cette offre. Je vous contacterai par téléphone. |
| *Bernard Cartier* | Il faudra, bien sûr, que vous nous rendiez une ou deux visites avant de prendre vos fonctions afin de rencontrer une ou deux personnes et vous familiariser un peu avec le terrain sur lequel vous travaillerez. |
| *Janine Hinault* | Oui, bien sûr. Ce sera pour moi un plaisir. |
| *Bernard Cartier* | Très bien; il ne me reste plus qu'à demander au service du personnel de vous envoyer l'offre écrite. Vous devriez la recevoir d'ici deux jours. |
| *Janine Hinault* | Merci beaucoup de m'avoir offert le poste. |
| *Bernard Cartier* | Ce sera un plaisir pour moi de travailler avec vous. Au revoir, à bientôt. |
| *Janine Hinault* | Oui, au revoir. |

1 Literally, 'bring to a conclusion'.

# 32  Planning a budget

| | |
|---|---|
| *Managing director* | All right, if I can open the meeting. This need not be too formal but I hardly need to say how important it is. The balance sheet for last year is for our eyes only, for a start. |
| *Director 2* | It makes very pleasant reading, 11 per cent growth on the preceding year... |
| *Managing director* | Don't get carried away, Derek. I've looked at our orders and would suggest that we should not budget for more than 5 per cent growth in the coming year. |
| *Director 2* | Does that mean an average 5 per cent increase in expenditure all round? |
| *Director 3* | Most of the increase will be forced on us. We have got to give the staff a cost of living increase, fuel for the vans is bound to increase by at least 5 per cent. |
| *Managing director* | What's certain is that we cannot recruit extra staff at this point so I agree with that. Is there any equipment we need to replace, Derek? |
| *Director 2* | The production stuff is in good nick and we have at least 20 per cent spare capacity. The vans are OK, not too much mileage. |
| *Director 3* | Rosemary needs a new printer and we could all do with a higher spec photocopier. We probably need to up our marketing effort. |
| *Managing director* | I am relying on you to watch the monthly cash flow like a hawk, Bill. Most of my time is taken looking for new business. What about production costs, Derek? |
| *Director 2* | I reckon we can increase production by 10 per cent with hardly any extra cost and no danger. How about that! |
| *Managing director* | And the bank is happy with the state of our overdraft. That all looks fairly satisfactory. As long as we continue to work hard. |

# 32  Définir un budget

| | |
|---|---|
| *Directeur général* | Eh bien, chers collègues. Nous allons ouvrir la séance. Il n'est pas nécessaire que cette réunion soit très formelle, toutefois, je suis sûr que chacun est conscient de son importance. Le bilan pour l'année dernière devra, pour le moment n'être connu que de nous. |
| *Directeur 2* | Cela fait plaisir à lire, 11 pour cent d'augmentation par rapport à l'année précédente ... |
| *Directeur général* | Ne t'emballe pas, Damien. J'ai regardé nos commandes et je suggérerais que nous ne budgétisions pas pour une augmentation supérieure à 5% pour l'année à venir. |
| *Directeur 2* | Est-ce que vous entendez par là une augmentation moyenne de 5% des dépenses en général? |
| *Directeur 3* | Une grande partie de cette augmentation nous sera imposée. Nous devrons attribuer au personnel une augmentation relative au coût de la vie, l'essence pour les véhicules augmentera à coup sûr de 5% au moins. |
| *Directeur général* | Ce qu'il y a de sûr, c'est que nous ne pouvons pas nous permettre de recruter en ce moment. Je suis tout à fait d'accord avec ce que vous venez de dire. Y a-t-il du matériel qui doit être remplacé, Damien? |
| *Directeur 2* | Le matériel de production est en bon état et nous avons 20% de capacité de production disponible. Il n'y a pas de problèmes au niveau des véhicules, ils n'affichent pas trop de kilomètres. |
| *Directeur 3* | Rosanne a besoin d'une nouvelle imprimante et il serait bon pour nous tous d'avoir une photocopieuse plus performante. Nous avons également probablement besoin de faire un plus grand effort au niveau marketing. |
| *Directeur général* | Guillaume, je te fais confiance pour surveiller la trésorerie[1] tous les mois de très près. Je passe la plupart de mon temps à développer de nouvelles affaires. Qu'en est-il des coûts de production, Damien? |
| *Directeur 2* | Je pense que nous pouvons augmenter la production de 10% pratiquement sans aucun coût supplémentaire ou risque. Pas mal, n'est-ce pas? |
| *Directeur général* | Et la banque est satisfaite de l'état de notre découvert. Tout m'a l'air relativement satisfaisant. Toujours à condition de continuer à travailler comme des forcenés. |

1  '*Le cash-flow*' is also used but, like other terms borrowed from the English, not encouraged by the French government.

# 33  Organizing a product launch

| | |
|---|---|
| *Albert Archer* | My suggestion is that we hire a river cruiser and take our key accounts for an evening cruise and dinner. After dinner we can unveil our new range of services. |
| *Brian Ball* | Do you think that'll be enough? |
| *Albert Archer* | Well, when we've informed the key accounts, we can do some promotion in the trade press – some ads and, if possible, a press release. The key accounts managers will be expected to keep in touch with their clients. We'll have to wait and see what response we get from the trade journals. |
| *Brian Ball* | OK, agreed. Do you want me to get Jim started on the arrangements? |
| *Albert Archer* | Yes, you might as well. By the way, what about hospitality for the press? Couldn't we invite them to the clubroom for a special presentation? |
| *Brian Ball* | Good idea! I'll get Jim to see to it. |

# 33  Organiser le lancement d'un produit

| | |
|---|---|
| *Albert Arletty* | Je serais d'avis que nous louions un bateau-mouche et organisions pour nos plus gros clients une soirée dîner-croisière. Après le dîner, nous pourrions dévoiler notre nouvelle gamme de services. |
| *Bruno Bertrand* | Crois-tu que ce sera suffisant? |
| *Albert Arletty* | Eh bien, une fois que nous aurons prévenu les clients principaux, nous pourrions faire une campagne dans la presse spécialisée – quelques annonces publicitaires, et si possible, un communiqué de presse. Les responsables des comptes principaux seront censés garder contact avec leurs clients. Nous devrons attendre de voir les réactions provoquées dans les journaux spécialisés. |
| *Bruno Bertrand* | OK, c'est d'accord. Veux-tu que je demande à Jim de commencer à organiser tout cela? |
| *Albert Arletty* | Oui, tant qu'à faire. Au fait, au niveau de l'hospitalité pour la presse? Ne pourrions-nous pas les inviter dans notre salle de réunion et faire une présentation spéciale? |
| *Bruno Bertrand* | Très bonne idée! Je vais veiller à ce que Jim s'occupe de l'organisation. |

# 34  Contacting official agencies

## (a) Chamber of Commerce

| | |
|---|---|
| *Roberto Comas* | How do you do? I'm Roberto Comas, from Textiles Paloma. |
| *Arturo Castro* | Pleased to meet you. Arturo Castro. My staff told me you were going to call in this morning. How can we help? |
| *Roberto Comas* | We are thinking of expanding the business, especially to focus on the '30 to 50' market. We were advised to seek your views on how and where best to establish retail outlets for our fashion products. |
| *Arturo Castro* | Well, Mr Comas. I hope you will join the Chamber as and when you set up in the city, but for the time being you are welcome to our assistance. |
| *Roberto Comas* | Yes, I understand, but right now we are keen to obtain some information on local retail figures, the competition, some data on the local population, available premises and so on. |
| *Arturo Castro* | That's no problem. We can provide you with what you request and much more. Are you likely to be creating any jobs through your new initiative? |
| *Roberto Comas* | We will inevitably need new staff, both in the factory and in the local shops. Do you happen to have a good contact at the Jobcentre? |
| *Arturo Castro* | Yes, of course. If you'd like to come through to my office, we'll have a coffee and get down to discussing things. |

# 34   Contacter des organismes publics

## (a) La Chambre de Commerce

| | |
|---|---|
| *Roberto Comas* | Comment allez-vous? Roberto Comas de chez Textiles Paloma. |
| *Arturo Castro* | Enchanté de faire votre connaissance. Arturo Castro. Ma secrétaire m'a prévenu que vous alliez venir ce matin. Que puis-je faire pour vous? |
| *Roberto Comas* | Nous pensons sérieusement à agrandir notre entreprise, et nous visons principalement le marché touchant les 'trente à cinquante ans'. On m'a conseillé de venir recueillir vos conseils quant à la meilleure localisation de nos magasins pour la vente de nos produits de mode. |
| *Arturo Castro* | Eh bien, M. Comas, j'espère que vous adhérerez à la Chambre de Commerce lorsque vous serez établis dans notre ville. En attendant, je me ferai effectivement un plaisir de vous aider. |
| *Roberto Comas* | Oui, je comprends. Pour le moment, nous aimerions obtenir des renseignements d'ordre général, les chiffres de ventes réalisés dans la région, des informations concernant la concurrence, la population locale, les locaux actuellement disponibles et ainsi de suite. |
| *Arturo Castro* | Il n'y a aucun problème. Nous pouvons vous procurer toutes ces informations et bien plus encore. Allez-vous créer de nouveaux emplois grâce à cette nouvelle initiative? |
| *Roberto Comas* | Nous aurons inévitablement besoin de personnel tant à l'usine que dans les magasins. Avez vous de bonnes relations avec l'ANPE?[1] |
| *Arturo Castro* | Oui, bien sûr. Mais, venez plutôt dans mon bureau. Nous boirons une tasse de café et discuterons affaires plus à notre aise. |

1  *Agence Nationale pour l'Emploi* (ANPE) – the French national employment exchange.

# (b) Customs and Excise

| | |
|---|---|
| *Customs and Excise officer* | Good morning, sir. |
| *Retailer* | Hello, I have a query regarding the import of meat products. I wonder if you can help me. |
| *Customs and Excise officer* | Certainly. Can you explain? |
| *Retailer* | We're a meat retailer based here in Dover, and we're intending to import a range of cooked meats and sausages from a German supplier. So far we've only been supplied by British companies. I need to know what the regulations are. |
| *Customs and Excise officer* | It's rather difficult and complex to explain briefly. There is a range of regulations and restrictions. They're contained in our information brochures. When are you intending to import these products? |
| *Retailer* | We'll get the first shipment in a couple of weeks. |
| *Customs and Excise officer* | Then you'd better move fast. I'll collect all the information for you. The best thing is for you to read it and then come back to us with any queries. |
| *Retailer* | Fine. I'll get down to it. |

# (b) La Douane

*Douanier*    Bonjour, Monsieur.

*Détaillant*    Bonjour, j'ai besoin de quelques renseignements concernant l'importation de produits à base de viande. Pouvez-vous m'aider?

*Douanier*    Bien sûr. Que voulez-vous exactement?

*Détaillant*    Nous vendons de la viande ici à Douvres et nous aimerions importer une sélection de viandes cuites et de saucisses qui nous viendraient d'un fournisseur allemand. Jusqu'à présent, nous étions approvisionnés par des fournisseurs britanniques. Je dois donc connaître les réglementations.

*Douanier*    C'est relativement complexe et difficile à expliquer brièvement. J'ai ici tout un tas de réglementations et de restrictions à respecter. Elles figurent toutes dans nos brochures d'information. Quand comptiez-vous importer ces produits?

*Détaillant*    Nous devrions recevoir notre première commande d'ici deux semaines.

*Douanier*    Il faut donc se dépêcher. Alors, je vais rassembler ces informations pour vous. La meilleure chose à faire est de les lire et de nous contacter si vous avez d'autres questions.

*Détaillant*    Très bien. Je vais étudier cela de près.

# 35　Presenting company policy

## (a) Location

| | |
|---|---|
| *Managing director* | As you know, it's the company's policy to set up new plants in areas which offer the most advantages. For this reason the liquid detergent plant here will close as soon as the new plant is operational in the south-east. There are both economic and social benefits in doing things this way. |
| *Journalist* | What will happen to the people currently working at the plant? Will they be made redundant? |
| *Managing director* | That's not the way we do things here. We'll look to natural wastage and early retirements throughout the company – nobody will be made redundant because of this. But it's clear that some people will have to be redeployed and there may be possibilities at the new plant for some of the specialist technicians if they are willing to relocate. |
| *Journalist* | How will you reorganize the remaining staff? Would they qualify for removal assistance if they agreed to move? |
| *Managing director* | Clearly we would offer them a relocation package if they agreed to move; that's standard practice here. |

# 35 Exposer la politique de l'entreprise

## (a) Localisation

*Directeur général*    Comme vous le savez, la politique de l'entreprise veut que de nouvelles usines soient construites dans les régions les plus propices.[1] Pour cette raison, cette usine de détergent liquide sera fermée dès que la nouvelle usine du sud-est sera opérationnelle. Il y a des avantages tant économiques que sociaux à faire les choses de cette façon.

*Journaliste*    Et qu'adviendra-t-il des employés de cette usine? Seront-ils licenciés?

*Directeur général*    Ce n'est pas notre façon de traiter le personnel. Il faut que nous considérions les départs naturels ainsi que les préretraites au niveau global de l'entreprise – cette opération n'entraînera aucun licenciement. Mais il est sûr qu'une partie du personnel devra être réaffectée et il y aura sûrement des possibilités offertes par la nouvelle usine pour certains techniciens spécialistes s'ils acceptent de se déplacer.

*Journaliste*    Comment allez-vous opérer avec le personnel restant? Bénéficieront-ils d'une aide au déménagement s'ils acceptent d'être déplacés?

*Directeur général*    Bien sûr, nous leur offrirons un forfait déménagement s'ils acceptent notre proposition, cela fait partie de nos principes.

1 Literally, 'the most favourable regions'.

# (b) Development

| | |
|---|---|
| *Personnel manager* | So, as we have seen during the last half-hour, the prospects for the next few years are quite encouraging. We now need to consider precisely how we are going to develop policies to benefit the firm and its employees. |
| *Managing director* | Can I just add before you continue, Alan, that the Board will be taking very seriously whatever conclusions are drawn by this group today. So it is essential that people speak their mind. |
| *Personnel manager* | Thanks for confirming that, Victor. Frankly, recent EU legislation means that our profit margins can be increased as long as we take into account from the start matters like Health and Safety, employee compensation, maternity benefits, etc. These items, that normally and quite properly cost us a percentage of raw profits, can be reclaimed if fully documented. |
| *Financial director* | Well, that's good news as in the past we've never been able to prepare very well for this sort of cost to the company. |
| *Personnel manager* | I am proposing, therefore, that we create a small unit within the company to cover the full range of benefits that can accrue to us under the new provisions. In addition, we should be able to demonstrate to the workforce that by our observing these criteria, they too will have an enhanced status. Before I continue to my next subject, are there any questions? |
| *Sales manager* | Alan, can anyone guarantee that our current level of sales is sustainable? What you are saying about the interests of the workforce and those of the company as a whole being convergent seems to me a rather optimistic interpretation. |
| *Personnel manager* | We've commissioned a report on this very question. If everybody is prepared to wait for a week longer I should be able to give you an honest answer. Frankly, whatever the precise outcome of that report, we have to make plans for a future in which we balance the financial well-being of the firm with that of all the individuals who work for it. |

# (b) Développement

| | |
|---|---|
| *Directeur du personnel* | Alors, si l'on en juge par ce qui a été dit pendant cette dernière demi-heure, les perspectives d'avenir pour les quelques années à venir sont plutôt encourageantes. Nous devons maintenant préciser la manière dont nous devrions développer notre politique afin qu'elle avantage tant l'entreprise que ses employés. |
| *Directeur général* | Avant de poursuivre, Alain, j'aimerais préciser que le conseil d'administration prendra très au sérieux les conclusions tirées de cette réunion, quelles qu'elles soient. Il est par conséquent très important que chacun dise ce qu'il pense. |
| *Directeur du personnel* | Merci d'avoir soulevé ce point, Victor. Pour être franc, les récentes législations de l'Union Européenne ne nous empêcheront pas de continuer à augmenter nos marges de bénéfice à partir du moment où nous tenons compte dès le début de la santé, la sécurité, des indemnités pour les employés, des allocations de maternité, etcetera. Ces charges, qui nous coûtent un certain pourcentage des bénéfices bruts, peuvent être récupérées si nous sommes munis des documents justificatifs. |
| *Directeur financier* | Eh bien, c'est une très bonne nouvelle, surtout si l'on considère que nous n'avons jamais été très bien préparés pour ce genre de coût imputé à notre entreprise. |
| *Directeur du personnel* | Je propose par conséquent de créer une petite unité au sein de l'entreprise, qui s'occuperait de tous les avantages dont nous pourrions bénéficier grâce aux nouvelles dispositions légales. De plus, nous devrions pouvoir démontrer à notre personnel qu'en observant ces critères, eux aussi verront leur statut s'améliorer. Avant que j'enchaîne sur la question suivante, avez vous d'autres questions? |
| *Directeur des ventes* | Alain, qui peut garantir que notre niveau de vente actuel peut être maintenu? Ce que tu viens de dire au sujet de la convergence des intérêts de notre force ouvrière et ceux de l'entreprise en général me semble être une interprétation relativement optimiste. |
| *Directeur du personnel* | Nous avons demandé un rapport sur la question. Si chacun a la patience d'attendre encore une semaine, je serai à même de vous donner une réponse honnête. De toute façon, quel que soit le résultat précis se dégageant du rapport, nous devons faire des projets pour arriver à équilibrer le bien-être financier de l'entreprise et celui des individus qui travaillent pour elle. |

# (c) Staffing

*Meeting between the personnel manager and a trade union representative*

| | |
|---|---|
| *Personnel manager* | I've called you in to tell you about our proposed staff changes. |
| *TU representative* | Yes, I know. I've heard that you're planning compulsory redundancies. |
| *Personnel manager* | No, that's not the case, but we do need to rationalize. |
| *TU representative* | Can you tell me why? |
| *Personnel manager* | Everyone knows why: production costs have been increasing because of outmoded plant. We've taken the decision to close one of our older plants. |
| *TU representative* | Has it been decided which one? |
| *Personnel manager* | We have a choice of either Sheffield or Gloucester. The precise figures are being worked out. |
| *TU representative* | And what happens to the workforce? |
| *Personnel manager* | We are going to see what possibilities there are for voluntary redundancies and early retirements. That should reduce the problem considerably. |
| *TU representative* | But not fully. You'll have to lay people off. |
| *Personnel manager* | We don't think we'll have to do that. The remaining staff can be relocated. We have other plants within 20 miles of both Sheffield and Gloucester. We're talking about streamlining production, not cutting it back. |
| *TU representative* | So what will be the total reduction in the workforce? |
| *Personnel manager* | In the region of 200 to 250. |
| *TU representative* | And when will the changes be made? |
| *Personnel manager* | We're hoping to have them complete by the end of January. |
| *TU representative* | Has the matter been discussed at board level yet? |
| *Personnel manager* | Of course – the board gave its approval last week. That's why we're moving on it now. |

# (c) Personnel

*Réunion entre le directeur du personnel et le représentant d'un syndicat*

| | |
|---|---|
| *Directeur du personnel* | Je vous ai appelé pour vous parler des changements proposés au niveau du personnel. |
| *Représentant du syndicat* | Oui, je sais. J'ai entendu dire qu'il y avait des projets de licenciements.[1] |
| *Directeur du personnel* | Non, ce n'est pas exactement le cas mais nous devons rationaliser. |
| *Représentant du syndicat* | Pouvez-vous me dire pourquoi? |
| *Directeur du personnel* | Tout le monde sait pourquoi: les coûts de production ont augmenté parce que nos usines sont démodées. Nous avons pris la décision de fermer l'une des plus vieilles. |
| *Représentant du syndicat* | A-t-on décidé de quelle usine il s'agit? |
| *Directeur du personnel* | Nous devons choisir entre Lyon et Nantes. Les chiffres précis sont en cours d'élaboration. |
| *Représentant du syndicat* | Et qu'adviendra-t-il de la main d'œuvre? |
| *Directeur du personnel* | Nous allons voir quelles sont les possibilités de départs volontaires et de préretraites. Ceci devrait réduire considérablement notre problème. |
| *Représentant du syndicat* | Mais pas entièrement. Il va falloir que vous licenciez. |
| *Directeur du personnel* | Nous ne pensons pas devoir le faire. Le personnel restant pourra être muté.[2] Nous avons d'autres usines à environ 20 kilomètres de Lyon et Nantes. Nous parlons de rationaliser la production pas de la réduire. |
| *Représentant du syndicat* | Alors quelle sera la réduction totale de la main d'œuvre? |
| *Directeur du personnel* | Environ deux cents (200) à deux cent cinquante (250). |
| *Représentant du syndicat* | Et quand ces changements auront-ils lieu? |
| *Directeur du personnel* | Nous espérons que tout sera fait d'ici fin janvier. |
| *Représentant du syndicat* | Est-ce que ce sujet a été discuté au conseil d'administration? |
| *Directeur du personnel* | Bien sûr. Le conseil a donné son accord la semaine dernière. C'est la raison pour laquelle nous essayons maintenant de progresser. |

1 *Licencier* 'to dismiss', 'to make redundant'. 2 *Muter* 'to transfer' (to another post).

# (d) Sales

| | |
|---|---|
| *Chairman* | I am pleased to open this first Board Meeting following our change of parent company. The first item on the agenda is sales policy. Over to you, Charles. |
| *Charles* | Thank you, Mr Chairman. I am instructed by the main board of our parent company to plan, with you, the introduction of a new sales policy. |
| *Director 2* | What view is taken of our existing policy? Too expensive? |
| *Charles* | In a nutshell, yes. The company's product lines are mostly good but the sales operation could be improved. |
| *Director 2* | I am not surprised. I have thought for some time that we have too large a sales force in too many regions. |
| *Charles* | That brings me to one of the proposals I have. To redraw the regions and slim down the workforce. |
| *Director 2* | By redundancy or natural wastage? |
| *Charles* | Probably a bit of both would be necessary. Also, some concern has been expressed about the size of the advertising budget. |
| *Director 3* | Hear, hear. For a company with good products we do a hell of a lot of advertising. |
| *Charles* | I gather it is proposed, subject to this board's approval, to appoint a top class Marketing Manager with the remit to review the whole operation. |
| *Director 2* | Is a system of dealerships on the cards? |
| *Charles* | Nothing is excluded based on the premise of a need to rationalize the sales operation. |

# (d) Ventes

| | |
|---|---|
| *Président-directeur général* | Je suis heureux d'ouvrir la première réunion du Conseil d'administration suite à notre changement de société-mère. Le premier point de notre ordre du jour est la politique de vente. Charles? |
| *Charles* | Merci, Monsieur le Président. Le Conseil Général de notre société-mère m'a chargé de planifier, avec vous, l'introduction d'une nouvelle politique de vente. |
| *Directeur 2* | Comment est perçue notre politique actuelle? Trop chère? |
| *Charles* | En un mot, oui. Les gammes de produits de l'entreprise sont bonnes d'une manière générale mais le fonctionnement des ventes pourrait être amélioré. |
| *Directeur 2* | Cela ne me surprend pas vraiment. Cela fait un certain temps que je pense que nous avons une force de vente trop importante dans de trop nombreuses régions. |
| *Charles* | Ceci m'amène à l'une des suggestions que j'avais à faire. Revoir les régions et réduire la main-d'œuvre. |
| *Directeur 2* | En licenciant ou grâce aux départs naturels? |
| *Charles* | Il faudra certainement un peu des deux. On m'a également fait part de certains soucis au sujet du budget de la publicité. |
| *Directeur 3* | Entendu, entendu. Pour une entreprise comme la nôtre produisant de si bons produits, nous faisons effectivement bien trop de publicité! |
| *Charles* | Il semble qu'il soit proposé, proposition assujettie à l'approbation de ce conseil, de nommer un très bon directeur du marketing ayant la mission de revoir l'opération entière. |
| *Directeur 2* | A-t-on pensé à un système de concessions? |
| *Charles* | Rien n'est exclu en partant du principe que l'on a besoin de rationaliser. |

# 36  Visiting the bank manager

*Bank manager*    Good morning, Mrs Ansell. I'm pleased to see you again.

*Mrs Ansell*    Good morning, Mr Green. I have come to discuss our business plan with you. Our turnover has risen by 40 per cent for the last three years and our products have been selling really well. We'd like to open another shop in Loughborough.

*Bank manager*    Well, Mrs Ansell, I have followed the success of your company. The bank has been very happy to support its development. You've always stayed within your overdraft limits. How might we help you now?

*Mrs Ansell*    We're having to plough back most of our profits into the business in order to finance our growth. We've done market research in Loughborough and are convinced that it will be a success, what with Loughborough being a university town. What I've come to discuss with you is a loan to finance the lease of a shop and to buy start-up stock.

*Bank manager*    I'm sure the bank will be willing in principle to finance your business's future growth. If you send me your proposal for the shop in Loughborough, with details of the amount you wish to borrow, cash-flow projections – you know, all the usual information – I will consider it as quickly as possible.

*Mrs Ansell*    Thank you very much. I'll send you our proposal in the next few days.

# 36  Rendez-vous avec le directeur d'une agence bancaire

*Directeur d'agence*    Bonjour, Madame Anselle. Je suis content de vous revoir.

*Madame Anselle*    Bonjour, Monsieur Lebrun. Je suis venue discuter de notre plan d'entreprise avec vous. Notre chiffre d'affaires a augmenté de 40% ces trois dernières années! Nos produits se sont très bien vendus.[1] Nous aimerions ouvrir un nouveau magasin à Lyon.

*Directeur d'agence*    Et bien, Madame Anselle, j'ai suivi les progrès de votre entreprise. La banque était très contente d'avoir soutenu son développement. Vous avez toujours respecté votre découvert autorisé. Comment pourrions-nous vous aider cette fois?

*Madame Anselle*    Nous devons réinvestir la majeure partie de nos bénéfices afin de développer notre croissance. Nous avons fait une étude de marché à Lyon et sommes convaincus que ce sera un succès, surtout si l'on considère le fait que Lyon est une ville universitaire. Ce dont je suis venu discuter avec vous aujourd'hui est la possibilité d'un prêt pour financer le bail d'un magasin et acheter le stock dont j'ai besoin pour commencer.

*Directeur d'agence*    Je suis sûr que notre banque sera d'accord sur le principe pour financer la croissance de votre entreprise. Si vous m'envoyez votre proposition pour le magasin de Lyon, en y incluant les détails concernant le montant que vous souhaitez emprunter, les prévisions de cash-flow – vous savez, toutes les informations requises dans un tel cas – je considérerai la chose aussi rapidement que possible.

*Madame Anselle*    Merci beaucoup. Je vous enverrai notre proposition d'ici quelques jours.

---

1   Literally, 'have sold themselves very well'.

# 37  Selling a service to a client

| | |
|---|---|
| *Teresa Allison* | Good morning, Mr Tolson. I'm Teresa Allison from P and G Computer Maintenance Services. You answered one of our ads in the *Evening Mail*, so I have come to fill you in on what we have to offer to small businesses. |
| *Mr Tolson* | Ah yes, thank you for coming so soon. As you can see, we recently purchased a computer system which should maximize our efficiency in dealing with orders. |
| *Teresa Allison* | I assume that you have an initial service contract on the machines, but once that runs out you would be best advised to take out a plan like ours. We can provide a 24-hour breakdown cover, three-monthly servicing, immediate replacement of faulty equipment, regular updating of your software and a free consultancy service for the duration of the contract. |
| *Mr Tolson* | It sounds a good deal, but what are the conditions of payment? Is it possible to pay monthly via a standing order or does it have to be a lump sum? |
| *Teresa Allison* | You can pay either way, as long as your bank can guarantee that your account will bear it. I'll leave you some brochures to read at your leisure; you'll be able compare our prices and conditions with others, though I can assure you that it's the most favourable deal available at present. |
| *Mr Tolson* | OK, fair enough. Can you give me a ring in about a week and I'll let you know what I think. |
| *Teresa Allison* | I certainly will. Give me your number and I'll be in touch early next week. |

# 37  Vendre un service à un client

| | |
|---|---|
| *Thérèse André* | Bonjour, Monsieur Trudeau. Je suis Thérèse André de chez P et G Informatique. Vous avez répondu à l'une de nos annonces parues dans *Le Courrier du Soir*. Je suis donc venue pour vous donner davantage d'informations sur ce que nous pouvons offrir aux petites entreprises. |
| *M. Trudeau* | Ah, oui. Je vous remercie d'être venue aussi rapidement. Comme vous pouvez le voir nous venons de nous procurer un système informatique qui devrait maximiser notre compétence en matière de gestion des commandes. |
| *Thérèse André* | Je présume que vous avez pris un premier contrat d'entretien du matériel, mais lorsqu'il arrivera à échéance je vous conseillerais de prendre un contrat du style du nôtre. Nous offrons un service 24h/24h en cas de panne, une visite d'entretien tous les trois mois, le remplacement immédiat du matériel ayant des défauts, la mise à jour régulière de vos logiciels[1] et un service de consultation gratuit pour la durée du contrat. |
| *M. Trudeau* | Oui, ça a l'air d'être une très bonne idée. Quelles sont les conditions de paiement? Est-il possible de payer mensuellement par virement automatique ou doit-on payer comptant? |
| *Thérèse André* | L'un ou l'autre à partir du moment où la banque peut garantir votre solvabilité.[2] Je vais vous laisser des plaquettes d'information que vous pourrez lire lorsque vous aurez le temps. Vous pourrez comparer nos prix et conditions avec ceux des autres. Je peux quand même vous dire que nous proposons la meilleure offre sur le marché en ce moment. |
| *M. Trudeau* | Très bien. Pouvez-vous me passer un coup de fil d'ici une semaine et je vous dirai ce que j'en pense. |
| *Thérèse André* | OK. Bien sûr. Donnez-moi votre numéro et je vous appellerai en début de semaine prochaine. |

1  *Le logiciel* – a software package.
2  Literally, 'guarantee your solvency'.

## 38  Selling a product to a client

| | |
|---|---|
| *Salesman* | This motor is a very good buy, sir, if you prefer not to buy new. |
| *Max Chancellor* | It certainly looks to be in immaculate condition. About two years old is it? |
| *Salesman* | Eighteen months. It only has 6,000 miles on the clock. |
| *Max Chancellor* | That's unusual isn't it? Who was the previous owner? |
| *Salesman* | It's been a demonstration model. That explains the complete lack of any dents and no rust of course. |
| *Max Chancellor* | What sort of discount could I have? Can you offer a hire purchase deal? |
| *Salesman* | We are offering a 5 per cent discount off the list price and you could repay over one or two years. |
| *Max Chancellor* | That sounds quite interesting. And you would offer me the trade-in price for my present car that we discussed earlier? |
| *Salesman* | Yes indeed, sir. Would you like to try it out? |

## 39  Giving an informal vote of thanks

| | |
|---|---|
| *Speaker* | Ladies and gentlemen, I'd like to take this opportunity of thanking Leonard White and his colleagues for arranging the seminar over the last few days. I'm sure we've all found it most interesting and stimulating, and we all have good ideas to take back with us. |

I'd also like to thank them for their hospitality over the last two evenings, and I'm sure I speak for all of us when I say that the seminar has been a great success.

As you all know, we intend to hold a similar seminar next year at our headquarters, and that will give us the opportunity to return the hospitality. Thanks again, Leonard and colleagues, for a most successful event.

# 38  Vendre un produit à un client

| | |
|---|---|
| *Vendeur* | Cette voiture est un très bon achat, Monsieur, si vous préférez ne pas acheter neuf. |
| *Client* | Elle m'a certainement l'air en excellent état. Elle a deux ans, c'est ça? |
| *Vendeur* | Dix-huit mois. Elle a seulement 6 000 kilomètres au compteur. |
| *Client* | Ce genre d'occasion[1] est relativement rare, n'est-ce-pas? Qui était le propriétaire précédent? |
| *Vendeur* | C'était un modèle de démonstration. Ce qui explique qu'il n'y ait aucune marque sur la carrosserie et pas de rouille bien sûr. |
| *Client* | Quel genre de ristourne pourrais-je avoir et y aurait-il une possibilité de location-vente? |
| *Vendeur* | Nous offrons une ristourne de 5% sur le tarif figurant sur la liste des prix et vous auriez la possibilité de rembourser en un ou deux ans. |
| *Client* | Ceci m'a l'air très intéressant. Et m'offririez-vous la même valeur de reprise sur ma voiture que ce que vous m'aviez précédemment offert? |
| *Vendeur* | Oui, bien sûr, Monsieur. Voulez vous l'essayer? |

1   *Une occasion* is short for *une voiture d'occasion* 'a second-hand car'. *Une occasion* also means 'a bargain'.

# 39  Remerciements officieux

| | |
|---|---|
| *Orateur* | Mesdames et Messieurs, j'aimerais profiter de cette occasion pour remercier Léonard Blanc et ses collègues d'avoir organisé le séminaire qui s'est déroulé ces derniers jours. Je suis sûr que nous l'avons tous trouvé extrêmement intéressant et stimulant, et que nous repartirons tous avec de nouvelles idées. |
| | J'aimerais également les remercier de l'hospitalité dont ils ont fait preuve[1] au cours de ces deux dernières soirées et je suis sûr que nous sommes tous du même avis sur le fait que ce séminaire fut un grand succès. |
| | Comme vous le savez tous, nous aimerions organiser le même genre de séminaire l'année prochaine au siège, et ceci nous donnera l'occasion de vous rendre votre hospitalité. Merci encore Léonard, et vos collègues, pour cet événement très fructueux. |

1   *Faire preuve de quelque chose* – 'to show (give evidence of) something'.

# 40  Discussing contracts

## (a) Sales conditions

| | |
|---|---|
| *Client* | I'm pleased to inform you that we are prepared to include your company as one of our suppliers. Before we sign an agreement, we need to agree on terms and conditions. |
| *Supplier* | We're delighted. What in particular do we need to agree? |
| *Client* | Firstly, our terms of payment are 20 per cent on receipt of the goods and the remainder within 90 days. |
| *Supplier* | We normally expect to be paid in full within 60 days, but if we can have a two-year agreement, we could accept your conditions. |
| *Client* | Fine. We also want a 10 per cent discount for orders of over 5,000 parts. Deliveries must also be made by the specified date, with penalties for late delivery. I think you've been given some details. |
| *Supplier* | Yes, and I can assure you that we are accustomed to just-in-time delivery. I'm sure that you know already that we offer good service at a good price. We're ready to sign. |
| *Client* | That's good. I have the agreement here. |

# 40   Discuter de contrats

## (a) Conditions de vente

| | |
|---|---|
| *Client* | Je suis heureux de vous apprendre que nous sommes prêts à inclure votre entreprise sur la liste de nos fournisseurs. Avant de signer un contrat, nous devons nous mettre d'accord sur les termes et conditions. |
| *Fournisseur* | Nous en sommes enchantés. Sur quels aspects particuliers devons-nous nous mettre d'accord? |
| *Client* | Tout d'abord nos termes de règlement sont de 20% à la réception des marchandises et le solde sous 90 jours.[1] |
| *Fournisseur* | Normalement, nous préférons être réglés entièrement sous 60 jours, mais si nous avons un contrat de deux ans, nous pourrions accepter vos conditions. |
| *Client* | Très bien. Nous voulons également une ristourne de 10% pour les commandes supérieures à 5 000 pièces. Les livraisons doivent être effectuées à des dates spécifiées et soumises à des pénalités pour livraison tardive. Je crois que l'on vous a donné des détails à ce sujet, n'est-ce pas? |
| *Fournisseur* | Oui, je peux vous garantir que nous avons l'habitude des livraisons juste à temps. Je suis sûr que vous êtes tout à fait conscient que nous offrons un bon service à un prix raisonnable. Nous sommes prêts à signer. |
| *Client* | Parfait. Voici le contrat. |

1   Literally, 'under 90 days'.

# (b) Payment conditions

*Client*        When will I be required to complete the payment of the instalments on the new equipment?

*Supplier*    There are several plans under which you have maximum flexibility of conditions. Obviously, you can pay the full amount in a one-off sum, which would mean a substantial saving overall as interest costs are always high in the transport sector.

*Client*        Suppose I could pay you 50 per cent of the total cost now, what sort of arrangements would best suit us both for the other half over a couple of years?

*Supplier*    That would depend on how we structure our own borrowing requirement, but in principle there is no reason why payments cannot be adjusted exactly to suit your circumstances.

*Client*        Fine. Can you give me a few days to discuss this with my accountant? If the bank is willing to lend me more than I had first thought, I may perhaps be able to buy outright.

*Supplier*    Why not? With general interest rates as they are it could be worth risking a big outlay. But remember that whatever your decision, we can help as our own finances are secured by the parent company.

*Client*        Thanks for the reassurance. I'll let you know ASAP.

# (b) Conditions de paiement

*Client*  A quelle date voulez-vous que le règlement final soit effectué pour l'installation du nouveau matériel?

*Fournisseur*  Il y a plusieurs contrats qui offrent un maximum de souplesse au niveau des conditions. Bien sûr, vous pouvez régler la somme d'un seul coup, ce qui vous permettrait de faire pas mal d'économies car comme vous le savez, les intérêts sont toujours élevés dans le domaine du transport.

*Client*  Supposons que je puisse vous payer 50% du montant total dès maintenant, quel genre de contrat nous conviendrait le mieux, à vous tant qu'à moi, si l'on voulait échelonner[1] la somme restante sur deux ans?

*Fournisseur*  Cela dépend de la façon dont nous structurerions notre propre endettement, mais en principe il n'y a aucune raison pour que les règlements ne puissent pas être ajustés pour convenir à vos circonstances.

*Client*  Très bien. Pouvez-vous me donner quelques jours pour discuter de tout cela avec mon comptable? Si la banque accepte de me prêter plus que je ne le pensais au départ, je pourrais peut-être faire cet achat comptant.[2]

*Fournisseur*  Pourquoi pas? Avec des taux d'intérêts généraux tels qu'ils sont il serait peut-être valable de risquer une grosse dépense. Mais souvenez-vous que quelle que soit votre décision, nous pouvons vous aider car nos propres finances sont garanties par notre société-mère.

*Client*  Je vous remercie de m'avoir rassuré. Je vous ferai connaître ma décision dès que possible.

1  To spread or stagger payments.
2  Literally, 'make this purchase in cash'.

# (c) Breach of contract

*Client*      Well, here we have the order contract that you wanted to discuss.

*Supplier*    Yes, thanks. The paragraph I wanted to look at was this one, 9b.

*Client*      Is there a problem?

*Supplier*    It indicates that unless we deliver within three days of the date indicated, we are in breach of contract, and the order can be cancelled.

*Client*      That's part of our normal contract. Would you have a problem with that?

*Supplier*    I find it a bit unusual.

*Client*      We've had to introduce it, because in the past we had lots of problems with suppliers missing the delivery dates by weeks. We have lost customers because of that. Since we introduced this new clause we've had far fewer problems with delay.

*Supplier*    Is it possible to vary it a little?

*Client*      In what way?

*Supplier*    Well, I find three days very restrictive. We'd be much happier with one week.

*Client*      I'm sure you would! Any particular reason? Have you had difficulties meeting dates in the past?

*Supplier*    Only rarely, but it does happen. And it's usually because a supplier has let us down. I'd like to modify that paragraph a bit, to give us a little more time.

*Client*      Let me check it out with my manager. I'll get back to you in the next 24 hours.

*Supplier*    Thanks.

# (c) Rupture d'un contrat

| | |
|---|---|
| *Client* | Bon, voici le contrat d'achat dont vous désiriez discuter. |
| *Fournisseur* | Oui, merci. Le paragraphe qui m'intéresse est celui-ci, 9b. |
| *Client* | Y a-t-il un problème? |
| *Fournisseur* | Il est dit que si nous ne livrons pas sous les trois jours après la date indiquée, il y aura rupture de contrat et que la commande sera annulée. |
| *Client* | Cela fait partie des clauses normales de nos contrats. Cela vous créera-t-il un problème? |
| *Fournisseur* | J'ai rarement vu cela. |
| *Client* | Il a fallu que nous prenions ce genre de mesure car il nous est arrivé d'avoir beaucoup de problèmes avec des fournisseurs qui avaient jusqu'à plusieurs semaines de retard. Nous avons perdu des clients à cause de cela. Depuis que nous avons adopté cette nouvelle clause, nous avons eu beaucoup moins de problèmes au niveau des retards. |
| *Fournisseur* | Serait il possible de la modifier un petit peu? |
| *Client* | Dans quel sens? |
| *Fournisseur* | Eh bien, je trouve que trois jours c'est un petit peu trop restrictif. Nous serions bien plus satisfaits s'il s'agissait d'une semaine. |
| *Client* | Je suis sûr que vous le seriez! Avez-vous des raisons particulières? Avez-vous déjà eu des difficultés à respecter les délais imposés? |
| *Fournisseur* | Rarement, mais c'est arrivé. Et c'est généralement parce qu'un de nos fournisseurs n'a pas respecté les siens. J'aimerais que ce paragraphe soit un peu modifié, pour nous donner un peu plus de temps. |
| *Client* | Laissez-moi en parler avec mon directeur. Je vous contacterai d'ici 24 heures. |
| *Fournisseur* | Merci. |

# 41  Meeting visitors at the airport

| | |
|---|---|
| *John Andrew* | Messrs Martin and Bertot from Toulouse? |
| *M. Martin* | Are you Mr Andrew from Perkins Industrial? |
| *John Andrew* | Yes, hello. I am glad to hear that you speak English, I was trying to remember my schoolboy French on the way to the airport. |
| *M. Martin* | My colleague Bertot cannot speak English I am afraid, so you may need some of your schoolboy French, or perhaps an interpreter, when we come to discuss the contract. |
| *John Andrew* | Right, I'll see to it. Are these your bags? My car is just outside. Did you have a good journey? |
| *M. Martin* | We had quite a good journey. For some reason our plane from Toulouse to Paris was delayed so we nearly missed the Paris–Birmingham flight. |
| *John Andrew* | I am sure our Chairman will be pleased that you made it. We have high hopes for our proposed deal. Would you like to have a coffee before we leave? |
| *M. Martin* | Don't worry, we had an excellent breakfast on the plane. |
| *John Andrew* | Before we get back to talking shop can I just ask you what time you need to check in for this evening's return flight? |

# 41  Rencontrer des visiteurs à l'aéroport

| | |
|---|---|
| *John Andrew* | Messieurs Martin et Bertot de Toulouse? |
| *M. Martin* | Êtes-vous Monsieur Andrew de chez Perkins Industrial? |
| *John Andrew* | C'est cela. Je suis très content de voir que vous parlez anglais; j'essayais de me souvenir, en venant à l'aéroport, de mes leçons de français lorsque j'étais écolier. |
| *M. Martin* | Mon collègue Bertot ne parle pas anglais; il faudra donc que vous retrouviez certains éléments de votre français scolaire, ou peut-être devrons-nous utiliser les services d'un interprète lorsque nous en viendrons à discuter du contrat. |
| *John Andrew* | Très bien. Je vais m'en occuper. Ce sont vos bagages? Ma voiture est juste en face. Vous avez fait bon voyage? |
| *M. Martin* | Oui, nous avons fait un relativement bon voyage. Je ne sais pas pourquoi mais notre avion de Toulouse à Paris a eu du retard et nous avons failli rater notre vol pour Birmingham. |
| *John Andrew* | Je suis sûr que notre président sera très content que vous soyez arrivés. Nous avons de grands espoirs pour notre affaire. Voulez-vous prendre un café avant de partir? |
| *M. Martin* | Ne vous inquiétez pas, nous avons pris un excellent petit déjeuner pendant le vol. |
| *John Andrew* | Avant de reparler affaires, puis-je vous demander à quelle heure vous devez être de retour à l'aéroport pour reprendre votre avion ce soir? |

# Business Correspondence

# French business correspondence

## Professional letter layout

1
> Etablissements Dolla
> 24, rue Anatole France
> 33000 Bordeaux
> Téléphone: 33 90 04 04
> Télécopieur: 33 90 04 05

2
> Augustin SA,
> Service commercial,
> Zone Industrielle de l'Empereur,
> 19 200 Ussel,
> France

3  [  A l'attention de M. Xavier Martin, Attaché commercial.

4  [                              Bordeaux, le . . . . . . . . . .

5
> V/Réf.:
> N/Réf.:

6  [  Objet:

7
> Monsieur,

8
> Pierre Mancini
> Directeur Commercial

9
> P.J. (2): - Un catalogue
>              - Une liste de nos tarifs

10  [

## 1 Sender details

Placed at the top of the letter, on the left-hand side, this section gives the name, the address, the telephone/fax/telex numbers.

A company would give these details preceded by its logo. The presentation would vary but always remain at the top of the letter.

## 2 Addressee details

These are always placed on the right-hand side of the page (ranged right). They can either be aligned left (as shown on the example) or aligned right on the longest line.

They can include the name and the title of the addressee, followed by the company name, the department to which the addressee belongs and the address, in that order.

## 3 Addressee

If the name and title of the addressee have not been mentioned in 2, they can be set as *A l'attention de ...* ('for the attention of'). This is a more formal layout.

## 4 Date

This is positioned on the right-hand side, below the addressee's address. The place of writing always appears, followed by the date. Two solutions are possible: *Bordeaux, le 18/04/199-* or *Bordeaux, mardi 18 avril 199-*.

## 5 References

*V/Réf.* (*Votre référence*/Your reference)
*N/Réf.* (*Notre référence*/Our reference)
Code references are given here.

## 6 Object of the letter

Gives information on subject treated in the letter.

## 7 Body of the letter

The title appears in full only if it is official (*Monsieur le Président*). For all other cases, only mention *Monsieur* or *Madame* or *Mademoiselle*. Make sure you use the same title in the formal ending.

If you do not know the name of the addressee, start your letter with *Messieurs* or *Madame, Monsieur.*

In French, *cher* is much less used than its English equivalent 'Dear' and indicates a friendship, although it can be used as *Cher collègue* when writing to a member of your confraternity, e.g. another architect, or *Cher Client* (a customer to be buttered up).

Each paragraph of the letter is separated from the previous one by a double space. The last paragraph is always a formal ending, using one of the many possible formulas (see list pp. 285–6).

## 8 Signing off

A space of 5 lines is left for the handwritten signature. Underneath will be typed the name of the author of the letter and the title will be mentioned on the line below.

## 9 Enclosures

*P.J.* means *Pièces Jointes*/enclosures. Always mention the number and the designation of the documents enclosed with your letter.

*P.J.* can be replaced by *Annexe(s)* if the letter is the introduction to the enclosed document.

*P.J.* can be followed by *P.S.* (*post-scriptum*/postscript) to add further details.

## 10 Company data

Companies have to include some information on the bottom of their letterheads. The following items would have to appear:

(a)  Status of the company (*Forme juridique*)
(b)  Initial Company Capital (*au capital de . . .*)
(c)  Chamber of Trade Registration Number (*Numéro d'inscription au répertoire des métiers*)
      Example: N°RCS: BORDEAUX A 596 145 524
(d)  Code APE (*Activité principale exercée* – Main company activity number)
      Example: Code APE 7502
(e)  SIREN Number (*Système Informatique du Répertoire des Entreprises*) made up of 9 digits.
      Example: N° SIREN: 596 145 524
(f)  SIRET Number if applicable (*Système Informatique du Répertoire des Etablissements*).
      This number is issued when a company is comprised of more than one establishment. To all establishments depending on the same firm will be attributed a 14-digit number made up of the firm SIREN number (9 digits) plus 5 digits which will be specific to each establishment.
      Example: N° SIRET: 596 145 524 75 001
(g)  VAT Number if applicable (*Numéro Opérateur TVA*)
      Example: N° Opérateur TVA: FR97 596 145 524
(h)  Bank details if wished by the company

Head Office address and details if applicable can also be mentioned.

Please note that all numbers for the same company are originated from the SIREN Number.

# Note on translations

The documents presented here in parallel text are not a word-for-word translation of each other. Owing to obvious differences in letter-writing style in France and the business terminology used, it is possible to offer only an equivalent version of the French documents in the English text.

# 1  Enquiry about a product

Augustin SA
Z.I. de l'Empereur
F-19200 Ussel
France

Dear Sir/Madam

RE: TOOTHPICK MAKING & PACKAGING MACHINE

We represent a major distributor of foodstuffs and related materials in Kenya.

We have found your name in *Kompass* under the category of suppliers of toothpick-making machinery. Our present requirement is for a special toothpick-making and packaging machine. If you do produce such equipment or can supply it we would be pleased to receive your earliest quotation CIF Mombasa, prices for this machine and its equipment, together with a stated delivery time.

Please would you also quote for the installation of this machine in the Ususu factory in Mombasa.

We look forward to your earliest reply and remain

Yours faithfully


John Mason
Technical Director

# 1  Demande d'information concernant un produit

Augustin S.A.[1]
Z.I. de l'Empereur[2]
19200 Ussel
France

Agrate Brianza, le –/–/199-[3]

Objet: Fabrication de cure-dents et machines à conditionner[4]

Madame, Monsieur,[5]

Nous représentons l'un des plus grands distributeurs de produits alimentaires et produits associés au Kenya.

Nous nous sommes procuré votre nom par l'intermédiaire du *Kompass*[6] dans la catégorie 'fournisseurs de machines à fabriquer des cure-dents'. Ce que nous recherchons actuellement est une machine spéciale capable de fabriquer et conditionner des cure-dents. Si vous produisez un tel outillage ou êtes en mesure de le fournir, nous serions heureux de recevoir votre devis CIF[7]/Mombasa dans les meilleurs délais (prix pour cette machine, l'outillage ainsi que la mention d'une date de livraison).

Nous vous serions également reconnaissants[8] de nous indiquer le coût de l'installation de cette machine dans l'usine d'Ususu à Mombasa.

Dans l'attente de votre prompte réponse, je vous prie d'agréer, Madame, Monsieur, l'expression de mes salutations distinguées.[9]

Gianni Mussini,
Directeur technique[10]

1 Addressee on the right.
2 *Z.I.*: *zone industrielle.*
3 It is standard practice to give place and date. (See layout notes p. 115.)
4 Subject of the correspondence, before the 'Dear Sir, etc'.
5 No word for 'dear' is included, unless there is a real friendship.
6 A business reference book.
7 CIF is the international code. It can translate into French as CAF: *coût, assurance, fret.*
8 The usual word for 'grateful'.
9 A standard ending. (See pp. 285–6.)
10 Typically, the writer's position in the company.

# 2  Enquiry about prices

Bandani Detergenti SpA
Via A. Lamarmora 75
20093 COLOGNO MONZESE (MI)
Italy

Dear Sir/Madam

RE: QUOTATION RMS34/16 JAN 199-/TOILET CLEANSER

On 16 January we received a quotation from your company for the supply of 4,000 litres of industrial toilet cleanser and disinfectant. We were unable to justify ordering this at the time, because we had sufficient stocks remaining from our previous order at the end of last year.

We would like to enquire now if the prices quoted at the time are still valid for this commodity.

If you are unequivocably able to confirm that this is the case, please take this letter as an order for a further 10,000 litres. If there has been any increase in these prices, please fax this to us or phone the undersigned to enable us to proceed and agree a price in due course.

Yours faithfully

Dick DeZwart
Buyer

# 2 Demande de renseignements au sujet des prix

Détergents Bandini S.A.
10 promenade du Fort
14000 Caen[1]
France

Lauwe-Menen, le –/–/199-

Objet: Devis[2] RMS34/16 jan 199-/ Détergent pour toilettes

Madame, Monsieur,

Nous avons reçu de votre part, le 16 janvier dernier, un devis pour la fourniture de 4000 litres de détergent et désinfectant industriels pour toilettes. Nous ne pouvions pas justifier une telle commande à l'époque pour la bonne raison qu'il nous restait de notre commande de l'année précédente des stocks suffisants.

Nous aimerions savoir si les prix indiqués à cette époque sont toujours en vigueur pour ces produits.

Si vous pouvez confirmer sans équivoque que cela est le cas, veuillez considérer cette lettre comme une nouvelle commande de 10 000 litres. Si ces prix ont été sujets à une augmentation, veuillez les télécopier ou téléphoner au soussigné afin que nous puissions[3] aviser[4] et nous mettre d'accord sur un prix en temps voulu.[5]

Vous en remerciant par avance, nous vous prions d'agréer, Madame, Monsieur,[6] l'expression de nos salutations distinguées.

F. DeZwart
Responsable des achats

1 Postcode (*indicatif*) and town.
2 *Un devis*: 'a quote', 'an estimate of cost'.
3 'So that we might': subjunctive (see Reference Grammar, pp. 318–19).
4 *Aviser*: 'to consider', 'to take stock'.
5 *En temps voulu*: a useful translation for 'in due course'.
6 *Madame, Monsieur*: you must reproduce exactly the form of address used at the beginning of the letter.

# 3 Enquiry about a company

Giardin Prati spa
Via Cassia Km 89
Val di Paglia
53040 RADICOFANI
Siena
Italy

Dear Sir/Madam

RE: ORDER LAWN-IND/CZ28

We refer to your quotation for 30 industrial mowing machines, model CZ28.

Our client is now eager to proceed with finalizing the order for this equipment as we are slowly approaching spring time. As we have never placed an order with your company, we would be grateful if you would provide us with your full audited accounts for the last four trading years.

Please ensure that the above accounts reach us within the next five working days, as we are eager not to miss the six-week delivery time which will enable us to have the equipment in our hands as soon as possible.

Yours faithfully

Sales Department

# 3  Demande de renseignements au sujet d'une entreprise

Le Tout Jardin
89 rue de Courtalain
28200 Châteaudun
France

Robbio Lomellina, le –/–/199-

Objet: Commande de tondeuses. Ref: Gazon-IND/CZ28

Messieurs,[1]

Nous nous référons à votre devis pour trente tondeuses industrielles, modèle CZ28.

Notre client est maintenant désireux de faire avancer cette commande du fait que nous nous rapprochons du printemps. Etant donné que nous n'avons encore jamais passé commande auprès de votre entreprise, nous vous serions reconnaissants de bien vouloir nous faire parvenir vos comptes contrôlés des quatre derniers exercices comptables.[2]

Nous vous serions très reconnaissants de vous assurer que ces derniers nous parviennent sous les cinq jours ouvrables[3] car nous sommes désireux de ne pas outrepasser les délais[4] de livraison de six semaines afin d'être en possession du matériel[5] le plus rapidement possible.

Vous en remerciant par avance, nous vous prions d'agréer, Messieurs, l'expression de nos salutations distinguées.

Luigi Ravanelli
Directeur des ventes

1  'Dear Sirs' is used when you do not know the name(s) of the people.
2  *Exercice (comptable)*: 'financial year'.
3  *Jours ouvrables*: 'working days', from the verb *ouvrer*.
4  *Délai* means 'time lapse' allowed for something, 'time limit'.
5  *Matériel* means 'equipment' rather than 'material'.

# 4  Enquiry about a person

27 September 199-

ROPER Industriale
Viale San Benedetto 39–43
20084 Lacchiarella
Milano

Dear Sirs

RE: Mr Samuel Smith

We write to you as a fellow producer of machine tools. We have recently received an application from Mr Samuel Smith of Reading (England) who is applying for a post as technical support engineer with our company. This gentleman has given us your company's name both as a previous employer and as a character referee.

From our reading of Mr Smith's CV he would appear most suitable for the post. However we are also keen that people should fit into our factory and we are most concerned that in his early twenties Mr Smith was a very active member of the European Pro-Whale Organization. We would appreciate your comments on this as we are keen to be better informed about this candidate.

Yours faithfully


Carlo Ruggeri
Personnel Manager

# 4  Demande de renseignements au sujet d'un candidat

Roper Industriel,
39–43 rue Saint Benoît,
77000 Melun,
France

Castelfranco, le 27 septembre 199-

Objet: M. Samuel Smith

Messieurs,

Je vous écris en tant que confrère fabricant de machines-outils. Nous avons récemment reçu la candidature de M. Samuel Smith, de Reading, qui désire pourvoir[1] chez nous le poste d'ingénieur du support technique. Ce monsieur nous a donné le nom de votre entreprise non seulement en tant qu'employeur précédent mais également comme étant à même de fournir une lettre de recommandation.

D'après la lecture du C.V. de M. Smith, il semblerait tout à fait approprié pour le poste à pourvoir. Cependant nous attachons beaucoup d'importance à ce que nos employés s'intègrent bien à l'usine. Le fait qu'il ait été, alors qu'il avait une vingtaine d'années,[2] un membre actif de l'Association Européenne pour la Protection des Baleines nous inquiète quelque peu. Nous aimerions connaître votre opinion à ce sujet car nous sommes très désireux d'en savoir plus sur ce candidat.

Vous en remerciant par avance, nous vous prions d'agréer, Messieurs, l'expression de notre meilleure considération.

Carlo Ruggeri
Propriétaire

1  *Pourvoir un poste*: 'to fill a (vacant) position'.
2  Literally, 'when he was about twenty'. (NB **j'ai** *vingt ans*: 'I **am** twenty'.)

# 5 Enquiry asking for a specific quote

15 September 199-

Sales Manager
OFFICE 2000
89–91 Scott Road
Olton
Solihull
West Midlands
B92 7RZ

Dear Sir/Madam

RE: LASER PHOTOCOPIER PR3000

We have been in correspondence with your company over the last six months and have in that time received a number of different quotations for different models of the industrial laser photocopying machines produced by your company. We have decided that the most suitable machine for our requirement is the PR3000.

We note however that your price of £4,000 is for one machine only. We are keen to purchase 20 printers of this particular model and we would like to know what discount you would make on an order of this magnitude.

We are also keen to know the delivery time for this equipment. If it were possible to deliver the printers in two separate batches of 10 each, we would require the first delivery in three months' time and the second some two months after that, when our new British office is set up in Cromer.

Yours faithfully

Luca Evangelista
Sales Manager

# 5  Demande d'un devis

Directeur des ventes,
OFFICE 2000,
89–91 Scott Road,
Olton,
Solihull,
West Midlands,
B92 7RZ

Paris, le 15 septembre 199-

Objet: Photocopieuse laser PR3000

Madame, Monsieur,

Voici six mois que nous sommes en communication avec votre entreprise et nous avons reçu, pendant cette période, plusieurs devis pour différents modèles de photocopieuses laser industrielles que vous fabriquez. Nous avons décidé que la machine la plus adaptée à nos besoins est la PR3000.

Nous avons cependant noté que votre prix de £ 4000,00[1] correspond à l'achat d'une seule machine. Nous aimerions acquérir 20 imprimantes du même modèle et aimerions connaître le montant de la ristourne[2] que vous pourriez appliquer pour une commande de cette importance.

Nous aimerions également connaître les délais de livraison pour ce matériel. S'il vous était possible de livrer les imprimantes en deux lots de 10, nous demanderions une première livraison dans trois mois et une seconde deux mois plus tard, lorsque nos bureaux britanniques de Cromer seront terminés.

Dans l'attente de votre réponse, nous vous prions d'agréer, Madame, Monsieur, l'expression de nos salutations distinguées.

Luc Evangéliste
Directeur des ventes

1  The French use a comma (*la virgule*) for a decimal point.
2  There are various words for 'discount': *ristourne, rabais, remise*.

# 6  Soliciting an agency

17 November 199-

Erwin Page plc
Electrical applicances & supplies
29 Landon Place
London
SE45 9AS

Dear Sirs

We have heard from business associates that you are looking for an agency for the promotion of your products in the US. We feel that we may be of assistance to you: we are a long-established agency with offices in the Midwest and on the West Coast, and we are experienced in the sale and promotion of domestic electrical equipment. We have helped several British firms to boost their US sales, and are convinced that you too could benefit from our experience. Our UK representative, Charles J Parker, would be pleased to call on you to discuss your needs further. You can contact him on 0171 745 4756. He will in any event be in your locality in the coming week, and will certainly take the opportunity of calling on you.

Yours faithfully


Peter Bowles

# 6  Proposer ses services

Eric Lang et Associés[1]
45 boulevard des Pyrénées
64000 Pau
France

Lawrence, le 17 novembre 199-

Messieurs,

Nous avons appris de nos associés que vous cherchez une agence qui puisse[2] se charger de la promotion de vos produits aux Etats-Unis. Nous pensons que nous pouvons vous aider: nous avons créé cette agence voici de nombreuses années et nous possédons des bureaux dans le Midwest et sur la côte ouest, et nous avons acquis une certaine expérience de la vente et promotion des appareils ménagers électriques. Nous avons aidé plusieurs entreprises anglaises à relancer leurs ventes aux Etats-Unis et nous sommes convaincus que vous aussi, vous pourriez bénéficier de notre expérience. Notre représentant en Grande-Bretagne, Charles J. Parker, se ferait un plaisir de vous rendre visite afin de discuter plus amplement de vos besoins. Vous pouvez le contacter au numéro de téléphone suivant: 1 97 45 47 56. De toute manière, il sera dans votre région la semaine prochaine et passera très certainement vous voir.

Nous vous prions de croire, Messieurs, à l'expression de nos sentiments les plus dévoués.

Peter Bowles

1  *Associés*: 'partners'.
2  'An agency which could/might promote' . . . (subjunctive). For an explanation of the uses of the subjunctive, see the relevant section, on pp. 318–19 of the Reference Grammar.

# 7  Requesting information about agents

Duperrier SA
24 avenue des Sylphides
Brignoles
83170 Var
France

Dear Sirs

RE: LÜTTICH GmbH

We have heard from colleagues that you have recently used the services of
Lüttich GmbH as agents for your products in Germany. We are in a different line
of business from yourselves, but I believe that Lüttich represents companies of
various kinds. We are looking for agents in Germany and Switzerland for our
stationery products. I should be grateful if you could let us have further
information on the above named firm. Any information you send us will be
treated with the strictest confidence.

Yours faithfully


P Brandauer

# 7  Demande de renseignements concernant les dépositaires

Duperrier S.A.,
24 avenue des Sylphides
Brignoles
83 170 Var
France

Douvres, le –/–/199-

<u>Objet:</u> Lüttich GmbH

Messieurs,

Certains collègues nous ont appris que vous avez récemment utilisé les services de Lüttich GmbH comme dépositaires de vos produits en Allemagne. Nous sommes dans une branche différente de la vôtre, mais je crois que Lüttich représente des entreprises ayant différentes activités. Nous sommes à la recherche de dépositaires[1] en Allemagne et en Suisse pour nos fournitures de bureau.[2] Je vous serais donc très reconnaissant de bien vouloir nous communiquer[3] toute information que vous puissiez avoir sur l'entreprise mentionnée ci-dessus. Nous vous garantissons de garder l'information communiquée strictement confidentielle.

Vous en remerciant par avance, nous vous prions d'agréer, Messieurs, l'expression de nos salutations distinguées.

P Brandauer

1  An agent carrying stock.
2  Literally, 'office supplies'.
3  *De bien vouloir*: 'to be so good as to' . . .

# 8  Giving information about agents

17 December 199-

Herrn H Pike
Heinrich Pittmann GmbH
Ofterdingenstraße 69
6800 Mannheim
Germany

Dear Mr Pike

RE: DIETER & HELLER

Thank you for your enquiry about the company Dieter and Heller, who have been agents for our products for several years. The company has represented our interests in Eastern and Central Europe very effectively and our sales in those regions have been buoyant as a result. You will find their Bonn-based manager, Max Lettmann, particularly helpful, and I am sure he will be interested in co-operating with you.

If you do contact him, don't hesitate to mention my name.

Yours sincerely

Maria Fischer

# 8  Donner des renseignements au sujet d'agents

M. Henri Brochet
Entreprise Pitmann
69 rue des Dieux
44110 Châteaubriant
France

Durham, le 17 décembre 199-

Objet: Dieter et Heller

Monsieur,

Nous vous remercions de votre lettre nous demandant des renseignements concernant l'entreprise Dieter et Heller, qui sont les agents que nous utilisons pour nos produits depuis[1] plusieurs années. L'entreprise a représenté nos intérêts en Europe de l'Est et Centrale de manière très efficace et grâce à elle,[2] nos ventes dans ces régions ont été très actives. Vous vous rendrez compte[3] que le Directeur de Bonn, Max Lettmann, est très serviable, et je suis sûre que la perspective d'une coopération[4] avec vous l'intéressera.

Si vous décidez de le contacter, je ne vois aucun inconvénient à ce que vous mentionniez[5] mon nom.

Veuillez agréer, Monsieur, l'expression de mes sentiments respectueux.

Maria Fischer

1  *Que nous utilisons depuis*: that we have been using.
2  Literally, 'thanks to her', i.e. *l'entreprise* (f.).
3  *Se rendre compte*: 'to realize'.
4  'That the prospect of co-operation . . .'.
5  'That you should (subjunctive) mention' . . .

# 9  Request for a business reference

CONFIDENTIAL

Mr G Le Blanc
Sales Director
Curtains & Blinds Ltd
PO Box 181
Croydon
CR0 5SN

Dear Mr Le Blanc

RE: CASELLACCI SpA

We would like to introduce our company as a major supplier of castors for office furniture. We have been approached by Casellacci SPA of Pisa as potential distributors of our products in the Italian market. Mr Casellacci has explained that he has been supplying your range of curtain fittings in the market for some fifteen years and has gained a proven track record of both successful sales and prompt payment with your company.

We are eager to proceed in the Italian market, but we wish to have some reassurance about this company, as we do not know either the company or the individuals concerned. It would appear that they are selling only high-quality products and that our range of castors would fit very well into their sales range.

We would appreciate your earliest comments and thank you in advance for providing this information, which we would treat in the utmost confidence.

Yours sincerely


Steve Watwood
Export Manager

# 9  Demande d'une lettre de recommandation concernant une entreprise

M. G. LE BLANC
Directeur des ventes,
Rideaux et Stores S.A.
B.P. 45
29900 Concarneau
France

New Malden, le –/–/199-

Objet: Casellacci S.P.A.[1] (Confidentiel)

Monsieur,

Notre entreprise est l'un des plus importants fournisseurs de roulettes pour meubles de bureau. Nous avons été contactés par Casellacci SpA de Pise qui se proposait de distribuer nos produits sur le marché italien. M. Casellacci nous a expliqué qu'il était le fournisseur de votre gamme d'équipements pour rideaux depuis plus de quinze ans et avait acquis une bonne réputation auprès de votre entreprise pour avoir vendu ces articles avec succès et avec des paiements à court délai.[2]

Nous sommes désireux d'aborder le marché italien, mais nous aimerions être tout à fait rassurés non seulement au sujet de cette entreprise que nous ne connaissons pas, mais aussi en ce qui concerne les personnes qui la composent. Il paraîtrait qu'ils ne vendent que des produits de haute qualité et que notre gamme de roulettes s'intégrerait parfaitement dans la gamme de produits offerts. Nous vous serions reconnaissants de nous faire parvenir vos vues dans les plus brefs délais[2] et vous assurons que ces informations seront traitées de manière strictement confidentielle.

Avec nos remerciements anticipés, veuillez recevoir, Monsieur, l'expression de mes salutations distinguées.

Steve Watwood
Directeur Exportation

1  S.P.A. or SpA: Italian abbreviation for *Società per Azioni*: 'limited company'.
2  Note use of phrases with *délai*.

# 10  Favourable reply to request for a business reference

Mr S Watwood
CASTASSIST
158–161 Cressex Estate
New Malden
Surrey
KT13 4EY

Dear Mr Watwood

RE: CASELLACCI SpA of Pisa

We thank you for your letter of 11 March, regarding the company Casellacci of Italy as potential distributors of your range of castors.

We have indeed been working with Casellacci now for 23 years and know both Andrea Casellacci and his son Antonio, who has become more active in the company over the last few years. Casellacci have a number of most competent sales personnel covering the whole of Italy and the surrounding islands and have obtained excellent results for our company against our large German competitors within the market. Casellacci have over this period of time proven to be most prompt in their payment. At the time of writing I cannot recall any undue delay in the settlement of their bills.

I have some awareness of your company and its products and I am sure they are suited to the Italian market. I hope the Casellacci company will prove a dependable and successful distributor for your product.

We hope you find this information sufficient to your requirements. Should you need any further details please do not hesitate to contact us.

Yours sincerely


George Le Blanc
Sales Director

# 10  Lettre de recommandation favorable au sujet d'une entreprise

Mr S Watwood,
Castassist
158–161 Cressex Estate,
New Malden,
Surrey,
KT13 4EY

Concarneau, le –/–/199-

Objet: CASELLACCI S.P.A. de Pise

Monsieur,

Nous vous remercions de votre lettre du 11 mars dernier concernant l'entreprise Casellacci en Italie comme distributeur potentiel de votre gamme de roulettes.

Nous travaillons effectivement avec Casellacci depuis maintenant 23 ans et nous connaissons bien Andrea Casellacci ainsi que son fils Antonio qui a pris une part de plus en plus active dans l'entreprise ces dernières années. Casellacci possède une équipe de vendeurs des plus compétents couvrant l'Italie entière ainsi que les îles environnantes et ils ont obtenu d'excellents résultats pour notre entreprise, et ce, battant la concurrence allemande sur le marché qui nous préoccupe.[1] Casellacci a prouvé pendant cette période qu'il était très rapide au niveau des paiements. A l'heure où je vous écris, je ne peux me souvenir d'aucun rappel concernant leurs règlements.[2]

Je connais votre entreprise et ses produits et je suis sûr qu'ils sont adaptés au marché italien.[3] J'espère que Casellacci se révélera être[4] sérieux et distribuera vos produits avec succès.

J'espère que vous jugerez ces informations suffisantes. Si toutefois vous aviez besoin de plus amples détails,[5] n'hésitez pas à nous contacter.

Vous en souhaitant bonne réception, je vous prie d'agréer, Monsieur, l'expression de mes salutations distinguées.

Georges le Blanc
Directeur des ventes

1  Literally, 'in the market that concerns us'.
2  *Régler* and *règlement*: 'to settle' and 'settlement' (of debt).
3  With words describing nationality, only the country and the inhabitant begin with capital letters.
4  Literally, 'will reveal itself to be'.
5  'If however you had need of . . .'.

# 11  Unfavourable reply to request for a business reference

Mr S Watwood
CASTASSIST
158–161 Cressex Estate
New Malden
Surrey
KT13 4EY

Dear Mr Watwood

RE: CASELLACCI SpA OF PISA

We are in receipt of your letter regarding the company of Andrea Casellacci with whom you have been discussing the potential distribution of your products in the Italian market.

We must first ask you to accept our comments on this company in the most confidential terms. We have indeed been working with Casellacci for many years, but unfortunately six months ago Mr Andrea Casellacci was detained by the Italian police and certain irregularities within the company have come to light. A direct result of this situation, in our particular case, is that we have not received payment for the last three major shipments of goods to Casellacci, which were due at different times. We are at the moment in discussions with our solicitors who will be undertaking the appropriate action on our behalf.

As a result of this, therefore, although this company has performed successfully in the past, it is obviously not in a position to continue this work on our behalf and therefore would not be a suitable partner for you at this time.

Yours sincerely


George Le Blanc
Sales Director

# 11  Lettre de recommandation défavorable au sujet d'une entreprise

Mr S Watwood,
Castassist,
158–161 Cressex Estate,
New Malden,
Surrey,
KT 13 4EY.

Concarneau, le –/–/199-

Objet: CASELLACCI S.P.A. de Pise

Monsieur,

Nous avons bien reçu votre lettre concernant l'entreprise Andrea Casellacci avec qui vous avez discuté des possibilités de distribution de vos produits sur le marché italien.

Nous devons tout d'abord vous demander de considérer nos commentaires sur cette entreprise en toute confidentialité. Nous avons effectivement travaillé avec Casellacci pendant de longues années, mais malheureusement, il y a six mois, M. Andrea Casellacci a été interpellé[1] par la police italienne et certaines irrégularités au niveau de l'entreprise ont été découvertes. Le résultat direct de ce problème, pour notre part, fut[2] que nous n'avons pas été réglés pour les trois dernières livraisons de matériel à Casellacci qui étaient relativement importantes, et qui étaient payables à différentes dates. Nous sommes actuellement en discussion avec nos avocats qui prendront les mesures nécessaires en notre nom.

Ainsi nous pensons que, bien que cette entreprise ait obtenu des résultats tout à fait satisfaisants dans le passé, elle n'est, de toute évidence, pas apte à poursuivre ce travail pour nous et n'est pas actuellement un bon partenaire pour vous.

Vous souhaitant bonne réception de cette lettre,[3] je vous prie d'agréer, Monsieur, l'expression de mes salutations distinguées.

Georges le Blanc
Directeur des ventes

1  Literally, 'questioned'.
2  A past historic (*passé simple*): 'was'. (See Reference Grammar, p. 317.)
3  This phrase is added to give the following *formule de politesse* ('courtesy formula') a little more substance.

# 12   Evasive reply to request for a business reference

Mr S Watwood
CASTASSIST
158–161 Cressex Estate
New Malden
Surrey
KT13 4EY

Dear Mr Watwood

RE: CASELLACCI SpA OF PISA/ITALY

We are in receipt of your letter regarding the company Casellacci SpA with whom you have been discussing the distribution of your products in the Italian market.

Casellacci is a very good company, but we are concerned that they might have already stretched themselves with the selling of our products in Italy and we feel that, if they did take on your range of products, they would probably have to employ a further product manager and perhaps another half a dozen regional sales people in order to cover the Italian market adequately.

We trust this information is sufficient, but should you require any further comments please do not hesitate to contact us.

Yours sincerely


George Le Blanc
Sales Director

# 12  Lettre de recommandation évasive au sujet d'une entreprise

Mr S. Watwood
CASTASSIST
158–161 Cressex Estate,
New Malden,
Surrey
KT13 4EY

Concarneau, le –/–/199-

Objet: CASELLACCI S.P.A. de Pise

Monsieur,

Nous avons bien reçu votre lettre concernant l'entreprise CASELLACCI S.P.A. avec qui vous avez discuté de la distribution de vos produits sur le marché italien.

Casellacci est une très bonne entreprise mais nous sommes inquiets car ils se sont déja peut-être surpassés avec la vente de nos produits en Italie et nous pensons que s'ils prenaient en charge votre gamme de produits, il leur faudrait[1] probablement employer un chef de produits supplémentaire et peut-être même une autre demi-douzaine de vendeurs régionaux s'ils voulaient couvrir le marché italien correctement.[2]

Nous espérons que vous trouverez ces renseignements suffisants mais si vous souhaitez de plus amples informations, n'hésitez pas à nous contacter.

Vous souhaitant bonne réception de cette lettre, je vous prie d'agréer, Monsieur, l'expression de mes salutations distinguées.

Georges le Blanc
Directeur des ventes

1 Literally, 'it would be necessary to them'.
2 Literally, 'properly'.

# 13  Placing an order

Jenkins Freeman plc
Unit 36
Heddington Industrial Estate
Birmingham
B34 9HF

Dear Sirs

We thank you for your catalogue and price list, which we have read with interest. On the basis of your current prices, we wish to order the following:

50 electric drills, model 1456/CB
50 chain saws, model 1865/CH

Delivery is required by 3.5.199-, and the goods should be delivered to our warehouse in Riddington Way, Battersea. As agreed, payment will be by banker's draft.

Yours faithfully


Gillian Brookes
Purchasing Department

# 13  Passer une commande

Dupont Bonhomme S.A.
120 avenue Berthelot
69000 Lyon
France

Coventry, le –/–/199-

Messieurs,

Nous vous remercions de votre catalogue et liste des prix que nous avons étudiés[1] avec intérêt. Sur la base des prix mentionnés,[2] nous aimerions vous passer la commande suivante:

50 perceuses électriques, modèle 1456/CB
50 tronçonneuses, modèle 1865/CH

La livraison est requise le 03/05/199- au plus tard,[3] et les articles commandés devraient être livrés dans notre entrepôt se situant à Riddington Way, Battersea. Comme convenu, le paiement se réglera par chèque de banque.

Dans cette attente, veuillez agréer, Messieurs, l'expression de nos salutations distinguées.


Gillian Brookes
Service des achats

1  This past participle is agreeing with the preceding direct object.
2  Literally, 'the prices referred to' (in your price list).
3  'At the latest' (equivalent of 'by').

# 14  Cancellation of order

21 June 199-

Porzellanfabrik Hering
Langauer Allee 18
7000 Stuttgart
Germany

Dear Sirs

RE: ORDER NO. HGF/756

We recently placed an order for 60 bone china coffee sets (model 'Arcadia'). The order reference: HGF/756.

We greatly regret that due to circumstances beyond our control, we now have to cancel the order. We apologize for any inconvenience that this cancellation may cause you.

Yours faithfully


D Grey

# 14  Annulation de commande

Fabrique de Porcelaine
18 allée des Lilas
34000 Montpellier
France

Leeds, le 21 juin 199-

Messieurs,

Nous vous avons récemment passé une commande de 60 services à café en porcelaine (modèle 'Arcadia'). La référence de la commande est : HGF/756.

Nous sommes désolés d'avoir à l'annuler pour des raisons entièrement indépendantes de notre volonté.[1] Nous vous prions de bien vouloir nous excuser pour tous les inconvénients que cette annulation peut causer.

Vous remerciant par avance de votre compréhension, nous vous prions d'agréer, Messieurs, nos salutations distinguées.

D. Grey

1   This is the French version of the hallowed phrase: 'due to circumstances beyond our control . . .'.

# 15  Confirming a telephone order

18 May 199-

Henning & Söhne GmbH
Schillerstraße 45
4300 Essen
Germany

Dear Mr Hartmann

Following the visit of your representative Dieter Höne last week, we are writing to confirm our telephone order for

  250 car seat covers, model AS/385/c

The total price of the order, inclusive of your discount, is £4,600. Payment will follow immediately upon delivery. The covers should be delivered no later than Tuesday 3 February, to our warehouse on the Pennington Industrial Estate, Rochdale.

Yours sincerely


Derek Batty

# 15  Confirmer une commande passée par téléphone

Monsieur Jean Dutourd
45 rue Verlaine
63000 Clermont-Ferrand
France

Newcastle upon Tyne, le 18 mai 199-

Cher Monsieur,[1]

A la suite de la visite de votre représentant M. Eric Braque la semaine dernière, nous vous écrivons pour confirmer notre commande passée par téléphone de:

250 Housses pour sièges de voiture modèle AS/385/c.

Le montant total de la commande, votre ristourne[2] comprise, s'élève à 4 600,00 Livres Sterling. Notre règlement suivra immédiatement la livraison. Les housses devraient être livrées mardi 3 février au plus tard dans notre entrepôt situé à Pennington Industrial Estate, Rochdale.

Dans cette attente, veuillez recevoir, cher Monsieur, nos salutations distinguées.

Derek Batty

1  They know each other well.
2  Alternative: *rabais* (m).

# 16  Making an order for specific items of office equipment

7 July 199-

Your ref.
Our ref. HB/LP

Garzón y Hijos
Plaza de la Catedral 8
Bogotá

Dear Sir/Madam

We would be grateful if you would supply the following items, using the Order Number E183, to the above address at your earliest convenience. Payment will be made within 14 days of receipt of your invoice and of the goods as ordered.

6 artists' stools (aluminium)

20 sets of 5 painting brushes

10 reams of A5 drawing paper

2 drawing tables: 2m × 1m

1 Sanchix camera: FB4x model

1 QRM computer: portable TGS model

Before you prepare the order and invoice us for these goods, please inform us by telex or phone of the cost per item, for, on several occasions in the past, we have received bills for unexpectedly high amounts.

We thank you in anticipation of your prompt reply.

Yours faithfully

Herberto Baza
Studio Supervisor

# 16   Faire une commande pour des articles de bureau bien précis

Frères Dutilleul
2 rue Portfroid
66000 Perpignan
France

Votre Réf.: HB/LP
Notre Réf.: HB/LP

Port Bou, le 7 juillet 199-

Madame, Monsieur,

Nous vous serions reconnaissants de bien vouloir nous fournir les articles suivants, en utilisant le numéro de commande E183. Ils devront être livrés à l'adresse ci-dessus le plus tôt possible. Vous recevrez notre règlement 14 jours après réception de votre facture et des marchandises conformes à notre commande.

6 tabourets d'artistes (aluminium)

20 jeux de pinceaux (à 5)

10 rames de papier à dessin format A5

2 tables à dessin: 2m × 1m

1 appareil photographique Sanchix: modèle FB4x

1 ordinateur portatif QRM: modèle TGS

Avant de préparer cette commande et de nous envoyer votre facture, nous vous serions reconnaissants de bien vouloir nous faire parvenir[1] par télex ou téléphone le prix de chaque article car à plusieurs reprises[2] par le passé nous avons reçu des notes d'un montant extrêmement élevé totalement inattendu.

Vous remerciant par avance de votre prompte réponse, je vous prie d'agréer Monsieur, Madame, l'expression de mes meilleures salutations.

Herberto Baza
Responsable du studio

1   *Nous faire parvenir*: 'let us have'.
2   *A plusieurs reprises*: 'on several occasions'.

# 17  Acknowledgement of an order

18 November 199-

Mr Henry Putton
33 Flintway
West Ewell
Surrey
KT19 9ST

Dear Mr Putton

Thank you for your signed order given to our Adviser for a bed to be constructed to your specific requirements.

We shall now pass your order to our Design Department complete with your personal specification.

Delivery time will be in approximately seven weeks and we will advise you of the exact date in due course.

Once again many thanks for your order.

Yours sincerely



Janet Craig
Customer Relations Manager

# 17   Confirmation de la réception d'une commande

M. Henri François
410 avenue de l'Hippodrome
14390 Cabourg
France

Headington, le 18 novembre 199-

Cher Monsieur,

Nous vous remercions de votre commande signée remise[1] à notre conseiller pour un lit à fabriquer spécialement pour vous.

Nous allons maintenant faire passer votre commande ainsi que toutes vos spécifications personnelles à notre service de conception.

Il faudra compter environ 7 semaines pour la livraison. Nous vous ferons part de la date exacte en temps voulu.[2]

Vous remerciant une nouvelle fois de votre commande, nous vous prions d'agréer, cher Monsieur, l'expression de nos salutations respectueuses.

Janet Craig
Directrice du service clientèle

1   *Remettre*: 'to hand over/in' etc.
2   This is the equivalent set phrase in French.

# 18   Payment of invoices

## Letter accompanying payment

Dr V Meyer
Neue Marktforschung GmbH
Kastanienallee 14
D–45023 Osnabrück
Germany

Dear Dr Meyer

I enclose an international money order to the value of 450DM as payment for the three market research reports on dairy products published by your organization this year.

As agreed during our telephone conversation on 15.1.199-, the sum enclosed includes postage.

I look forward to receiving the reports as soon as possible.

Yours sincerely


Maria Meller

Enc.

# 18   Règlement de factures

## Lettre accompagnant le règlement

Etudes de Marché Meyer
14 allée des Marronniers
67500 Haguenau
France

Dublin, le 18 janvier 199-

A l'attention de Dr. V. Meyer

Cher Monsieur,

Vous trouverez ci-joint un mandat international d'un montant de 1556,00 francs pour le règlement des trois rapports sur les études de marchés des produits laitiers publiés par votre organisme cette année.

Comme nous l'avons convenu[1] lors de notre conversation téléphonique du 15 janvier, la somme ci-jointe[2] comprend les frais de port.

Dans l'attente des rapports, qui nous l'espérons arriveront dans les plus brefs délais, je vous prie d'agréer, cher Monsieur, l'expression de mes sentiments distingués.


Maria Meller

P.J.[3] (1): Mandat international

1   Literally, 'as we agreed (it)'.
2   Agreeing with *la somme*.
3   Abbreviation for *pièce jointe*: 'enc(losure)'.

# 19  Payment of invoices

## Request for deferral

South East Finance Ltd
Alton Court
Cleeve Road
London W11 1XR

Dear Sirs

RE: MAXITRUCK 2000

I refer to our recent agreement of 30 November 199- regarding payment for one 40-ton Maxitruck 2000.

As you will recall, we paid an initial instalment of £10,000 and agreed to 10 further monthly instalments of £3,000. The December and January instalments, as you will know, have been paid promptly.

However, owing to the serious economic situation we find ourselves in, we are at the moment unable to make payments of more than £2,000 a month. We would, therefore, appreciate the opportunity to discuss this matter with you and reach a mutually satisfactory arrangement.

Yours faithfully


Tom Page
Finance Manager

# 19   Règlement de factures

## Demande d'un règlement différé

South East Finance Ltd
Alton Court
Cleeve Road
London W11 1XR

Nantes, le 15 décembre 199-

Objet: Maxitruck 2000

Messieurs,

Nous faisons référence à notre récent accord du 30.11.199- concernant le règlement d'un maxitruck 2000 de 40 tonnes.

Comme vous vous en souviendrez certainement, nous avons payé un acompte de 10 000,00 livres sterling et pour la somme restante, vous nous aviez accordé un règlement de dix mensualités de 3 000,00 livres sterling. Les mensualités de décembre et janvier comme vous l'avez remarqué ont été réglées avec promptitude.

Cependant, étant donnée la situation économique dans laquelle nous nous trouvons actuellement, nous sommes malheureusement dans l'impossibilité de payer un montant supérieur à 2 000,00 livres sterling par mois. Nous aimerions par conséquent solliciter un rendez-vous afin de pouvoir en discuter avec vous et éventuellement convenir d'un nouvel accord.

Dans cette attente, et vous remerciant de votre compréhension, je vous prie d'agréer, Messieurs, l'assurance de nos meilleurs sentiments.


Thomas Pauger
Directeur Financier

# 20  Payment of invoices

## Refusal to pay

Johnson (Builders) Ltd
Nugget Grove
Christchurch
Dorset

Dear Sirs

RE: INVOICE NO. L28/4659

We refer to your invoice No. L28/4659 regarding repairs to the roof of workshop 17 at Heath End.

In spite of the repair work carried out by your employees the roof still leaked in a number of places during the recent rains, causing a shut-down of the workshop for safety reasons.

We look forward to a speedy response from you, in order to resolve this problem in a satisfying manner.

Yours faithfully


Martin Lowe
Financial Services

# 20  Règlement de factures

## Refus de payer

Johnson (Builders) Ltd,
Nugget Grove,
Christchurch,
Dorset

Christchurch, le 5 novembre 199-

Objet: Facture No. L28/4659

Messieurs,

Nous faisons référence à votre facture No. L28/4659 concernant les réparations effectuées sur le toit de notre atelier situé au No. 17 Heath End.

En dépit des travaux réalisés par vos employés, le toit fuit toujours à plusieurs endroits; ceci a été vérifié lors des dernières pluies, et a entraîné la fermeture de l'atelier pour des raisons de sécurité.

Nous vous serions reconnaissants de bien vouloir nous répondre dans les plus brefs délais afin de résoudre ce problème de manière satisfaisante.

Vous en remerciant par avance, nous vous prions d'agréer, Messieurs, l'expression de notre parfaite considération.


Martin Lowe
Service Financier

# 21  Apologies for non-payment

18 August 199-

Mr I Sahani
Michigan Lake Trading Co.
974 South La Salle Street
Chicago
Illinois 60603
USA

Dear Mr Sahani

I refer to our telephone conversation yesterday.

I must apologize once again for the fact that you have not yet received payment for order No. 072230/5310.

Payment was duly authorized by me on 10 July, but owing to staff holidays the paperwork appears to have gone astray between our sales and finance departments.

We have now traced the relevant documentation and I can assure you that the matter is being attended to with the utmost urgency.

If you have not received payment by Monday, 22 August, I would be grateful if you would contact me immediately.

I apologize once again for the inconvenience this has caused you and assure you of our best intentions.

Yours sincerely


Jack Andrews
Finance Director

# 21   Excuses pour faute de règlement

M. I. Sahani,
Michigan Lake Trading Co.,
974 South La Salle Street,
Chicago,
Illinois 60 603,
Etats-Unis

Limoges, le 18 août 199-

Cher Monsieur,

Suite à notre conversation téléphonique d'hier, je dois une fois de plus vous demander de nous excuser pour ne pas vous avoir encore envoyé le règlement de notre commande no. 072230/5310.

J'ai autorisé moi-même le paiement en temps utile le 10 juillet mais il semble que du fait du départ en vacances de certains membres du personnel, certains dossiers se soient[1] égarés entre le service des ventes et celui de la comptabilité.

Nous avons maintenant retrouvé la documentation en cause et je peux vous assurer que nous nous occupons de cette affaire afin qu'elle soit[1] réglée le plus rapidement possible.

Si vous n'avez pas reçu votre règlement lundi 22 août, je vous serais reconnaissant de m'en faire part immédiatement.

Vous demandant une nouvelle fois de bien vouloir nous excuser, je vous prie d'agréer, cher Monsieur, l'expression de mes salutations distinguées.

Jacques André
Directeur Financier

1   The subjunctive is used after *il semble que* and *afin que* (see Reference Grammar pp. 318–19).

# 22  Request for payment

18 June 199-

Huron Motor Factors
6732 John Street
Markham
Ontario
Canada L3R 1B4

Dear Sir

RE: Invoice No. JE/17193

As per our invoice JE/17193 of 13.3.199-, we supplied your plant with 500 litres of AVC automotive base paint, payment due 60 days after receipt of our consignment.

This period of time has now elapsed and we request immediate settlement of the above invoice.

Yours faithfully


G McGregor
Finance Director

# 22  Demande de règlement

M. Jean Maréchal
Huron Motor Factors
6732 John Street
Drummondville
Québec
Canada

Birmingham, le 18 juin 199-

Objet: Commande No. JE/17193

Monsieur,

Comme le spécifiait notre facture JE/17193 du 13-03-199-, nous avons livré 500 litres de peinture à base d'apprêt[1] AVC pour automobiles, dont le règlement devait être effectué 60 jours après réception de notre marchandise.

Cette période est maintenant écoulée et nous exigeons le règlement immédiat de cette facture.

Dans cette attente, veuillez agréer, Monsieur, l'expression de mes salutations distinguées.


G. McGregor
Directeur Financier

1  Technical term in paint: 'sizing' etc.

# 23   Overdue account

## First letter

25 April 199-

Lota (UK) Ltd
93 Armstrong Road
Dudley
West Midlands DY3 6EJ

Dear Sir

Arrears on Finance Agreement No. 261079

I am writing to advise you that your bankers have failed to remit the April instalment of £8,373 on the above agreement and as a result the account is now in arrears.

This has incurred an additional £460.50 in interest and administration charges.

Please advise your bank to transfer £8,833.50 to our account to bring your account up to date and enable us to remove it from our arrears listing.

Yours faithfully


Mark Phillips
Financial Director

# 23   Compte arriéré

## Première lettre

Lota (UK) Ltd,
93 Armstrong Road,
Dudley,
West Midlands DY3 6EJ,
Angleterre

Clichy, le 25 avril 199-

Objet: Arriéré concernant le contrat de financement No. 261079

Monsieur,

Nous désirions[1] vous signaler que vos banquiers ne nous ont pas remis le versement d'avril s'élevant à £ 8 373,00 et que votre compte est actuellement arriéré.

Ceci a engendré un coût supplémentaire de £ 460,50 en intérêts et frais de dossier.

Nous vous serions très reconnaissants de bien vouloir ordonner à votre banque de verser £ 8 833,50 sur notre compte et ainsi de mettre votre compte à jour pour nous permettre de l'enlever de la liste des arriérés.

Dans cette attente, nous vous prions d'agréer, Monsieur, l'expression de nos salutations distinguées.


Marc-Philippe Wright
Directeur Financier

1   Imperfect tense: 'we wanted to advise you'.

# 24   Overdue account

## Final letter

10 June 199-

Lota (UK) Ltd
93 Armstrong Road
Dudley
West Midlands DY3 6EJ

Dear Sir

Arrears on Finance Agreement No. 261079

Our records show that despite our previous reminders, your account remains overdue.

We now insist that you clear the outstanding arrears by close of business on Friday, 26 June 199-.

Failure to comply with this request by the date specified will result in the termination of the agreement. We would then take steps to recover our property.

Yours faithfully


Mark Phillips
Finance Director

# 24  Compte arriéré

## Dernière lettre

Lota (UK) Ltd
93 Armstrong Road
Dudley
West Midlands DY3 6EJ
Angleterre

Clichy, le 10 juin 199-

Objet: Arriérés sur le contrat de financement No. 261079

Messieurs,

Nos registres montrent que malgré nos précédentes lettres de rappel, votre compte est toujours arriéré.

Nous insistons pour que vous régliez[1] le montant dû avant la fermeture des bureaux le vendredi 26 juin 199- au plus tard.

Si vous n'effectuez pas ce règlement à la date spécifiée, il en résultera la résiliation[2] de notre accord. Nous prendrions alors nos dispositions pour récupérer nos biens.

Dans l'espoir de recevoir le règlement de vos dettes avant l'échéance mentionnée ci-dessus, je vous prie d'agréer, Messieurs, l'expression de nos salutations distinguées.

**M.-Philippe Wright**
**Directeur Financier**

1  Subjunctive.
2  *La résiliation, résilier*: 'termination', 'to terminate' (a contract).

# 25  Job advertisement

## Letter to newspaper

20 August 199-

H J Marketing Services
County House
53 Stukely Street
Twickenham TW1 7LA

Dear Sir

Please would you insert the attached job advertisement in the January issues of *East European Marketing Monthly* and *Food Industry Digest*.

As usual we require a quarter-page ad, set according to our house style.

Please would you invoice us for payment in the usual way.

Yours faithfully


John Capstan
Personnel Director

Enc.

# 25   Offre d'emploi par petite annonce

## Lettre de demande de parution au journal

Services Publicitaires
*Monde Agricole*
3 rue de la Laiterie
76600 Le Havre
France

Epsom, le 20 août 199-

Messieurs,

Nous vous prions de bien vouloir insérer notre offre d'emploi que vous trouverez ci-joint dans votre parution de janvier des journaux *Monde Agricole* et *Agriculture Européenne*. Comme d'habitude, nous demandons une annonce de quart de page, composée selon le style de notre maison.

Nous vous serions reconnaissants de bien vouloir nous facturer selon les conditions habituelles.

Vous en remerciant par avance, nous vous prions d'agréer, Messieurs, l'expression de nos salutations distinguées.


John Capstan
Directeur du Personnel

P.J. (1): Texte de l'annonce

# 26  Newspaper advertisement

We are currently expanding our operations in Eastern Europe and require experienced people within the food processing industry who are looking for an opportunity to sell in Hungary and Bulgaria products of leading food companies. The products are of good quality and already enjoy a substantial international reputation.

The salary for the above position is negotiable dependent upon experience and qualifications. A competitive benefits package is offered.

For further details and application form please write to the Personnel Manager, EEF Ltd, Roman Road, Epsom, Surrey, KT72 7EF, quoting reference HB/127.

Closing date:    14 February 199-.

# 26 Annonce

Nous sommes actuellement en pleine phase de développement de nos activités dans les pays de l'Europe de l'Est et sommes à la recherche de gens expérimentés dans l'industrie agro-alimentaire qui seraient intéressés par la vente en Hongrie et en Bulgarie de produits venant des meilleures entreprises agro-alimentaires. Les produits sont de bonne qualité et ont déjà une réputation internationale.

Le salaire attribué au poste décrit ci-dessus est négociable et dépend de l'expérience, de l'aptitude et de la formation. De nombreux avantages salariaux sont également offerts.

Afin d'obtenir de plus amples informations ainsi qu'un dossier de candidature, veuillez écrire au directeur du personnel EEF S.A.R.L.,[1] Route des Romains, 67210 Obernai, en rappelant le numéro de référence suivant: HB/127.

Candidatures à soumettre avant le 14 février 199-.

1   Abbreviation for *Société à responsabilité limitée*.

# 27 Asking for further details and application form

7 September 199-

EEF Ltd
Roman Road
Epsom
Surrey KT72 7EF

Dear Sir

Ref. HB/127

I would be very grateful if you could send me further details and an application form for the post of sales manager as advertised in this month's *East European Marketing Monthly*.

Yours faithfully

Lorraine Russell

# 27   Demander de plus amples informations et un formulaire de candidature

EEF S.A.R.L.,
Route des Romains,
67210 Obernai,
France

Wissembourg, le 7 septembre 199-

Réf: HB/127

Messieurs,

Je vous serais très reconnaissante de bien vouloir me faire parvenir de plus amples informations ainsi qu'un dossier de candidature pour le poste de directeur des ventes dont l'annonce est passée dans la revue *Marché Est-Européen*[1] de ce mois.

Vous en remerciant par avance, je vous prie d'agréer, Messieurs, l'expression de mes salutations distinguées.

Lorraine Russell

1   The French for 'marketing' is of course *le marketing*.

# 28  Job application

25 January 199-

Black's (Automotive) Ltd
18 Dawson Street
Birmingham
B24 4SU

Dear Sir

Further to your recent advertisement in the *Daily Satellite* on 21 January 199-, I am applying for the post of market research officer.

I graduated from Chiltern University in June 199- with an upper second class degree in European Business. The following January I was awarded the Diploma of the Chartered Institute of Marketing. On my degree course I specialized in market research and I did a one-year work placement with Cox, Paton and Taylor in London.

Since leaving university I have been employed as a market research assistant in the Quantocks Tourist Agency. I am now seeking an opportunity to apply the knowledge and skills I have acquired in a larger, more market-orientated organization.

I enclose my CV and the names of two referees. I would be grateful if you would not contact my current employer without prior reference to me.

I look forward to hearing from you.

Yours faithfully

Michael Westwood

Enc.

# 28  Offre de candidature

Michel Noir Automobile
Z.I.[1] Les Cordeliers
54000 Nancy
France

Taunton, le 25 janvier 199-

Messieurs,

Suite à votre annonce parue dans *Le Satellite* du 21 janvier 199-, je me permets de vous proposer ma candidature pour le poste de responsable des études de marché.

J'ai quitté l'Université de Chiltern en juin 199- ayant obtenu une licence avec mention bien[2] en Commerce Européen. Au mois de juin suivant, j'ai obtenu le diplôme du CIM.[3] Au cours de mes études supérieures, je me suis spécialisé dans le secteur 'Etudes de marchés' et j'ai fait un stage d'un an chez Cox, Paton et Taylor à Londres.

Depuis que j'ai quitté l'université, j'occupe le poste d'assistant en études de marchés à l'agence de tourisme Quantocks. Je suis actuellement à la recherche d'opportunités pour utiliser les connaissances et l'expertise acquises dans une entreprise plus grande et plus orientée vers les marchés.

Vous trouverez ci-joint mon curriculum vitae ainsi que le nom de deux personnes pouvant fournir des lettres de recommandation. Je vous serais très reconnaissant de ne pas contacter mon employeur actuel sans m'en avoir tout d'abord fait part.[4]

Je souhaite avoir retenu votre attention et vous remercie de la suite que vous voudrez bien donner à mon offre de candidature.

Veuillez agréer, Messieurs, l'expression de mes salutations distinguées.


Michael Westwood

P.J. (1): Curriculum vitae

1  Z.I.: abbreviation for *Zone Industrielle*.
2  A first class degree would be *avec mention très bien*.
3  Abbreviation for Chartered Institute of Marketing.
4  *Faire part de qch. à qn.*: 'to inform s.o. of s.th.'.

# 29  Curriculum vitae

| | |
|---|---|
| Name: | Michael Westwood |
| Address: | 14 Bicknolles Road |
| | Taunton |
| | Somerset TA4 71E |

| | |
|---|---|
| Date of Birth: | 14/05/196- |
| Nationality: | British |
| Marital status: | Single |

EDUCATION AND QUALIFICATIONS

BA (Hons) Business Studies (Leeds, 1981)
MBA(1) (Warwick, 1985)

PREVIOUS EMPLOYMENT:

| | |
|---|---|
| October 1988 – | Marketing Manager |
| | Cockpit Industries Ltd |
| | 8 Wendover Road |
| | Accrington |
| | Lancs BB7 2RH |
| January 1986 – September 1988 | Marketing Assistant |
| | Spurlands Ltd |
| | 71 Misbourne Road |
| | Northallerton |
| | Yorks DL5 7YL |
| October 1981 – December 1985 | Marketing Assistant |
| | Tutton Enterprises Ltd |
| | Wye House |
| | Cores End |
| | Wolverhampton WV6 8AE |
| September 1978 – September 1981 | Sales Assistant (part time) |
| | J. V. Ansell & Co. |
| | Moortown |
| | Leeds |
| | Yorks |

# 29  Curriculum vitae

| | |
|---|---|
| Nom: | MICHAEL WESTWOOD |
| Adresse: | 14 Bicknolles Road, |
| | Taunton, |
| | Somerset TA4 7IE |
| Né le: | 14/05/196- |
| Nationalité: | Britannique |
| Situation de famille: | Célibataire |

EXPÉRIENCE
PROFESSIONNELLE:

| | |
|---|---|
| Octobre 1988 – actuellement: | Responsable du marketing |
| | Cockpit Industries Ltd, |
| | 8 Wendover Road, |
| | Accrington, |
| | Lancs, BB7 2RH |
| Janvier 1986 – septembre 1988: | Assistant du service marketing |
| | Spurlands Ltd., |
| | 71 Misbourne Road, |
| | Northallerton, |
| | Yorks. DL5 7YL |
| Octobre 1981 – décembre 1985: | Assistant du service marketing |
| | Tutton Enterprises Ltd |
| | Wye House, |
| | Cores End, |
| | Wolverhampton WV6 8AE |
| Septembre 1978 – septembre 1981: | Assistant du service des ventes (à temps partiel)[1] |
| | J. V. Ansell & Co. |
| | Moortown, |
| | Leeds, |
| | Yorks. |

ETUDES ET DIPLÔMES:

Licence ès lettres en études commerciales (B.A. Honours)
(Leeds, 1981)
MBA[2] (Warwick, 1985)

LANGUAGES

Fluent French and German

PRACTICAL SKILLS

Knowledge of the following software: Lotus, Word for Windows, Excell

DRIVING LICENCE SINCE 1980

LANGUES

Français et allemand courants (parlés, lus, écrits)

CONNAISSANCES PRATIQUES

Connaissance des logiciels[3] suivants: Lotus, Word for Windows, Excell.

PERMIS DE CONDUIRE[4] OBTENU EN 1980.

1  'Part time', i.e. while studying.
2  Abbreviation for Master of Business Administration.
3  *Un logiciel*: 'a software package'.
4  'Driving licence'.

# 30  Unsolicited letter of application

17 September 199-

Executive Agency plc
22 Ellison Place
London WC1B 1DP

Dear Sirs

I have recently returned to Britain after working in Canada and the Gulf States for the last 15 years.

In Canada, I spent five years as chief financial accountant of Bourges-Canada in Montreal, before moving to the Gulf. I have worked as financial director for Jenkins-Speller for the last ten years. During this period the company's number of clients and turnover have quadrupled.

I have returned to Britain for family reasons and I am now seeking an appropriate position in a company that can capitalize on my expertise in financial management and strategy.

I enclose a detailed CV for your further information and look forward to hearing from you soon.

Yours faithfully


R Bennett

Enc.

# 30  Lettre de candidature spontanée

Consultants Financiers Kléber
57 square Kléber
75016 Paris

Londres, le 17 septembre 199-

Messieurs,

Après quinze ans au Canada et dans les Etats du Golfe, je suis récemment rentré en Grande-Bretagne.

Au Canada, j'ai travaillé cinq ans en tant que comptable financier chez Bourges-Canada à Montréal. Je suis ensuite parti dans les Etats du Golfe[1] où j'ai depuis travaillé pendant 10 ans comme Directeur Financier chez Jenkins-Speller. Pendant ce laps de temps, le nombre de clients et le chiffre d'affaires ont quadruplé.[2]

Je suis rentré en Europe pour des raisons familiales et je suis à la recherche d'un nouveau poste au sein d'une entreprise pouvant utiliser pleinement et apprécier à sa juste valeur mon expertise dans le secteur de la gestion financière et de la stratégie.

Vous trouverez ci-joint mon curriculum vitae qui vous apportera davantage d'éclaircissements.

Souhaitant avoir retenu votre attention et vous remerciant de la suite que vous voudrez bien donner à mon offre de candidature,[3] je vous prie d'agréer, Messieurs, l'expression de mes salutations distinguées.

R. Bennett

P.J. (1): Curriculum vitae

1  Le Golfe Persique.
2  One of a series of verbs: *doubler, tripler, quintupler,* etc.
3  Literally, 'Thanking you for any follow-up you may give to my application'.

# 31   Interview invitation

19 February 199-

Ms F Jones
23 Park View
Colchester
Essex CO4 3RN

Dear Ms Jones

Ref. PS/2021: Personnel assistant

Interviews for the above position will take place on Friday, 22 February 199-, beginning at 10 a.m.

We expect to conclude the interviews after lunch, at approximately 2.30 p.m.

Please can you confirm whether you will be able to attend the interview.

Yours sincerely


Mr C Smith
Personnel Officer

# 31   Invitation à une entrevue

Mlle F. Jones,
23 rue du Parc,
79000 Niort,
France

Lowestoft, le 19 février 199-

Objet: PS/2021 – Assistant au Service du Personnel

Chère Mademoiselle

Les entretiens pour le poste vacant mentionné ci-dessus auront lieu le vendredi 22 février 199- à partir de 10h00.

Nous espérons terminer ces entretiens après déjeuner, vers 14h30 environ.

Nous vous serions reconnaissants de bien vouloir nous confirmer votre présence.

Vous en remerciant par avance, je vous prie d'agréer, chère Mademoiselle, l'expression de nos salutations distinguées.


C. Smith
Directrice du Personnel

# 32  Favourable reply to job application

15 March 199-

Mrs L Flint
7 Fisherman's Way
Okehampton
Devon EX12 0YX

Dear Mrs Flint

I am writing to offer you formally the position of personal assistant to the operations director at Farnbury.

As discussed at the interview the normal working hours are 8.30 a.m.–5 p.m., Monday to Friday, although the position requires a flexible approach and on occasions you will be expected to work outside these times. The annual salary is £18,000.

You will receive further details if you accept the position.

Please confirm in writing by first post, Monday 3 April at the latest, whether you accept the offer of the position.

We look forward to hearing from you.

Yours sincerely

F Jones

# 32  Réponse favorable à une offre de candidature

Mme L. Flinte,
7 rue du Pêcheur,
92150 Suresnes,
France

Fermont, le 15 mars 199-

Chère Madame,

L'objet de cette lettre est de vous annoncer officiellement que nous vous offrons le poste de secrétaire personnelle du directeur d'exploitation à Fermont.

Comme nous vous l'avons mentionné lors de l'entretien, les horaires journaliers sont de 8h30 à 17h00, du lundi au vendredi. Nous avons également précisé que le poste demande une certaine souplesse à cet égard, ce qui vous amènera donc parfois à travailler au-delà des horaires cités ci-dessus. Le salaire est de 180 000,00 francs par an.

Si vous acceptez ce poste, nous vous ferons parvenir une description détaillée.

Nous vous serions reconnaissants de bien vouloir nous faire connaître votre réponse par courrier le 3 avril au plus tard.

Dans cette attente, je vous prie d'agréer, chère Madame, l'expression de nos respectueuses salutations.


F. Gérard

# 33   Unfavourable reply to job application

16 March 199-

Mr R Smith
15 Adams Way
Reading
Berks
RG23 6WD

Dear Mr Smith

RE: POSITION AS SALES DIRECTOR

I am writing to inform you that your application was unsuccessful on this occasion.

We thank you for the interest you have shown in our company and we wish you every success with your career.

Yours sincerely

F Jones

# 33  Réponse défavorable à une offre de candidature

M. R. Sert,
15 voie Adamov,
78000 Versailles,
France

Fermont, le 16 mars 199-

<u>Objet: Poste de Directeur Commercial</u>

Monsieur,

L'objet de cette lettre est de vous informer que nous n'avons malheureusement pas pu retenir votre candidature.

Nous le regrettons vivement et vous remercions de l'intérêt et de la confiance que vous avez bien voulu nous manifester. Nous vous souhaitons tout le succès possible en ce qui concerne votre carrière.

Nous vous prions d'agréer, Monsieur, l'expression de nos sentiments distingués.

F. Gérard

# 34  Requesting a reference for an applicant

Your ref. AS/
Our ref. FG/JL

2 February 199-

The Manager
First Class Bank
1–6, King's Square
BURY

Dear Mr Swift

RE: MISS STEPHANIE BOSSOM

This branch of the Safety First has recently received an application for employment as an accounts clerk from Ms Stephanie Bossom. She has quoted your name as a referee to whom we might address ourselves in the event of our wishing to interview her.

I believe that Ms Bossom has been working in your bank for several years and that her desire to change employment is prompted largely by her intention to marry and settle in this area. From her application it would seem that she would be a valuable asset to us. We should therefore be most grateful if you could confirm our impression in writing (by fax if possible) as soon as is convenient.

Please feel free to comment on any aspect of Ms Bossom's work that you deem to be of likely interest to us.

I thank you in advance for your co-operation.

Yours sincerely


Frank Graham
Branch Manager

# 34 Demande d'une lettre de recommandation pour un candidat

Monsieur le Directeur,
First Class Bank,
1 à 6 Place du Roi,
69000 Lyon,
France

Lancaster, le 2 février 199-

Votre Réf.: AS
Notre Réf.: FG/JL

Objet: Mlle Stéphanie Bossom

Monsieur,

Cette succursale de Safety First a récemment reçu la candidature de Mlle Stéphanie Bossom pour le poste d'aide comptable. Mlle Bossom nous a indiqué votre nom au cas où[1] nous voudrions nous procurer une lettre de recommandation si nous avions l'intention de lui faire passer un entretien d'embauche.[2]

Il semble que Mlle Bossom ait[3] travaillé plusieurs années dans votre banque et que son désir de changer de poste provienne[3] en grande partie du fait qu'elle veut se marier et s'installer dans notre région. D'après sa lettre de candidature, il semblerait qu'elle puisse[3] être un sérieux atout pour notre entreprise. Nous vous serions donc très reconnaissants de bien vouloir confirmer nos impressions par écrit (via fac-similé[4] si possible) dès que cela vous sera possible.

N'hésitez pas à nous transmettre toute information que vous jugerez utile concernant le travail de Mlle Bossom.

Vous remerciant par avance de votre coopération, je vous prie d'agréer, Monsieur, l'expression de mes salutations distinguées.

Frank Graham
Directeur d'agence

1 Literally, 'in case we wanted to'.
2 *Embauche, embaucher*: 'recruitment', 'to recruit'.
3 Subjunctives.
4 Alternative: *par télécopie*.

# 35  Providing a positive reference for an employee

4 February 199-

Your ref. FG/JL
Our ref. AS/MN

Mr F Graham
Safety First Assurance plc
12, Bright Street
Lancaster

Dear Mr Graham

MS STEPHANIE BOSSOM

I hasten to reply to your request for a reference for Ms. Stephanie Bossom. Please accept my apologies for not being able to fax my reply, but at present we are experiencing problems with the machine.

I have to say that Stephanie has been an ideal employee, who started with us as an office junior straight from school and has been promoted on several occasions in recognition of her work. I understand her reasons for wishing to leave and would very soon have been promoting her myself if she were staying with us.

You will see from her application that she has sat and passed a number of professional examinations over the last two years. In that time she has taken responsibility for supervising the progress of trainees and has been involved in new initiatives relating to our office systems.

You will find Stephanie a pleasant, willing and talented person. She can be relied upon to carry out her professional duties to the best of her ability at all times.

I hope you will be able to offer her the post, which you imply is likely in your initial letter.

Yours sincerely


Alan Swift
(Manager, Town Centre Branch)

# 35  Fournir une lettre de recommandation positive pour un employé

M. F. Graham,
Safety First Assurance plc
12, Bright Street,
Lancaster
Angleterre

Lyon, le 4 février 199-

Votre Réf.: FG/JL
Notre Réf.: AS/MN

Objet: Mlle Stéphanie Bossom

Monsieur,

Je m'empresse de répondre à votre demande d'une lettre de recommandation pour Stéphanie Bossom. Je suis vraiment désolé de ne pas avoir pu vous envoyer ma réponse par fac-similé, mais nous avons actuellement quelques problèmes avec cet appareil.

Je dois dire que Stéphanie a été pour nous une employée idéale, qui a commencé dans notre entreprise en tant qu'employée de bureau dès sa sortie de l'école. Elle a été promue à plusieurs reprises grâce à son travail. Je comprends tout à fait les raisons pour lesquelles elle souhaite nous quitter et vous prie de croire qu'elle aurait été de nouveau promue dans de très courts délais si elle était restée chez nous.

Vous verrez en vous référant[1] à son dossier de candidature qu'elle a passé[2] et obtenu avec succès un certain nombre d'examens professionnels au cours des deux dernières années. Pendant cette période, elle avait la responsabilité de superviser les progrès des stagiaires[3] et elle était impliquée dans la restructuration de notre système administratif.

Vous vous rendrez compte[4] que Stéphanie est agréable, pleine de bonne volonté et talentueuse. On peut lui faire confiance et être sûr qu'elle fera tout son possible[5] pour remplir ses fonctions professionnelles.

J'espère que vous serez à même de lui offrir le poste comme vous l'aviez suggéré dans votre lettre.

Je vous prie d'agréer, Monsieur, l'expression de mes salutations distinguées.

Alan Swift
Directeur, Agence Centre Ville

1 'Referring yourself': *se référer* is a reflexive verb. 2 *Passer un examen* is French for 'to sit an exam'. 3 *Le* or *la stagiaire* is anyone following *un stage*, 'a training course'. 4 *Se rendre compte*: to realize. 5 'She will do her utmost'.

# 36  Acceptance letter

19 July 199-

Mrs Cornwell
Human Resources Department
Melton's Motor Factors Ltd
63 Station Road
Thirsk
N. Yorkshire
YO9 4YN

Dear Mrs Cornwell,

Thank you for your letter of 17 July offering me the post of parts manager.

I am delighted to accept your offer.

Yours sincerely


Oliver Marks

# 36  Lettre d'acceptation

Madame Cornwell
Service des ressources humaines
Melton's Motor Factors Ltd,
63 Station Road,
Thirsk,
N. Yorkshire Y09 4YN
Angleterre

Vannes, le 19 juillet 199-

Chère Madame,

Je vous remercie de votre lettre du 17 juillet dernier m'offrant le poste de directeur du service des pièces détachées.

C'est avec grand plaisir que j'accepte votre offre.

Je vous prie d'accepter, chère Madame, l'expression de mes salutations distinguées.

Olivier Dumarc

# 37  Contract of employment

Dear

Following our recent discussions we are pleased to offer you employment at our Company as Area Manager on the following terms and conditions:-

### Remuneration
Your salary will be £15,000 per annum plus commission on the basis we have already discussed with you. As with all our staff your salary will be paid monthly on the last Thursday in each month, your first review being in July 199-.

### Notice
As with all our staff, you will be employed for an initial trial period of six months, during which time either you or we may terminate your appointment at any time upon giving seven days' notice in writing to the other. Provided that we are satisfied with your performance during the trial period, we will thereafter immediately confirm your appointment as a permanent member of our staff and the seven-day period of notice referred to above will be increased to one month.

### Sickness Pay
During any reasonable absence for illness the Company, at its discretion, will make up the amount of your National Insurance Benefit to the equivalent of your normal salary, although it should be noted that this will be essentially relative to your length of service.

### Holidays
Your normal paid holiday entitlement will be 20 working days in a full year, the holiday year running from 1 January to 31 December.

### Car
We will provide you with a suitable Company car (cost circa £14,000), which is to be mainly for your business use but also for your private use. The Company will meet all normal running expenses associated with the car such as road tax, insurance, repairs, servicing and petrol.

### Pensions
The Company operates a Pension Plan. You can either decide to join the Company Scheme after six months' service at the Scheme's next anniversary date (July 199-), or alternatively choose a Personal Pension Plan to which the Company would contribute.

# 37  Contrat de travail

Monsieur,

A la suite de nos récentes discussions, nous sommes heureux de vous offrir le poste de directeur régional au sein de notre entreprise, selon les termes et conditions suivants:

Rémunération:
Votre salaire s'élèvera à 150 000,00 francs par an plus une commission relevant des points déjà discutés avec vous. Comme tout le personnel, votre salaire sera payé mensuellement le dernier jeudi de chaque mois. La première réévaluation sera en juillet 199-.

Préavis:
Comme tous nos employés, vous serez employé pendant une période initiale de six mois pendant lesquels chacune des deux parties pourra mettre un terme à son engagement en en avisant l'autre partie par écrit sept jours au préalable. Si nous sommes satisfaits de vos performances pendant la période d'essai, nous vous confirmerons, dès son échéance, votre engagement permanent et la période de préavis d'une semaine sera prolongée à un mois.

Indemnisation de maladie:
Toute absence raisonnable pour cause de maladie sera indemnisée par nos soins, à la hauteur de votre salaire normal, pour la partie non prise en charge par la sécurité sociale. Toutefois, il est à noter que cette participation sera relative à votre durée de service chez nous.

Vacances:[1]
Vous aurez droit à 20 jours ouvrables de vacances payées dans une année entière, la période normale des congés étant comprise entre le 1er janvier et le 31 décembre.

Voiture:[2]
Nous vous fournirons une voiture d'entreprise appropriée (coût environ 140 000,00 francs), qui est prévue pour un usage principalement lié à vos activités d'entreprise mais dont vous pourrez également vous servir pour votre utilisation personnelle. L'entreprise prendra en charge tous les coûts normaux engendrés par ce véhicule: vignette, assurance, réparations, entretien et essence.

Retraite:
L'entreprise est à même d'offrir un régime de retraite. Vous aurez ainsi la possibilité soit d'y souscrire après six mois de service lors de l'anniversaire de la mise en place de ce régime en juillet 199-, soit de choisir un régime de retraite indépendant auquel l'entreprise contribuerait.

### Hours

Normal office hours are from 9.00 a.m. to 5.15 p.m. from Monday to Friday with one hour for lunch. However, it is probable that additional calls will be made upon your time.

### Grievance and Disciplinary Procedure

Should you wish to seek redress for any grievance relating to your employment, you should refer, as appropriate, either to the Company Secretary or to the Managing Director. Matters involving discipline will be dealt with in as fair and equitable a manner as possible.

### Health & Safety at Work Act

A copy of the Staff Notice issued under the Health & Safety at Work etc. Act 1974 will be given to you on the first day of your employment. Your acceptance of the appointment will be deemed to constitute your willingness to comply with these regulations.

### Start Date

The date on which your employment by the Company is to commence remains to be agreed and we look forward to establishing a mutually acceptable date with you as soon as possible.

Will you kindly provide us with your acceptance of this offer of employment by signing and returning to us the enclosed duplicate copy of this letter.

We trust that you will have a long, happy and successful association with our Company.

Yours sincerely


B. Foster
Managing Director

Enc.

Horaires:[3]
Les heures de bureau normales sont de 9h00 à 17h15 du lundi au vendredi avec une heure pour le déjeuner. Il se peut cependant que vous soyez parfois amené à travailler au-delà de ces horaires.

Différends et procédures disciplinaires:

Si vous avez quelque plainte que ce soit vous devrez la soumettre soit au Secrétaire Général, soit au Directeur Général. Les problèmes de discipline seront réglés de la manière la plus équitable et juste possible.

Santé et Sécurité sur le lieu de travail:
Un exemplaire de la 'Notification au personnel' publié suivant la loi 1974 'Santé et sécurité au Travail' vous sera donné le jour de la prise de vos fonctions. L'acceptation du poste vous engage également à accepter et respecter ces consignes.

Date d'entrée en fonction:
Votre date d'entrée en fonction n'a toujours pas été déterminée. Nous serions heureux de la fixer avec vous dans les plus brefs délais.

Nous vous serions reconnaissants de bien vouloir nous faire parvenir votre acceptation de cette offre d'emploi et de nous retourner un exemplaire[4] dûment signé de cette lettre.

Nous espérons que votre association à notre entreprise sera de longue durée, heureuse et pleine de succès.

Je vous prie d'agréer, Monsieur, l'assurance de mes meilleurs sentiments.


B. Foche
Directeur Général

P.J.: Exemplaire du contrat

1   *Vacances*: in France depending on the collective agreement (*convention collective*) normal paid holidays are 25 working days (if Saturday is not considered a working day) and 31 working days (if Saturday is considered a working day). Also, and still depending on the collective agreement, the holiday year runs from 1 May to 30 April or 1 June to 31 May.
2   Please note that in France it is very unusual for a company to offer a company car as a benefit unless it is absolutely indispensable for the job. Even in the latter case, it is not rare to see in the job advertisement *voiture indispensable*, which implies that the candidate must already possess a vehicle.
3   *Horaires*: French office working hours are from 9 a.m. to 6 p.m. in most cities with one hour for lunch between 12 p.m. and 1 p.m. or 1 p.m. and 2 p.m. Elsewhere from 8 a.m. to 7 p.m. with a two-hour lunch break between 12 p.m. and 2 p.m.
4   *Exemplaire*: 'a copy'.

## 38 Enquiring about regulations for purchase of property abroad (memo)

Internal memorandum

From:        Terry Baddison (Customer Services)
To:          Guillermo Estuardos (Legal Department)

Date:        20 October 199-

Message:     I urgently need some information on current rules and regulations
             concerning the purchase and renting of property in Spain. We have
             some clients interested in the new complex at Carboneras, but there
             seems to be doubt over whether they can sublet part of the premises
             without paying local tax on the rental.

             P.S. I'm in the office every afternoon this week.

             Terry

# 38  Demande de renseignements concernant les règlementations pour l'achat de propriétés à l'étranger (mémo)

MEMORANDUM

De la part de:   Terry Baddison (Service clientèle)
Destiné à:       Guillermo Estuardos (Service juridique)

Date:            20 octobre 1993

J'ai un besoin urgent d'informations concernant les statuts régissant l'achat et la location de propriétés mobilières en Espagne. Nous avons certains clients intéressés par le nouveau complexe immobilier de Carboneras, mais il semble y avoir des doutes au sujet de la sous-location d'une partie des locaux sans avoir à payer de taxes locales sur le loyer. Pourriez-vous vérifier tout cela le plus rapidement possible?

P.S. Je serai au bureau tous les après-midi cette semaine.

# 39  Advising of delay in delivery (telex)

TELEX:       Expofrut (Almería, Spain) to Henshaw Bros. (Wolverhampton, England)

Subject:     Delay in delivery

Sender:      Pablo López
Addressee:   Mary Henshaw
Date:        1 May 199-

Message:     APOLOGIES FOR FAILING TO DELIVER USUAL ORDER THIS WEEK.

DOCKS STRIKE CALLED FROM TODAY THROUGHOUT SPAIN.

YOUR CONSIGNMENT OF FRUIT AND VEGETABLES ON QUAYSIDE. STILL POSSIBLE TO SEND GOODS BY ROAD, BUT COULD NOT GUARANTEE DELIVERY BY WEEKEND.

PLEASE INFORM BY TELEPHONE (00 3451 947583) THIS P.M. IF TO PROCEED WITH ORDER BY ROAD.

REGARDS

Pablo López
(Export Manager)

# 39  Avis de retard de livraison (telex)

Expofruit (Valflaunès, France)
Destiné à Henshaw Bros (Wolverhampton, Angleterre)

Objet: Retard de livraison

Expéditeur: Pierre López

Destinataire: Mary Henshaw

Date: 1er mai 199-

Message:
Désolé de ne pas avoir pu vous livrer votre commande habituelle cette semaine. Une grève des dockers sévit actuellement dans la France entière. Votre commande de fruits et légumes est à quai. Il est toujours possible d'envoyer la marchandise par transport routier, mais nous ne pouvons pas promettre l'arrivage avant le week-end. Veuillez nous informer de votre décision par téléphone (00 33 67 42 89) cet après-midi si vous voulez que nous acheminions la commande par transport routier.

Cordialement,


Pierre López
Directeur Exportation

# 40  Seeking clarification of financial position (fax)

To:      Accounts Section, MULTIBANK,
         Prince's Square, Crewe

From:    John Turket, PERLOANS
         High Street, Tamworth

Date:    17 August 199-
No. of pages, including this: 1

Dear Sir

This company has been approached by a Mr Alan Thomas, who wishes to secure a loan in order to finance a family visit to relatives living overseas. He has given his approval to my contacting your branch of Multibank, where he holds two accounts, in order to verify and clarify information he has proffered about his financial position.

Once you have satisfied yourselves that Mr Thomas is willing that you divulge facts about his finances, can you please provide the following information?

1  Has Mr Thomas incurred major overdrafts since 1990?

2  Do both Mr Thomas and his wife have salary cheques paid directly each month into their current account?

3  Does your bank have any reason to believe that Mr Thomas will not be able to repay a £3,000 loan to Perloans over 3 years from July 199-?

We hope you feel able to respond to our request, and thank you for your assistance in this matter.

Yours faithfully


John Turket
Loans Manager

# 40  Demande de renseignements concernant la situation financière d'un client

## TELECOPIE

De:          Jean Touraine
Tél:         0827 872 132
Fax:         ⟍ 0827 872 395

A:           Service comptable
Fax No.:     (00 33) 143 86 75 95

SOCIETE:     MULTIBANK FRANCE

Date:        17 août 199-

Nombre de pages, y compris celle-ci: 1

Message:

Nous venons d'être contactés par Monsieur Alain Thomas qui désire obtenir un emprunt afin de financer un voyage avec sa famille pour aller rendre visite à de proches parents vivant à l'étranger. Il m'a donné son accord pour contacter votre agence de Multibank où il possède deux comptes; ceci afin de vérifier et clarifier ce qu'il nous a dit de sa situation financière.

Une fois que vous aurez vérifié que M. Thomas veuille[1] bien divulguer les faits concernant ses finances, nous vous serions très reconnaissants de bien vouloir nous faire parvenir les informations suivantes:

1-    M. Thomas a-t-il été en situation de découvert important depuis 1990?
2-    Les salaires de M. et Mme Thomas[2] sont-ils tous deux versés sur leur compte courant?
3-    Votre banque a-t-elle, pour quelque raison que ce soit, lieu de croire que M. Thomas ne soit pas en mesure de rembourser 30 000,00 à Perloans en trois ans à partir du mois de juillet 199-?

Nous espérons que vous serez en mesure de nous répondre et vous remercions par avance de votre coopération.

Nous vous adressons, Messieurs, nos salutations distinguées.

Jean Touraine
Responsable des prêts

1   Subjunctive.
2   *M.* but *Mme* and *Mlle* (no full stop is used when the last letter of the abbreviated word is present).

# 41   Reporting to client on availability of particular property (fax)

To:      Ms L Topcopy
         Trendset Printers
From:    Mrs D Russell
         Smith & Jones

Date:    20 August 199-

No. of pages, including this: 1

Re:      Office for lease

Dear Ms Topcopy

I am faxing you urgently to let you know that office premises have just become available in the area of town you said you liked. The lease on a street-front shop with upstairs office has been cancelled early by another client who is moving south. If you would like to see the property, please get back to us this afternoon and we will arrange a visit.

Best wishes


Dorothy Russell

# 41  Prévenir un client de la disponibilité de locaux d'activité (télécopie)

## TELECOPIE[1]

Date:     20 août 199-

Dest.:    Mme Dubonnet      Tel: (00 33) 43 87 75 86
          Topcopy           Télécopie: (00 33) 43 87 75 85

Exp.:     Mme D. Russell    Tel: (19 44) 1772 743901
                            Télécopie: (19 44) 1772 742900

Re:       Location de bureaux

Nombre de pages, y compris la page de garde: 1

Message:

Je vous envoie cette télécopie afin de vous faire savoir le plus rapidement possible que des bureaux viennent de se libérer dans le quartier où vous désiriez vous installer. Le bail d'un fond de commerce à devanture ayant des bureaux à l'étage vient d'être annulé par l'un de nos clients qui a décidé de s'installer dans le sud. Si vous désirez visiter les locaux, nous vous serions reconnaissants de nous le faire savoir cet après-midi et nous organiserons un rendez-vous.

Cordialement,


Dorothy Jenkins

1  Example of a different standard fax layout very much in use in France.

# 42  Complaining about customs delay (fax)

| | |
|---|---|
| To: | HM Customs and Excise |
| | London |
| From: | Ordenasa, Madrid |
| Date: | 21/2/9- |
| No. of pages: | 1 |

Dear Sirs

On behalf of my director colleagues of this computer software business I wish to lodge a complaint about customs clearance at British airports.

On several occasions since October 199- materials freighted from Madrid to retailers in Great Britain have been subject to unexplained and unjustifiable delays. This company depends for success on its ability to respond quickly to market demand; furthermore, at all times the requisite export licences have been in order.

This communication by fax is prompted by the latest and most frustrating hold-up we have experienced, at Gatwick Airport yesterday, which has allowed a market competitor to secure a valuable contract ahead of us.

If the Single Market is to function effectively this is precisely the type of situation that must be avoided. I intend to contact the relevant Chamber of Commerce, but in the meantime I insist on an explanation from your officers of why consignment AT/463 was not permitted immediate entry on 20 February 199-.

Yours faithfully


Dr. Norberto Mateos
(Managing Director)

# 42  Plainte au sujet des services de dédouanement (télécopie)

## TELECOPIE

| | |
|---|---|
| De: | Dr. Norberto Mareos |
| Tél: | 32 275 6580 |
| Fax: | 32 275 7821 |

| | |
|---|---|
| A: | HM Customs and Excise, Londres |
| Fax No.: | (44) 71 731 4846 |

Date:        21 février 199-

Nombre de pages, y compris celle-ci: 1

Message:

Messieurs,

De la part de mes collègues directeurs de cette société de services et d'ingénierie informatiques, je désire formuler une plainte visant les services de dédouanement dans les aéroports britanniques.

A plusieurs reprises depuis le mois d'octobre 199-, les matériaux envoyés de Bruxelles à des distributeurs en Grande-Bretagne ont subi des retards inexplicables et injustifiables. Afin de réussir, cette entreprise se doit[1] de répondre très rapidement à la demande du marché; de plus, les différents documents requis et notre licence d'exportation ont toujours été en règle.

Cette communication par télécopie a été précipitée par le retard le plus long et le plus frustrant que nous ayons[2] eu jusqu'à présent à l'aéroport de Gatwick hier, ce qui a permis à l'un de nos concurrents de signer un important contrat à notre place.

Si le marché unique veut fonctionner correctement, c'est précisément le genre de situation que l'on veut éviter. J'ai l'intention de contacter la chambre de commerce compétente, mais en attendant j'exige de la part de vos douaniers une explication écrite de la raison pour laquelle l'envoi AT/463 n'a pas été autorisé à entrer immédiatement dans le pays le 20 février 199-.

Dans l'attente de votre réponse, je vous prie d'agréer, Messieurs, ma parfaite considération.


Dr. Norberto Mateos
(Président Directeur Général)

1  Literally, 'owes to itself (to)'.
2  Subjunctive.

# 43 Stating delivery conditions

1 August 199-

Your Reference: AD/LR
Our Reference: TH/PA

Sr José Escalante
Managing Director
Escalante e Hijos
Avenida del Sol
San Sebastián
SPAIN

Dear Mr Escalante

Thank you for your fax communication of yesterday regarding the delivery of the chickens and other poultry ordered by you from this company in early July. As we indicated in our original quote to Mr Salas, who first contacted us, the delivery can only be guaranteed if your bank is able to confirm that debts owed to us will be cleared this week.

Please note that our drivers would much appreciate assistance with overnight accommodation and that any costs they incur should be charged directly to Bury Farm on completion of the delivery next week.

We look forward to hearing from you on both matters.

Yours sincerely

Tom Holbrook
Transport Manager

# 43   Exposer ses conditions de livraison

M. Joël Escalante
Directeur Général
Escalante et Fils
Avenue du Soleil
64000 Pau
France

Craven Arms, le 1er août 199-

Votre Réf.: AD/LR
Notre Réf.: TH/PA

Monsieur,

Nous vous remercions de votre communication télécopiée d'hier concernant votre commande de poulets et autres volailles datant de début juillet. Comme nous vous l'avons précisé dans notre devis adressé à M. Salas qui nous a contactés dès le début, la livraison pourra être livrée sous la seule condition que votre banque nous confirme que vos dettes seront réglées cette semaine.

Nous vous serions reconnaissants de bien vouloir aider nos chauffeurs à trouver un logement pour la nuit. Les frais engendrés devront être facturés directement à Bury Farm une fois la livraison effectuée la semaine prochaine.

Dans l'attente de vos réponses sur les deux points soulevés ci-dessus, je vous prie d'agréer, Monsieur, l'expression de mes meilleurs sentiments.

Tom Holbrook
Directeur du service transport

# 44  Confirming time/place of delivery

12 June 199-

Your Reference: RCG/LP
Our Reference: FG/JD

Dr Rosa Castro Giménez
Subdirectora
Departamento de Relaciones Exteriores
Ministerio de Industria
Quito
ECUADOR

Dear Madam

Further to our communication of 9 May in which we outlined to your department the likely oil needs of the companies we represent, it is with some concern that we have heard indirectly that your Ministry may be unable to fulfil its immediate responsibilities. We would be most obliged to hear, at your earliest convenience, that the draft agreement signed recently by our representatives remains valid.

In spite of our concern we are fully committed to the trading relations discussed and as such wish to confirm details of the first delivery of the manufactured goods which are being exchanged for the above-mentioned oil imports. Carlton Excavators plc have confirmed this week that the consignment of earthmovers, tractors and diggers bound for Constructores Velasco was loaded on Monday of this week. It should reach the port of Guayaquil by the end of the month. We will, of course, provide you with more precise details nearer the time.

Meanwhile, please accept our best wishes for the continuation of our collaborative venture as we await your confirmation regarding the deliveries of your oil to the New South Wales terminal.

Yours faithfully


Frank Gardner
SENIOR PARTNER

# 44 Confirmer la date et le lieu d'une livraison

Dr. Rossa Castro Giménez,
Directrice Adjointe,
Département de Relations Extérieures,
Ministère de l'Industrie,
Cayenne,
Guyane Française[1]

Sydney, le 12 juin 199-

Votre Réf.: RCG/LP
Notre Réf.: FG/JD

Chère Madame,

A la suite de notre communication du 9 mai par laquelle nous vous avons fait part du besoin approximatif de nos entreprises en pétrole, c'est avec une certaine inquiétude que nous avons appris indirectement que votre ministère ne sera pas à même d'assurer ses responsabilités. Nous vous serions très obligés de bien vouloir nous faire savoir le plus rapidement possible que le projet d'accord récemment signé par nos mandataires demeure valable.

Malgré notre inquiétude, nous sommes totalement engagés au niveau des relations commerciales dont nous avons discuté et nous désirons ainsi confirmer les détails de la première livraison des marchandises fabriquées qui doivent être échangées avec les importations de pétrole mentionnées ci-dessus. Carlton Excavators plc a confirmé cette semaine que la commande de bulldozers, tracteurs et pelleteuses était prête à partir pour Constructeurs Vauban lundi prochain. Elle devrait arriver à Cayenne d'ici la fin du mois. Nous vous donnerons de plus amples détails dès que possible.

Je vous prie d'agréer, chère Madame, l'expression de nos meilleurs voeux pour la poursuite de notre coopération tout en attendant votre confirmation au sujet des livraisons de votre pétrole au terminal pétrolier de New South Wales.

Frank Gardner
Associé majoritaire

1 French Guiana.

# 45    Checking on mode of transportation

19 February 19-

Your ref. SM/MB
Our ref. TS/PU

Mr Sebastián Morán
Sales Manager
Hermanos García SA
Carretera Luis Vargas, 24
CUENCA
Spain

Dear Mr Morán

Thank you for your letter sent on Tuesday last in which you refer to the kitchen equipment we ordered from García Brothers in December. As you know, our market has been rather depressed, but there are recent signs of improvement, and as a result we now need to receive the cupboard doors and worktops much more promptly than hitherto.

Can you please confirm that where necessary you would be able to deliver some items by road, or even by air if very urgent, rather than by the sea route you currently use?

We have checked that from Valencia it would be possible to airfreight at a reasonable price to East Midlands Airport on a Monday afternoon and a Thursday evening.

I would be grateful if you could send us a reply once you have been able to ascertain whether our proposal is viable.

Yours sincerely


Trevor Sharp
Warehouse Manager

# 45  Choix d'un moyen de transport

M. Sebastien Moren,
Directeur des ventes,
Frères Garcia SA,
150 rue des Barricades,
84300 Cavaillon,
France

Leicester, le 19-02-199-

Votre Réf.: SM/MB
Notre Réf.: TS/PU

Cher Monsieur,

Nous vous remercions de la lettre que vous nous avez envoyée mardi dernier dans laquelle vous vous référiez aux aménagements de cuisines que nous avons commandés aux Frères Garcia en décembre. Comme vous le savez, notre marché a récemment été en crise mais est maintenant en passe d'amélioration et nous avons donc besoin de recevoir les portes de placards et les plans de travail beaucoup plus rapidement que nous en avions l'habitude.

Pourriez-vous nous confirmer que, si nécessaire, il vous serait possible d'acheminer la marchandise voulue par transport routier ou aérien pour les demandes urgentes, plutôt que par transport maritime utilisé jusqu'ici?

Nous avons vérifié la possibilité d'envoyer la marchandise par avion à un prix raisonnable de Marseille à l'aéroport des East Midlands le lundi après-midi et le jeudi soir.

Nous vous serions très reconnaissants de bien vouloir nous donner votre réponse quant à la réalisation de notre proposition.

Vous en remerciant par avance, nous vous prions d'agréer, cher Monsieur, nos salutations distinguées.


Trevor Sharp
Chef magasinier

# 46 Claiming for transportation damage

24 January 199-

Claims Department
Lifeguard Assurance plc
Safeside House
High Street
Bromsgove
Worcs.

Dear Sir/Madam

POLICY NO. AL 78/2139B

My letter concerns a claim I wish to make on behalf of this firm, Anchor Lighting. We have had a policy with your company for many years, and rarely have needed to call upon your services. This time, however, we have suffered a serious financial loss due to damage incurred during the transit of goods.

Last week a whole consignment of lamps and other fittings was lost when our delivery truck ran off the road and turned over. The retail value of the merchandise ruined was in the region of £7,000, a sum equivalent to an entire quarter's profit.

I would be most grateful if you could send at your earliest convenience a major claim form and some general information on your settlement procedures.

Our policy number is as follows: AL 78/2139B.

I look forward to hearing from you soon.

Yours sincerely


Brian Tomkinson
(Proprietor)

# 46  Demande d'indemnité pour dégâts à des marchandises en transit

Service Indemnités,
Cabinet d'Assurances Ange
53 rue de la République,
25300 Pontarlier,
France

Granville, le 24 janvier 199-

Objet: Police d'assurance no. AL 78/2139B

Monsieur, Madame,

Nous aimerions formuler une demande d'indemnité au nom de notre entreprise Luminaires Ancre. Nous avons souscrit chez vous une police pendant plusieurs années en n'utilisant vos services que[1] très rarement. Cette fois, cependant, nous avons souffert d'importantes pertes financières à cause de dommages subis par des marchandises en transit.

La semaine dernière, un envoi complet de lampes et autres équipements a été perdu lors de l'accident d'un de nos camions de livraison qui a quitté la route et s'est renversé. La valeur marchande[2] de la marchandise perdue s'élevait à environ 70 000,00 francs, une somme équivalente aux bénéfices d'un trimestre[3] entier.

Nous vous serions donc très reconnaissants de bien vouloir nous envoyer le plus rapidement possible un formulaire de déclaration de sinistre[4] et les informations générales concernant les procédures pour le règlement.

Notre numéro de Police d'Assurance est le suivant: AL 78/2139B.

Dans l'attente d'une prompte réponse, nous vous prions d'agréer, Monsieur, Madame, nos respectueuses salutations.

Bertrand Tellier
(Propriétaire)

1  *n'... que*: stands for *ne ... que*: 'only', e.g. *Je ne pars que demain.*
2  'Market value'.
3  *Un trimestre* is literally a three-month period.
4  *Un sinistre*: 'disaster', 'fire'.

# 47  Enquiring about customs clearance

10 August 199-

Your ref.
Our ref. TC/LJ

The Customs and Excise Branch
Chilean Trade Ministry
SANTIAGO
Chile
South America

Dear Sirs

I have been advised to write to you directly by the Commercial Section of the Chilean Embassy in London. My company produces high-tech toys for the world market; at a recent trade fair in Barcelona several Chilean retailers expressed interest in importing our products, but we were unable to provide information on customs formalities in your country. Similarly, the London Embassy has recommended that I consult your Branch to seek up-to-date information.

The situation is as follows: our products include computer games, remote-control toy cars, mini-sized televisions etc. It seems that goods made in the EU are subject to a customs process rather more restrictive than those from Japan or the USA. As my company is a wholly-owned subsidiary of a US parent firm, would it be easier and cheaper to export to Chile from the USA rather than from Britain?

My intention is not merely to circumvent regulations but to optimize our operations, particularly at a time when such matters as customs clearance can result in costly delays.

I thank you for your attention and look forward to an early reply.

Yours sincerely,


Thomas Carty
MANAGING DIRECTOR

# 47  Demande de renseignements concernant les formalités douanières

Le Service des Douanes,
Ministère du Commerce,
SANTIAGO,
Chili,
Amérique du Sud

Evry, jeudi 10 août 199-

Messieurs,

Le service commercial de l'Ambassade Chilienne à Paris m'a conseillé de vous écrire directement. Mon entreprise fabrique des jouets de technologie avancée pour le marché mondial. Lors d'un récent salon à Barcelone, plusieurs détaillants chiliens ont exprimé l'intérêt d'importer nos produits mais nous sommes dans l'incapacité de leur fournir quelque information que ce soit[1] sur les formalités douanières de votre pays. L'ambassade de Paris nous a également conseillé de contacter votre service afin de nous donner les renseignements les plus à jour.[2]

La situation est la suivante: nos produits comprennent des jeux informatiques, des voitures modèles réduits télécommandées, des télévisions miniatures, etc. Il semble que les produits fabriqués en Europe soient soumis à des vérifications douanières beaucoup plus sévères que ceux provenant du Japon ou des Etats-Unis. Du fait que cette entreprise est une filiale entièrement possédée par une maison mère située aux Etats-Unis, serait-il plus facile et moins cher d'exporter au Chili à partir des Etats-Unis au lieu de la France?

Mes intentions ne sont pas d'outrepasser les règlements mais d'optimiser nos opérations surtout lorsque l'on sait que de nos jours les démarches de dédouanement peuvent entraîner de coûteux retards.

Je vous remercie de votre attention et espère recevoir très prochainement votre réponse.

Dans cette attente, nous vous prions de recevoir, Messieurs, nos salutations distinguées.

Thierry Cartier
Directeur Général

1  'Any information at all'.
2  Cf. *mettre à jour*: 'to bring up to date', 'to update'.

# 48  Undertaking customs formalities

27 November 199-

Your ref.
Our ref. RM/AP

HM Customs and Excise
Government Offices
LONDON WC2

Dear Sir/Madam

I write to inform you of a business operation in which my company is to be involved for the first time and to request your advice in the case of any misapprehension on my part.

As sole director of Leatherlux I have recently been able to conclude a deal with a firm of suppliers in Tunisia. I imagine that as a non-EU nation Tunisia cannot trade with complete freedom from import/export levies. I wish therefore to inform you that I intend to import from Nabeul in the next fortnight the following articles:

```
150 men's leather jackets
 50 pairs of ladies' leather trousers
250 leather belts
100 pairs of leather sandals
 50 pairs of men's leather boots
```

I anticipate paying approximately £3,000 for the consignment. Can you please provide me with official documentation (if required) or confirm by fax that I shall be required to pay some form of duty on these imports?

I thank you in anticipation of your assistance.

Yours faithfully

Royston McAughey
Managing Director

# 48   Se familiariser avec les formalités douanières

Bureaux des Douanes,
CDP Contrôle Douanier,
52 rue du Louvre,
75001 Paris

Angoulême, le 27/11/199-

Votre Réf.
Notre Réf: RM/AP

Messieurs,

Je vous écris pour vous informer d'une transaction dans laquelle mon entreprise sera impliquée pour la première fois et vous demander conseil afin d'éviter tout déboire.[1]

En tant qu'unique directeur de 'Cuirlux' j'ai récemment conclu un marché avec une entreprise de fournisseurs en Tunisie. J'imagine qu'étant un pays ne faisant pas partie de l'Union Européenne, la Tunisie ne peut pas opérer de transactions non soumises à l'imposition[2] Import/Export. Je désire par conséquent vous informer de mon intention d'importer de Nabeul d'ici quinze jours les articles suivants:

    150 vestes d'hommes en cuir
     50 paires de pantalons en cuir pour femmes
    250 ceintures en cuir
    100 paires de sandales en cuir
     50 paires de bottines en cuir pour hommes

Je pense devoir une somme d'environ 25 000 francs pour cet envoi. Vous serait-il possible de m'envoyer les formulaires et la documentation officielle (si nécessaire) ou au moins me confirmer par télécopie, si possible, que je devrai être imposé d'une manière ou d'une autre sur ces importations?

Vous remerciant par avance de votre coopération, je vous prie d'agréer, Messieurs, l'assurance de mes meilleurs sentiments.


Raymond Arlery
Directeur Général

1   'To avoid any mishap'.
2   'Subject to taxation'.

# 49  Informing of storage facilities

13 June 199-

Your ref. JG/TK
Our ref. JS/PI

Hurd's (International) Removals
34-36, Wesley Avenue
CROYDON
Surrey

Dear Mrs Gordon

I am pleased to inform you that the container of household goods your company contracted us to transport from Australia to England has now been delivered to our depot here in Kent.

We will need by the end of this week to complete the official formalities, but you are welcome to pick up the unloaded contents for onward delivery to your customer from next Monday.

If you prefer to leave the goods here in store until further notice, please consult our price list (enclosed) for storage facilities and let us know your intention by fax.

When your driver does come to pick up the goods, he should enter the terminal by the side entrance which will lead him straight to the relevant loading area, marked DOMESTIC.

I trust these arrangements meet with your approval.

Yours sincerely


Jim Smith
Depot Manager

Enc.

# 49  Informer un client d'une possibilité d'entreposage

Déménageurs Demongeau,
106 avenue de la Forêt,
60500 Chantilly,
France

Bordeaux, le 13 juin 199-

Votre Réf.: JG/TK
Notre Réf.: JS/PI

Messieurs,

Je suis heureux de vous informer que le conteneur d'appareils ménagers dont vous nous avez confié le transport d'Australie en France vient d'être livré ici dans notre entrepôt de Bordeaux.

Nous devrons, d'ici la fin de la semaine, effectuer les démarches officielles mais il vous est tout à fait possible de venir récupérer les produits déchargés afin de pouvoir honorer la commande de votre client lundi prochain.

Si vous préférez laisser les marchandises en dépôt ici jusqu'à nouvel ordre, veuillez consulter nos tarifs pour entreposage en annexe et veuillez nous faire part de votre décision par télécopie.

Quand votre chauffeur viendra chercher les marchandises, il devra accéder au terminal par l'entrée latérale et arriver directement dans la zone de chargement appropriée, signalisée "METROPOLE".[1]

En espérant que ces arrangements vous conviendront, je vous prie de croire, Messieurs, à l'expression de nos sentiments respectueux.

Jacques Sautelle
Chef magasinier

P.J. (1): Tarifs d'entreposage

1   *La métropole* is metropolitan (mainland) France.

# 50  Assuring of confidentiality of information

1 November 199-

Your ref. EF/LJ
Our ref. HE/PI

Dr Ernesto Furillo
University Hospital
University of Managua
Managua
República de Nicaragua

Dear Dr Furillo

<u>MISS ALICIA BARTOLOMÉ</u>

Thank you for your letter of last month in which you sought confirmation that the reference you provided for Miss Alicia Bartolomé and her personal details would remain confidential.

It is the policy of the Government and of this Ministry to maintain total discretion when dealing with citizens from other countries who come here in order to develop their professional studies. Miss Bartolomé's course begins in three weeks' time, by which time her curriculum vitae will have been duly stored on computer in this Ministry and will be accessible only to those with the due authorization.

As you will be well aware the need for confidentiality in matters such as these is paramount, so you may rest assured that all proper measures will be taken to protect the interests of your organization and of its employees.

Yours sincerely


Hortensia Enríquez Castro
Personnel Supervisor

# 50  Promettre la confidentialité au sujet de renseignements donnés

Dr Ernesto Furlllo,
CHR de Créteil,
94000 Créteil,
France.

La Habana, le 1er novembre 199-

Votre Réf.: EF/LJ
Notre Réf: HE/PI

Cher Monsieur,

Nous vous remercions de votre lettre du mois dernier, dans laquelle vous nous demandiez la confirmation d'avoir traité dans la plus stricte confidentialité la lettre de recommandation et les informations personnelles concernant Mlle Alicia Bartholémy que vous nous avez si gentiment fait parvenir.[1]

Il est du devoir du gouvernement et de son ministère, de garder la plus grande discrétion concernant les citoyens provenant d'autres pays qui viennent approfondir leurs études professionnelles. Les cours de Mlle Bartholémy commencent dans trois semaines; d'ici là, son curriculum vitae aura été saisi[2] sur le système informatique de ce ministère et sera uniquement accessible par les personnes munies d'une autorisation.

Comme vous devez le savoir, la nécessité d'une stricte confidentialité dans des cas comme celui-ci est d'une suprême importance; vous pouvez ainsi être rassuré des mesures prises afin de protéger l'intérêt de votre organisme et celui de vos employés.

Je vous prie de recevoir, cher Monsieur, nos salutations distinguées.

Hortensia Enríquez Castro
Chef d'équipe du personnel

1  'That you (have) so kindly sent'.
2  Note the special use here of *saisir*, the basic meaning of which is 'to seize'.

# 51  Informing a client on conditions of loans/mortgages available

14 July 199-

Your ref. GB/LK
Our ref. PH/VE

Mr G Brookham
Managing Director
MultiCast
Floor 11
Forum House
Dukeries Avenue
Mansfield

Dear Mr Brookham

Since receiving your letter of 23 June we have been making enquiries on the matter of financing that you raised. You will find enclosed three leaflets containing information about properties you may find interesting. They are self-explanatory and we shall await your reaction to them.

More pressing, perhaps, is the question of finance. Having consulted local banks as well as our own finance broker, we have concluded that you would do best to arrange a meeting with the latter, Charles Element, who will be pleased to outline a variety of mortgage as well as short-term loan plans.

All the four major banks in town offer facilities for loans, so you may prefer to try them before meeting Mr Element. However, it certainly appears that our broker can secure more favourable conditions if you are interested principally in a short-term loan.

Please see our broker's details below:

Element Financial Services, Star Chambers, High Street, Worksop, Nottinghamshire.

Yours sincerely


Percy Hartshorn
Customer Liaison

Encs

# 51   Informer la clientèle des prêts logement[1] disponibles sur le marché

M. Gilles Bourdieu,
Multicast,
11 rue Gambetta,
12000 Rodez.

Millau, le 14 juillet 199-

Monsieur,

Depuis la réception de votre lettre du 23 juin, nous avons fait des recherches concernant les problèmes de financement que vous avez soulevés. Vous trouverez ci-joint trois brochures contenant les informations au sujet des propriétés que vous pourriez juger intéressantes. Elles parlent d'elles-mêmes et nous attendons de savoir ce que vous en pensez.

Le plus pressant est peut-être la question du financement. Ayant consulté les établissements bancaires de la région ainsi que notre propre courtier, nous en avons conclu que la meilleure solution serait que vous preniez rendez-vous avec ce dernier, Gérard Element, qui se fera un plaisir de vous exposer les différentes possibilités en ce qui concerne les prêts logement ainsi que les prêts à court terme.

Les quatre banques principales de cette ville offrent toutes des prêts, ainsi préférerez-vous les contacter avant de rencontrer M. Element. Cependant, il semble que sans aucun doute, notre courtier pourrait garantir de meilleures conditions si vous êtes principalement intéressé par le prêt à court terme.

Veuillez trouver ci-dessous les coordonnées de notre courtier:
Services Financiers Element,
10 rue de l'Etoile,
34000 Montpellier

Veuillez agréer, Monsieur, l'assurance de nos meilleurs sentiments.

Laurent Carlton
Relations clientèle

P.J. (3): Brochures descriptives de propriétés.

1   Another word for mortgage is *une hypothèque*.

# 52   Circulating local businesses with property services available

12 January 199-

Our ref. CE/MB

To: Directors of all businesses in the Castilla-León region

Dear Colleague

I take the opportunity to write to you on behalf of myself and my partner, Ana Martiarena, in order to publicize as widely as possible the property services we can make available to businesses in the region.

Since establishing our company here in 1976 we have gradually expanded our range of activities and clients. Most recently we have opened a free advice centre in Puentenorte for any member of the public to obtain up-to-date information on the property market.

As regards the needs of business, we offer the following services:

- a weekly guide to premises for rent and sale
- a direct link to sources of finance
- rent-collection service
- legal and insurance consultancy
- assistance in securing mortgages
- technical support in planning space and furbishment
- computer database linked to the national property network

These and many more services are available from us, and all are on your doorstep. Don't hesitate – call us today on 234 56 71 or come in person to 69 Calle Balbita, Puentenorte, where you can be sure of a warm welcome.

Yours sincerely


Carlos Estévez

# 52   Circulaire adressée aux entreprises de la région concernant les services immobiliers disponibles

Moulins, le 12 janvier 199-

A l'attention de tous les Directeurs de toutes les entreprises de la région d'Auvergne

Notre Réf.: CE/MB

Cher Collègue,

Mon associée, Anne Montaigu et moi-même vous adressons cette lettre afin de diffuser aussi largement que possible les services immobiliers que nous pouvons offrir aux entreprises de la région.

Depuis la création de cette entreprise en 1976, nous avons progressivement développé notre gamme d'activités et de clients. Nous venons d'ouvrir un centre d'informations à accès libre à Moulins destiné à tout membre du public désirant obtenir les dernières informations sur le marché immobilier.

En ce qui concerne les besoins particuliers des entreprises, nous pouvons offrir les services suivants:

- une brochure hebdomadaire donnant tous les renseignements concernant les locaux à vendre et à louer;
- une liaison directe avec les établissements de financement;
- un service de gestion des locations;[1]
- un cabinet de conseil en droit et assurances;
- une aide à l'obtention de prêts immobiliers;[2]
- un soutien technique pour la planification de l'espace et la décoration;
- une base de données informatiques reliée au réseau immobilier national.

Nous pouvons mettre à votre disposition tous ces services et bien d'autres encore. N'hésitez pas à nous appeler dès aujourd'hui au 44 56 23 71 ou à nous rendre visite personnellement au 45 Avenue du Général Leclerc, Moulins, où le meilleur accueil vous sera réservé.

Dans cette attente, veuillez recevoir, cher Collègue, nos respectueuses salutations.


Charles Eluard

1   Literally, 'management of lettings'.
2   Another word for 'a mortgage' is *une hypothèque*.

# 53  Advertising maintenance services available for office equipment

30 January 199-

Your ref.
Our ref. TH/JY

To:  Office Managers:
     Motor Sales businesses
     in South London area

Dear Colleague

You may be aware from press advertising that our firm offers a new service to the motor trade, particularly to maintain equipment used in processing stores supplies. Most large dealerships with service and accessories departments have installed a fully-integrated system that reduces drastically the need for large numbers of warehousemen.

The service charge is £350 per quarter, irrespective of visits made or problems solved; this figure also includes a component of insurance that covers both the dealership and ourselves against major breakdowns.

In recent months we have signed such service contracts with more than 40 dealerships whose names we are happy to supply if you are interested in checking our claims.

Thank you for your attention. Please do not hesitate to ring or fax us this week if the enclosed information leaflet is relevant to your needs.

Yours sincerely


Tom Henderson
Managing Director

Enc.

# 53 Promouvoir ses services d'entretien pour le matériel de bureau

A l'attention de la Direction de tous les concessionnaires de la région de Lyon

Notre réf.: TH/JY

Lyon, le 30 janvier 199-

Cher Collègue,

Vous avez très certainement appris par la publicité parue dans la presse que nous offrons un nouveau service à l'industrie automobile, particulièrement en ce qui concerne l'entretien du matériel utilisé par les fournisseurs de pièces. La plupart des concessionnaires offrant services et accessoires disposent de systèmes de traitement de données intégrés[1] qui réduisent considérablement le nombre des magasiniers nécessaires.

Le coût de ce service est de FF 3 500,00 par trimestre quels que soient les visites faites ou les problèmes résolus; ce chiffre comprend également une assurance couvrant le concessionnaire, et nous-mêmes, en cas de grosses pannes.

Au cours des derniers mois, nous avons signé de semblables contrats avec près de 40 concessionnaires dont nous sommes prêts à communiquer les noms si vous désiriez faire des vérifications.

Si vous trouvez les informations contenues dans la brochure ci-jointe intéressantes, n'hésitez pas à nous contacter.

Vous remerciant de votre attention, nous vous prions d'agréer, cher Collègue, l'assurance de nos meilleurs sentiments.


Thomas Hendaye
Président Directeur Général

P.J. (1): Brochure

1    Literally, 'have at their disposal integrated data-processing systems'.

# 54  Arranging a meeting for further discussions

4 October 199-

Our ref: TSS/EHK

Mr Angelo Ricasso
Cuscinetti SAS
Via Alessandro Manzoni, 32
20050 Triuggio (MI)
Italy

Dear Mr Ricasso

RE: THRUST BEARINGS

In 1989 we met in order to discuss the addition of our thrust bearings to the Dudley range for sale in your country.

We regret that due to many changes which have occurred in this company and in our parent company no progress was made with our arrangements, and we understand that it must have been disappointing for you not to have heard from us for such a long time.

We are now willing to try again, if you have not made other arrangements and we would like to arrange a meeting with you in Cologne at the Hardware Fair next March.

We look forward to hearing from you,

Yours sincerely


Thomas Stone
SALES DIRECTOR

# 54  Organiser une réunion pour de plus amples discussions

M. André Ricard,
Mécaniques du Nord,
200 rue Fernand Forest,
59000 Lille,
France

Dudley, le 4 octobre 199-

N/Ref.: TSS/EHK

Objet: Roulements de butée

Cher Monsieur,

En 1995, nous nous sommes rencontrés afin de discuter de nos projets d'ajouter nos roulements à la gamme de produits que nous vendons dans votre pays.

Nous regrettons beaucoup que suite à des restructurations réalisées au sein de cette entreprise et de la maison mère, nous n'avons pas pu faire avancer ces projets et comprendrions fort bien que vous ayez été[1] déçus de ne pas avoir eu de nos nouvelles pendant un laps de temps aussi long.

Nous désirons maintenant faire un nouvel essai si vous n'avez pas pris d'autres dispositions entre-temps et aimerions beaucoup organiser une réunion avec vous lors du Salon de la Quincaillerie à Cologne en mars prochain.

Dans l'attente de vos nouvelles, je vous prie d'agréer, cher Monsieur, l'assurance de notre parfaite considération.

Thomas Stone
Directeur des ventes

1  Literally, 'we would understand that you may have been'.

# 55   Reservations

## Enquiry about hotel accommodation (fax)

17 April 199-

Hotel Lucullus
Amadeusplatz 27
Hannover
Germany

Dear Sirs

I am attending the trade fair in Hanover in May with two colleagues, and we shall need rooms for three nights. Please could you confirm availability and price of the following:

– three single rooms with bath/shower from 3 to 6 May.

Yours faithfully


Fred Garner

# 55  Réservations

## Demande de renseignements au sujet de chambres d'hôtel (télécopie)

Hotel Lucullus,
Square Amédée,
21000 Dijon,
Bourgogne,
France.

Coventry, Angleterre, le 17 avril 199-

Chers Messieurs,

J'assisterai, en compagnie de deux de mes collègues, au salon professionnel de Dijon en mai et nous aurions à cette occasion besoin[1] de chambres d'hôtel pendant trois nuits. Vous serait-il possible de nous indiquer vos prix et disponibilités pour les dates et chambres suivantes:

– trois chambres à une personne avec salle de bain/douche du 3 au 6 mai.

Vous en remerciant par avance, nous vous prions d'agréer, chers Messieurs, l'assurance de nos meilleurs sentiments.


Fred Garner

1  Literally, 'we would have need'.

# 56  Reservations

## Confirmation of reservation (fax)

6 June 199-

Ms G Cole
Ledington Parker plc
Moreton Avenue
Birmingham
B37 9KH

Dear Ms Cole

Room reservation 15–18 November

We confirm that we are able to offer the following accommodation:

Four single rooms with shower/WC @ £150 per night, inclusive of breakfast and service.

We should be grateful if you could confirm the booking in writing as soon as possible.

Yours sincerely


H Japer
Manager

# 56  Réservations

## Confirmation d'une réservation

Mme G. Cole,
Ledington Parker plc,
Moreton Avenue,
Birmingham B37 9KH,
Angleterre

Pau, le 6 juin 199-

Objet: Réservation de chambres du 15 au 18 novembre

Chère Madame,[1]

Nous vous confirmons la disponibilité des chambres suivantes:

4 chambres pour une personne
avec douche et toilettes
à 1 245 Frs par nuit, petit déjeuner et service compris.

Nous vous serions très reconnaissants de bien vouloir nous confirmer cette réservation par écrit le plus rapidement possible.

Vous en remerciant par avance, nous vous prions d'agréer, chère Madame, l'assurance de nos salutations distinguées.

H. Japer
Gérant

1  A 'Ms' is a *Mlle* (*Mademoiselle*) but the hotel is playing safe in case the correspondent is a *Madame*.

# 57  Reservations

## Change of arrival date

3 March 199-

Ms J Hinton
Hotel Bonner
46 Southampton Way
London
SE39 8UH
England

Dear Madam

We have today received your confirmation of our booking of three single rooms from 18 to 23 March.

Unfortunately, we have had to change our plans, and shall not now arrive in London until the morning of 20 March. We would be grateful if you could change the reservation accordingly. We now require three rooms from 20 to 23 March.

With thanks for your assistance.

Yours faithfully


Jacques Duclos

# 57  Réservations

## Modification d'une arrivée

Ms J. Hinton,
Hotel Bonner,
46 Southampton Way,
London SE39 8UH,
Angleterre

Amiens, lundi 3 mars 199-

Chère Madame,

Nous venons de recevoir votre confirmation de notre réservation pour trois chambres à une personne du 18 au 23 mars.

Nous devons malheureusement modifier nos projets et n'arriverons pas à Londres avant le 20 mars au matin. Nous vous serions très reconnaissants de bien vouloir changer, en conséquence, notre réservation. Nous voudrions donc trois chambres du 20 au 23 mars.

Vous en remerciant par avance, je vous prie d'agréer, chère Madame, l'expression de nos salutations distinguées.

Jacques Duclos

# 58  Reservations

## Request for confirmation of reservation

19 June 199-

Ms J Petersen
45 Dorrington Terrace
Bradford
Yorkshire
England

Dear Ms Petersen

You made a telephone reservation one week ago for a single room for two nights (20–22 July). We indicated to you when you made the reservation that we would hold it for one week, but that we required written confirmation.

If you still wish to reserve the room, we would be grateful if you would please confirm by fax within 24 hours, or we shall have to reserve the room for other clients.

Thank you for your cooperation.

Yours sincerely


John Bromwich
Manager

# 58  Réservations

## Demande de confirmation d'une réservation

Ms Petersen,
45 Dorrington Terrace,
Bradford,
Yorkshire,
Angleterre

Strasbourg, le 19 juin 199-

Chère Mademoiselle,

Vous avez réservé par téléphone, voici une semaine, une chambre pour une personne pour deux nuits (20 au 22 juillet). Lorsque vous avez effectué cette réservation, nous vous avions dit que nous la maintiendrions pendant une semaine et qu'une confirmation écrite était nécessaire.

Si vous désirez toujours retenir cette chambre, nous vous serions très reconnaissants de bien vouloir nous le confirmer par télécopie sous[1] 24 heures à défaut de quoi[2] nous réserverons cette chambre pour d'autres clients.

Vous remerciant par avance de votre coopération, nous vous prions d'agréer, chère Mademoiselle, l'expression de nos sentiments respectueux.

Jean Baumgertner
Gérant

1  Literally, *under*, meaning 'within'.
2  'Failing which'.

# 59  Insurance

## Request for quotation for fleet car insurance

7 October 199-

Hartson Insurance Services
24 Westbury Way
Sheffield
S12 9JF

Dear Sirs

We understand from colleagues that you specialize in insurance for company fleet cars. We have a large fleet of executive saloons, and are currently obtaining quotations for insurance cover.

If you are interested in giving us a quotation, could you please contact Ms Helen Bridges, our fleet manager, who will give you the appropriate details.

Yours faithfully


D J Herbert

# 59  Assurance

## Demande d'un devis pour assurer des véhicules de fonction

Assurance Alliance,
24 boulevard Jourdain,
75000 Paris

Paris, le 7 octobre 199-

Messieurs,

D'après certains de nos collègues, il semble que vous soyez spécialisés dans les assurances pour voitures de fonction. Nous possédons un bon nombre de ces véhicules et sommes actuellement en train de formuler la demande d'un certain nombre de devis.

Si vous pensez être intéressés par nos besoins, nous vous serions très reconnaissants de bien vouloir contacter Mme Hélène Brun, la responsable des véhicules, qui vous donnera de plus amples informations.

Veuillez recevoir, Messieurs, l'expression de nos salutations distinguées.


Dennis Hébert
Président

# 60  Insurance

## Reminder of overdue premium

21 November 199-

Mr R Collins
45 Delta Road
Stoke-on-Trent

Dear Mr Collins

Your vehicle, registration no H351 AWL is currently insured by us. We sent you several days ago a reminder that the insurance renewal premium was due. We have still not received this from you. We have to write to inform you that unless we receive payment within 72 hours, the insurance cover will lapse.

We would be most grateful if you would send your payment directly to our office in Gower Street, London.

Yours sincerely

Gerald Smith

# 60  Assurance

## Rappel pour le règlement d'une prime

Mr R. Collins,
45 rue des Remparts,
62000 Boulogne sur Mer,
France

Leeds, le 21 novembre 199-

Monsieur,

Nous assurons actuellement votre véhicule immatriculé 4639 XX 62.[1] Voici plusieurs jours de cela, nous vous avons envoyé une note de rappel de votre cotisation pour votre police d'assurance. Nous ne l'avons toujours pas reçue. Nous devons vous informer qu'à moins de recevoir le montant de cette cotisation d'ici 72 heures, vous ne serez plus couvert par l'assurance.

Nous vous serions donc très reconnaissants de bien vouloir nous faire parvenir votre règlement par retour, adressé à notre agence de Gower Street à Londres.

Dans cette attente, veuillez agréer, Monsieur, l'assurance de notre parfaite considération.

Gerald Smith

1   A French number plate (*la plaque d'immatriculation*) with the number of the *département* (Nord, 62) as part of it. Could this be a Channel Tunnel commuter?

# 61  Insurance

## Submission of documents to support claim

6 October 199-

Darton Insurance Services
59 Tristan Road
Uttoxeter
Staffordshire

Dear Sirs

I submitted to you several days ago a claim form under the terms of my motor vehicle insurance (policy number CDF 9486756 UY 94766). Your head office has since requested from me the original policy document. I regret to inform you that this is no longer in my possession, and I enclose herewith a photocopy. I trust that this will meet with your requirements.

Yours faithfully


A Lightowlers

Enc.

# 61  Assurance

## Soumission de documents pour la déclaration d'un accident de voiture

Cabinet d'assurances Daumier
107 rue du Château,
14000 Caen

Cabourg, mercredi 6 octobre 199-

Messieurs,

Je vous ai fait parvenir voici quelques jours un formulaire de déclaration d'accident concernant ma police d'assurance pour mon véhicule (police no. AA 9489 6756 bb/am). Depuis, les bureaux de votre siège m'ont demandé l'original de mon contrat d'assurance. Je suis désolé de vous apprendre que ce document n'est plus en ma possession et j'en joins à cette lettre une photocopie.

Dans l'espoir que cela sera suffisant pour l'usage que vous voulez en faire, je vous prie d'agréer, Messieurs, mes salutations distinguées.

André Lalumeau

P.J. (1): Photocopie de mon contrat d'assurance

# 62  Insurance

## Taking out third party vehicle insurance

18 November 199-

Uxbridge Insurance
Grosvenor House
12b Weston Terrace
Bournemouth
Hants

Dear Sirs

RE: QUOTATION RC28FO

Thank you for sending me your quotation. I confirm that I wish to take out Third Party car insurance, and I enclose the appropriate fee in the form of a cheque.

I should be grateful if you could send me confirmation of receipt and the policy certificate as soon as possible.

Yours faithfully


Oliver Gissing

# 62   Assurance

## Prendre une assurance voiture au tiers

Assurances Rhône et Saône,
87 rue du Vieux Quartier,
13000 Marseille

Cannes, le 18 novembre 199-

Objet: Devis no. RC28FO

Messieurs,

Ayant reçu votre devis, dont je vous remercie, j'aimerais contracter une police d'assurance au tiers. Vous trouverez ci-joint mon règlement sous forme de chèque bancaire.

Je vous serais très reconnaissant de bien vouloir m'en confirmer réception et de me faire parvenir mon attestation d'assurance dès que possible.

Vous en remerciant par avance, je vous prie d'agréer, Messieurs, l'expression de ma parfaite considération.


Olivier Gérard

# 63  Insurance

## Refusal to meet claim

Ms D Leach
29 Janison Avenue
York

Dear Ms Leach

RE: CLAIM NO. JH 8576/HY

We acknowledge receipt of your claim form (reference JH 8576/HY) for water damage to your stock on the night of 27 March. We regret, however, that we are unable to meet the claim, as our policy (section 3, paragraph 5) specifically excludes this form of damage, particularly since the premises were unoccupied for a period of two weeks before the damage occurred.

Yours sincerely


P Hartwell

# 63  Assurance

## Refus d'allocation d'indemnités

Mme D. Loque,
29 avenue des Acacias,
14800 Deauville,

Lyon, vendredi 10 avril 199-

Objet: Demande d'indemnités JH 8576/HY

Chère Madame,

Nous accusons réception de votre demande d'indemnités pour les dommages causés par les eaux à votre stock pendant la nuit du 27 mars. Nous avons cependant le regret de vous annoncer qu'il ne nous a pas été possible de l'honorer car notre police (section 3, paragraphe 5) ne couvre pas ce genre de dommages, surtout si l'on considère que les locaux étaient inoccupés pendant une période de plus de deux semaines avant le sinistre.

Nous vous adressons, chère Madame, nos salutations distinguées.


P. Halévy

# 64   Considering legal action

24 May 199-

Cabinet Rossignol
4 rue des Glaïeuls
75009 Paris
France

<u>For the attention of Maître Patelin</u>

Dear Maître Patelin

Your name was given to us by Robert Mackenzie of Canine Crunch Ltd for whom you acted last year.

We have a complaint against the French newspaper *The Daily Rocket* who have, in our opinion, seriously defamed us in the enclosed article dealing with the closure of our plant at Roissy-en-France.

We would wish to take legal action against the said journal but first would like to have your professional advice on the strength of our case. Could you also let us know how long our case might run and give us an idea of the likely scale of our legal costs.

Yours sincerely


Lionel E Bone
Managing Director

Enc.

# 64  Informer du désir d'intenter une action en justice

Cabinet Rossignol,
4, rue des Glaïeuls,
75009 Paris
France

West Hampstead, le 24 mai 199-

A l'attention de Maître[1] Patelin

Cher Maître,

Votre nom nous a été communiqué par Robert Mackenzie de chez Canine Crunch Ltd pour qui vous avez travaillé l'année dernière.

Nous avons une plainte à formuler contre le journal *La Fusée* qui nous a sérieusement diffamés dans l'article que nous joignons à cette lettre concernant la fermeture de notre usine de Roissy-en-France.

Nous désirons intenter une action en justice contre ledit journal mais nous aimerions tout d'abord avoir votre avis professionnel concernant la solidité de notre cas. Pourriez-vous également nous faire savoir la durée probable de cette action et nous donner une idée du montant des frais judiciaires que cette poursuite pourrait engendrer.

Vous en remerciant par avance, veuillez recevoir, cher Maître, nos salutations distinguées.

Lionel E. Bone
**Président Directeur Général**

**P.J.: article**

1  Title and form of address for a lawyer.

# 65  Requesting information on setting up a plant abroad

23 May 199-

Office Notarial
84 rue du Grand Pineau
85000 Olonnes sur Mer
France

Dear Sirs

Our company is proposing to set up a dairy produce processing plant in western France and we would like you to find us a suitable site.

We need either freehold or leasehold premises of 2,000 square metres on a plot with easy access for large vehicles.

Can you help us in finding the site and act for us in its acquisition? This is our first venture into France so we would appreciate any additional information about property purchase or leasing that you could send us.

Yours faithfully


Arthur Sturrock
Managing Director

# 65  Demande d'informations au sujet de l'implantation d'une usine à l'étranger

Office Notarial,
84 rue du Grand Pineau,
85000 Olonnes-sur-Mer,
France

Ludlow, le 23 mai 199-

Messieurs,

Notre société se propose de créer une usine productrice de produits laitiers dans l'ouest de la France et nous aimerions trouver un site propice.[1]

Nous désirerions des locaux de 2000 mètres carrés, qu'il s'agisse d'une propriété foncière libre de toute obligation ou d'une propriété louée à bail, sur un terrain d'accès facile aux gros véhicules.

Vous serait-il possible de nous aider à trouver ce site et d'agir en notre nom lors de l'acquisition? Ceci est notre première implantation[2] en France et nous vous serions très reconnaissants de bien vouloir nous donner toutes les informations en votre possession concernant l'achat ou la location de propriétés foncières.[3]

Dans l'attente de votre réponse, veuillez recevoir, Messieurs, nos salutations distinguées.


Arthur Sturrock
Président Directeur Général

1  Literally, 'propitious'.
2  Literally, 'setting up'.
3  *Foncier* relates essentially to leasing land.

# 66 Complaint about delay in administering an account

18 September 199-

Société Bancaire Générale
4 boulevard Leclerc
76200 Dieppe
France

For the attention of the Manager

Dear Sir

RE: ACCOUNT NO. 654231

We have received the July statement of our above account no. 654231 and are surprised that the balance shown is so low.

We have been assured by two of our major customers, Alligand SA and Berthaud Etains, that they settled large outstanding invoices by bank transfer to that account four weeks and five weeks ago respectively.

Will you please check very carefully and let us know by fax the exact balance of our account. If as we think, work is being processed by you in a dilatory fashion, please could you let us know the reason for this.

Yours sincerely


Eric Smith
Finance Director

# 66   Plainte concernant un retard de gestion d'un compte

Société Bancaire Générale,
4, boulevard Leclerc,
76200 Dieppe,
France

Blackburn, le 18 septembre 199-

A l'attention du Directeur

Concerne: Compte no. 654231

Monsieur,

Nous venons de recevoir notre relevé de compte du mois de juillet et sommes surpris de constater que le solde soit[1] si bas.

Deux de nos plus gros clients, Alligand S.A. et Berthaud Etains, nous assurent qu'ils ont bien réglé leurs factures arriérées dont le montant était très important. Ce règlement a été effectué par virement bancaire sur le compte cité en référence il y a respectivement quatre et cinq semaines.

Vous serait-il possible de vérifier très consciencieusement les opérations de notre compte et de nous en faire parvenir par fax le solde exact? Nous vous serions très reconnaissants de bien vouloir nous faire connaître les raisons de cette erreur, si, comme nous le pensons, tel est le cas.

Veuillez agréer, Monsieur, l'assurance de notre parfaite considération.

Eric Smith
Directeur Financier

1   Subjunctive.

# 67  Complaint about mail delivery

19 November 199-

The Central Post Office
Place Centrale
53000 Laval
France

Dear Sirs

We have made some enquiries in England and it appears that there are serious delays in the delivery of our mail to our subsidiary in Cossé le Vivien which are being caused at the Laval sorting office.

Since our business is being seriously inconvenienced by postal delays we would be most grateful if you could look into the matter.

It should not take 10 days for orders and invoices to get from us to our colleagues in Cossé. You will find enclosed a sample mailing with dates clearly marked.

Yours faithfully


Jeremy P Johnson
Director

Enc.

# 67 Plainte au sujet de la distribution du courrier

The Central Post Office,
Place Centrale,
53000 Laval,
France

Bridlington, le 19 novembre 199-

Messieurs,

Nous avons fait une enquête en Angleterre et il semble qu'il y ait[1] d'importants retards dans la distribution de notre courrier adressé à notre filiale de Cossé le Vivien. Il semble que les problèmes viennent du centre de tri de Laval.

Du fait que nos activités sont sérieusement perturbées par les retards postaux, nous vous serions très reconnaissants de bien vouloir redresser la situation.

Il ne devrait pas prendre plus de 10 jours à nos commandes et factures pour arriver à nos collègues de Cossé à partir d'ici. Vous trouverez ci-joint un exemple de courrier affranchi dont les dates sont clairement inscrites.

Vous en remerciant par avance, nous vous prions d'agréer, Messieurs, l'assurance de notre parfaite considération.


Jeremy P. Johnson
Directeur

P.J.: exemple de courrier

1 Subjunctive.

# 68  Complaint about wrong consignment of goods

21 September 199-

Dessous Dessus
14 rue Legrand
80000 Amiens
France

For the attention of Mr A Malraux

Dear Mr Malraux

RE: INVOICE NO. 13322/08/92

We regret to inform you that the garments you sent us in your consignment of 25 August were not what we had ordered.

Please refer to our order (copy enclosed) and to your invoice (N.13322/08/92). You will see that the briefs, slips and bras are mostly the wrong sizes, colours and materials.

We are at a loss to explain this departure from your normally reliable service. Will you please contact us immediately so that we can put matters right?

Yours sincerely


Fred Smith
Manager

Enc.

# 68  Plainte au sujet de l'envoi des mauvaises marchandises

Dessous Dessus
14, rue Legrand,
80000 Amiens,
France

Wolverhampton, le 21 septembre 199-

A l'attention de Mr Malraux

Objet: facture no. 13322/08/92

Cher Monsieur,

Nous regrettons d'avoir à vous informer que les articles que vous nous avez envoyés le 25 août n'étaient pas ceux que nous avions commandés.

Nous vous demandons de bien vouloir vous reporter à notre commande (copie ci-jointe) et à votre facture (no. 13322/08/92). Vous verrez que les slips, jupons et soutiens-gorge ne sont pas de la taille, des couleurs et des qualités de tissus demandées.

Nous sommes vraiment étonnés d'avoir pu constater de telles erreurs alors que vous êtes d'habitude si compétents. Vous serait-il possible de nous contacter dans les plus brefs délais afin de pouvoir rectifier ce malentendu?

Veuillez agréer, cher Monsieur, l'expression de nos salutations distinguées.


Fred Smith
Directeur

P.J. (1): Copie de notre bon de commande

# 69  Complaint about damage to goods

3 April 199-

Transports Transmanche SA
Quai des Brumes
14000 Caen
France

For the attention of Mr Gérard Dispendieux

Dear Monsieur Dispendieux

We have received a complaint from John Ferguson of Amex Insurance concerning the company's removal to Beauvais three weeks ago. You will remember that we subcontracted this removal to your company.

Mr Ferguson claims that several of the items of furniture and office equipment were damaged on arrival at the premises in Beauvais.

Although he immediately complained to your deliverymen, he has still not heard from you. In the interests of our future business relations I would be grateful if you could clarify this situation.

Yours sincerely


Gerald Wagstaffe
French Area Manager

# 69   Plainte au sujet de dégâts subis par des marchandises

Transports Transmanche S.A.,
Quai des Brumes,
14000 Caen,
France

Birmingham, le 3 avril 199-

A l'attention de Mr Gérard Dispendieux

Cher Monsieur,

Nous avons reçu une plainte de John Ferguson des Assurances Amex concernant leur déménagement à Beauvais voici maintenant trois semaines. Vous vous souviendrez certainement que nous avons sous-traité ce déménagement à votre entreprise.

Mr Ferguson se plaint d'avoir constaté que plusieurs meubles et du matériel de bureau étaient endommagés à leur arrivée dans les locaux de Beauvais.

Bien qu'il ait[1] formulé une plainte immédiatement à votre livreur, il n'a toujours pas eu de vos nouvelles.[2] Dans l'intérêt de nos relations professionnelles, je vous serais très reconnaissant de bien vouloir rectifier la situation.

Veuillez agréer, cher Monsieur, l'expression de notre parfaite considération.


Gerald Wagstaffe
Directeur du secteur France

1   Subjunctive.
2   Literally, 'news from you'.

# 70  Informing customers that a company has been taken over

24 July 199-

Produits Chimiques SA
89 rue Jules Barni
80330 Longueau
France

Dear Sirs

Thank you for your order dated 17 July. We have to inform you, however, that our company has recently been taken over by a larger concern, INTERNATIONAL CHEMICALS Inc.

As a result of this, we are sorry to tell you that we no longer produce the polymers that you request at this site. We have, however, passed on your order to our parent company and are confident that you will be contacted soon.

In the interests of our future business relations we enclose the latest catalogue of our total range of products, indicating which subsidiary manufactures which product.

Yours faithfully


Frederick Herriot
Plant Director

Enc.

# 70   Informer la clientèle que l'entreprise a été reprise

Produits Chimiques S.A.,
89, rue Jules Barni,
80330 Longueau,
France

Knottingley, le 24 juillet 199-

Messieurs,

Nous vous remercions de la commande que vous nous avez passée le 17 juillet. Nous devons vous informer que notre entreprise vient d'être reprise par une grande société: International Chemicals Inc.

De ce fait, nous avons le regret[1] de vous annoncer que nous ne produisons plus les polymères que vous nous demandez. Nous avons cependant fait suivre votre commande à notre société mère et sommes sûrs que l'on vous contactera d'ici peu.

En vue d'entretenir nos relations commerciales, vous trouverez ci-joint notre dernier catalogue exposant notre gamme complète, vous indiquant également le lieu de production de chaque produit.

Nous vous prions de croire, Messieurs, à l'expression de nos sentiments distingués.

Frederick Herriot
Directeur de l'usine

P.J. (1): Catalogue

1   Literally, 'we (have the) regret to'.

# 71 Informing customers of change of name and address

**EUROPEAN COMMERCIAL INSURANCE Ltd**
**47 Broad Walk**
**Preston**
**Lancashire United Kingdom**

(Formerly PRESTON INSURERS Inkerman Street, Preston)

1 June 199-

The Export Manager
Nouveaux Textiles
342 chaussée Baron
59100 Roubaix
France

Dear Sir

RE: CHANGE OF COMPANY NAME AND ADDRESS

We are writing to all our valued customers to inform them of our change of registered name and address.

We are still located in Preston and operating as commercial insurers as before. However, we have acquired new partners who have invested fresh capital in the business.

It is our firm intention to increase our European business, hence the new name. Enclosed is our brochure setting out our range of services and tariffs. Do not hesitate to contact us if you have any queries about these changes.

Yours faithfully

Nancy Wilton
Customer Liaison Manager

Enc.

# 71  Informer la clientèle d'un changement de nom et d'adresse

EUROPEAN COMMERCIAL INSURANCE Ltd,
47 Broad Walk
Preston
Lancashire
United Kingdom

(Anciennement PRESTON INSURERS Inkerman Street, Preston)

> Directeur du Service Export,
> Nouveaux Textiles,
> 342 chaussée Baron,
> 59100 Roubaix,
> France.
>
> Preston, le 1er juin 199-[1]

Monsieur,

Nous écrivons à toute notre fidèle clientèle afin de l'informer de notre changement de nom déposé[2] et d'adresse.

Nous sommes toujours à Preston et exerçons toujours en tant qu'assureurs. Toutefois, nous avons de nouveaux associés qui ont investi de nouveaux capitaux dans notre entreprise.

Nous avons la ferme intention de développer nos affaires en Europe, d'où notre nouveau nom. Vous trouverez ci-joint notre brochure exposant notre gamme de services et nos tarifs. N'hésitez pas à nous contacter pour toutes informations concernant ces modifications.

Nous vous prions d'agréer, Monsieur, l'expression de nos sentiments respectueux.


Nancy Wilton
Directeur de la communication avec la clientèle

P.J. (2): Brochure
         Liste des tarifs

1  Remember that in dates 'the first' is *le premier*, but 'the second', 'third', 'twelfth' etc. are *le deux, trois, douze* and so on.
2  Cf. *marque déposée*: 'registered brand name'.

# 72 Informing customers of increased prices

2 November 199-

Epicerie Fine
9 rue Dutour
72100 Le Mans
France

Dear Monsieur Olivier

In reply to your letter of the 5th I am sending you a new price list.

You will note that all of our prices have increased by some 6.3 per cent. This was unfortunately made necessary by our continuing inflation as well as the British Chancellor's recent decision to increase the general rate of VAT to 17.5 per cent.

I hope that the quality of our produce will continue to engage your loyalty. (It is also the case that the pound sterling has reduced in value against the franc.)

Yours sincerely


Michael McDermott
Marketing Manager

Enc.

# 72 Informer la clientèle d'une augmentation des prix

Epicerie Fine,
9 rue Dutour,
72100 Le Mans,
France.

Birmingham, le 2 novembre 199-

Cher Monsieur,

En réponse à votre lettre du 5 novembre, nous vous envoyons la liste de nos nouveaux tarifs.

Vous remarquerez que tous nos nouveaux prix ont subi une augmentation de 6,3%. Celle-ci est malheureusement due à une inflation en hausse constante ainsi qu'à la décision du Ministre des Finances britannique d'augmenter la TVA qui s'élève maintenant à 17,5%.

Nous espérons que vous nous resterez fidèle grâce à la qualité de nos produits. (Il est à noter aussi que la livre sterling a subi une baisse de valeur par rapport au franc français.)

Nous vous prions d'agréer, cher Monsieur, nos sentiments respectueux et dévoués.

Michael McDermott
Directeur Commercial

**Annexe: liste des nouveaux tarifs**

# 73  Requesting information about opening a business account

23 October 199-

The Manager
Crédit Mercantile
89 rue Béranger
69631 VÉNISSIEUX
France

Dear Sir

We are proposing to open an office and refrigerated storage facility at Vénissieux in the new year and would appreciate some information about opening a bank account at your branch.

Initially we would be transferring funds to finance the setting up of our new business premises. Thereafter we would expect to use the account to receive payments from French customers and to pay local suppliers etc.

We would be most grateful if you could inform us of all the formalities that we need to observe, both public and particular to Crédit Mercantile. Could you also inform us of your charges on business accounts?

Yours faithfully


Eric Wise
Commercial Manager

# 73  Demande de renseignements concernant l'ouverture d'un compte bancaire pour entreprise

Monsieur le Directeur,
Crédit Mercantile
89 rue Brager
69631 Vénissieux,
France

Melton Mowbray, le 23 octobre 199-

Monsieur,

Nous pensons ouvrir un bureau et un local[1] réfrigérant à Vénissieux d'ici l'année prochaine et nous aimerions obtenir des informations concernant l'ouverture d'un compte bancaire dans votre agence.

Pour commencer, nous transférerions les fonds servant à financer les locaux de notre nouveau commerce. Ensuite, le but de ce compte serait de recevoir les règlements de nos clients français, de payer nos fournisseurs locaux etc.

Nous vous serions très reconnaissants de bien vouloir nous informer de toutes les formalités que nous devrons observer, tant publiques que[2] particulières au Crédit Mercantile. Pourriez-vous également nous renseigner sur les frais incombant aux comptes commerciaux.

Vous en remerciant par avance, je vous prie d'agréer, Monsieur, l'assurance de nos meilleurs sentiments.


Eric Wise
Directeur Commercial

1  *Un local*: 'premises'.
2  *Tant ... que*: 'both ... and'.

# 74   Requesting information about opening a personal bank account

4 November 199-

The Manager
Banque Nationale
146 boulevard Haussmann
75016 Paris
France

Dear Sir

My British employers are posting me to their French subsidiary as of the beginning of January. I will therefore be moving to Paris with my family and I expect to be resident in France for two years.

I would be grateful if you could inform me about opening a personal current account at your bank. My salary would be paid into the account and both my wife and myself would wish to draw money from it and to pay bills by cheque etc. We may also wish to transfer money to a bank account in England.

Please send me any documentation you have.

Yours faithfully


Stuart Smith

# 74   Demande d'information concernant l'ouverture d'un compte personnel

Le Directeur,
Banque Nationale,
146, boulevard Haussmann,
75016 Paris,
France

Altrincham, le 4 novembre 199-

Monsieur,

Muté par mon employeur britannique, je travaillerai dans sa filiale française à partir de début janvier. Ainsi je serai dans l'obligation de déménager à Paris avec ma famille et je devrai résider en France pendant deux années.

Je vous serais très reconnaissant de bien vouloir me renseigner au sujet de l'ouverture d'un compte personnel au sein de votre banque. Mon salaire serait versé sur ce compte et j'aimerais que ma femme puisse[1] y faire les mêmes opérations que moi-même: retirer de l'argent, payer les factures, émettre des chèques,[2] etc. Il se pourrait que nous voulions[1] également faire des virements sur notre compte bancaire en Angleterre.

Je vous serais donc très reconnaissant de bien vouloir m'envoyer toute la documentation disponible à ce sujet.

Vous en remerciant par avance, je vous prie de recevoir, Monsieur, mes salutations distinguées.

Stuart Smith

1   Subjunctives.
2   'Withdraw money', 'pay bills', 'issue cheques', etc.

# 75  Letter re overdrawn account

9 March 199-

Mr J H Duke
47 Narrow Bank
Lichfield
Staffordshire

Dear Mr Duke

We regret to inform you that your account, number 62467840, is overdrawn by £21.09.

We would appreciate your rectifying this situation as soon as possible since you have no overdraft arrangement with us.

Yours sincerely


F E Jones
Manager

# 75  Lettre au sujet d'un compte à découvert

Monsieur J. Duhameau,
47 rue Gambetta,
Bergerac

Bergerac, le 9 mars 199-

Monsieur,

Nous avons le regret de vous informer que votre compte numéro 62467840 est à découvert d'un montant de 221,09 francs.

Nous vous serions très reconnaissants de bien vouloir régulariser cette situation dans les plus brefs délais car vous n'avez pas fait de demande d'autorisation de découvert.

Vous en remerciant, nous vous prions d'agréer, Monsieur, l'assurance de notre parfaite considération.


J.-F. Janneau
Directeur

# 76   Bank's letter to customer

2 May 199-

Mr Bernard J Mann
4 Beauchamp Mews
London SW3 6LZ
England

Dear Mr Mann

We are writing to inform you that we have today received a cheque payable to you for the sum of $124,035.00 and sent by J et P Barraud Notaires, 307 rue du Château, Luxembourg.

Can you please confirm as soon as possible that you were expecting this deposit and let us know your instructions concerning it?

Enclosed is a photocopy of this cheque and its accompanying letter.

Yours sincerely


Amélie Dupont
Head Cashier

Encs

# 76   Lettre d'une banque adressée à un client

M. Bernard J. Mann,
4 Beauchamp Mews,
London SW3 6LZ,
England

Vannes, le mercredi 2 mai, 199-

Cher Monsieur,

Nous vous écrivons pour vous informer que nous venons de recevoir un chèque d'un montant de $ 124 035,00 libellé à votre nom et émis par J. et P. Barraud Notaires, demeurant 307 rue du Château, Luxembourg.

Nous vous serions très reconnaissants de bien vouloir nous confirmer que vous attendiez bien ce chèque et de nous donner vos instructions.

Vous trouverez ci-joint une photocopie du chèque et de la lettre l'accompagnant.

Dans l'attente de vos instructions, nous vous prions de recevoir, cher Monsieur, nos salutations distinguées.

Amélie Dupont
Caissière principale

P.J. (2): – Photocopie du chèque reçu
          – Photocopie de la lettre accompagnant ce chèque

# 77   General query about banking

Monsieur J. Delor
Président-Directeur Général
Mouton-Poulenc
7 rue du Trocadéro
75016 Paris
France

Dear Sir

In response to your general query about banking in England there are two main types of bank, merchant banks and commercial banks. The former are very numerous and deal with companies generally. The latter are mainly the four big groups, Lloyds, National Westminster, Barclays and Midland.

The enclosed leaflet will give you further details, including information about banking in Scotland. Our office is mainly concerned with complaints about banks.

You should note that The Post Office in England also has some banking and money transfer facilities.

I hope that the enclosed information is of use to you.

Yours faithfully


C D Prettyman
For the Ombudsman

Enc.

# 77  Demande d'informations d'ordre général concernant les opérations bancaires courantes

Monsieur J. Delor,
Président Directeur Général,
Mouton-Poulenc,
7, rue du Trocadéro,
75016 Paris,
France

Londres, le 28 mai 199-

Monsieur,

En réponse à votre demande de renseignements concernant les opérations bancaires courantes en Angleterre, il faut savoir qu'ici il y a deux types de banques, les banques d'affaires et les banques de dépôt. Les premières sont très nombreuses et traitent avec les entreprises en général. Les autres sont constituées pour la plupart des quatre groupes principaux: Lloyds, National Westminster, Barclays et Midland.

La brochure ci-jointe vous donnera de plus amples informations, y compris des renseignements au sujet des opérations bancaires courantes en Ecosse. Notre bureau se charge principalement des plaintes au sujet des banques.

Nous tenions également à vous faire savoir que la Poste anglaise réalise aussi des opérations bancaires et peut effectuer des virements.

En espérant que les informations apportées vous seront utiles, nous vous prions d'agréer, Monsieur, l'expression de nos sentiments respectueux.


C. D. Prettyman
Pour le Médiateur

P.J. (1): Brochure

# 78  Enquiry about post office banking facilities

2 February 199-

La Poste Centrale
Place du Général De Gaulle
16000 Angoulême
France

Dear Sirs

I am intending to open a second business in Angoulême and would like to enquire what services you offer to small businesses.

I have in mind giro banking; can you tell me how your post office bank accounts work? Secondly, is it to you that I should apply to have a telephone? Thirdly, do you have special rates for business mail?

I would be most grateful for any information you can send me.

Yours faithfully


Mostyn Evans
Proprietor

# 78  Demande de renseignements au sujet des opérations bancaires courantes réalisées par la Poste

La Poste Centrale,
Place du Général de Gaulle,
16000 Angoulême,
France

Pontypridd, mardi 2 février 199-

Messieurs,

J'ai l'intention d'ouvrir une seconde affaire à Angoulême et j'aurais aimé savoir[1] quels sont les services bancaires que vous offrez aux petites entreprises.

Je pensais aux comptes-chèques postaux.[2] Vous serait-il possible de m'expliquer le fonctionnement de vos comptes d'opérations bancaires? Etes-vous l'organisme que je dois contacter afin d'obtenir un téléphone? Offrez vous des tarifs préférentiels pour l'affranchissement du courrier d'entreprise?

Je vous serais très reconnaissant de bien vouloir me faire parvenir toute information que vous pourriez juger utile.

Vous en remerciant par avance, je vous prie d'agréer, Messieurs, mes respectueuses salutations.


Mostyn Evans
Propriétaire

1  Literally, 'I would have liked to know'.
2  Abbreviated as *CCP.*

# 79  Enquiry about opening a post office account

8 March 199-

Bureau Central
Postes et Télécommunications
Paris
France

Dear Sirs

I do not know exactly who to write to but hope nevertheless that this letter will reach the right service.

I would like to obtain information about opening a Post Office account to enable my French customers to settle my invoices in France and permit me to pay certain of my French suppliers by cheque.

I would be grateful if you would inform me of the formalities involved and send me the necessary forms.

Yours faithfully

Eric Clifford
Managing Director

# 79 Demande de renseignements au sujet de l'ouverture d'un compte-chèques postaux

Bureau Central,
Postes et Télécommunications,
Paris,
France

Wirral, lundi 8 mars 199-

Messieurs,

Je ne sais malheureusement pas à quel service écrire exactement et espère néanmoins que cette lettre atteindra la personne à même de me répondre.

J'aurais aimé obtenir des renseignements concernant l'ouverture d'un compte-chèques postaux afin de permettre à mes clients français de régler mes factures en France, tout en me permettant de payer certains de mes fournisseurs par chèque.

Je vous serais très reconnaissant de bien vouloir m'informer des formalités à remplir et de bien vouloir me faire parvenir les formulaires nécessaires à l'ouverture du compte correspondant à mes besoins.

Vous en remerciant par avance, je vous prie d'agréer, Messieurs, mes salutations distinguées.


Eric Clifford
Directeur Général

# 80  Opening poste restante

26 March 199-

La Poste Centrale
Place Bellecour
69001 Lyon
France

Gentlemen

We are in the process of moving our French subsidiary from Villeurbanne to Saint Priest; the move should be completed at some time in the next month.

We would like to ask you on receipt of this letter, and until further notice, to retain all mail addressed to us poste restante at your central office.

Please inform us if there are any other formalities to observe. Enclosed is an addressed envelope and international reply coupon for your reply.

Thank you in advance.


Arthur T Goldberg
On behalf of Software Supplies Inc.

Enc.

# 80  Demander le service Poste Restante

Poste Centrale,
Place Bellecour
69001 Lyon,
France

New York, le 26 mars 199-

Messieurs,

Nous sommes actuellement en phase de déménagement. En effet, nous déplaçons notre filiale de Villeurbanne à Saint-Priest. Le déménagement devrait être terminé dans le courant du mois prochain.

Nous aimerions vous demander s'il vous serait possible, et ceci à partir du moment où vous recevrez[1] cette lettre et jusqu' à nouvel ordre, de garder tout le courrier qui nous est adressé poste restante dans vos bureaux de la poste centrale.

Veuillez nous informer de toutes autres formalités auxquelles nous devrions nous conformer.[2] Vous trouverez ci-joint une enveloppe adressée et un coupon-réponse international pour votre réponse.

Vous en remerciant par avance, je vous prie d'agréer, Messieurs, l'expression de ma parfaite considération.

Arthur T. Goldberg
Pour Software Supplies Inc

P.J.: Enveloppe adressée et coupon-réponse international

1  Literally, 'will receive'.
2  Note the use of the reflexive verb *se conformer*: 'to adapt oneself'.

# Business Practice

# 1 Addressing people

When speaking to someone you do not know, you can address them as *Monsieur/Madame/Mademoiselle*; and in the plural *Messieurs/Mesdames/ Mesdemoiselles*. In French there are two ways of saying and writing 'you': a formal *vous* and an intimate *tu* (plural *vous*). You would only use *tu* with close friends, children – and animals.

A letter to someone who is not your friend would begin *Monsieur/Madame/ Mademoiselle*. A letter to a firm in which you know no one by name would begin *Messieurs*.

You can be friendly in manner by combining *cher* with a role name, e.g. *Cher Client* ('customer'), *Cher Collègue* or *Confrère* (a fellow professional), *Cher Camarade* (a person from the same school or political party). *Chère Cliente* etc., if the correspondent is a woman.

If the addressee has a title you may write (or say) *Monsieur le Président* or *Madame le Ministre* (note there is no feminine form) or *Monsieur l'Ambassadeur* (addressed as *Votre Excellence* in the letter). Other quite frequent titles are *Maître* (for a lawyer) and *Docteur* (a medical doctor).

Abbreviations of any of these words have no full stop if the last letter of the word is present, so: *M.*, *Mme*, *Mlle*, *MM.* (*Messieurs*), *Mmes* (*Mesdames*), *Me* (*Maître*), *Pr* (*Professeur*), *Mlles*, etc. Increasingly the abbreviation *Mr* is used for *Monsieur*.

One final point to remember is that the form of address used at the beginning of a letter must also be used at the end, in the so-called *formule de politesse*.

## Belgium

It should not be assumed that a Belgian national is a French speaker and wishes to speak French; s/he may prefer Flemish (Dutch) or German (or even English). See Section 2 on written communications.

# 2 Written communications

## The letter

The letters section gives numerous variations on the concluding part of a formal letter in French. It generally links with the body of the letter. It begs the recipient (addressed in the same manner as at the beginning) to receive the writer's more or less cordial or respectful sentiments. You will find below the most commonly used concluding expressions:

(a) When addressing a superior:
* *Je vous prie d'agréer, Monsieur le . . . (Président, Directeur), l'expression de mes respectueuses salutations.*
* *Veuillez agréer, Monsieur le . . ., l'expression de mes sentiments respectueux.*
* *Je vous prie d'agréer, Monsieur le . . ., l'expression de mes sentiments dévoués.*

- *Je vous prie d'agréer, Monsieur, l'expression de ma respectueuse considération.*
- *Nous vous prions d'agréer, Monsieur, nos sentiments respectueux et dévoués.*
- *Je vous prie d'agréer, Monsieur, l'expression de ma haute considération.*

(b)  When addressing an equal:
- *Je vous prie d'agréer, Monsieur, l'expression de mes salutations distinguées.*
- *Nous vous prions de recevoir, Monsieur, nos salutations distinguées.*
- *Veuillez recevoir, Monsieur, nos salutations distinguées.*

(c)  When addressing an inferior:
- *Veuillez agréer, Monsieur, l'assurance de mes meilleurs sentiments.*
- *Je vous prie d'agréer, Monsieur, l'assurance de ma parfaite considération.*

(d)  From a man to a woman:
- *Je vous prie de croire, Madame, à l'expression de mes sentiments respectueux.*
- *Je vous prie d'agréer, Madame, l'expression de mes hommages respectueux.*

(e)  From a woman to a man:
- *Veuillez recevoir, Monsieur, mes salutations distinguées.*

(f)  From a woman to a woman:
- *Veuillez recevoir, Madame, l'expression de mes sentiments distingués.*

## Addresses

The address (set on the right-hand side of the envelope) has the usual features and a post-code. Full details of the codes of all 36,000 **French** communes can be obtained from any French post office. They begin with the two or three digits of the *département*, for example Ain 01, Aisne 02, Allier 03. (There are some 100 *départements* including overseas, *départements d'outre-mer*, like Martinique.)

Possible abbreviations for addresses which are very often used:

| | | | |
|---|---|---|---|
| ALL: | Allée (Lane) | IMP: | Impasse (no through road) |
| AV: | Avenue (Avenue) | PAS: | Passage (passage way) |
| Bd: | Boulevard (Boulevard) | PL: | Place (Square) |
| CHE: | Chemin (Path) | QU: | Quai (Quay) |
| CRS: | Cours (Walk) | RTE: | Route (Road) |
| SQ: | Square (Public Gardens) | | |

| | |
|---|---|
| St: | Saint (e.g. St-Cloud) |
| Ste: | Sainte (e.g. Ste-Marie) |

## Faxes

These are better known as *télécopies* (f.). You will find below a standard French fax sheet:

---

[*NOM SOCIETE*]
[*Adresse exp.*]
[*Code postal Ville*]

# Première page de télécopie

| Date: | xx [*mois*] xxxx | | Heure: | xxhxx |
|---|---|---|---|---|

| Dest.: | [*Noms*] | | Tél.: | [*Leur num. de téléphone*] |
|---|---|---|---|---|
| | [*Nom société*] | | Télécopie: | [*Leur num. de télécopie*] |
| Exp.: | [*Noms*] | | Tél.: | [*Votre num. de téléphone*] |
| | [*Nom société*] | | Télécopie: | [*Votre num. de télécopie*] |
| RE: | [*Objet*] | | | |
| CC: | [*Noms*] | | | |

Nombre de pages, y compris la page de garde: [*Tapez le nombre de pages ici*]

## Message

[*Tapez votre message ici*]

---

## Telexes

These are still used a great deal in French business. A telex can be written in full, but has traditionally used a lot of abbreviations. Here are some common ones (French and international):

| | |
|---|---|
| CIE | *compagnie* |
| CREDOC | *crédit documentaire* ('documentary credit') |
| EEE | 'error' |
| ETS | *établissements* ('company') |
| GA | 'go ahead' ('transmit') |
| HT | *hors taxe* ('exclusive of tax') |
| OCC | *occupé* ('engaged') |
| OK | OK |
| PV | *procès-verbal* ('report') |
| RAP | *rappeler* 'call back' |

| RDV | *rendez-vous* |
| RPT | *répéter* 'repeat' |
| SVP | *s'il vous plaît* |
| TPR | 'teleprinter' (*téléimprimeur*) |
| TTC | *toutes taxes comprises* ('all taxes included') |
| WRU | 'who are you?' |

## Memoranda

*Le mémorandum* (plural *-s*) or *le mémo* is also international in format: A (lower case à: to), DE (From), Date, Objet (Subject), CC (Copies), Message.

## Belgium

The kingdom of Belgium is divided into three federal states (with a political apparatus and control over much policy) and ten provinces. Flanders (Flemish speaking) contains the provinces of West Flanders (capital Bruges, post-code 8000), East Flanders (Ghent, 9000), Antwerp (Antwerp, 2000), Limburg (Hasselt, 3500) and Flemish Brabant (Leuven or Louvain, 3000). Wallonia (La Wallonie – French speaking) contains the provinces of Hainaut (capital Doornik, 7500) Namur (Namur, 5000), Liège (Liège, 4000), Luxembourg (Arlon, 6700) and Walloon Brabant (its new capital has not yet been decided). Eupen-Malmédy in the east is part of Liège and home to some 60,000 Flemish speakers. Brussels is officially bilingual (French and Flemish), but is in fact multilingual and comes under the jurisdiction of Flanders. (There is an informative magazine called *W+B* published jointly by La Région Wallonne and La Communauté française Wallonie-Bruxelles, address Avenue Louise 65, Bte 9, B–1050 Brussels).

# 3 Telecommunications

### (a) Telephoning

A typical call would be something like this:

A    *Bonjour, Etablissements Dupont.*

B    *Bonjour, je voudrais parler à Pierre Dupont, s'il vous plaît.*

A    *C'est de la part de qui?* (Who is calling?)

B    *Je m'appelle Clive Smith.*

A    *Ne quittez pas, je vous passe M. Dupont.* (Hold the line, I am putting you through.)

B    *Merci bien.*

A    *Je suis désolé. Son poste est occupé/Il n'est pas dans son bureau* (I am sorry. His line is engaged/He is not in his office.)

B    *Ce n'est pas grave. Puis-je laisser un message?* (Never mind. Can I leave a message?)

### (b) Some stock telephone phrases

*M. Dupont est en congé/en vacances/en déplacement/en réunion.*
(Mr Dupont is on leave (today)/on holiday/on a business trip/in a meeting.)
*Je cherche le numéro de Monsieur André Dupont à Versailles dans les Yvelines.*
(I am seeking the number of Mr Dupont who lives in Versailles, in Yvelines.)
*Je vous appelle au sujet de . . .*
(I am calling you about . . . )
*Pourriez-vous demander à M. Dupont de me rappeler?*
(Could you ask Mr Dupont to call me back?)
*Pourriez-vous répéter, je vous entends très mal?*
(Could you repeat please, I can hardly hear you?)
*Je ferai la commission/Je lui passerai le message.*
(I will pass on the message/to him or her.)
*Pourriez-vous m'indiquer le nom de la personne qui s'occupe de . . . ?*
(Could you tell me the name of the person who deals with . . .?)
*Est-ce que vous pourriez m'aider?*
(Can you help me?)
*Je ne vous comprends pas très bien.*
(I cannot understand you very well.)

### (c) Telephone numbers

The French and Belgian French verbal equivalents of three numbers are not the same as can be seen in the following examples: seventy/*soixante-dix* (French)/*septante* (Belgian), eighty/*quatre-vingts*/*huitante* (or possibly *octante*), ninety/*quatre-vingt-dix*/*nonante*. A Walloon would say *nonante-cinq* (95) etc.

### (d) Telephone facilities

For French Directory Enquiries (*renseignements*) dial (*composer*) 12. When asking for a subscriber number, give surname, Christian name, town and county. Full address is not necessary. Green numbers (*numéros verts*) are freephone services. The 'Red List' (*liste rouge*) is for ex-directory numbers. French *Yellow Pages* (*pages jaunes*) give businesses in categories. French *White Pages* (*pages blanches*) give names in alphabetical order by city. The *annuaire* is the telephone directory.

Most telephone booths (*cabines téléphoniques*) use *cartes téléphoniques* or *télécartes* ('phonecards'), available from tobacconists and newsagents (*buralistes* or *tabacs*).

### (d) Minitel

This is a combination of telephone and computer terminal present in many thousands of French homes and offices and giving easy access to some 20,000 services. For example:

*L'annuaire électronique*, a national (11) and international (3619) electronic telephone directory
*MGS (Minitel Guide des Services)*, a listing of all Minitel services
*Minicom 3612*, for exchanging written messages

You can also use the following numbers:

| | | |
|---|---|---|
| 3615 | SECAM | to book a hotel room |
| 3615 | OFFI | to find out about entertainments |
| 3615 | METEO | to check the weather forecast |
| 3615 | HORAVION | for air travel information |

NB: A Minitel is always at your disposal in any post office. The Minitel telephone directory service is free of charge when consulted in a post office.

# 4 Business culture

## Protocol

There is much courtesy (*la politesse*) in business practice, between firms, with suppliers (*les fournisseurs*), with customers (*les clients*). It begins with the respectful and unobsequious use of *Monsieur, Madame, Mademoiselle*. Appointments are made (*on prend rendez-vous*); one is generally punctual, but appointments may be cancelled (owing to *circonstances indépendantes de ma propre volonté* – 'circumstances beyond my control', etc.). Disagreements will, initially at least, be polite: *je ne partage pas entièrement votre opinion* (I do not entirely share you opinion). Visiting cards will be exchanged. There is time to respect the formalities.

## The firm

There are still old-style firms, often family firms, run by a *patron*, the PDG (*Président-Directeur Général*), who is much deferred to and addressed as *Monsieur le Président*. Decisions are taken by him and there are clear demarcations of grade. There is little informality – colleagues address each other by family name and *vous* not *tu*. The firm may well close for lunch from 12 to 2 and for the holidays during all of July or August (a shop might close in August).

The whole system, however, is fast modernizing itself, even the thousands of small family firms. Many do not now close for lunch, and the *cadres* ('executives') only have time for a *casse-croûte* ('a snack') – unless there is a visitor who must be taken out to lunch. This is all part of the courtesy referred to above: the visitor may be no more important than a university lecturer coming to visit his students during their *stages* ('industry placements'). On the other hand, the lunch may be designed to clinch a deal. The once multi-layered hierarchy is being rationalized. An *organigramme*, a 'plan of management structure', shows the management functions, many of them equal in rank. The systems and documentation are computerized, the staff are trained and retrained. Personnel has become *Ressources Humaines*. Colleagues in the same section may even call each other by first names and *tu*. They socialize; there may perhaps even be socializing among different grades of staff in the context of events organized by the *Comité d'Entreprise* ('Works Committee').

## Higher education

In particular, since the creation of the Ecole Nationale d'Administration to train top civil servants, there has been a Grande Ecole vogue. (*Grandes Ecoles* are prestigious, competitive-entry higher education institutes, originally designed to train the technical élites of France.) It seems that a large proportion of senior managers of larger companies are products of ENA (having perhaps been bought out of their civil service contract), HEC (L'Ecole des Hautes Etudes Commerciales), Centrale (L'Ecole Centrale), Arts et Métiers (L'Ecole Nationale des Arts et Métiers), L'Ecole Polytechnique, etc., or one of the network of Higher Commercial Schools (*Ecoles Supérieures de Commerce*, popularly known as *Sup de Co*). These managers are bright, cultured, confident, having emerged from a highly selective, high-level and very project-oriented training, that there is a French solution to a given problem.

It should also be said that the educational underpinning of the *Grandes Ecoles* is reasonably impressive. Students intending to work in commerce or industry could opt for a technical stream (*filière technique*) and sit a technical Baccalauréat at 18 or 19. Students who are not academically inclined can opt at the age of 14 for a Lycée d'Enseignement Professionnel (L.E.P.) where they gain practical experience. Once the CAP ('Certificat d'Aptitude Professionnelle') is passed, they can either opt for another CAP in a different trade, a Baccalauréat technique, a Brevet de Technicien Supérieur or leave school. Alternatively, they could gain entry to an IUT (Institut Universitaire de Technologie) and take two-year courses, leading to the DUT qualification, in, say, Techniques de Commercialisation ('marketing skills'). If they enter commerce or industry and subsequently discover a bent or a need for further study, they can then follow the *formation continue* ('further training') track among the many part-time courses offered by university departments or *Chambres de Commerce*. Those artistically inclined can join an Art School ('Ecole des Beaux-Arts') and once they have passed their degree, if they wish to further their artistic studies, they can join the 'Ecole supérieure des Beaux-Arts de Paris' subject to entry examination.

## Recruitment

Candidates for managerial posts are often recruited by specialized agencies called *chasseurs de têtes* (literally, 'headhunters') which examine them in depth. They are usually asked to send a manuscript letter of application (*lettre de motivation*) so that a graphologist can examine it. And there is much psychometric testing (*les tests psychométriques*). Employment procedure starts in France with a 3- or 6-month trial period (*période d'essai*) which in most cases is completed with the signature of the contract of employment (*contrat à durée indéterminée*). This is to enable the employee to know and assess his/her ability to fulfil the job offered and vice-versa before commitments are made. This system seems to be necessary as French laws make dismissals (*licenciements*) very difficult to achieve. If a dismissal is considered by the employer, whilst the contract of employment is valid and the dismissal is considered unfair, the employee might well turn to Occupational Safety and Health Administration (l'Inspection du Travail) or the Industrial Court (le Conseil des Prud'hommes – see page 302).

## Style of dress

There are fewer uniforms in France than in some countries. In shops the sales staff may be recognized by a badge. For men, the wearing of a suit and tie is not obligatory except perhaps for appointments with customers. In general the French are quite relaxed (*décontractés*) where dress is concerned.

## Invitations and presents

Main clients may be invited out to dine, to the theatre, to the opera, to a concert, to a *vernissage* ('paintings exhibition', literally 'varnishing'), to a sporting occasion (the tennis at Roland Garros, for example). It would be normal to invite a customer and his/her spouse. It is considered a particularly friendly act to invite a business contact to your home. If this happens it would be normal to take some *douceur* – chocolates or flowers – for the hostess. The practice of giving presents, say at Christmas, is widespread, and the presents vary with the importance of the client from a bottle to a case of wine.

## Belgium

A peculiarity of Belgium is that it is part of an economic union with Luxembourg (since 1921) and with The Netherlands (since 1958 – hence the name Benelux. See below under banking). It is said that Belgians like to keep work separate from social life. In work they are also very courteous – it would be rude not to shake hands for example. They tend to conduct a lot of business *à table*. (The story goes that at a particular international conference the Belgian delegates were little in evidence at the workshops, very active in the restaurants and snaffled most of the contracts at the end.) They like punctuality and swiftness, even preferring the telephone or fax to the letter. Managerially, they consider it a good thing to delegate to subordinates, to talk to subordinates as they would to equals, to be informal with a purpose. It is generally considered that languages are very important. It is commonly accepted that you will write in your own, native language and receive your correspondent's reply in his/hers. On many occasions English may be used to defuse tension between Flemish and French speakers. Brussels is a multilingual town; it not only has branches of many foreign companies, it is also the site of the very large administration of the EU (the European Commission) and also of NATO headquarters. Not surprisingly, about half of the Brussels population is foreign. For purposes of large contracts, except in defence or heavy industry, it should be borne in mind that Belgium is regionally organized and contractors would be dealing with Flanders, Wallonia or possibly Eupen-Malmédy.

# 5 Office and shop hours

## (a) Shops

In the provinces they generally open from Tuesday to Saturday 9 a.m.–12 noon and 2 p.m.–7 p.m. In general they are closed on Mondays. In Paris shops open 10 a.m. to 7 p.m. On Sundays, food shops and tobacconist-newsagents (*tabacs* or *buralistes*) are open from 9 to 12.30.

In Paris and other cities most shops are open all day from 9.30 a.m. to 7 p.m. and close only on Sundays. Some department stores (*grands magasins*) and shopping centres (*centres commerciaux*) may stay open until 10 p.m. once or twice a week.

## (b) Firms

Offices in Paris are normally open from 9 a.m. to 6 p.m., with a lunchtime break from 12 noon to 2 p.m. Elsewhere, they are open from 8 a.m. to 7 p.m. with a lunchtime closure between 12 and 2 p.m.

## (c) Banks

Banks are open from Monday to Friday 9.30 a.m.–5 p.m., with a Wednesday early closing at 4 p.m., and sometimes a Friday closing at 4.30 p.m. Banks that open on Saturday close on Monday.

## (d) Post offices

Post office counters (*guichets*) are open Monday to Friday 9 a.m.–7 p.m. and Saturdays from 9 till 12.30. In the provinces some post offices may close at 6 p.m. and over lunchtime. Last collections from a public letterbox (*une boîte aux lettres*) are 6 p.m. for another *département* or abroad, or 7.30 for the same town and *département*. Collections are later at a sorting office (10 p.m. for the same town, 9 p.m. for the same *département*, 8 p.m. for other destinations).

### Belgium

In Belgium commercial establishments may open at 8.30 a.m., but in general the opening hours are very similar to those in France. The regular breaks allowed in the working day tend to be co-ordinated between departments for the recognized purpose of informal communication of information, 'formalized gossip' as it were.

# 6 Business organizations
# (See also Trade unions below)

**INSEE** (Institut National de la Statistique et des Etudes Economiques), 12 Rue Boulitte, 75001 Paris (tel. 1 45 39 22 77) has all sorts of information about economic matters.

Information may be obtained from national employers' organizations like the **CNPF** (Conseil national du patronat français) or the **CGPME** (Confédération générale des petites et moyennes entreprises – small and medium-sized enterprises) representing big and small business respectively.

Chambers of Commerce and Industry are like their British counterparts but better funded – for example they are entitled to receive the tax paid by firms to finance training – and more influential. They have good facilities, resources and information about national and local affairs. They would be an excellent first port of call when seeking information about a town or region.

The national address for these is: **APCCI** (Assemblée Permanente des Chambres de Commerce et d'Industrie), 45 avenue d'Iéna, 75116 Paris. The address of the **Paris CCI** is: La Chambre de Commerce et d'Industrie de Paris, 27 avenue de Friedland, 75382 Paris Cedex 08.

In the sphere of regional development **DATAR** (Délégation à l'aménagement du territoire et à l'action régionale), 1 avenue Charles Floquet, 75700 Paris) is very influential.

**COFACE** (Compagnie française d'assurance pour le commerce extérieur) and **BFCE** (Banque française du commerce extérieur) both guarantee risks and provide loans for overseas trade.

Customs information is provided by the Service de Renseignements Douaniers, 182 rue St Honoré, 75001 Paris.

The Rotary Club is very widespread, very active and usually very congenial in France.

The Ministry of Labour is La Direction Générale du Travail, de l'Emploi, et de la Formation Professionnelle, 1 place Fontenoy, 75007, Paris.

### Belgium

In Belgium the Brussels Chamber of Commerce is at: Avenue Louise 50, 1050 Brussels (tel. 02 648 50 02). The National Federation of Chambers of Commerce and Industry (Fédération nationale des Chambres de Commerce et d'Industrie) is at: Rue du Congrès 40, 1000 Brussels (tel. 02 217 36 71). The National Employers Federation (La Fédération des Entreprises de Belgique) is at Rue Ravenstein 4, 1000 Brussels (tel. 02 511 58 80). The address of the National Institute of Statistics is given below (under banking). There is no national employment agency; an important agency for French-speakers is the Office Communautaire et Régional de la Formation et de l'Emploi.

# 7 Banks

## Types and establishments (in France)

- **Deposit Banks** (*banques de dépôt*) offer deposit, withdrawal and credit facilities to the public.
- **Investment Banks** (*banques d'affaires*) buy shares, manage share holdings, provide credits, set up businesses.

- **Credit Banks** (*banques de crédit*) offer credits over at least two years and can normally only receive deposits for a minimum two years.
- **Nationalized Banks** (*banques nationalisées*) are limited companies whose capital belongs to the State; however, the law of 4 January 1974 allows them to distribute shares to the value of a quarter of the capital to their staff or certain approved organizations, e.g. La Caisse des Dépôts, and some pension funds.
- **La Caisse des Dépôts et Consignations** is a State organization which principally manages savings monies collected by La Poste and the Caisses d'épargne.
- **La Banque de France** (The Bank of France) has the exclusive privilege of issuing banknotes (made by the Mint – La Monnaie) and in general supervises the banking system.
- **Mutualist or Cooperative Banks** are led by **Crédit Agricole** (originally providing credit for the farming sector, now one of the biggest banks in the world), **Banque Populaire** (its branches now have a wider clientele than the original SMEs), **Crédit Mutuel** (principally financing housing), **Crédit Coopératif** (principally public amenities), **Crédit Maritime Mutuel** (principally for the fishing industry).
- **Savings Banks** (*caisses d'épargne et de prévoyance*) are non-profitmaking organizations at the service of individuals and non-business organizations.
- **Municipal Credit Banks** (*caisses de crédit municipal*) are principally concerned with local community organizations and civil servants (*fonctionnaires*).
- **Finance Companies** (*sociétés financières*) offer various services in the spheres of mortgage (*prêts immobiliers, hypothèques*), lend-lease (*crédit-bail*), hire-purchase, factoring (*affacturage*), etc.

Other specialized financial institutions include the **Crédit National**, founded in 1919 and offering long-term credit and credit refinancing for major plant investment, and the **Crédit Foncier**, offering state-supported land or property loans in different sectors.

Le **Comptoir des entrepreneurs** (Enterprise Fund) offers state-aided special loans (PAPs) for construction etc.

Le **Crédit Local de France** also offers long- or medium-term loans particularly in the property area (*crédits fonciers*).

Regional Development is overseen by 19 *sociétés de développement régionales* supporting economic and employment investment, for example **SFIPARIC** for the Paris region and **SOFIMAC** in the Massif Central.

SME funds: The **CPME** and the **SOFARIS** offer credit and capital insurance respectively to the SME sector (PME: *Petites et Moyennes Entreprises*).

Le **Trésor Public** is the equivalent of the British Treasury. The Central Economic Cooperation Fund (**Caisse centrale de coopération économique**) supports overseas development particularly in the French Départements d'Outre-Mer (DOM) and the Territoires d'Outre-Mer (TOM).

La **Société des Bourses de Valeurs** (Stock Exchange Company) regulates stock exchange activities.

Post Office financial services: **La Poste** manages Post Office accounts (*comptes-chèques postaux*) and the **Caisse Nationale d'Epargne** (National Savings Fund).

Other useful addresses are:

Banque de France
Service de l'Information
39, rue Croix des petits champs
75049 Paris Cédex 01
tel. 49 92 42 92

Ministère de l'Economie
139, rue de Bercy
75572 Paris Cédex 12
tel. 40 04 04 04

A useful publication worth consulting is:

Annuaire des Banques et de la Finance
Publications Mandel
3, rue de l'Arrivée
75749 Paris Cédex 15
tel. 45 38 71 50

## Belgium

In Belgium there is a national supervisory **Commission Bancaire** (Bank Commissie). The central bank is **La Banque Nationale de Belgique** (Nationale Bank van België) which is 50 per cent government-owned and 50 per cent public. (It issues a monthly 'synthetic index' of sectoral economic performance.) There are some 80 commercial banks offering the usual services. There are also a number of public credit institutions like the **Caisse Générale d'Epargne et de Retraite** (Algemene Spaar en Lijfrente Kas), the **Société Nationale de Crédit à l'Industrie** (Nationale Maatschapij voor Kredit aan de Nijverheid) and **Crédit Communal de Belgique** (Algemene Kredit van België). Under the Convention on Economic Union of 1921 (renewed 1992) the Belgian and Luxembourg francs are fixed at parity and foreign currency holdings are pooled and form a single customs area. Under the 1958 treaty, Benelux (with The Netherlands) was created as an economic union. Belgium is the centre for the **SWIFT** system of international monetary transfers; a very large number of commercial banks are part of this network. The following addresses may be useful:

Association belge des Banques
Rue Ravenstein 36 bte 5
1000 Brussels
(tel. 02 512 58 68)

Ministère des Affaires Economiques – Institut National des Statistiques
Rue de Louvain 44
1000 Brussels
(tel. 02 513 96 50)

# 8 Legal practitioners

## France

There are various areas of justice: administrative/social, civil/commercial, criminal (*pénal*). There are also various types and levels of court, for example, at the first stage: *tribunaux* (singular: *le tribunal*) *administratifs, tribunaux d'instance/tribunaux de commerce/conseils des prud'hommes* (see 12 below), *tribunaux de police*. At the second stage there is *la Cour d'Appel*. At the third stage *la Cour de Cassation* or even *le Conseil d'Etat*.

Among the practitioners the judges, who may be called *magistrats* or *juges*, preside over courts or act as prosecutors on behalf of the state (*procureurs*). The French legal system being inquisitorial, as opposed to accusatorial, there is additionally the important role of examining magistrate, *le juge d'instruction*. She or he examines complex criminal cases before they come to court.

The *avocats* are registered at the bar (*le barreau*) and must be employed to represent the parties at a trial at the level of *tribunal de grande instance* or *cour d'appel*. An *avocat* offers a legal advice service as well as one of representation in court. This profession has now subsumed that of *conseiller juridique* ('legal adviser').

The *avoués* are employed by the Justice Ministry and draw up the findings of the *cour d'appel*.

The *greffiers* assist judges (*magistrats*) by running courts, arranging hearings, recording debates and drawing up decisions. The *huissiers de justice* have various tasks: to serve writs or other documents, to execute decisions of the court (seizures, expulsions), to act as court ushers, etc.

The *notaires* are formally appointed by the Justice Ministry and have the function of giving authenticity to documents, like wills, mortgages, deeds of sale, marriage contracts. With the increasing internationalization of the legal profession, their range of activity is tending to widen.

Readers will not be surprised to learn that the French legal system is full of special terminology. They may wish to obtain a copy of *Les 200 mots-clés de la Justice* (which summarizes the essential terminology) published by the Service de l'Information et de la Communication, 13 place Vendôme, 75001 Paris.

## Belgium

In Belgium the legal system is based in all regions on the Code Napoléon dating from 1804, and so is essentially similar to the French system.

# 9  Accounting and auditing

## France

In France accountancy (*la comptabilité*) practices and principles are in line with European Directives, Number Four (the presentation of company accounts) and Number Seven (consolidated accounts) and French accountants use the historic cost convention (as opposed to current cost accounting). An *expert-comptable* is more highly qualified than a *comptable*. The accountants' professional body is called the Ordre des Experts-Comptables et des Comptables Agréés ('approved').

An accountancy firm, quite often a member of an international accountancy group, will give accountancy advice, carry out an audit (*un audit*), give taxation advice (*conseil fiscal*) and advise on acquisitions and mergers (*acquisitions et fusions*), etc. Companies must file annual financial statements (*le rapport annuel*) with the Tribunal de Commerce, including a balance-sheet (*un bilan*) showing fixed assets (*les immobilisations, l'actif immobilisé*), current assets (*les actifs*), expenses (*les frais* or *les charges*), equity capital (*le capital-actions*), provision for losses (*les provisions*), credits (*les crédits*), etc. There should also be a statement of income (*revenu*). These statements should give 'a true and fair view' (*une image fidèle*) of the company's financial position.

Companies are required by law to appoint at least one independent auditor (*un commissaire aux comptes*). Publicly quoted companies (*sociétés cotées en Bourse*) must appoint two independent auditors.

A company having control of, or significant influence over, another company is required to produce consolidated accounts (*comptes consolidés*).

## Belgium

Belgian accountancy law incorporates the EC 4th Directive (mentioned above) and is falling into line with Directive Number Seven also. Audit requirements are less demanding on small companies, not exceeding two of the following: 50 employees; turnover of BF145 m.; balance sheet of BF70 m. Otherwise, companies must appoint an auditor from the Belgian Institute of Certified Public Accountants. Auditors must report annually to shareholders and the Works Council (companies with 100 or more employees). The tax authorities normally audit all corporation tax returns every two years.

# 10  Advertising media

## France

One distinguishes in French between media (*un média, les médias*) and advertising media (*les supports publicitaires*). The five main advertising media are the written press, the radio, television (including satellite and cable TV), the cinema and posters (or billboards). There is also ex-media advertising at the point of sale (PLV: *publicité sur le lieu de vente*), by mailshot (*les mailings* – the French for 'junk mail' is *les imprimés publicitaires*), sponsorship (*la sponsorisation, le parrainage*), etc. It almost goes without saying that advertising and publicity (*la pub*) are constantly and rapidly evolving. The industry is also evolving fast with the formation of communications conglomerates e.g. Hachette which is involved both in France and abroad in publishing, the press, radio, television, distribution and services.

Since the media ('the Fourth Estate') are so influential, politically, economically and culturally, France has constantly been concerned to define and redefine their relationship with the State. Today the State has some control over TV and radio via its control of the air waves (*le spectre hertzien*) and the Conseil Supérieur de l'Audiovisuel (CSA). It has some control over the written press via laws concerning ownership. Apart from state constraint and legality, advertising is self-regulating in France via bodies like L'Union des Annonceurs (the advertisers' union), Le Bureau de Vérification de la Publicité (advertisers, advertising agencies, media and consumers) and Le Conseil National de la Publicité (advertisers, agencies and media).

## Major French advertising media

### Press titles

*Télérama* , a TV magazine.
News magazines: *Le Nouvel Economiste, Le Point, Capital*.
National newspapers: *Le Figaro, Le Monde, Libération, la Tribune, les Echos*.
Provincial dailies: (examples) *La Nouvelle République* (Central Region), *La Montagne* (Auvergne).
Other magazines: *Elle, Marie-Claire, Studio, Cuisine & Vins de France, Marie-Claire Maison*, etc.

### Television

National public channels: France 2, France 3.
Private channels: TF1, M6, Canal+ (encoded), la 5 (from 6.15 a.m. to 7 p.m.), Arte, an equally shared Franco-German channel (from 7 p.m. to 2 a.m.).
Cable and satellite: RTLTV, Monte Carlo, TV 5 Europe, Ciné Cinémas, Ciné Cinéfil, Paris Première, Planète, Eurosport, Canal J, Canal Jimmy, MCM, TMC, MTV, Euronews, BBC, etc.

### Radio channels

RTL, Europe 1, France Inter, France Culture, France Musique, and various 'peripheral' stations.

### Cinema

There are about 3,000 cinemas in France with some three million cinema visits per week. At the last count there were two main distribution companies: Médiavision and Circuit A.

## Affichage

Advertising by posters is a very important mass advertising medium in France, with some 12 per cent of market share. Big communications groups like Havas, Publicis, Hachette are involved with poster advertisers like Avenir, Giraudy, Dauphin and Métrobus.

Worth consulting:

Tarif Média (5 rue de la Boétie, 75008 Paris – Tel: (1) 44 56 31 56 – Fax: (1) 42 66 49 05 – Minitel: 3617 TARIFMEDIA).

Tarif Média indexes more than 6,000 media (for France); that is the near-totality of existing advertising medium/*supports existants* (press/*la presse*, poster advertising/*l'affichage*, radio/*la radio*, television/*la télévision*, etc.). On each of those, it can provide information and figures (circulation, distribution, broadcasting/*diffusion*, sales general terms/*conditions générales de vente*, media audience/*audience des médias*).

### Belgium

In Belgium the Flemish national TV (BRT, radio and television, two TV channels) and the French-language TV (Radio et Télévision Belge Francophone, two TV channels) do not take advertising. Only the fifth channel (VTM, Flemish) does so. In radio the same policy applies; local, private stations take advertising. On the other hand most homes are 'cabled', enabling them to take all television programmes (and advertising) from neighbouring countries. The most influential French-language national newspaper is *Le Soir*, which takes advertising, as does the rest of the press. The Belgian national press agency is called **Belga**.

# 11 Holidays

## Public holidays in France

1 January (*le jour de l'an*)
Easter Monday (April)
Ascension Thursday (May)*
Whit Monday (May–June)
1 May
8 May (celebrating the 1945 victory in Europe)
14 July (*la fête nationale*)
15 August (*Assomption*)
1 November (All Saints – *la Toussaint*)
11 November (celebrating the 1918 victory)
25 December (*le jour de Noël*)

*Most companies also take the Friday off (*faire le pont*).

If the bank holiday falls on a normal closing day, there is no extension.

### Annual holidays in France

Holidays from work (*congés payés*) are set and depend on activity sectors. They figure in national collective agreements (*conventions collectives nationales*). There are many such conventions, among others a national collective agreement for bank employees (*convention collective nationale du personnel de banque*) or the national collective agreement for advertising (*convention collective nationale de la publicité*). The holiday year can run either from 01/05 to 30/04 or from 01/06 to 31/05.

There are inducements to encourage employees to take at least part of their holidays outside a certain period. If some days are taken between 1/11 and 30/04, the holidays entitlement is increased (up to a week if 20 days are taken within this period, depending on the convention). These are called *hors période* (out of season). This is probably to encourage people to work during the summer-time when France is known to be working in slow motion.

### Leave of absence

This is also catered for in the way of sabbaticals (*congés sabbatiques*), economic/social/trade union training and leave to carry out public, social or professional functions – for example service on a *Prud'hommes* tribunal.

### Other holiday benefits

(a) the French Railways (La Société Nationale des Chemins de Fer – SNCF) offers all wage earners, trainees and registered unemployed persons, together with their families, a yearly return rail journey of 200km. or more at a reduction of 25 per cent.

(b) This reduction could be more if you pay with a 'holiday cheque' (*un chèque vacances*) to which you are entitled if you pay less than a certain figure in income tax. The cheque can be used for other holiday expenses also.

(c) There are numerous holiday facilities for workers' children subsidized by firms or other organizations, e.g. open-air centres (*centres aérés*) and *colonies de vacances* ('holiday camps').

### Belgium

In Belgium the national day is not 14 July but the 21st. It celebrates the separation of Belgium from Holland, thanks in part to British pressure on the Dutch, in 1830. Government departments and some business houses may, in addition, be closed on 2 and 15 November. When a public holiday falls on a Sunday, the Monday following is usually a holiday. Most employees have 20 days of holiday a year (as well as the 10 statutory public holidays) and receive a vacation allowance of about 85 per cent of a month's salary. Many employers, as in France, pay their staff for a '13th month' (*un treizième mois*) as a bonus.

## 12 Trade unions and industrial relations

### France

In France the historical desire of working-class activists to federate the working class has meant that trade unions (*syndicats*) are mostly merged in federations (*fédérations, confédérations, centrales syndicales*). The main ones are:

**CGT** (Confédération générale du travail), the oldest, the largest (with some 750,000 members) and close in its outlook to the PCF (Parti communiste français)

**FO** (Force ouvrière) was formerly part of the CGT; it does not advocate worker control and favours collective bargaining – it has a membership of some 500,000

**CFTC** (Confédération française des travailleurs chrétiens) seeks peaceful collaboration between labour and capital – it has c. 100,000 members

**CFDT** (Confédération française et démocratique du travail) with c. 500,000 members (*adhérents*) has wished to combine radicalism (e.g. *autogestion*: 'worker control') with a willingness to bargain

**CGC** (Confédération générale des cadres) represents managerial and supervisory staff (c. 100,000 members) and considers itself politically neutral

These five *centrales syndicales* are usually represented in national collective agreements (*conventions collectives*). One should however also mention **FEN** (Fédération de l'Education Nationale) representing teachers, and **FNSEA** (Fédération Nationale des Syndicats d'Exploitants Agricoles) representing farmers.

French union membership has long been in decline. Nevertheless by strikes, bargaining and political affiliation the unions have won certain benefits. All firms with 10 or more employees must have an elected *délégué du personnel* to represent them. Unions are entitled by law to set up union branches (*sections syndicales*) within firms. All firms with 50 or more employees must have a *comité d'entreprise* which is elected, has certain inspection powers and receives from the firm a sum equivalent to a fraction of the wages bill. The *Conseils des Prud'hommes* are industrial tribunals with lay judges (two employers and two employees, elected) which settle disputes between individual employees and their employers. There is a minimum wage called **le SMIC** (see below). All employees have at least 5 weeks' annual holiday and a 39-hour week.

### Belgium

In Belgium there is a tendency to cut the normal 40-hour week to 37 or 38 and there is a maximum working day of 12 hours. Some two-thirds of the workforce belong to a trade union, so that although there are no 'closed shops' (*un monopole syndical*), the unions are influential. Given the divided nature of Belgian society, the unions are not national but 'socialist', 'Catholic', 'liberal', with professional subdivisions (metalworkers, hotelworkers, etc.). All employees must receive a contract of employment, usually with a probationary period (*période d'essai*). In the interests of job security unions have been known to recommend wage reductions. Minimum wages have been agreed in most industries by joint Labour–Management Councils. The cost of sacking an employee increases in line with his/her period of employment, as does the length of notice of dismissal. Companies with 100 or more employees must form a Works Council.

# 13 Taxes

- **Income Tax** (*impôt sur le revenu*) is progressive and calculated in bands. Taxpayers (*contribuables*) declare their income annually before the beginning of March. The income tax is paid in February, May and September, based on the declared income for the previous year. Any adjustment is settled in September.
- **Company Tax** (*impôts sur les sociétés*) is also progressive and paid in estimated tranches in May, June, September and December. The last payment includes the balance owed (*le solde*).
- **Direct Local Taxes** are collected by *communes*, *départements* and *régions*. They include the Dwelling Tax (*taxe d'habitation*), Land and Property Taxes (*taxes foncières*), the Business Tax (*taxe professionnelle*, on property used for business), etc.
- **Registration Duties** (*droits d'enregistrement*) on sales, donations, leases (*le bail, les baux*), setting up of companies, etc.
- **Stamp Duties** (*droits de timbre*) are likewise connected with the documentation of certain formalities like transport contracts, bills and securities, identity cards, passports, driving licences (*permis de conduire*), hunting permits (*permis de chasse*), etc.
- **Value Added Tax** (*taxe sur la valeur ajoutée*, TVA) in principle affects all goods and services and has a common rate of 20.6 per cent. There is a reduced rate of 5.5 per cent on such goods as most foodstuffs, books, medicines and original works of art.
- **Axle and Aircraft Tax** (*taxe à l'essieu et taxe sur les aéronefs*): this affects road and air transport.
- **Differential Automobile Tax** known as *la vignette* applies to all motor vehicles and varies according to the horsepower (*chevaux fiscaux*: 'fiscal horses'), the vehicle's age and the *département* in which it is registered (*immatriculé*).

## Belgium

Belgium additionally has a **Withholding Tax** on dividend income and interest (*un précompte mobilier*). Value Added Tax in Flemish abbreviates to BTW; there are several rates of VAT (TVA, BTW) with 19 per cent as the standard. VAT can be as high as 33 per cent, which may be expressed as 25 per cent plus 8 per cent luxury goods tax. Coordination Centres (see below) enjoy a range of tax advantages (e.g. exemption from withholding taxes). Tax treaties (based on the OECD model) signed with some 50 countries mean that corporation tax (*impôt sur les sociétés*) on non-resident companies or companies that are more than 50 per cent foreign-owned is limited to the local rate (*c.* 40 per cent). The tax year is the calendar year and tax pre-payments (estimates) are due in April, July, October and December. Income from property is taxed by both the state and the municipality. Expatriates benefit from special income tax allowances. Stamp duty is payable on insurance contracts. Gains on capital are taxed at income tax rates. It is said to be a national hobby to evade tax, which is facilitated by the fact that a large proportion of Belgians (and Belgian companies) have one or more foreign bank accounts.

# 14 Types of company

## France

Companies in France fall into one of the types described below:

- **Une entreprise individuelle** is owned and run by an individual, for example a baker or a plumber. The individual is responsible for all the debts incurred by the company and its 'profits' are taxed as personal income.
- **Une société en nom collectif** (SNC) is a company in which the partners bear unlimited responsibility for any debts.
- **Une entreprise unipersonnelle à responsabilité limitée** (EURL/SRL) has legal company status, normally a single official director and a legally determined minimum registered capital.
- **Une société à responsabilité limitée** (SRL) requires at least two partners (*associés*) and a certain sum of registered capital. Accounts have to be audited by an official *commissaire aux comptes* above a certain level. In the case of receivership (*dépôt de bilan*) the *tribunal de commerce* may contest the limitation of liability to the amount of the registered capital. Readers will also come across the acronym SARL.
- **Une société en commandite simple** (SCS) has some partners (*commandités*) who are not limited in their liability but others (*commanditaires*) who are only responsible to the extent of their share of the registered capital.
- **Une société anonyme** (SA) requires at least seven partners and a quite high amount of registered capital (*capital social*). The capital is divided into shares (*actions*) which can be freely sold to third parties. The SA must have a board of directors (*un conseil d'administration*). It may or may not be quoted at the Stock Exchange (*coté en Bourse*).
- **Une société en commandite par actions** (SCA) is like the SCS above but with shares that can be freely sold.
- **Une société du secteur public** is a registered company whose capital belongs in whole or in part to the state.
- **Un groupement d'intérêt économique** (GIE) is a group in which any profits are considered (and taxed) as income of the individual members.
- **Un groupement européen d'intérêt économique** (GEIE) is the same as a GIE, with members from different countries of the European Union.
- **Une société d'habitation à loyer modéré** (HLM) is a state-funded housing association.
- **Une société immobilière pour le commerce et l'industrie** (SICOM) is a type of property company.
- **Une mutuelle** is a sort of provident society.
- **Une société d'aménagement foncier et d'établissement rural** (SAFER) is a

company originally set up to reorganize the small farms of its region into larger units.

(And many others!)

## Belgium

In Belgium various tax concessions have been accorded to so-called **Coordination Centres** (often finance centres of multinational firms), which are required to have a consolidated equity of US$25 million. These Centres cannot hold shares. The major types of company are:

- **Une société anonyme** (SA, or NV, *naamlooze vennootschap*) is a public limited company. It must have a minimum capital of BF1.25 million.
- **Une société privée à responsabilité limitée** (SPRL, or BVBA, *besloten vennootschap met beperkte aansprkelijkheid*) is a private limited company. It has a minimum of two shareholders and capital of BF750,000.
- **Une société en nom collectif** (SC, or *vennootschap onder firma*) is one type of general partnership.
- **Une société en commandite simple** (SC, or CV, *gewone commanditaire vennootschap*) is another.
- **Une société en commandite par actions** (or *commanditaire vennootschap op aandelen*) is a limited partnership with shares.
- **Une société coopérative** (or *cooperative vennootschap*) is a cooperative.

Many foreign companies set up branches in Belgium. To do so, articles of association must be filed with the Clerk (*le Greffe/de Griffie*) of the Commercial Court.

One particular, major Belgian company is the **Hoge Raad voor Diamant** (the High Council for Diamonds) in Antwerp (Flemish: Antwerpen, French: Anvers), which oversees the four diamond exchanges (of 13 worldwide) in Belgium.

# 15  Red tape

The term 'red tape' probably comes from the red ribbon used to tie the bulging files of bureaucrats. Its French equivalent is *la paperasserie* meaning 'lots of paper'. Another term might be *la bureaucratie*, which implies an abusive use of administrative powers.

## Company regulations

Companies are heavily regulated where employees are concerned. They pay a lot on top of wages (even small wages) in *charges sociales* for social security and retirement benefits. They also have many regulations to observe concerning safety (*la sécurité*). They must pay a tax for training (*la taxe de formation professionnelle*). They must also finance any company Works Committee (*le comité d'entreprise*) and elected trade union delegates must be allowed time from their 39 statutory hours for trade union activity (*les activités syndicales*).

## Official forms

French people spend a lot of time filling in forms. Everything that involves paperwork seems to be difficult to achieve. Dealing with the administration is not a pleasant or easy task. However prepared you might be, you can be sure there will always be something missing from your file (*pièce manquante à votre dossier*), preventing the *fonctionnaire* from proceeding. Here is a small example of what is required from an EU member to be able to obtain a resident's card (which, by the way, is compulsory): birth certificate of applicant, spouse and children if applicable (all copies must be less than three months old), original marriage certificate (*certificat de mariage original*), photos of all involved (black and white), employment contract (*contrat de travail à durée indéterminée*), letter from employer (for husband and wife if both work) stating conditions of employment, giving reasons why the applicant must stay, stating position held, and salary. If you decide, once in possession of the precious card, to move to another French *département*, you will be pleased to find out that all this has to be repeated! Similar requirements will apply for affiliation to the Social Security (*Sécurité sociale*), family allowance applications (*allocations familiales*), etc. However, you will be pleased to know that you will not have to do anything to receive your local tax form (*taxe d'habitation*)! This will somehow find its own way to your home address! But as far as your income tax form (*déclaration des revenus*) is concerned, you are expected to know that the first year, you will have to get it from your local Town Hall. Do not wait until 28 February to do so as it has to be sent by 18 March (also you may find that you will have to do quite a bit of reading first as mistakes on your part are not allowed!).

## Personal documentation

Citizens may well be required to produce various papers at various times, like their identity card (*la carte d'identité*); birth certificate (*l'extrait d'acte de naissance*); 'family book' (*le livret de famille* which officially registers spouses and children); tax receipt (*la feuille d'impôt*); rent receipt (*la quittance de loyer* – to prove that one has a regular *domicile*); pay-slip (*la feuille de paye* – to prove that one has a regular income) and even one's police file (*l'extrait de casier judiciaire*). (A lot of red tape is involved in replacing any of these if they are lost!)

## Vehicles

If you are in charge of a vehicle the insurance sticker must be displayed, as must the road tax (*la vignette* – which also must be bought during November only) and the driver must have the vehicle registration document (*le certificat d'immatriculation* or *la carte grise*). The French equivalent of the British MOT certificate is the official Technical Verification (*le contrôle technique*), which must be passed by all vehicles aged five years or more.

## Traffic wardens

Everyone at some time will be irritated by the traffic wardens, *les contractuel(le)s*, now also called (the women at least) *les pervenches* ('periwinkles', after their blue uniforms. They were formerly *les aubergines*). You may also be fined on the spot by the *contrôleur* ('inspector') of the train or the metro.

### Belgium

Belgians may try to avoid paying tax but they become accustomed, from the age of 12, to carrying an identity card. Less acceptable is the fact that you can be arrested as a vagrant (*un vagabond/een zwerver*) if you do not have on your person enough money for a loaf of bread and a pint of milk (the same applies in France, where you would be deemed a *clochard*). The police are not generally disliked, but tax officials and social workers are, both professions being considered to be interfering in people's personal affairs. Many foreign nationals work in Belgium. If they work for one of the co-called Coordination Centres or are EU nationals they do not need a work permit. Otherwise they do require this ever-scarcer document.

# 16 Wages and salaries

### France

*Le salaire* of a manager would often be called *le traitement*. If you are a member of *les professions libérales* you will be paid fees or *honoraires*. France has traditionally had a wide spectrum of salaries and wages (*l'éventail des salaires*). You will find that French people do not like to be asked any questions about the contents of their pay-slips.

There is in France a national minimum wage called the SMIC (*le salaire minimum interprofessionnel de croissance*) which is indexed to the cost of living. There is also a minimum five weeks' paid holiday.

Semi-skilled workers, often called *ouvriers spécialisés* (OS), are paid 10 or 20 per cent more than the national minimum wage. Skilled workers (*ouvriers qualifiés*) will get 40 or 50 per cent, whilst middle managers (*cadres moyens*) may earn up to six times the national minimum wage.

### Belgium

Belgium, like France, has a minimum wage for workers aged 21 years. Starting salaries may well be low and differentials between grades, or between managers and workers, high. A factor keeping wage costs down is the relatively low cost of housing which may be the result of a kind of parochialism, conditioned in part by language.

# 17 The Stock Exchange

### France

In France there are seven Stock Exchanges: in Paris, Bordeaux, Lille, Lyon, Marseille, Nancy and Nantes. La Bourse de Paris does the lion's share of the business.

The primary market (*le marché primaire*) of the Stock Exchange allows companies to be publicly quoted (*cotées en Bourse*) and to issue (*émettre*) securities (*valeurs mobilières, titres*) for sale to investors. The closely associated secondary market (*le marché secondaire*) displays the (fluctuating) prices (*les cours*) of securities (stocks or shares: *les actions*, bonds: *les obligations*) and allows their resale. (In addition bonds earn interest: *les intérêts*, shares earn dividends: *les dividendes.*) The Stock Exchange therefore facilitates the raising of capital (*augmentation de capital*), restructuring (*la restructuration*), mergers (*les fusions*), takeovers (*les rachats*), takeover bids (*les OPA, offres publiques d'achat*), capital gains (*les plus-values*) and capital losses (*les moins-values*) and so on. The COB (Commission des Opérations de Bourse) is the independent watchdog body which supervises the financial markets, and attempts to prevent insider dealing (*le délit d'initiés*).

In 1983, a second market for medium-sized companies (*les entreprises moyennes*) was created. In 1986 the MATIF (*le marché à terme d'instruments financiers* – a futures market for financial instruments) was created, giving the possibility of protection against variations in interest rates (*les taux d'intérêt*). In 1987 the MONEP (*Marché d'Options Négociables de Paris* – Paris options market) was created.

In the several years before the Crash (*le Krach*) of October 1987 La Bourse grew rapidly, e.g. fourfold between 1981 and 1986, as shown by the CAC index (Chambre Syndicale des Agents de Change – the stockbrokers' association).

There are currently two principal changes taking place: growing institutionalization with more investment by institutional investors (*investisseurs institutionnels*) like insurance companies (*compagnies d'assurance*) or pension funds (*caisses de retraite*), and more collectively managed funds with similarities to Unit Trusts like SICAV (*sociétés d'investissement à capital variable*: 'variable capital investment companies') and FCP (*fonds communs de placement*: 'common investment funds'). The second change is internationalization, either of portfolios (*le portefeuille*) or of stocks quoted. Important stocks are likely to be quoted in various stock exchanges and may therefore be traded around the clock, thus creating a global equity market (*un marché mondial d'actions*).

### Belgium

The main Belgian stock exchange is in Brussels and accounts for 85 per cent of turnover. There are also minor exchanges in Antwerp, Ghent, and Liège. The Banking Commission must approve any listing. Disclosure requirements for foreign companies must comply with those of 'home' exchanges. There is a second market for smaller companies.

# 18 Women at work

### France

The law of 22 December 1972 (part of French Labour Law – *le Code du Travail*) laid down the requirement for employers to give equal pay for equal work. *A travail égal, salaire égal.* Following the law of 13 July 1983 there must be equality at work (*égalité professionnelle*) between men and women. Companies with 300 or more staff were required to produce a detailed comparative report together with a set of solutions to inequalities, in what is called *Un Plan d'Egalité Professionnelle.*

In 1984 a national supervisory body was set up – *Le Conseil Supérieur de l'Egalité Professionnelle.*

Various abuses on the grounds of sex are outlawed: refusal to hire (*refus d'embauche*); transfer or refusal to transfer (*mutation ou refus de mutation*); cancellation or non-renewal of work contract (*résiliation ou non-renouvellement de contrat de travail*); discrimination based on family situation (*discrimination à cause de situation de famille*) and so on.

In 1986 an official circular published rules for the feminization of trades (*le métier*), functions (*la fonction*), ranks (*le grade*) and titles (*le titre*). The following equivalents were suggested: *un architecte/une architecte, un délégué/une déléguée, un médecin/une femme médecin, un mécanicien/une mécanicienne, un acheteur/une acheteuse* (the 't' belongs to the verb *acheter*, 'to buy'), *un animateur/une animatrice* (the 't' is not part of the verb *animer* – 'to lead a group'), *un vendeur/une vendeuse, un ingénieur/une femme ingénieur.* Note that **un** *secrétaire* is likely to have a very different job, more administrative and less subordinate, than **une** *secrétaire.* (The French novelist Christiane Rochefort once jokingly suggested *écrevisse* ('crayfish') as a feminine form for *écrivain.*) In modern France women executives (usually called *femmes cadres* despite attempts to feminize terms) would probably be amused by 'male chauvinism' (*la phallocratie* or *le machisme*) and dismissive of attempts at sexual harassment (*le harcèlement sexuel*). However they are convinced that there *are* problems for women wanting a career in business. For example if they wish to have children as well as a career they have to plan their pregnancies (*les grossesses*) and maternity leaves (*les congés de maternité*) at opportune moments if possible. They have to teach the men around them in the workplace about the relatively new situation in which women are the bosses (*les problèmes relationnels*). If the job involves *déjeuners, dîners, déplacements* ('lunches, dinners and trips'), they may have to make arrangements for their families in order to fulfil these commitments. Women in subaltern positions may be off sick, but women managers, it often seems, need extra physical and psychological resources. It remains to be seen when there will be equality of opportunity (*égalité des chances*) to match legal equality, or if and when *harcèlement sexuel* in the workplace will ever stop.

## Belgium

In Belgium there appears to be a more traditional relationship between the sexes. There is respect, but on the other hand Belgian women may more readily accept that the 'female professions' are less well-paid and, as a result, their expectations of reaching manager status will not be as great as those of their neighbours in France or Germany.

# 19  Social Security

## France

In France, employees contribute a proportion of their salary to the Social Security (*Sécurité sociale*) and to a complementary health insurance (*une mutuelle*) which is also compulsory. The individuals pay their health care and drugs (*médicaments*) bills. The Social Security pays a certain percentage back and the *mutuelle* tops up the reimbursement. If your company subscribes to a good *mutuelle*, you can be reimbursed up to 100 per cent of all your health care bills, including opticians and dentists.

Some *mutuelles* offer a payment method which enables the employee to receive drugs without making any payment (this system is called the *tiers payant*). This can be done in different ways. The most common one is that the *mutuelle* has an agreement with a network of chemists who deal directly with them and the Social Security (the patient in this case only has to show his/her *mutuelle* and Social Security card). The other method is for the *mutuelle* to provide the employee with a special cheque book. In this case, the patient will pay the chemist using those cheques called Santé-Pharma (this enables the employee to go to any chemist).

When the employee has to receive treatment in hospital or in a clinic, the *mutuelle* will have to be informed straight away and they will look after all costs incurred.

As for visits to the doctor or specialist (*consultations*), in most cases the fee has to be advanced by the patient. Some surgeries have agreements with the Social Security and in this case, the patient will only have to pay the remaining 30 per cent (this system is called *paiement du ticket modérateur*).

## Belgium

In Belgium Social Security is compulsory and is all dealt with through *mutuelles* which are, like trade unions, organized along political, ethnic or religious lines. The social insurance companies may even own their own hospitals. The employer's contribution is almost as high as in France, on average some 30 per cent of salary.

# Reference Grammar

# Brief notes on French grammar

## Days and months

Note that these are written with a small, not capital, initial letter.

| | |
|---|---|
| **lundi** | Monday |
| **mardi** | Tuesday |
| **mercredi** | Wednesday |
| **jeudi** | Thursday |
| **vendredi** | Friday |
| **samedi** | Saturday |
| **dimanche** | Sunday |
| **janvier** | January |
| **février** | February |
| **mars** | March |
| **avril** | April |
| **mai** | May |
| **juin** | June |
| **juillet** | July |
| **août** | August |
| **septembre** | September |
| **octobre** | October |
| **novembre** | November |
| **décembre** | December |

Some typical dates:

**le premier septembre**
**le deux mars (not deuxième)**
**le vingt-trois janvier**
**le vingt-neuf février (une année bissextile: a leap year)**

**mardi, le dix avril**
**le mardi dix avril**

## Numbers

| | | | |
|---|---|---|---|
| **un(e)** | one | **onze** (11) | zéro (0) |
| **deux** | two | **douze** (12) | |
| **trois** | three | **treize** (13) | |
| **quatre** | four | **quatorze** (14) | |
| **cinq** | five | **quinze** (15) | |
| **six** | six | **seize** (16) | |
| **sept** | seven | **dix-sept** (17) | |
| **huit** | eight | **dix-huit** (18) | |
| **neuf** | nine | **dix-neuf** (19) | |
| **dix** | ten | **vingt** (20) | |

**vingt et un** (21), **vingt-deux** (22), **vingt-trois** (23), etc.
**trente** (30), **trente et un** (31), etc.
**quarante** (40), **quarante et un** (41), etc.
**cinquante** (50), **cinquante et un**, (51), etc.
**soixante** (60), **soixante et un**, (61), etc.

**soixante-dix** (70), **soixante et onze** (71), **soixante-douze** (72), etc. **quatre-vingts** (80), **quatre-vingt-un** (81), **quatre-vingt-deux** (82), etc. **quatre-vingt-dix** (90), **quatre-vingt-onze** (91), etc., **cent** (100), **cent-un** (101), etc., **deux cents** (200), **deux cent trois** (203), etc.

*Note:*
Belgian French has **septante** (70) and **nonante** (90). Swiss French also has those, plus **octante** (80).

**mille** (1000)
**un million** ( 1 000 000)
**un milliard** (1 000 000 000) (a billion)

*Note:*
The comma (**virgule**) is strictly used as a decimal point in numbers.

**premier** (first)
**deuxième** (second)
**neuvième** (ninth)
**quarante-septième** (47th)
**soixante-seizième** (76th)
**cent unième** (101st), etc.

## Fractions

**la moitié** (half)
**le quart** (quarter)
**le tiers** (third)
**les trois-quarts** (three-quarters)
**le cinquième** (fifth)
**le quatre-vingt-treizième** (93rd), etc.

# Gender of nouns

All nouns are either masculine or feminine and the accompanying 'the' or 'a' will consequently be either **le** (m.) or **la** (f.), **un** or **une**. Or **l**' if the noun begins with a vowel or mute **h**:

| | |
|---|---|
| la compagnie | une compagnie |
| le directeur | un directeur |
| la directrice | une directrice |
| l'entreprise (f.) | une entreprise |
| l'hôtel (m.) | un hôtel |

There is sometimes a masculine and feminine form of a word and sometimes not:

| | |
|---|---|
| **le docteur** | no feminine |
| **le président** | **la présidente** |
| **la personne** | no masculine |
| **un administrateur** | **une administratrice** |
| **le maire** (mayor) | no feminine |
| **le directeur** | **la directrice** |

# Singular and plural forms

Most plurals are made by adding **s** (which is almost never pronounced):

| | |
|---|---|
| **les firmes** | the firms |
| **des firmes** | (some) forms |

There are however other plural forms:

| | |
|---|---|
| **le bijou** | **les bijoux** |
| **le bateau** | **les bateaux** |
| **l'animal** | **les animaux** |
| **le bail** (lease) | **les baux** |
| **le chef-lieu** (county town) | **les chefs-lieux** |
| **le chemin de fer** (railway) | **les chemins de fer** |
| **le gratte-ciel** (skyscraper) | **les gratte-ciel** |

# Verb forms

**Present tense:**

| | *1st conj.* | *2nd conj.* | *3rd conj.* | *Irregular* |
|---|---|---|---|---|
| je | **parle** | **finis** | **vends** | **fais** |
| tu | **parles** | **finis** | **vends** | **fais** |
| il/elle | **parle** | **finit** | **vend** | **fait** |
| nous | **parlons** | **finissons** | **vendons** | **faisons** |
| vous | **parlez** | **finissez** | **vendez** | **faites** |
| ils/elles | **parlent** | **finissent** | **vendent** | **font** |

The conjugation of a verb can usually be judged by the form of its infinitive: **parler, finir, vendre.** Among common *irregular* verbs are:

**être** (to be, **je suis** etc.)
**avoir** (to have)
**aller** (to go)
**conduire** (to lead)
**écrire** (to write)
**faire** (to make, to do)
**mettre** (to put)
**prendre** (to take)

**pouvoir** (to be able)
**tenir** (to hold)
**voir** (to see)
**vouloir** (to want)

The forms are often, but not always, similar to standard forms. Here are the present tenses of **avoir** and **être**:

| *être* | *avoir* |
|---|---|
| **je suis** | **j'ai** |
| **tu es** | **tu as** |
| **il/elle est** | **il/elle a** |
| **nous sommes** | **nous avons** |
| **vous êtes** | **vous avez** |
| **ils/elles sont** | **ils/elles ont** |

(Note: **c'est**: 'it is')

### The perfect tense (le passé composé)

With most verbs this is formed using the verb **avoir** and the past participle of the other verb, e.g. **j'ai mangé**, 'I have eaten'/'I ate'. Some verbs use **être** e.g. **je suis allé**, 'I have gone'/'I went'. All reflexive verbs use **être**, e.g. **je me suis lavé**, 'I have washed'/'I washed' (myself):

Here are some examples of the perfect tense

**j'ai parlé** (I have spoken, I spoke)
**tu as choisi** (chosen)
**elle a vendu** (sold)
**nous avons mangé** (eaten)
**vous avez obéi** (obeyed)
**ils ont répondu** (replied)

**je suis venu** (I have come)
**tu es arrivé** (arrived)
**il est parti** (left)
**nous sommes entrés** (entered)
**vous êtes nés** (you were born)
**ils se sont tués** (they have killed themselves)

Here are most of the verbs (not counting reflexive verbs) that form their composed past tense with **être**:

| | |
|---|---|
| **aller** | to go |
| **venir** | to come |
| **arriver** | to arrive |
| **partir** | to depart |
| **entrer** | to enter |
| **sortir** | to go out, leave |
| **monter** | to go/come up |

| | |
|---|---|
| **descendre** | to go/come down |
| **revenir** | to come back, return |
| **retourner** | to go back, return |
| **rentrer** | to go home |
| **tomber** | to fall |
| **rester** | to remain |
| **devenir** | to become |
| **naître** | to be born |
| **mourir** | to die |

(*Note:* the past participle will agree with the subject: **elles sont mortes.**)

## The past historic

This tense is called in French **le passé simple** and is a literary and historic past tense probably little used in a business context, but readers ought to be familiar with it. The forms are briefly as below:

| **manger** | **boire** | **partir** |
|---|---|---|
| **je mangeai*** | **je bus** | **je partis** |
| **tu mangeas** | **tu bus** | **tu partis** |
| **il/elle mangea** | **il but** | **il partit** |
| **nous mangeâmes** | **nous bûmes** | **nous partîmes** |
| **vous mangeâtes** | **vous bûtes** | **vous partîtes** |
| **ils/elles mangèrent** | **ils burent** | **ils partirent** |

(*The 'extra' **e** after the **g** is to keep it 'soft'. A **g** is always 'hard', as in **gamin**, before **a/o/u**.)

## The imperfect tense

This tense is used to describe continuous or habitual past action: 'it was raining', 'we used to visit Granny'. Add the following endings to the **nous** form of the present tense without its ending: e.g. **nous achet(ons), nous attend(ons), nous finiss(ons):**

- – ais
- – ais
- – ait
- – ions
- – iez
- – aient

(An example of the use of the imperfect and perfect tenses in the same sentence is as follows: **La directrice embrassait le comptable quand son mari est arrivé:** 'the manageress was kissing the accountant when her husband arrived'.)

## The future tense

It is common to use **aller** plus an infinitive to convey future meaning, e.g. **je vais écrire une lettre demain** ('I am going to write a letter tomorrow'); **nous allons faire le reste la semaine prochaine** ('we will do the rest next week'). There is also a future tense with the following endings added usually to the infinitive of the verb (without the **e** in the case of **-re** infinitives):

| | |
|---|---|
| – ai | **je travaillerai** |
| – as | **tu finiras** |
| – a | **elle attendra** |
| – ons | **nous partirons** |
| – ez | **vous écrirez** |
| – ont | **ils vendront** |

Watch out for irregulars like **j'aurai, je serai, je ferai, je pourrai**. The expression **il y a**, meaning 'there is/are', becomes **il y aura**: 'there will be'.

## The conditional tense

Meaning 'I would eat', etc., this tense is formed by adding the same endings as the imperfect to the same stem as the future tense:

| | |
|---|---|
| **je finirais** | I would finish |
| **tu vendrais** | you would sell |
| **il ferait** | he would do |
| **elle aurait** | she would have |
| **ce serait** | it would be |
| **nous mangerions** | we would eat |
| **vous attendriez** | you would wait |
| **elles diraient** | they would say |

A couple of examples are: **Je voudrais visiter les ateliers**: 'I would like to visit the workshops'. **Si j'avais de l'argent j'achèterais des actions Rolls Royce**: 'If I had the money I would buy Rolls Royce shares.'

The past conditional meaning 'I would have eaten' etc., is formed by the conditional of **avoir** or **être** with the past participle of the other verb e.g. **j'aurais mangé**: 'I would have eaten'; **je serais parti**: 'I would have left'. Study the following example: **Si le directeur financier avait fait son travail, nous aurions pu racheter Rolls Royce**: 'If the financial director had done his work we would have been able to buy (could have bought) Rolls Royce'.

## The subjunctive

This is called a 'mood' and it expresses uncertainty, or the wish (that something should happen) or an emotion. The present subjunctive is formed by adding the following endings to the stem of the present participle (without its ending **–ant**): **-e, -es, -e, -ions, -iez, -ent**.

Some irregular verbs have a single subjunctive stem:

| faire | que je fasse/que nous fassions |
|---|---|
| falloir | qu'il faille |
| pouvoir | que je puisse/que vous puissiez |
| savoir | que je sache/qu'ils sachent |

Some others have two stems:

**que j'aille/que nous allions,**
**que je prenne/que nous prenions**
**que je veuille/que nous voulions**

The present subjunctive of **avoir** and **être** (with irregular endings) are:

| avoir | être |
|---|---|
| que j'aie | que je sois |
| que tu aies | que tu sois |
| qu'il/elle ait | qu'il/elle soit |
| que nous ayons | que nous soyons |
| que vous ayez | que vous soyez |
| qu' ils aient | qu'ils/elles soient |

Here are some typical examples of subjunctive use:

**il faut que nous préparions les chiffres** we must prepare the figures
**il semble que cette entreprise soit au bord de la faillite** it seems this firm is close to bankruptcy
**il se peut que ce modèle plaise mieux aux femmes** it may be that this model is more pleasing to women
**que voulez-vous que nous fassions?** what do you want us to do?
**nous sommes très heureux que vous ayez été reçu au bac** we are very happy that you have passed your bac

As the last example illustrates, the past subjunctive is made by combining the present subjunctive of **avoir** or **être** with the past participle. Note this final example: **je crains qu'elle ne soit morte** (I fear she may have died).

There are numerous examples of use of the subjunctive in the letters section, usually signposted by a footnote.

# Present and past participles/infinitives

To translate 'going' (allant) 'waiting' (attendant), etc. and 'killed' (tué), 'gone' (allé, parti), etc., the present participle is formed by adding **-ant** to the **nous** form of the present tense without the ending, e.g. **nous continuons: continuant** ('continuing'). **Etre, avoir** and **savoir** are irregular, producing **étant, ayant** and **sachant** ('being', 'having' and 'knowing'). The past participle is usually the infinitive of a verb without the **-er/-ir/-re** and with **-é/-i/-u**, e.g. **parlé, choisi, vendu** ('spoken', 'chosen', 'sold').

Infinitives are expressed in English as 'to go', 'to do', 'to play': **aller, faire, jouer.** Quite often the 'to' is expressed by an additional **à** or **de**, e.g. **je voudrais voir** ('I would like to see') but **je continue à penser** ('I continue to think'); **nous avons décidé de partir** ('we have decided to go'). Note also **j'ai cessé de fumer** ('I have stopped smoking').

# The passive voice

This is a way of focusing on the object of a process, e.g. 'machined parts are produced in our factory in the north-east'. It is commonly constructed in two ways in French:

1  **les pièces usinées sont produites dans notre usine dans le nord-est**
2  **on produit les pièces usinées dans notre usine du nord-est**

Both constructions are equally valid. The first uses the appropriate tense and form of the verb **être** plus the past participle (which agrees in gender and number with the subject). The second uses the pronoun **on** (which has none of the social class connotation that it may have in English).

# Adjectives

Descriptive adjectives agree in gender and number with the nouns they modify and usually, but not always, have distinct masculine, feminine, singular and plural forms, e.g.:

| masc. sing. | fem. sing. | masc. pl. | fem. pl. |
|---|---|---|---|
| petit | petite | petits | petites |
| noir | noire | noirs | noires |
| or: | | | |
| utile | utile | utiles | utiles |
| or: | | | |
| bon | bonne | bons | bonnes |

or, an extra form before a masculine noun beginning with a vowel or mute **h**:

| | | | |
|---|---|---|---|
| nouveau/nouvel | nouvelle | nouveaux | nouvelles |
| or: | | | |
| naïf | naïve | naïfs | naïves |
| blanc | blanche | blancs | blanches |
| menteur | menteuse | menteurs | menteuses |
| légal | légale | légaux | légales |
| régulier | régulière | réguliers | régulières |

Unlike English, adjectives very often follow the noun they modify. Here are some examples of typical use:

**une grande entreprise**
**une firme multinationale**

**le PDG et le chef comptable son très intelligents**
**dernier entré, premier sorti**
**l'ancien directeur** (N.B. 'the former manager')
**une meilleure performance**

**Meilleur** is the comparative of **bon**. Good, better, best: **bon, meilleur, le/la meilleur(e)**. With most adjectives the comparative and superlative forms (e.g. 'best') are made by **plus** and **le/la plus**, e.g. **froid, plus froid** ('colder'); **le plus froid** ('coldest').

## Possessive adjectives

Like other adjectives, 'his', 'her', 'my', 'your', 'our', etc. agree with the nouns they are attached to, e.g. **elle est dans son lit** ('she is in her bed'). Another point to note is that **mon**, **ton** and **son** are used instead of **ma**, **ta** and **sa** before feminine singular nouns beginning with a vowel or mute **h**, e.g. **il déjeune avec son assistante** ('he is lunching with his PA'). Compare this with **il déjeune avec sa secrétaire**.

Here are the forms:

| English | Singular (m/f) | Plural |
|---|---|---|
| my | **mon/ma** | **mes** |
| your (fam.) | **ton/ta** | **tes** |
| his/her/its | **son/sa** | **ses** |
| our | **notre** | **nos** |
| your | **votre** | **vos** |
| their | **leur** | **leurs** |

## Demonstrative adjectives

'This', 'that', 'these', 'those'. As in the following examples:

**ce responsable de service**
**cet appareil** (masculine beginning with a vowel)
**cette personne**
**ces personnes**
**ces appareils**

*Note:* **C'est ma voiture. Là-bas ce sont les voitures de Claude et Janine** ('This is my car'. 'Over there are the cars of Claude and Janine').

## Interrogative adjectives

'Which', 'what'. As in the following examples:

**Quel fromage est le meilleur?**
**Quelle est la différence?**
**Quels employés vont être licenciés?** (Which employees will be made redundant?)

**Quelles sont les factures en litige?** (Which are the disputed invoices?)

*Note:* also: **Quelle pagaille!** What a shambles!

# Adverbs

Words like 'quickly', 'intelligently' – i.e. usually ending in 'y' in English, but not always (e.g. 'he works fast'). Adverbs do not agree. They modify verbs, adjectives or other adverbs, e.g.:

**Il travaille rapidement**
**Elle est moins rapide**
**Nous attendons depuis bien longtemps** (we have been waiting quite some time)

Most adverbs are formed by adding -**ment** to the adjective, using its feminine form when it ends in a consonant, e.g.:

| | |
|---|---|
| **probable** | **probablement** |
| **général** | **généralement** |
| **doux** | **doucement** ('gently', 'softly') |

Note the construction of **intelligent/intelligemment; constant/constamment**, etc.
    There are other common adverbs like: **aussi, bien, encore, mal** (badly), **peu, si, toujours**, etc.
    The comparative and superlative are formed by **plus** and **le plus** (or **moins** and **le moins**), e.g.:

**vite**
**plus vite**
**le plus vite**

or

**brillamment**
**moins brillamment**
**le moins brillamment**

To go with the adjectives **bon, meilleur(e), le/la meilleur(e)** there are the adverbs **bien, mieux, le mieux: C'est lui qui a le mieux travaillé** 'he has worked best'.

# Pronouns

| Subject | Object | Indirect object | Reflexive |
|---|---|---|---|
| **je** (I) | **me** (me) | **me** (to me) | **me** |
| ***tu** (you) | **te** (you) | **te** (to you) | **te** |
| **elle** (she) | **la** (her) | **lui** (to him/her) | **se** |
| **il** (he) | **le** (him) | **se** (to him/her/oneself) | **se** |
| **on** (one) | **se** (him/her/oneself) | | |
| **nous** (we) | **nous** (us) | **nous** | **nous** |

| | | | |
|---|---|---|---|
| **vous** (you) | **vous** (you) | **vous** | **vous** |
| **ils** (they) | **les** (them, m. & f.) | **leur** (to them) | **se** |
| **elles** (they) | **se** (themselves) | **se** (to themselves) | **se** |

\*Tu is the familiar form of 'you', used with friends, relatives, animals and sometimes between colleagues. **Vous** is the more formal method of address, and also the plural. So, if you were speaking to several friends you would say '**Vous êtes mes meilleurs amis.**'

The indirect object is not always obvious in English, e.g. 'he wrote her a letter': **il lui** ('to her') **a écrit une lettre.**

Note the following examples of reflexive pronouns and the pronouns **en** and **y**: **il se lève** ('he gets up' – literally, 'he raises himself'); **nous nous dépêchons** ('we hurry'); **je m'en occupe** ('I'll take care of it' – **en** meaning 'of it', etc.); **ils s'y habituent** (they are getting used to it – **y** meaning 'to it').

### Disjunctive pronouns

These can stand separately from verbs. They are **moi** ('me'), **toi** ('you'), **lui** ('him'), **elle** ('her'), **nous** ('us'), **vous** ('you'),  **eux** ('them'), **elles** ('them' – female). Examples:

**c'est moi**
**chez eux**
**toi et moi nous sommes les champions**
**il est plus fort que moi**

### Possessive pronouns

Expressions such as 'its his', 'that's ours', 'where is yours', are as follows:

| English | masculine | feminine | mascl. pl. | fem. pl. |
|---|---|---|---|---|
| mine | **le mien** | **la mienne** | **les miens** | **les miennes** |
| yours | **le tien** | **la tienne** | **les tiens** | **les tiennes** |
| his/hers/its | **le sien** | **la sienne** | **les siens** | **les siennes** |
| ours | **le nôtre** | **la nôtre** | **les nôtres** | **les nôtres** |
| yours | **le vôtre** | **la vôtre** | **les vôtres** | **les vôtres** |
| theirs | **le leur** | **la leur** | **les leurs** | **les leurs** |

Here are some examples:

**le mien est bleu**
**ces enfants sont les tiens je crois**
**cette maison est la nôtre**
**ces appareils sont les leurs**

### Demonstrative pronouns

Words meaning 'this one', 'that one', 'this', 'these,' 'those', 'this one here' etc., are:

| masc. sing. | fem. sing. | masc. pl. | fem. pl. |
|---|---|---|---|
| **celui** | **celle** | **ceux** | **celles** |

Examples:

**ce produit et celui de nos concurrents** this product and that of our competitors . . .

**celle** (fem.) **de gauche est ma préférée** the one on the left is my favourite, **ceux qui disent** those who say . . .

You can add **-ci** or **-là** to these pronouns to make 'this one here' (or perhaps 'the latter') and 'that one there' (or perhaps 'the former'). **Ceux-ci sont plus intelligents que celles-là**: 'the latter are brighter than the former'. Note also **cela** (often **ça**) and **ceci** are used for 'that' and 'this'.

### Relative pronouns

Phrases like 'the firm that Rupert created', 'the figures from which this balance was created', 'the person to whom I wrote', etc., are constructed in French using

| **qui** | 'who'/'which'/'that' (subject of the relative clause) |
|---|---|
| **que** | 'whom'/'which'/'that' (object . . .) |
| **quoi** | 'what'/'which' (with a preposition) |
| **lequel** | 'whom'/'which' (with a preposition) |
| **laquelle** | |
| **lesquels** | |
| **lesquelles** | |
| **dont** | 'whose'/'of whom'/'of which' |

Examples:

**la compagnie qui a remplacé Starbrite** 'which has replaced' (= subject)
**la compagnie que Starbrite a remplacée** 'which Starbrite has replaced' (= object)
**le monsieur qui vous reçoit** 'the gentleman who receives you'
**les dames qui sont en face** 'the ladies who are opposite'
**le truc avec lequel vous ouvrez** . . . 'the whatsit with which you open . . .'
**les difficultés auxquelles vous vous référez** 'the difficulties to which you refer'
**le sujet/la personne dont vous parlez** 'the subject/the person of which/whom you are speaking'

The interrogative pronouns are: **qui?** ('who'/'whom'); **que?** ('what'); **quoi?** ('what'); **qui est–ce qui?** ('who' – person); **qu'est-ce-qui?** (what' – thing); **qui est-ce qui?** ('whom'), **qu'est-ce que?** ('what' – object), **lequel/laquelle/lesquels/lesquelles?** ('which'/'which one(s)').
Here are some examples:

**Qui est à la porte?**

**Que voulez-vous?**
**A qui parlez-vous?**
**Quoi?**
**Qui est-ce qui a dit ça?**
**A qui est-ce que vous adressez cette proposition?** (To whom are you sending this proposal?)
**Qu'est-ce qui ne va pas?** (What's up?)
**Qu'est-ce que vous dites?**
**Laquelle de ces voitures est la tienne?**

# Prepositions

These are **de, à, avec, par, pour, en, dans, chez, devant** ('in front of'), **avant** ('before'), **en face de** ('opposite'), etc. **De** ('of', 'from') with **le** or **les** becomes **du** or **des**, e.g. **le directeur du personnel. A** (no accent when it is a capital) means 'at'/'to'/'in'; when combined with **le** or **les** it becomes **au** or **aux**, e.g. **aller aux toilettes. Dans** ('in') is more like the English 'inside' than **en** or **à**.

# Negatives

**Ne ... pas** ('not'), **ne ... jamais** ('never'); **ne ... plus** ('no longer'), **ne ... rien** ('nothing'); **ne ... guère** ('hardly'), **ne ... personne** (nobody), **ne .. aucun(e)** ('not one'), **ne ... que** ('only') surround the finite part of the verb.
    Examples:

**je ne sais pas** (I don't know)
**je n'ai rien fait** (I haven't done anything)
**cela ne plaît à personne** (nobody likes that)
**elle n'a plus de temps** (she has no time left)
**je n'ai que cinq minutes** (I only have five minutes)

# A last word about French grammar

There are many more aspects of French grammar than we have room for in this short section. It is hoped that this introduction will enable readers, with the help of the dual-language versions of the letters and situations and the footnotes in both sections, to understand the relevant text.

# Business Glossary

# Key to glossary

Grammatical abbreviations

| | |
|---|---|
| abbr | abbreviation |
| adj | adjective |
| adv | adverb |
| conj | conjunction |
| det | determiner |
| n | noun |
| nf | feminine noun |
| nfpl | plural feminine noun |
| nm | masculine noun |
| nmpl | plural masculine noun |
| pp | past participle |
| pref | prefix |
| prep | preposition |
| pron | pronoun |
| vb | verb |

Symbols

* denotes slang term
(GB) term particular to Great Britain
(US) term particular to USA

NB: Contexts are given in parentheses after term and part of speech
    or before multiple translations

   Parts of speech are provided for all headwords and for translations
   where appropriate. Subterms are only supplied with parts of speech
   where it is considered necessary to indicate gender or to avoid
   ambiguity

# French–English

**abandon** *nm* waiver *n*, abandonment *n*
**abandonner** *vb* abandon *vb*, waive *vb*
**abattement** *nm* reduction *n*, discount *n*
  **abattement fiscal** tax allowance
**abolir** *vb* abolish *vb*
**abolition** *nf* abolition *n*
**abondance** *nf* abundance *n*
**abonné** *nm* subscriber *n*
**aboutir** *vb* lead to *vb*, result in *vb* **aboutir à
un compromis** reach a compromise
**abrégé** *adj* abbreviated *adj*
**abréger** *vb* abbreviate *vb*
**abréviation** *nf* abbreviation *n*
**abroger** *vb* rescind *vb*
**absence** *nf* non-attendance *n*, absence *n*
**absent** *adj* absent *adj*
**absentéisme** *nm* absenteeism *n*
**absentéiste** *adj* absentee *adj*
**absolu** *adj* absolute *adj*
**absorber** *vb* absorb *vb*
**abus** *nm* abuse *n* **abus de confiance** breach
of trust **abus de pouvoir** abuse of power
**abuser** *vb* abuse *vb*
**accéder (à)** *vb* access *vb*
**accélération** *nf* acceleration *n*
**accélérer** *vb* expedite *vb*, accelerate *vb*
**acceptation** *nf* acceptance *n* **acceptation par
les consommateurs** consumer acceptance
**acceptation du produit par le marché** market
acceptance
**accepter** *vb* agree *vb*
**accès** *nm* access *n*
**accessibilité** *nf* accessibility *n*
**accident** *nm* accident *n* **accident du travail**
industrial accident
**accomplir** *vb* achieve *vb*, accomplish *vb*
**accord** *nm* agreement *n*, consent *n* **être
d'accord** *vb* agree *vb* **accord de clearing**
exchange clearing agreement **accord commercial** trade agreement **accord commercial
réciproque** fair trade agreement **accord
contingentaire** quota agreement **accord
formel** formal agreement **accord global**
package deal **accord international** international agreement **Accord Monétaire Européen** European Monetary Agreement
(EMA) **accord salarial** wages settlement **par
accord tacite** by tacit agreement **accord de
troc** barter agreement **accord verbal** verbal
agreement **d'un commun accord** by mutual
agreement

**accorder** *vb* grant *vb*, award *vb* **accorder un
prêt** grant a loan **accorder un rabais** grant a
rebate
**accréditer** *vb* accredit *vb*
**accroissement** *nm* increase *n*, rise *n* **accroissement de la valeur** (in value)
appreciation **accroissement de valeur** gain
in value
**accroître** *vb* expand *vb*, extend *vb* **accroître
la gamme** extend the range
**accumulation** *nf* accrual *n*
**accumuler** *vb* accumulate *vb*
**accuser** *vb* **accuser qn de qch** charge sb with
sth **accuser réception de qch** acknowledge
receipt of sth
**achat** *nm* purchase *n*, purchasing *n* **achat
fictif** fictitious purchase **achats et ventes**
buying and selling **achat à terme** futures
buying **achat de terrain** land purchase
**acheter** *vb* purchase *vb*, buy *vb*, bribe *vb*
**acheter qch à crédit** buy sth on credit
**acheter qch en gros** buy sth wholesale
**acheter qch d'occasion** buy sth second hand
**acheteur** *nm* vendee *n*, buyer *n* **acheteur de
maison** home buyer
**achever** *vb* complete *vb*
**acier** *nm* steel *n*
**acompte** *nm* down payment *n*, advance
payment *n*, instalment *n*
**acquéreur** *nm* buyer *n*, purchaser *n*, vendee *n*
**acquérir** *vb* acquire *vb*
**acquisitif** *adj* acquisitive *adj*
**acquisition** *nf* acquisition *n*
**acte** *nm* (law) deed *n* **acte judiciaire** writ **acte
translatif de propriété** deed of transfer **acte
de vente** bill of sale, deed of sale
**actif** *nm* asset **actif disponible à court terme**
quick assets **actif fictif** nominal assets **actif
immobilisé** fixed assets **actif net** net(t)
assets **actif caché** hidden assets **actif disponible** liquid assets **actif financier** financial
assets **actif immobilier** capital assets **actif
incorporel** intangible assets
**action** *nf* share *n*, action *n* **action en justice**
legal action **action nominale** registered
share **action ordinaire** equity share, ordinary share **action au porteur** bearer share
**actions en circulation** outstanding stock
**actions gonflées** watered stock
**actionnaire** *nm* stockholder *n*, shareholder *n*
**activité** *nf* (line of) business *n* **activité**

**boursière** trading
**actuaire** nmf actuary n
**actualiser** vb bring sth up to date vb (records) update vb
**adapter** vb (adapt) tailor vb, adjust vb
**adjoint** 1. adj deputy adj 2. nm deputy n
**administrateur** nm administrator n
**administration** nf administration n, civil service n, management n **administration des douanes et accises** the Board of Customs and Excise
**administrer** vb administer vb **administrer par fidéicommis** hold sth in trust
**adresse** nf address n **adresse commerciale** business address **adresse personnelle** home address
**adresser** vb address vb **adresser une soumission** lodge a tender
**AELE (Association européenne de libre échange)** abbr EFTA (European Free Trade Association) abbr
**aérogare** nm air terminal n
**aéroport** nm airport n
**affacturage** nm factoring n
**affacturer** vb (debts) factor vb
**affaire** nf deal n **l'affaire des fausses factures** the scandal of the bogus invoices **les affaires** nfpl business n **l'affaire est dans le sac** it is in the bag **une bonne affaire** a good deal
**affairisme** nm wheeling and dealing n
**affectation** nf appropriation n, assignment (to, for) n
**affiche** nf (advertising) poster n
**affranchir** vb frank vb
**affréteur** nm shipper n
**agence** nf branch n, branch office n **agence immobilière** estate agency, real estate agency (US) **agence locale** regional office **agence de messageries** express agency **Agence nationale pour l'emploi (ANPE)** employment agency, job centre **agence de presse** news agency **agence de publicité** advertising agency **agence de voyages** travel agency
**agent** nm agent n, commission agent n **agent d'assurances** insurance broker **agent de change** broker, stockbroker **agent financier** financial officer **agent général** general agent **agent immobilier** estate agent, realtor, real estate agent (US) **agent libre** free agent **agent maritime** shipping agent
**agraire** adj agrarian adj
**agrandir** vb enlarge vb
**agriculture** nf farming n, agriculture n
**agronome** nm agronomist n
**aide** nf grant n, aid n **aide extérieure** foreign aid **aide financière** financial aid
**aiguilleur** nm **aiguilleur du ciel** air traffic controller
**aîné** adj senior adj
**ajournement** nm deferment n, adjournment n

**ajourner** vb defer vb, adjourn vb
**ajustement** nm adjustment n
**ajuster** vb adjust vb
**aller** vb **aller à l'étranger** go abroad **aller (et) retour** return ticket, round-trip ticket (US) **aller simple** (rail/flight) single/one-way ticket
**allocation** nf (social security) benefit n allowance n **allocation de chômage** unemployment pay **allocation familiale** family allowance **allocation de maladie** sickness benefit
**allouer** vb grant vb, allocate vb
**alpha-numérique** adj alphanumeric adj
**amarrer** vb moor vb
**ambassade** nf embassy n
**améliorer** vb improve vb (value) enhance vb
**améliorer (s')** vb (improve) pick up vb
**aménagement** nm amenity n, planning n **aménagement du territoire** regional planning
**amende** nf fine n **faire amende honorable** vb make amends vb
**amender** vb amend vb
**amical** adj friendly adj
**amont** nm **en amont** upstream
**amorcer** vb (computer) boot vb
**amortir** vb (machine) write off vb, depreciate vb, absorb vb, amortize vb
**amortissement** nm redemption n, amortization n (machine) depreciation n
**analyse** nf analysis n **analyse des coûts** cost analysis **analyse coûts-rendements** cost-benefit analysis **analyse économique** economic analysis **analyse fonctionnelle** functional analysis **analyse horizontale** horizontal analysis **analyse du marché** market analysis **analyse numérique** numerical analysis **analyse des risques** risk analysis **analyse de système** systems analysis **analyse des tâches** job analysis **analyse de la tendance** trend analysis
**analyser** vb analyze vb
**analyste** nmf analyst n **analyste-programmeur** program analyst
**ancienneté** nf seniority n
**année** nf year n **année budgétaire** financial year
**annonce** nf advertisement n **annonce dans la presse** newspaper advertisement
**annuaire** nm **annuaire du commerce** trade directory **annuaire téléphonique** telephone directory
**annulation** nf cancellation n, abatement n, annulment n
**annuler** vb (offer) revoke vb rescind vb, cancel vb, abate vb **annuler une commande** cancel an order **annuler un contrat** cancel a contract **annuler un rendez-vous** cancel an appointment
**antidater** vb **antidater un chèque** backdate a cheque
**apogée** nf zenith n, at the height (of sth)

**appel** *nm* appeal *n*, call *n* **appel gratuit** Freefone (R) (GB) **appel d'offres** call for tenders **appel avec préavis** person-to-person call **appel téléphonique** telephone call **faire un appel d'offres** put sth out for tender

**apprenti, -e** *nm,f* apprentice *n*

**apprentissage** *nm* apprenticeship *n*

**approbation** *nf* approval *n*

**approuver** *vb* approve *vb*

**approvisionnement** *nm* sourcing *n*, supplying *n*

**approvisionner** *vb* supply *vb*, provide *vb*

**approximatif** *adj* approximate *adj*

**approximativement** *adv* approximately *adv*

**aptitude** *nf* ability *n*

**arbitrage** *nm* arbitrage *n*, arbitration *n*, switching *n* **arbitrage industriel** industrial arbitration

**arbitraire** *adj* arbitrary *adj*

**arbitre** *nm* arbitrator *n*

**arbitrer** *vb* arbitrate *vb*

**argent** *nm* money *n* **argent cher** dear money **argent comptant** spot cash **argent liquide** cash

**arithmétique** *nf* arithmetic *n*

**arrangement** *nm* (agreement) arrangement *n*

**arrêt** *nm* **arrêt de travail** (strike) stoppage

**arrêter** *vb* (inflation) halt *vb*

**arrhes** *nfpl* deposit *n*, payment on account *n*, advance payment *n*, cash advance *n*

**arriéré** *nm* backlog *n*, arrears *npl*

**arriérer (s')** *vb* fall/get into arrears *vb*

**arrimage** *nm* stowage *n*

**arriver** *vb* **arriver à un compromis** come to an accommodation **arriver sur le marché** hit the market

**article** *nm* item *n*, good *n* **article d'appel** loss leader **articles à forte rotation** fast-selling goods **articles de luxe** luxury goods

**assemblée** *nf* meeting *n* **assemblée extraordinaire** extraordinary meeting **assemblée générale annuelle** AGM (Annual General Meeting)

**assiette** *nf* (taxation) basis of assessment *n*

**assigner** *vb* assign *vb* **assigner qn** issue a writ

**association** *nf* partnership *n*, general partnership *n* **association commerciale** trading partnership

**associé** *nm* associate *n*, partner *n*, business associate *n*, general partner *n*

**assouplir** *vb* (credit) ease *vb* (restrictions) relax *vb*

**assumer** *vb* **assumer la responsabilité de qch** take charge of sth

**assurance** *nf* insurance *n*, indemnity insurance *n* **assurance automobile** car insurance **assurance bagages** luggage insurance **assurance à capital différé** endowment insurance, endowment policy **assurance chômage** unemployment insurance **assurance pour le commerce extérieur** export credit insurance **assurance détournement et vol** fidelity bond, fidelity insurance **assurance contre incendie** fire insurance **assurance maladie** health insurance, medical insurance **assurance maritime** marine insurance **assurance nationale** national insurance (NI) (GB) **assurance tous risques** all-risks insurance, comprehensive insurance, comprehensive insurance policy **assurances sociales** national insurance (NI) (GB) **assurance au tiers** third-party insurance **assurance vie** life assurance/insurance **assurance voyage** travel insurance

**assuré, -e** *nm,f* policy holder *n*

**assurer** *vb* insure *vb*

**assureur** *nm* insurance underwriter *n*, insurance broker *n*

**atelier** *nm* workshop *n* **atelier ouvert aux non syndiqués** open shop

**atout** *nm* trump card *n*, asset *n*

**atteindre** *vb* reach *vb*, attain **atteindre un objectif** reach an objective **atteindre le plancher** bottom out

**attendre** *vb* (on phone) hold on *vb*, hang on *vb*

**attente** *nf* expectation *n* **attente du consommateur** consumer expectations

**attestation** *nf* testimonial *n*, attestation *n*

**attribuer** *vb* assign *vb*

**attribution** *nf* awarding *n*, granting *n*, assignment *n*

**aubaine** *nf* windfall *n*

**audit** *nm* audit *n* **audit externe** external audit **audit interne** internal audit

**auditeur** *nm* auditor *n* **auditeur interne** internal auditor

**augmentation** *nf* (in earnings) rise *n*, raise (US) **augmentation de salaire** pay rise, wage increase, wage rise **augmentation des ventes** sales growth

**augmenter** *vb* (interest rate) raise *vb* (price) mark up *vb* (taxation) increase *vb*, expand *vb* (value) enhance *vb* **augmenter la production** increase output

**auto-évaluation** *nf* self-assessment *n*

**autofinancé** *adj* self-financing *adj*

**autogestion** *nf* self-management *n*

**automatique** *adj* automatic *adj*

**automatisation** *nf* automation *n*

**autonome** *adj* autonomous *adj*

**autoriser** *vb* license *vb*, authorize *vb*

**autorité** *nf* (official) authority *n* **autorités portuaires** harbour authorities

**autosuffisant** *adj* self-sufficient *adj*

**auxiliaire** *adj* auxiliary *adj*

**aval** *nm* **en aval** downstream

**avance** *nf* advance payment *n*, cash advance *n* (on salary) advance *n*

**avancer** *vb* (salary) advance *vb*

**avant-projet** *nm* tentative plan *n*, pilot study *n*, draft project *n*

**avantage** *nm* benefit *n*, avantage *n* **avantage comparatif** comparative advantage **avantage concurrentiel** competitive avantage, competitive edge **avantages divers** fringe benefits **avantages en nature** perquisites (formal), perks (informal)

**avantageux** *adj* advantageous *adj*

**avarie** *nf* accidental damage *n* **avarie commune** general average **avaries de route** damage to goods in transit

**avenir** *nfpl* **les perspectives d'avenir** future prospects

**avérer (s')** *vb* turn out *vb*

**avertir** *vb* warn *vb*

**avertissement** *nm* reminder *n*, warning *n*

**avide** *adj* acquisitive *adj*

**avion** *nm* aeroplane *n*, airplane (US) **les voyages en avion** air travel

**avis** *nm* **avis de crédit** credit note **avis de débit** debit note **avis de versement** remittance advice

**avocat** *nm* solicitor *n*, barrister *n*, lawyer (US)

**avoirs** *nmpl* **avoirs en devises** foreign exchange holdings **avoirs fictifs** fictitious assets **avoirs gelés** frozen assets

**azimut** *nm* compass point *n* **tous azimuts** all directions

**bailleur** *nm* lessor *n* **bailleur de fonds** backer **bailleur de licence** licensor

**baisse** *nf* fall *n* **à la baisse** falling

**baisser** *vb* (price, interest rate) lower *vb*, mark down *vb*, knock down *vb*

**balance** *nf* (financial) balance *n* **balance commerciale** balance of trade, trade balance **balance commerciale déficitaire** adverse balance of trade, balance of payments deficit **balance commerciale excédentaire** balance of payments surplus, favourable balance of trade **balance des paiements** balance of payments **balance sterling** sterling balance

**bande** *nf* **bande magnétique** (DP) magnetic tape

**banlieue** *nf* suburb *n* **grande banlieue** outer suburbs

**banque** *nf* bank *n* **banque d'affaires** merchant bank **banque centrale** central bank **banque de dépôt** clearing bank, commercial bank **banque de données** data bank **banque d'émission** issuing bank **Banque Européenne d'Investissement** European Investment Bank (EIB) **Banque Mondiale** World Bank

**banquier** *nm* banker *n* **banquiers suisses** the Gnomes of Zurich

**baratin\*** *nm* sales talk *n*

**barrière** *nf* barrier *n* **barrière douanière** tariff barrier, trade barrier **barrière à l'importation** import barrier **barrière tarifaire** tariff wall

**bas** 1. *adj* (price) low *adj* **bas de gamme** (product) down-market **basse saison** low season 2. *nm* bottom *n* **au bas** at the bottom

**bâtiment** *nm* building *n*, housing *n*

**bâtir** *vb* build *vb* **bâtir une réputation** build a reputation

**battage** *nm* **battage publicitaire** hype

**bénéfice** *nm* profit *n* **bénéfice brut** gross/pre-tax profit **bénéfice net** net(t) profit, net(t) earnings **bénéfice nul** nil profit **bénéfices** (business) earnings, earnings yield **bénéfices en diminution** falling rate of profit **bénéfices exceptionnels** windfall profit **bénéfices d'exploitation** operating profit, operating income **bénéfices d'exploitation** operating profit, operating income **bénéfices non distribués** earned surplus **faire des bénéfices** make profits

**bénéficiaire** *nm* payee *n*

**bénéficier à** *vb* benefit *vb*

**besoin** *nm* requirement *n* **besoins matériels** material needs

**bidon\*** *adj* mock *adj*, bogus *adj*

**bien** 1. *adj* **bien connu** well-known **bien fait** well-made **bien informé** well-informed, knowledgeable **bien payé** well-paid **bien rénuméré** well paid 2. *nm* **bien corporel** tangible asset **biens** *nmpl* chattels, goods **biens en consignation** goods on consignment **biens (de consommation) durables** durable goods **biens en cours** goods in progress/process **biens domestiques** domestic goods **biens d'équipement** capital goods **biens à l'essai** goods on approval **biens d'exportation** export goods **biens importés** import goods **biens ménagers** household goods

**bien-être** *nm* welfare *n*, well-being *n*

**bienfaiteur** *nm* benefactor *n*

**biennal** *adj* biennial *adj*

**bilan** *nm* statement *n*, balance sheet *n* **bilan financier** financial balance

**billet** *nm* ticket *n*, note *n* **billet aller et retour** return ticket, round-trip ticket (US) **billet de banque** banknote **billet de complaisance** accommodation bill **billet à ordre** promissory note

**bimensuel** *adj* bimonthly *adj*

**bloc** *nm* block *n*

**blocage** *nm* **blocage des salaires** wage(s) freeze

**blocus** *nm* blockade *n*

**bloquer** *vb* block *vb*, blockade *vb* **bloquer un chèque** stop a cheque

**BNPA (bénéfice net par action)** *abbr* earnings per share *npl*

**bogue** *nf* (listening device) bug *n*

**boîte** *nf* box *n* **boîte postale (BP)** PO box

**bon** 1. *adj* good *adj* **bonne volonté** goodwill 2. *nm* voucher *n*, token *n* **bon de commande** order form **bon de livraison** advice note, delivery note **bon du Trésor** government bond, Treasury bill

**bonification** *nf* **bonification pour non-sinistre** no-claim(s) bonus

**bordereau** *nm* note *n*, invoice *n* **bordereau**

**d'expédition** dispatch note
**bourreau** *nm* **bourreau de travail** workaholic
**Bourse** *nf* Stock Exchange **Bourse de New York** NYSE (New York Stock Exchange) *abbr* **Bourse des valeurs** Stock Market
**boycottage** *nm* boycott *n*
**boycotter** *vb* boycott *vb*
**brader** *vb* sell off *vb*
**branche** *nf* line of business *n* **être dans la branche** be in the business
**brevet** *nm* patent *n*
**breveté** *adj* patented *adj*
**bric-à-brac** *nm* junk *n*
**briefing** *nm* briefing *n*
**briseur** *nm* **briseur de grève** strikebreaker
**britannique** *adj* British *adj*
**brochure** *nf* brochure *n*
**broyeur** *nm* shredder *n*
**brut** *adj* (salary, weight) gross *adj* **bénéfice brut** gross profit **brut-inexpérimenté** (unprocessed) raw **marge brute** *nf* gross margin
**BTP (bâtiments et travaux publics)** *abbr* building and civil engineering
**budget** *nm* budget *n* **budget fixe** fixed budget **budget flexible** flexible budget **budget d'investissement** capital budget **budget publicitaire** promotional budget **budget de publicité** advertising budget
**bulletin** *nm* newsletter *n*, bulletin *n* **bulletin d'informations** news bulletin
**bureau** *nm* office *n* **bureau de change** bureau de change **Bureau Fédéral** Federal Bureau (US) **bureau d'importation** import office **bureau local** regional office **bureau de location** box office **bureau des objets trouvés** lost-property office **bureau de placement** employment agency **bureau de poste** post office **bureau de renseignements** information office **bureaux de douane** customs office
**bureaucrate** *nmf* bureaucrat *n*
**bureaucratie** *nf* bureaucracy *n*
**bureaucratique** *adj* bureaucratic *adj*
**butin** *nm* spoils *npl*
**cabine** *nf* (phone) kiosk *n*, booth (US) **cabine téléphonique** telephone box, telephone booth (US)
**cabinet** *nm* agency *n*, office *n* **cabinet de conseil** consultancy, consulting (US)
**cadastre** *nm* land register *n*
**cadet** *adj* junior *adj*
**cadre** *nm* executive *n* **cadre en formation** trainee manager **cadre moyen** middle manager **cadre supérieur** top manager, executive
**CAF (coût, assurance et fret)** *abbr* c.i.f. (cost insurance and freight) *abbr*
**caisse** *nf* cash desk *n* **caisse d'épargne** savings bank **caisse de secours** emergency fund **faire la caisse** cash up
**caissier, -ière** *nm,f* cashier *n*, teller *n* **caissier**

**principal** chief cashier
**calcul** *nm* assessment *n*, calculation *n*
**calculatrice** *nf* calculator *n*
**calculer** *vb* assess *vb*, calculate *vb* **calculer le coût de** cost a job
**camarade** *nmf* **camarade de travail** workmate
**cambiste** *nmf* money trader *n*, foreign exchange dealer *n*, exchange broker *n*
**camembert** *nm* (informal) pie chart *n*
**campagne** *nf* campaign *n* **une campagne ciblée** targeted campaign **campagne de publicité** advertising campaign, publicity campaign **une campagne de recrutement** recruitment campaign **campagne de vente** sales campaign
**candidat** *nm* (for job) candidate *n*
**candidature** *nf* (for a post) application *n*
**CAO (conception assistée par ordinateur)** *abbr* CAD (computer-aided or assisted design) *abbr*
**capacité** *nf* capacity *n* **capacité bénéficiaire** earning capacity **capacité excédentaire** excess capacity **capacité d'expansion** expand capacity **capacité industrielle** industrial capacity **capacité inutilisée** idle capacity **capacité de mémoire** memory capacity **capacité de production** manufacturing capacity **capacités en calcul** numeracy **les capacités requises** necessary qualifications **capacité de stockage** storage capacity **capacité de stockage** storage capacity
**capital** *nm* capital *n* **capital-actions** share capital **capital de départ** initial capital **capital dilué** watered capital **capital engagé** invested capital **capital fixe** fixed capital **capital initial** start-up capital **capital limité** limited capital **capital à long terme** long-term capital **capital-obligations** debenture capital, debenture stock (US) **capital risque** risk capital **capital de roulement** trading capital **capital social** registered capital **capital vendeur** vendor capital **capital versé** paid-up capital **capitaux fixes** fixed assets **capitaux mobiles** floating assets **capitaux propres** equity capital **capitaux spéculatifs** hot money **capitaux en surplus** funds surplus
**capitaliser** *vb* capitalize *vb*
**capitalisme** *nm* capitalism *n*
**capitaliste** 1. *adj* capitalist *adj* 2. *nmf* capitalist *n*
**capitalistique** *adj* capital-intensive *adj*
**caractère** *nm* **caractère numérique** numeric character **en caractères gras** bold type **en gros caractères** large type **en petits caractères** small type
**cargaison** *nf* cargo *n* **cargaison en vrac** bulk cargo
**cargo** *nm* cargo ship *n*
**carnet** *nm* **carnet de chèques** cheque book,

checkbook (US) **carnet de commandes** order book

**carrière** nf career n

**carte** nf card n **carte d'abonnement** season ticket **carte bancaire** cheque card **carte de crédit** credit card, charge card **carte d'identité** identity card **carte à mémoire** smart card **carte professionnelle** business card **carte de séjour** green card

**cartel** nm cartel n

**cash-flow** nm cash flow n **cash-flow actualisé** discounted cash-flow

**casier** nm **casier de consigne** left-luggage locker

**catégorie** nf category n **catégorie socio-professionnelle (CSP)** socio-economic category

**cause** nf cause n **à cause d'une erreur** due to an oversight

**causer** vb cause vb, bring about vb, issue vb

**caution** nf bail n, caution money n **caution fiduciaire** fiduciary bond

**CEB (comité de réglementation bancaire)** abbr banking regulatory council n

**CECA (Communauté européenne du charbon et de l'acier)** abbr ECSC (European Coal and Steel Community) abbr

**cent** nm hundred n **cent pour cent** one hundred per cent

**centralisation** nf centralization n

**centraliser** vb centralize vb

**centre** nm centre n, center (US) **centre commercial** business centre, shopping centre, shopping mall **centre de coût** cost centre **centre de formation** training centre **centre informatique** computer centre **centre de traitement** (DP) central processing unit (CPU) **centre-ville** town centre

**certificat** nm certificate n, clearance certificate n **certificat d'assurance** insurance certificate **certificat d'emploi** certificate of employment **certificat de marriage** marriage certificate **certificat d'obligation** scrip, bond certificate **certificat d'origine** certificate of origin, statement of origin

**certifier** vb certificate vb, certify vb

**cesser** vb stop vb, discontinue vb **cesser le travail** knock off* work, stop work

**cession** nf assignment n **cession de propriété** (ownership) transfer

**cessionnaire** nmf assignee n

**chaîne** nf **chaîne de fabrication** production line **chaîne hôtelière** hotel chain **chaîne de magasins** chain of shops, retail shops **chaîne de montage** assembly line

**chambre** nf room n, chamber n **chambre de commerce** chamber of Commerce **chambre d'hôtel** hotel accommodation

**chancelier** nm chancellor n **chancelier de l'Echiquier** Chancellor of the Exchequer (GB)

**change** nm (action) foreign exchange n

**changer** vb **changer d'adresse** change address **changer d'avion/de train** (transport) transfer

**chantier** nm site n, depot n **chantier de construction** building site **chantier naval** dockyard, shipyard

**chapardage** nm pilferage n

**charge** nf load n, charge n **charges fixes** fixed charges **charges indirectes** indirect costs **charge de travail** workload **charge utile** (of vehicle) payload

**charger** vb load vb

**chaud** adj hot adj

**chef** nm head n, chief n **chef comptable** chief accountant, head accountant **chef de famille** householder **chef financier** chief financial officer **chef du gouvernement** head of government **chef de service** head of department

**chemin** nm path n, way n **chemin de fer** railway, railroad (US)

**chèque** nm cheque n, check (US) **chèque bancaire** treasurer check (US) **chèque de banque** bank draft **chèque barré** crossed cheque **chèque en blanc** blank cheque **chèque en bois** dud cheque **chèque de change** exchange cheque **chèque non barré** open cheque **chèque non débité** unpaid cheque **chèque au porteur** bearer cheque **chèque sans provision** bad cheque, dud cheque **chèque qui est refusé** bounce* a cheque **chèque pour la somme de £100** a cheque for the amount of £100 **chèque de voyage** traveller's cheque, traveler's check (US) **faire un chèque à l'ordre de qn** make out a cheque to sb

**cher** adj expensive adj

**chercher** vb search vb, look for vb **chercher du travail** look for work

**chevalier** nm **chevalier blanc** white knight

**chiffre** nm figure n **chiffre d'affaires** turnover, trade figures **chiffre d'affaires brut** gross sales **chiffres consolidés** consolidated figures **chiffre des ventes** sales figures

**chimique** adj chemical adj

**chômage** nm unemployment n **être au chômage** be out of work **chômage généralisé** mass unemployment **être en chômage partiel** be on short time

**chômeur, -euse** nm,f unemployed person n

**chronométrage** nm timing n

**cible** nf target n

**circonstance** nf circumstance n **circonstances imprévues** unforeseen circumstances **circonstances indépendantes de notre volonté** circumstances beyond our control

**circulaire** nf (letter) circular n

**circulation** nf **circulation de marchandises** freight traffic **circulation routière** road traffic

**circuler** vb (document) circulate vb

**cité** nf town n, housing estate n, housing tenement (US)

**clair** adj clear adj

classe *nf* class *n* **classe affaires** (plane) business class
**classer** *vb* file *vb*
**classeur** *nm* filing cabinet *n*
**clause** *nf* (in contract) clause *n* **clause d'abandon** waiver clause **clause d'exclusion** exclusion clause **clause de négligence** neglect clause, negligence clause **clause résolutoire** escape clause **clause de sauvegarde** hedge clause (US)
**clavier** *nm* keyboard *n*
**client** *nm* client *n*, customer *n* **client fidèle** regular customer **client régulier** regular customer
**clientèle** *nf* clientele *n*
**climatisé** *adj* air-conditioned *adj*
**clôturer** *vb* wind up *vb* **clôturer une réunion** close a meeting
**COB (commission des opérations de bourse)** *abbr* SIB (Securities and Investment Board) (GB) *abbr*
**code** *nm* code *n* **code (à) barres** bar code **code de bonne conduite** code of practice **code des impôts** tax code **code postal** post code, zip code (US)
**codétenteur** *nm* joint holder *n*
**coercition** *nf* enforcement *n*
**COFACE** *nf* export credit agency *n*
**cogestion** *nf* joint management *n*
**col** *nm* **col blanc** white-collar worker **col bleu** blue-collar worker
**colis** *nm* parcel *n*
**collaborer** *vb* collaborate *vb*
**collatéral** *nm* collateral *n*
**collecte** *nf* **collecte des données** information retrieval
**collecter** *vb* collect *vb*
**collectif** *nm* collective *n*
**collection** *nf* collection *n*
**collègue** *nmf* colleague *n*
**colloque** *nm* colloquium *n*, conference *n*
**colporter** *vb* peddle *vb*
**comité** *nm* board *n*, committee *n* **comité consultatif européen** European Advisory Committee **comité d'entreprise** works committee, works council **comité exécutif** executive committee **comité de viligance** watchdog committee
**commande** *nf* order *n* **commande renouvelée** repeat order **commande urgente** rush order
**commanditaire** *nm* backer *n*, silent partner *n*, sleeping partner *n*
**comme** *prep* **comme prévu** according to plan
**commentaire** *nm* comment *n*
**commerçant, -e** *nm,f* trader *n*
**commerce** *nm* commerce *n*, trade *n* **commerce des armes** arms trade **commerce bilatéral** bilateral trade **commerce de détail** retail trade **commerce extérieur** foreign trade, overseas trade **commerce de gros** wholesale trade **commerce international**

export trade, international trade **commerce loyal** fair trade, fair trading
**commercial** *adj* commercial *adj*
**commercialisation** *nf* marketing *n* **commercialisation de masse** mass marketing
**commercialiser** *vb* market *vb*
**commissaire** *nm* commissioner *n* **commissaire aux comptes** auditor **commissaire-priseur** auctioneer
**commission** *nf* board *n*, committee *n*, commission *n*, commission fee *n* **commission consultative** advisory committee **Commission Européenne** European Commission
**commissionnaire** *nm* agent *n*, broker *n* **commissionnaire inportateur** import agent
**commode** *adj* convenient *adj*, handy *adj*
**communauté** *nf* community *n* **Communauté Européenne** European Community (EC)
**communication** *nf* communication *n* **communication interurbaine** long distance telephone call **communication en PCV** reverse-charge call, collect call (US)
**compagnie** *nf* company *n* **compagnie d'aviation** airline **compagnie en concurrence** competing company **compagnie de crédit** credit company **compagnie étrangère** foreign company **compagnie financière** financial company, finance company **compagnie de navigation** shipping line **compagnie à responsabilité limitée** limited company **compagnie de transport** transport company
**comparatif** *adj* comparative *adj*
**compatible** *adj* compatible *adj*
**compensation** *nf* compensation *n*
**compenser** *vb* compensate for *vb*, offset *vb* **compenser un chèque** clear a cheque
**compétence** *nf* ability *n*, expertise *n*, qualification *n*
**compétitif** *adj* competitive *adj*
**compétitivité** *nf* competitiveness *n*
**complet** *adj* comprehensive *adj*
**compléter** *vb* complete *vb*
**complexe** *adj* complex *adj*, intricate *adj*
**comportement** *nm* (behaviour) performance *n*
**compression** *nf* trimming *n*
**compromis** *nm* compromise *n*
**comptabilité** *nf* accountancy *n*, book-keeping *n* **comptabilité analytique** management accounting **comptabilité générale** financial accounting, general accounting **comptabilité en partie double** (bookkeeping) double-entry
**comptable** *nmf* accountant *n*, book-keeper *n*
**compte** *nm* account **compte en banque** bank account **compte chèque postal** post office (giro) account **compte clients** charge account **compte courant** current account **compte à découvert** overdrawn account **compte d'épargne** savings account **compte**

**d'exploitation** operating statement, trading account **compte joint** joint account **compte de profits et pertes** profit and loss account **comptes définitifs** final accounts **comptes d'exploitation trimestriels** quarterly trade accounts **comptes fournisseurs** accounts payable **faire le compte** do the sums
**compteur** *nm* meter *n* **compteur à gaz** gas meter
**comptoir** *nm* counter *n* **comptoir de liquidation** clearing house
**concepteur** *nm* designer *n*
**conception** *nf* design *n* **conception assistée par ordinateur (CAO)** computer-aided design (CAD)
**concerner** *vb* (be of importance to) concern *vb*
**concession** *nf* franchise *n*
**concessionnaire** *nmf* dealer *n*, authorized dealer *n*
**concevoir** *vb* design *vb*
**conclure** *vb* clinch *vb* **conclure un marché** clinch a deal **conclure un traité** make a treaty **conclure une transaction** close a deal
**concordat** *nm* winding-up arrangements *npl*
**concurrence** *nf* competition *n* **concurrence acharnée** cut-throat competition **concurrence déloyale** unfair competition **concurrence étrangère** foreign competition **concurrence internationale** international competition **concurrence loyale** fair competition **concurrence au marché** market competition **faire concurrence** compete
**concurrent** *nm* competitor *n*
**concurrentiel** *adj* competitive *adj*
**condition** *nf* term *n*, condition *n* **sans condition** unconditional **conditions avantageuses** favourable terms **conditions contractuelles** the terms of the contract **conditions de paiement** credit terms **conditions de travail** working conditions, working environment **conditions de vente** conditions of sale, conditions of purchase **conditions de vie** living conditions
**conditionnel, -elle** *adj* conditional *adj* **acceptation conditionnelle** qualified acceptance
**conditionnement** *nm* packaging *n*
**confection** *nf* **la confection** the rag trade
**conférence** *nf* conference *n* **conférence de presse** press conference
**confiance** *nf* trust *n*
**confidentiel** *adj* confidential *adj*
**confidentiellement** *adv* in strictest confidence *adv*
**confirmation** *nf* confirmation *n*
**confirmer** *vb* confirm *vb* **confirmer réception de qch** confirm receipt of sth
**conflit** *nm* dispute *n* **conflit social** labour dispute **conflit du travail** industrial dispute
**conformément** *adv* **conformément à** in accordance with
**congé** *nm* leave of absence **congé de mala-**

**die** sick leave **congé de maternité** maternity leave **congé payé** paid holiday
**conglomérat** *nm* conglomerate *n*
**congrès** *nm* congress *n*
**conjoncture** *nf* economic trend *n*
**connaissance** *nf* knowledge *n*
**connaissement** *nm* bill of lading *n*, export bill of lading *n* **connaissement de transitaire** forwarding note
**connecté** *adj* on-line *adj*
**connecter** *vb* **connecter en réseau** network *vb*
**conseil** *nm* advice *n*, board *n*, consultant *n* **conseil d'administration** board of directors, factory board **Conseil Européen** European Council **conseil financier** financial consultancy **conseil en gestion** business consultant **conseil en marketing** marketing consultant **conseil municipal** town council **Conseil de prud'hommes** industrial tribunal **conseil de surveillance** supervisory board
**conseiller** **1.** *nm* adviser/advisor *n* **conseiller financier** financial consultant **conseiller en gestion** management consultant **2.** *vb* **conseiller qn sur qch** advise sb about sth
**consentement** *nm* consent *n*
**consentir** *vb* agree *vb*, consent *vb*
**conséquence** *nf* consequence *n*
**conservation** *nf* retention *n*
**conserver** *vb* (goods) keep *vb*, retain *vb*
**conserverie** *nf* packing house (US) *n*
**considérer** *vb* consider *vb* **considérer l'affaire comme conclue** call it a deal
**consignataire** *nmf* consignee *n*
**consignateur** *nm* consigner/or *n*, shipper *n*
**consigne** *nf* left-luggage office *n*
**consigné** *adj* (deposit) returnable *adj*
**consolider** *vb* consolidate *vb*
**consommateur, -trice** *nm,f* consumer *n*
**consommation** *nf* consumption *n* **consommation mondiale** world consumption
**consortium** *nm* consortium *n*, syndicate *n*
**constructeur** *nm* builder *n*
**construction** *nf* **construction navale** ship-building
**consul** *nm* consul *n*
**consulat** *nm* consulate *n*
**consultant** *nm* consultant *n*
**consultatif** *adj* advisory *adj*
**consulter** *vb* consult *vb*
**consumérisme** *nm* consumerism *n*
**contacter** *vb* contact *vb*
**conteneur** *nm* container *n*
**contingent** *nm* quota *n* **contingent d'importation** import quota
**continuer** *vb* continue *vb* **continuer l'activité** keep the business running
**contourner** *vb* bypass *vb*
**contracter** *vb* **contracter une assurance** take out insurance
**contrat** *nm* contract *n* **contrat en bonne et due forme** formal contract **contrat d'hy-**

pothèque mortgage deed **contrat de location** hire contract **contrat de prêt** loan agreement **contrat à terme** forward contract, futures contract **contrat de travail** employment contract **contrat type** standard agreement

**contre** prep against prep **contre-réaction** negative feedback **contre espèces** for cash

**contrefaçon** nf forgery n, counterfeit n

**contrefaire** vb counterfeit vb

**contremaître** nm supervisor n, foreman n

**contresigner** vb witness a signature vb countersign vb

**contribuable** nm taxpayer n

**contribuer** vb contribute vb

**contribution** nf contribution n **contributions directes** direct tax

**contrôle** nm inspection n **contrôle des changes** exchange control **contrôle douanier** (customs) inspection, customs check **contrôle financier** financial control **contrôle de la production** production control **contrôle de qualité** quality control **contrôle des stocks** inventory control

**contrôler** vb make a check on sth vb, monitor vb

**convention** nf covenant n **convention collective** collective agreement **convention de fiducie** trust agreement **convention salariale** wage(s) agreement

**convenu** adj agreed adj

**conversion** nf conversion nf **conversion au système métrique** metrication

**convivial** adj user-friendly adj

**convoquer** vb call vb, summon vb **convoquer une assemblée** convene a meeting

**copie** nf copy n

**copropriété** nf joint ownership n

**copyright** nm copyright n

**coque** nf hull n

**corporation** nf guild n, trade n

**correspondance** nf correspondence n

**correspondre (à)** vb tally with vb

**corriger** vb correct vb, adjust vb **corriger les statistiques** adjust the figures

**corruption** nf bribery n, corruption n

**cosignataire** nmf cosignatory n

**costume** nm suit n

**cotisation** nf contribution n **cotisation à la Sécurité Sociale** social security contributions

**coup** nm **coup de pouce** boost n

**coupon** nm coupon n, voucher n

**cour** nm court n **cour d'appel** Court of Appeal, Court of Appeals (US) **Cour internationale de justice** World Court **Cour de Justice Européenne** European Court of Justice (ECJ)

**courant** adj normal adj, standard adj

**courbe** nf curve n **courbe d'expérience** experience curve **courbe de rendement** yield curve

**couronne** nf (Danish, Norwegian) krone n

**courrier** nm mail n, post n **courrier électronique** email, electronic mail **courrier exprès** express service **courrier recommandé** registered mail

**cours** nm currency n, price n, rate n **cours acheteur** buying rate **cours de clôture** closing price **cours légal** legal tender **cours d'ouverture** opening price **cours à terme** futures price

**coursier** nm courier n

**court** adj short adj

**courtage** nm brokerage n

**courtier** nm broker n, commission broker n, floor broker n **courtier d'assurances** insurance broker **courtier maritime** shipping broker **courtier de placement** investment adviser

**coût** nm cost n **coût estimatif** estimate of costs **coût d'immobilisation** capital cost **coût initial** original cost **coût marginal** marginal cost **coûts fixes** fixed costs **coûts de la main-d'oeuvre** labour costs **coûts de production** factory costs **coûts variables** variable costs **coût de la vie** cost of living

**coûter** vb cost vb

**couverture** nf insurance cover n **couverture à terme** forward cover

**créance** nf accounts receivable npl **créance fiscale** tax claim **créance irrécouvrable** bad debt

**créancier** nm covenantee n, creditor n **créancier hypothécaire** mortgagee

**création** nf **création d'emplois** job creation

**crédit** nm credit n **crédit à la consommation** consumer credit **crédit à l'exportation** export credit **crédit fixe** fixed credit **crédit illimité** unlimited credit **crédit libre** open credit **crédit à longue échéance** long credit **crédit relais** bridging loan, bridge loan (US) **crédits gelés** frozen credits **encadrement du crédit** credit control

**créditer** vb **créditer un compte** credit sth to an account

**créer** vb **créer une mode** set a trend

**créneau** nm niche n, market opportunity n **créneaux sur un marché** market opportunities

**crise** nf (economic) crisis n, slump n **crise monétaire** financial crisis

**critiquer** vb (disparage) knock vb

**croissance** nf growth n **croissance économique** economic growth **croissance entraînée par les exportations** export-led growth **croissance du marché** market growth **croissance zéro** zero growth

**cumulé** adj accumulated adj

**curriculum vitae (CV)** nm curriculum vitae (CV) n, résumé (US)

**cycle** nm **cycle économique** economic cycle, trade cycle

**dactilographier** vb type vb

**dactylographe** *nmf* typist *n*
**dactylographie** *nf* typing *n*
**date** *nf* **date d'expédition** date of dispatch
  **date d'expiration** expiry date, expiration
  date (US) **date de fraîcheur** best-before date
  **date de licenciement** termination date **date
  de livraison** delivery date **date prévue** target
  date
**déballer** *vb* unpack *vb*
**débit** *nm* debit *n*
**débiter** *vb* (account) debit *vb*
**débiteur** *nm* covenantor *n*, debtor *n*
**débouché** *nm* market opportunity *n*, market
  outlet *n*
**débourser** *vb* disburse *vb*
**décharger** *vb* unload *vb*
**déchet** *nm* spoilage *n* **déchets de fabrication**
  waste products **déchets industriels** industrial waste
**déclaration** *nf* statement *n* **déclaration en
  douane** customs declaration **déclaration
  sous serment** affidavit
**déclin** *nm* decline *n* **déclin économique**
  economic decline
**décomposition** *nf* (of figures) breakdown *n*
**déconseiller** *vb* **déconseiller à qn de faire qch**
  warn sb against doing sth
**décote** *nf* discount on share price *n*
**découvert** *nm* overdraft *n*, bank overdraft *n*
  **demander un découvert** request an
  overdraft **mettre un compte à découvert**
  overdraw on an account **mettre à découvert**
  overdraw
**dédit** *nm* (penalty) forfeit *n*
**dédommagement** *nm* compensation *n*
**dédommager** *vb* pay compensation *vb*
**dédouanement** *nm* customs clearance *n*
**dédouaner** *vb* clear sth through customs *vb*
**déductible** *adj* deductible *adj* **déductible des
  impôts** tax-deductible
**déduction** *nf* deduction *n*
**déduire** *vb* deduct *vb*
**défaut** *nm* defect *n*, default *n*, fault *n* **défaut
  caché** hidden defect **défaut grave** serious
  fault
**défectueux** *adj* defective *adj*
**défectuosité** *nf* defect *n*
**déficit** *nm* deficit *n* **déficit budgétaire** budgetary deficit **déficit commercial** trade gap
  **déficit démographique** population gap
**déflation** *nf* deflation *n*
**déflationniste** *adj* deflationary *adj*
**dégât** *nm* damage *n* **causer des dégâts** cause
  damage
**dégraissage** *nm* trimming **dégraissage d'actifs** asset stripping
**dégrèvement** *nm* **dégrèvement fiscal** tax
  alleviation
**délai** *nm* time limit *n* **délai de grâce** period of
  grace **délai de livraison** delivery time **délai
  de préavis** term of notice, notice period
  **délai prévu** due warning **dans les meilleurs**

**délais** as quickly as possible
**délégation** *nf* delegation *n*
**délégué** *nm* delegate *n* **délégué d'atelier**
  shop steward **délégué syndical** union
  representative
**déléguer** *vb* delegate *vb*
**délit** *nm* **délit d'initié** insider dealing, insider
  trading (US)
**délivrance** *nf* (of a patent) grant *n*
**délivrer** *vb* (tickets, policy) issue *vb*
**demande** *nf* request *n*, demand *n*, enquiry *n*
  **demande des consommateurs** consumer
  demand **demande d'emploi** letter of
  application **demande de règlement** request
  for payment **faire une demande** apply for
  **être en forte demande** be in great demand
  **l'offre et la demande** supply and demand
**demandeur** *nm* claimant *n*
**démarrage** *nm* start-up *n*
**démettre** *vb* **se démettre de ses fonctions**
  resign from office **démettre de ses fonctions** dismiss
**demi** *adj* half *adj* **demi-pension** half-board
  **demi-salaire** half-pay
**démission** *nf* resignation *n*
**démissionner** *vb* resign *vb*, quit (US)
**démocratie** *nf* democracy *n* **démocratie industrielle** industrial democracy
**démodé** *adj* out of date *adj*
**démographie** *nf* demography *n*
**dénationaliser** *vb* denationalize *vb*
**deniers** *nmpl* **deniers publics** public money
**denrée** *nf* commodity *n*, foodstuff *n* **denrées
  de base** staple commodities **denrées périssables** perishable goods
**déontologie** *nf* (professional) code *n*
**dépanner** *vb* repair *vb*, help out (in
  difficulty) *vb*
**départ** *nm* **départ entrepôt** ex store/
  warehouse **départ magasin** ex stock **départ
  usine** ex factory/works
**département** *nm* department *n*
**dépassé** *adj* obsolete *adj*
**dépasser** *vb* exceed *vb*
**dépense** *nf* expenditure *n*, expense *n* **dépenses d'exploitation** operating expenditure
  **dépenses d'investissement** capital outlay
  **dépenses des ménages** household
  expenditure **dépenses publiques** state
  expenditure
**dépenser** *vb* spend *vb*
**dépensier** *adj* spendthrift *adj*
**déposer** *vb* **déposer son bilan** go into
  voluntary liquidation
**dépôt** *nm* depository *n* **dépôt à long terme**
  long deposit
**dépression** *nf* (economic) depression *n*,
  slump *n*
**DEPS (dernier arrivé premier sorti)** *abbr*
  LIFO (last in first out) *abbr*
**député** *nm* Member of Parliament (MP) (GB)
**député européen** Member of the European

Parliament (MEP)

**dérapage** *nm* **dérapage sur les bénéfices** earnings drift

**dernier** *adj* last *adj* **dernier avertissement** final notice **dernière facture** final invoice **dernière offre** final offer, closing bid **dernier rappel** final demand

**dès que** *conj* **dès que possible** a.s.a.p. (as soon as possible) *abbr*

**description** *nf* **description du poste** job description

**designer** *nm* (commercial) designer *n*

**dessinateur** *nm* designer *n*

**dessous** *adv* below *adv, prep* **dessous-de-table** (bribe) sweetener* **au-dessous du pair** below par

**dessus** *adv* above *adv, prep* **au-dessus du pair** above par

**destinataire** *nmf* addressee *n*, recipient *n*, sendee *n*

**destiné** *adj* **destiné à promotion rapide** fast track

**détachement** *nm* secondment *n*

**détaillé** *adj* comprehensive *adj*, detailed *adj*

**détailler** *vb* itemize *vb*

**détenir** *vb* **détenir qch en garantie** hold sth as security

**détenteur** *nm* holder *n*

**détournement** *nm* **détournement de fonds** embezzlement

**détourner** *vb* embezzle *vb*

**dette** *nf* debt *n*, outstanding debt *n* **dette consolidée** funded debt **dette publique** national debt **dettes à court terme** current liabilities

**dévalorisation** *nf* depreciation *n*

**dévaloriser (se)** *vb* depreciate *vb*

**dévaluation** *nf* devaluation *n*

**devancer** *vb* forestall *vb*

**développement** *nm* development *n* **développement économique** economic development

**devis** *nm* quotation *n*, estimate of costs *n*

**devise** *nf* (currency) foreign exchange *n*, foreign currency *n* **devise convertible** convertible currency **devise faible** soft currency **devise forte** hard currency **devises étrangères** foreign currency

**devoir** *vb* owe *vb*

**diagramme** *nm* diagram *n*, chart *n* **diagramme de circulation** flow chart

**diffamation** *nf* libel *n*

**différé** *adj* (tax) deferred *adj* **paiement différé** deferred payment

**différer** *vb* (postpone) defer *vb*

**difficulté** *nf* **difficulté financière** financial difficulty

**diffuser** *vb* broadcast *vb*

**digne** *adj* **digne de confiance** creditworthy, reliable

**dilapider** *vb* squander *vb*

**dilué** *adj* watered *adj*

**diminuer** *vb* decrease *vb* **diminuer les impôts** reduce taxes

**diminution** *nf* shrinkage *n*, decrease *n*

**diplôme** *nm* academic qualification *n*

**diplômé** 1. *adj* qualified *adj* 2. *nm* (of university) graduate *n*

**direct** *adj* direct *adj*

**directeur** *nm* manager *n*, director *n* **directeur adjoint** associate director, assistant manager, deputy director **directeur de banque** bank manager **directeur financier** company treasurer **directeur général** general manager **directeur régional** area manager **directeur de succursale** branch manager **directeur d'usine** works manager **directeur d'usine** plant manager, works manager

**direction** *nf* management *n* **direction commerciale** sales management **direction générale** general management **direction par objectifs** management by objectives

**diriger** *vb* (manage) run *vb* (department) head *vb*

**diriger (se) (vers)** *vb* head for *vb*

**disponible** *adj* available *adj*

**disposer** *vb* arrange *vb*, display *vb* **disposer des données en tableau** tabulate data

**disposition** *nf* (stipulation) provision *n* **disposition facultative** option clause

**disque** *nm* disk *n* **disque dur** hard disk **disque magnétique** magnetic disk **disque souple** floppy disk

**disquette** *nf* disk *n*

**distributeur** *nm* distributor *n* **distributeur automatique** vending machine **distributeur de billets** cash machine/dispenser, automatic cash dispenser

**distribution** *nf* distribution *n*

**diversification** *nf* diversification *n*

**diversifier (se)** *vb* diversify *vb*

**dividende** *nm* dividend *n* **dividende de fin d'exercice** year-end dividend

**diviser** *vb* split *vb* **diviser en zones** zone *vb*

**diviser (se)** *vb* split *vb*

**division** *nf* (of company) division *n* **division du travail** division of labour

**dock** *nm* (for berthing) dock *n*

**document** *nm* document *n* **les documents** *nmpl* paperwork *n* **document de travail** working paper

**dollar** *nm* dollar *n*, buck* (US)

**DOM-TOM (départements et territoires d'outre-mer)** *abbr* overseas departments and territories

**dommage** *nm* damage *n* **dommages matériels** damage to property

**donnée** *nf* fact *n* **données** *nfpl* data *npl* **données disposées en tableau** tabulated data **données d'essai** test data

**donner** *vb* give *vb* **donner sa démission** hand in one's resignation **donner des instructions (à qn)** brief *vb* **donner sa parole** give one's word

**dossier** *nm* file *n*, brief *n* **d'après notre dossier** according to our records **dossier de candidature** application form

**dotation** *nf* appropriation *n*, endowment *n*

**douane** *nf* customs *npl*

**douanier** *nm* customs inspector *n*, customs officer *n*

**double** *adj* double *adj* **double de la facture** duplicate invoice

**douteux** *adj* (dealings) shady* *adj*

**droit** *nm* right *n* **droit d'auteur** copyright **droit civil** civil law **droit contractuel** law of contract **droit de copyright** copyright law **droit coutumier** common law **droit international** international law **droit pénal** criminal law **droit de propriété** (goods) title **droit public** public law **droit de recours** right of recourse **droits acquis** vested rights **droits d'amarrage** mooring rights **droits (de douane)** (customs) duty **droits exclusifs** sole rights **droit de sociétés** business law **droit des sociétés** company law **droits de port** harbour fees, harbour dues **droit du travail** employment law **droit de vote** voting right

**DTS (droits de tirage spéciaux)** *abbr* SDRs (special drawing rights) *abbr*

**ducroire** *adj* decredere *adj*

**dumping** *nm* dumping *n*

**durée** *nf* time frame *n* **durée de vie** life cycle

**durement** *adj* **durement gagné** hard-earned **durement touché** hard-hit

**dynamique** 1. *adj* dynamic *adj* 2. *nf* dynamics *npl*

**écart** *nm* difference *n* **écart d'inflation** inflationary gap

**échange** *nm* exchange *n* **échange avantageux** favourable exchange

**échanger** *vb* barter *vb* **échanger ses impressions** compare notes

**échantillon** *nm* sample *n*

**échantillonnage** *nm* sampling *n*

**échec** *nm* failure *n*

**échelle** *nf* scale *n* **échelle mobile** sliding scale **échelle des salaires** salary scale **à grande échelle** large-scale

**échelon** *nm* level *n* **à l'échelon national** at the national level

**échelonner** *vb* (payments) spread *vb*

**échouer** *vb* fail *vb*

**économe** 1. *adj* economical *adj* 2. *nm* bursar *n*

**économétrie** *nf* econometrics *n*

**économie** *nf* economics *n* **économie avancée** advanced economy **économie libérale** free market, free economy, free market economy **économie de marché** free market economy, market economy **économie mixte** mixed economy **économie mondiale** global economy **économie nationale** national economy **économie planifiée** planned economy **économies d'échelle** economies of scale **économie sous-développée** under-

developed economy

**économiste** *nmf* economist *n*

**écoute** *nf* **écoutes téléphoniques** phone tapping **heures de grande écoute** peak listening times

**écouter** *vb* **écouter (clandestinement) un appel téléphonique** bug a call

**écran** *nm* screen *n* **écran de visualisation** visual display unit (VDU)

**écu** *nm* ECU (European Currency Unit) *abbr*

**édition** *nf* publishing *n*

**édulcorer** *vb* water down *vb*

**effectif** *nm* workforce *n* **les effectifs** payroll

**effet** *nm* effect *n*, bill *n* **effet de commerce** bill of exchange **effet négociable** negotiable bill **effets escomptés** bills discounted **effets financiers** financial effects

**efficace** *adj* efficient *adj*, businesslike *adj*

**efficacité** *nf* efficiency *n*

**efficience** *nf* efficiency *n*

**effondrement** *nm* (of economy, company) collapse *n*

**effondrer (s')** *vb* collapse *vb*

**égaliser** *vb* equalize *vb*

**égalité** *nf* equality *n* **égalité des salaires** equal pay

**élaborer** *vb* (agreement, policy) work out *vb*, develop *vb*

**élasticité** *nf* (of prices) flexibility *n* elasticity *n* **élasticité de la demande** elasticity of demand **élasticité de la production** elasticity of production **élasticité-revenu** income elasticity

**élection** *nf* election *n* **élections législatives** general election **élections municipales** local election

**électronique** *adj* electronic *adj*

**électrotechnique** *nf* electrical engineering *n*

**élément** *nm* **élément d'actif** asset

**élever** *vb* raise *vb* **s'élever à** amount to *vb* **élever une objection** object, make/raise an objection

**élimination** *nf* **élimination des tarifs** elimination of tariffs

**emballage** *nm* packaging *n*

**embargo** *nm* embargo *n*, trade embargo *n*

**embauche** *nf* recruitment *n* **embauche de personnel** staffing

**embaucher** *vb* (person) hire *vb*

**émettre** *vb* (notes, cheques, shares) issue *vb*, broadcast *vb* **émettre un emprunt** raise capital *vb*, loan *vb*

**émigration** *nf* emigration *n*

**émission** *nf* flotation *n*, broadcast *n* **émission de droits de souscription** rights issue **émission de titres** share issue, stock issue (US)

**emplacement** *nm* location *n*

**emploi** *nm* use *n*, employment *n* **emploi permanent** permanent employment **emploi du temps** work schedule, timetable

**employé** *nm* employee *n* **employé de ban-**

que bank clerk **employé de bureau** clerk, clerical worker **être employé par une entreprise** be on the payroll **employé de magasin** shop assistant

**employer** *vb* employ *vb*

**employeur** *nm* employer *n*

**emprunt** *nm* loan *n* **emprunt d'état** government loan **emprunt extérieur** foreign loan **emprunt obligataire** debenture loan

**emprunter** *vb* borrow *vb*

**en** *prep* **en attente** (on phone) on hold **en circulation** in circulation **en ce qui concerne** with regard to **en cours de négociation** under negotiation **en-tête** letterhead **en ligne** on-line **en panne** out of action **en tant que (président)** in my capacity as (chairman)

**encaissement** *nm* cashing *n*, collection *n*

**encaisser** *vb* cash *vb* **encaisser un chèque** cash a cheque

**enchère** *nf* (auction) bid *n*

**enchérir** *vb* **enchérir sur** outbid

**encourir** *vb* (expenses) incur *vb*

**endetté** *adj* indebted *adj*

**endettement** *nm* **endettement des entreprises** corporate debt

**endetter (s')** *vb* get into debt *vb*

**endommager** *vb* damage *vb*

**endossement** *nm* endorsement *n*

**endosser** *vb* (cheque) endorse *vb*

**énergétique** *adj* energy *adj*

**énergique** *adj* high-powered *adj*

**enfreindre** *vb* contravene *vb*

**engagement** *nm* undertaking *n*, commitment *n*, bond *n*

**engager** *vb* commit *vb*

**enjeu** *nm* stake *n*

**enquête** *nf* enquiry *n* **enquête sur les ménages** household survey **enquête de solvabilité** credit enquiry **enquête sur le terrain** field investigation

**enseignement** *nm* **enseignement assisté par ordinateur** computer-aided learning (CAL)

**ensemble** *nm* complex *n*

**entamer** *vb* **entamer des pourparlers** begin negotiations

**entente** *nf* understanding *n*, working agreement *n*

**enterrer** *vb* **enterrer un projet** kill a project

**entraver** *vb* block *vb*

**entrée** *nf* **entrée libre** free entry

**entreposage** *nm* warehousing *n*

**entrepôt** *nm* warehouse *n*, entrepôt *n* **entrepôt-conteneurs** container depot **entrepôt de douane** customs warehouse **entrepôt frigorifique** cold storage plant **entrepôt sous douane** bonded warehouse

**entreprendre** *vb* undertake *vb*

**entrepreneur** *nm* entrepreneur *n*, contractor *n* **entrepreneur en bâtiment** building contractor **entrepreneur de transports** haulage contractor **entrepreneur de transports routiers** haulier

**entreprise** *nf* (project) enterprise *n*, company *n* **entreprise commerciale** trading company **entreprise familiale** family business, family corporation, family industry **entreprise gouvernementale** government enterprise **entreprise jointe** collaborative venture **entreprise leader** market leader **entreprise moyenne** medium-sized firm **entreprise privée** private enterprise **entreprise publique** state-owned enterprise **entreprise de transports routiers** haulage company, freight company (US) **petites et moyennes entreprises** small and medium enterprises (SME)

**entrer** *vb* **entrer aux docks** *vb* dock *vb*

**entretien** *nm* interview *n*, talk *n*, maintenance *n*

**entrevue** *nf* interview *n*

**enveloppe** *nf* enveloppe *nf* **enveloppe de paie** wage packet, salary package (US)

**envergure** *nf* scale *n*

**envoi** *nm* dispatch *n* **envoi recommandé** recorded delivery

**envoyer** *vb* send *vb* **envoyer par coursier** courier *vb* **envoyer un message par télex** (message) telex *vb*

**épargne** *nf* savings *npl* **épargne nette** net(t) saving

**éprouver** *vb* experience *vb*, suffer *vb*

**épuisé** *adj* out of stock *adj*

**épuisement** *nm* depletion *n*, exhaustion *n*

**épuiser** *vb* (stocks) run down *vb* (reserves) exhaust *vb*

**équilibre** *nm* equilibrium *n*, balance *n*

**équilibrer** *vb* balance *vb*

**équipe** *nf* team *n* **équipe de chercheurs** research team

**équipement** *nm* kit *n*, equipment *n* (installation) facility *n* **équipements** *nmpl* amenities *npl* **équipement vidéo** video facilities

**équiper** *vb* equip *vb*

**équité** *nf* (fairness) equity *n*

**ergonomie** *nf* ergonomics *n*

**erratique** *adj* (prices) volatile *adj*

**erreur** *nf* oversight *n*, mistake *n* **erreur de calcul** miscalculation **erreur d'écriture** clerical error

**escalade** *nf* (prices) escalation *n*

**escalier** *nm* **escalier roulant** escalator

**escompte** *nm* discount *n* **escompte de caisse** cash discount

**escroc** *nm* swindler\* *n*, shark\* *n*, embezzler *n*

**escroquerie** *nf* swindle\* *n*, racket *n*

**escudo** *nm* escudo *n*

**espèces** *nfpl* cash *n*, hard cash *n*

**essai** *nm* attempt *n* **à l'essai** on trial **essai sur le terrain** field test

**essayer** *vb* try out *vb*

**essor** *nm* expansion *n* **essor économique** economic boom

**établir** *vb* (company) set up *vb* **établir le**

**budget** draw up a budget **établir un budget pour qch** budget for (sth) **établir le solde** balance the budget

**établissement** *nm* establishment *n* **établissement de crédit** credit agency **établissement financier** financial institution

**étalage** *nm* (of goods) display *n*

**étaler** *vb* (holidays) stagger *vb* (payments) spread *vb*

**étalon** *nm* **étalon or** gold standard

**étanche** *adj* watertight *adj*

**état** *nm* state *n*, condition *n* **état financier** financial statement **état providence** welfare state

**étiqueter** *vb* label *vb*

**étiquette** *nf* label *n*

**étranger** *adj* foreign *adj*

**étroit** *adj* narrow *adj*

**étude** *nf* study *n* **étude de consommation** consumer research, consumer survey **étude de marché** market research, market research survey **étude des méthodes de travail** work study **études de gestion** business studies **étude sur le terrain** field research

**euro-capital** *nm* eurocapital *n*

**euro-obligation** *nf* eurobond *n*

**euro-sceptique** *nmf* eurosceptic *n*

**eurochèque** *nm* eurocheque *n*

**eurocrate** *nm* eurocrat *n*

**eurocratie** *nf* eurocracy *n*

**eurodevises** *nfpl* euromoney *n*, eurocurrency *n*

**eurodollar** *nm* eurodollar *n*

**euromarché** *nm* euromarket *n*

**européen, -enne** *adj* European *adj*

**évaluation** *nf* valuation *n*, estimate *n*, assessment *n*, appraisal *n* **évaluation des besoins** needs assessment **évaluation des performances** performance appraisal **évaluation des risques** risk assessment

**évaluer** *vb* estimate *vb*, assess *vb*

**évasion** *nf* **évasion fiscale** tax evasion/avoidance

**éviter** *vb* evade *vb*, avoid *vb*

**exact, -e** *adj* accurate *adj*

**exactitude** *nf* accuracy *n*

**examen** *nm* test *n*, examination *n*

**examiner** *vb* examine *vb*

**excédent** *nm* surplus *n* **excédent de bagages** excess luggage **excédent budgétaire** budget surplus **excédent commercial** trade surplus **excédent d'exportation** export surplus **excédent d'importation** import surplus **excédent de poids** excess weight

**exclure** *vb* exclude *vb*

**exécuter** *vb* carry out *vb*

**exécutif** *nm* (body) executive *n*

**exécution** *nf* accomplishment *n*

**exemplaire** *nm* copy *n*

**exempt** *adj* exempt *adj*

**exempté** *adj* duty-free *adj*

**exempté, -e** *adj* **exempté de droits de**

**douane** (goods) duty-free *adj*

**exemption** *nf* exemption *n*

**exercice** *nm* trading year *n* **exercice comptable** accounting period, fiscal year, financial year **exercice financier** financial year **exercice fiscal** tax year

**exigence** *nf* requirement *n*, demand *n*

**exiger** *vb* demand *vb* **exiger le remboursement d'un prêt** demand the repayment of a loan

**exonéré** *adj* **exonéré d'impôts** tax-exempt, tax-free

**exorbitant** *adj* exorbitant *adj*

**expansion** *nf* expansion *n* **expansion du capital** expansion of capital **expansion des échanges** expansion of trade **expansion économique** economic expansion **en pleine expansion** booming

**expédier** *vb* forward *vb* (goods) dispatch *vb*

**expéditeur** *nm* shipper *n*, sender *n*, freight forwarder *n*, dispatcher *n*

**expédition** *nf* shipment *n* dispatch *n*, consignment *n* **expédition partielle** part shipment

**expérience** *nf* **expérience professionnelle** track record, employment/work history

**expérimenté** *adj* experienced *adj*

**expert** 1. *adj* expert *adj* **expert comptable** chartered accountant **expert immobilier** chartered surveyor 2. *nm* expert *n*

**expiration** *nf* expiration *n*, expiry *n*, expiration (US)

**expirer** *vb* expire *vb*

**exploit** *nm* achievement *n*

**exploitation** *nf* (of business) operation *n* **exploitation minière** mining

**exploiter** *vb* exploit *vb* **exploiter un marché** tap a market

**exportateur** *nm* exporter *n*

**exportation** *nf* export *n*, export operations *npl* **exportations invisibles** export of capital, invisible exports **exportations mondiales** world exports

**exporter** *vb* export *vb*

**exposer** *vb* exhibit *vb*

**exposition** *nf* show *n*, exhibition *n*

**expropriation** *nf* expropriation *n*

**exproprier** *vb* expropriate *vb*

**expulsion** *nf* eviction *n*

**extérieur** *adj* external *adj*

**extorsion** *nf* extortion *n*

**FAB (franco à bord)** *abbr* FOB (free on board) *abbr*

**fabricant** *nm* manufacturer *n*

**fabrication** *nf* manufacture *n* **fabrication assistée par ordinateur** computer-aided manufacture (CAM) **fabrication en série** mass production

**fabriquer** *vb* manufacture *vb* **fabriqué en France** made in France

**facilité** *nf* facility *n*

**façonner** *vb* (adapt) tailor *vb*

**facsimile** *nm* facsimile *n*, fax *n*
**facteur** *nm* (general) factor *n* **facteur de limitation** limiting factor **facteur de production** factor of production
**facture** *nf* invoice *n*, bill *n* **facture impayée** unpaid bill
**facturer** *vb* invoice *vb*, charge *vb*
**faillite** *nf* bankruptcy *n* **en faillite** bankrupt
**fainéant** *nm* shirker* *n*
**faire** *vb* **faire appel** appeal *vb* **faire campagne** run a campaign **se faire une clientèle** win customers **faire concurrence (à)** compete, compete with a rival **faire la connaissance de qn** make the acquaintance of sb **faire défaut** default *vb* **faire une enchère** (auction) bid **faire une erreur** make a mistake **faire fortune** make a fortune **faire grève** strike *vb* **faire de la publicité (pour)** advertise
**faisabilité** *nf* feasibility *n*
**faisable** *adj* feasible *adj*
**falsification** *nf* falsification *n*
**faute** *nf* error *n*, offence *n*, fault *n* **faute de frappe** typing error **faute grave** gross negligence **faute professionnelle** malpractice **faute de renseignements** in the absence of information
**faux 1.** *adj* wrong *adj*, fake *adj*, false *adj* **fausse déclaration** *nf* false representation **faux frais** *nmpl* incidental expenses **faux numéro** *nm* (phone) wrong number **2.** *nm* counterfeit *n*, fake *n*, forgery *n*
**fax** *nm* fax (facsimile) *n*
**fédéral** *adj* federal *adj*
**fédération** *nf* federation *n*
**fermer** *vb* close *vb* **fermer boutique** (informal) shut up shop, go out of business **fermer un compte** close an account **fermer une entreprise** close a business
**fermeture** *nf* shutdown *n*, closure *n* **fermeture d'une entreprise** closure of a company
**ferraille** *nf* (metal) scrap *n*
**feuille** *nf* **feuille d'instructions** instruction sheet
**fiabilité** *nf* reliability *n*
**fiable** *adj* reliable *adj*
**fiche** *nf* form *n*, slip *n*, card *n*
**fichier** *nm* (computer) file *n* **fichier d'adresses** mailing list **fichier informatique** computer file
**fictif** *adj* fictitious *adj*
**fidéicommis** *nm* trusteeship *n*
**fidélité** *nf* fidelity *n* **fidélité du client** customer loyalty
**fiduciaire** *nm* trustee *n*
**file** *nf* **file d'attente** queue *n*
**filiale** *nf* subsidiary *n*, subsidiary company *n*, branch *n*, affiliated company *n* **filiale à cent pour cent** wholly-owned subsidiary **filiale offshore** offshore company
**fin** *nf* end *n* **fin de l'année budgétaire** fye (fiscal year end) *abbr*
**finance** *nf* finance *n*

**financé** *adj* funded *adj*
**financement** *nm* funding *n*, financing *n* **financement par capitaux propres** equity financing **financement déficitaire** deficit financing **financement par émission d'actions** equity trading **financement excédentaire** financing surplus
**financer** *vb* fund *vb*, finance *vb* **financer un projet** back a venture
**financier 1.** *adj* financial *adj* **2.** *nm* financier *n*
**fisc** *nm* Inland Revenue *n*
**fiscalité** *nf* taxation *n*, tax system *n* **fiscalité à taux zéro** zero-rate taxation
**fixer** *vb* **fixer un objectif** set a target **fixer un prix** fix a price
**FLB (franco le long du bord)** *abbr* FAS (free alongside ship) *abbr*
**fléchir** *vb* (market) weaken *vb*
**florin** *nm* guilder *n*
**fluctuation** *nf* fluctuation *n* **fluctuation des ventes** fluctuation in sales
**fluctuer** *vb* fluctuate *vb*
**fluide** *adj* fluid *adj*
**flux** *nm* **flux des capitaux** funds flow **flux de capitaux vers l'extérieur** capital exports
**foire** *nf* **foire-exposition** trade fair
**foncier** *adj* **propriété foncière** landed property
**fonction** *nf* (role) function *n* **fonction publique** civil service **fonctions de cadre** executive duties
**fonctionnaire** *nmf* civil servant *n*
**fonctionnement** *nm* (of machine) operation *n*
**fondateur** *nm* founder *n*
**fondation** *nf* (of company) formation *n*
**fonder** *vb* (company) found *vb*
**fonds** *nm* funds *npl* **fonds d'assurance** insurance fund **fonds commun de placement** investment fund, mutual fund (US) **Fonds de Développement Européen** European Development Fund (EDF) **Fonds Européen de Coopération Monétaire** European Monetary Cooperation Fund (EMCF) **Fonds Européen de Developpement Régional** European Regional Development Fund (ERDF) **fonds en fidéicommis** trust fund **Fonds Monétaire International** International Monetary Fund (IMF) **fonds propres** capital funds **fonds publics** public funds, public money **fonds de retraite** pension fund **fonds de roulement** working capital **Fonds Social Européen** European Social Fund (ESF)
**force** *nf* **forces du marché** market forces
**forfait** *nm* fixed sum *n*, set price *n*
**forfaitaire** *adj* flat-rate *adj*
**formalité** *nf* **formalités douanières** customs formalities
**formation** *nf* educational qualification *n*, employee training *n*, formation *n*, training *n* **formation des cadres** management training **formation de capital** capital formation **formation élémentaire** basic training

**formel** adj formal adj
**former** vb (staff) train vb
**formulaire** nm (document) form n **formulaire de déclaration de sinistre** claim form
**formulation** nf wording n
**fort** adj strong adj **fort en calcul** numerate **forte concurrence** tough competition
**fourchette** nf bracket n
**fournir** vb supply vb **fournir qch à qn** issue sb with sth **fournir des références** act as referee
**fournisseur** nm supplier n **fournisseur principal** main supplier
**fraction** nf fraction n
**fragile** adj handle with care
**frais** nm charge n **frais administatifs** administrative costs **frais d'annulation** cancellation charge **frais bancaires** bank charges **frais de banque** bank charges **frais de contentieux** legal charges **frais de déplacement** travelling expenses, travel expenses (US) **frais de douane** customs charges **frais d'entretien** maintenance costs **frais d'expédition** forwarding charges **frais d'expertise** consultancy fees, consulting (US) **frais fiscaux** fiscal charges **frais fixes** standing charges **frais de fonctionnement** running costs **frais généraux** overheads **frais indirects** indirect expenses **frais de location** hire charges **frais de manutention** handling charges **frais de port** delivery charges, carriage costs, carriage charge **frais professionnels** business expenses **frais de représentation** entertainment expenses **frais de transport** travelling expenses, travel expenses (US)
**franc** nm **franc belge** Belgian franc **franc français** French franc **francs constants** inflation-adjusted **franc suisse** Swiss franc **franc symbolique** nominal damages
**franchisage** nm franchising n
**franchisé** nm franchisee n
**franchiser** vb franchise vb
**franchiseur** nm franchisor n
**franco** adv free adv **franco à bord** free on board (FOB) **franco domicile** franco domicile **franco de fret** free of freight **franco le long du bord (FAS)** free alongside ship (FAS) **franco à quai** free on quay
**fraude** nf fraud n
**frauder** vb defraud vb
**frauduleux** adj fraudulent adj
**fréquence** nf frequency n
**fret** nm freight n **fret chargé sur palette** palletized freight
**frontière** nf frontier n
**fuite** nf **fuite de capitaux** flight capital
**fuseau** nm **fuseau horaire** time zone
**fusion** nf merger n, amalgamation n **fusion d'entreprises européennes** euromerger
**fusionner** vb amalgamate vb, merge vb
**gage** nm pledge n
**gagner** vb gain vb, earn vb, net vb **gagner de**

l'argent make money **gagner du soutien** win support **gagner sa vie** make a living
**gain** nm gain n **gains de productivité** productivity gains
**galopant** adj galloping adj
**gamme** nf product line n **gamme de produits** range of products **haut de gamme** top-of-the-range, up-market
**garant** nm underwriter n, guarantor n
**garanti, -e** adj secured adj
**garantie** nf warranty n, guarantee n **étendue de la garantie** extent of cover **garantie de qualité** quality guarantee
**garantir** vb (risk) underwrite vb
**garder** vb retain vb **garder sa parole** keep one's word **garder qch en réserve** hold sth in reserve
**gardien** nm warden n, caretaker n
**gare** nf station nf **gare routière** bus station
**gaspillage** nm waste n, wastage n
**gaspiller** vb waste vb
**gaz** nm gas nm **gaz naturel** natural gas
**gazoduc** nm gas pipeline n
**géant** adj king-size(d) adj
**gel** nm (on prices, wages) freeze n
**geler** vb (prices, wages) freeze vb
**générateur** adj **générateur de marge** profitable
**générer** vb **générer des revenus** generate income
**générosité** nf generosity n
**génie** nm engineering n **génie civil** civil engineering **génie maritime** marine engineering
**géographie** nf **géographie économique** economic geography
**gérer** vb manage vb, administer vb (money) handle vb **gérer une affaire** operate a business
**gestion** nf (of business) operation n management n **gestion de bureau** office management **gestion d'entreprise** business management **gestion financière** financial management **gestion hôtelière** hotel management **gestion de l'information** information management **gestion du personnel** personnel management **gestion des ressources humaines** human resources management (HRM) **gestion des stocks** stock control, inventory control (US) **gestion du temps de travail** time management **gestion transactionnelle** transaction management
**gisement** nm **gisement de pétrole** oilfield
**global** adj global adj
**gloire** nf kudos n
**goulot** nm **goulot d'étranglement** bottleneck
**gouvernement** nm government n
**gouverner** vb govern vb
**gracieux** adj complimentary adj
**grand** adj **grand ensemble** housing complex **grand livre des achats** bought ledger **grand**

livre de l'usine factory ledger **grand livre des ventes** sales ledger **grand magasin** department store **grand magasin à succursales multiples** chain store

**Grande-Bretagne** nf Great Britain n

**graphique** nm graph n, chart n **graphique en barres** bar chart **graphique circulaire** pie chart

**gras** adj **en caractères gras** in bold

**gratuit** adj free adj, complimentary adj

**grève** nf strike n, industrial action n **grève générale** general strike **grève légale** official strike **grève sauvage** unofficial strike, wildcat strike **grève sur le tas** sit-in strike **grève du zèle** work to rule, go-slow strike

**gréviste** nmf striker n

**grief** nm grievance n

**grille** nf scale n **grille des salaires** wage scale

**gros** adj big adj **en gros** in general, wholesale **gros ordinateur** mainframe computer **gros utilisateur** heavy user

**grossiste** nm wholesaler n

**groupe** nm group n **groupe de pays** group of countries **groupe de travail** working party

**grouper** vb bundle up vb

**guerre** nf war n **guerre commerciale** trade war **guerre des prix** price war

**guichet** nm ticket office n

**habitude** nf habit n **habitudes d'achat** spending patterns **habitudes de consommation** consumer habits

**hall** nm **hall d'exposition** exhibition hall

**hasard** nm chance n **au hasard** at random

**hasardeux** adj hazardous adj

**hausse** nf rise n **à la hausse** rising **hausse du taux d'escompte** rise in bank rate

**haut** adj high adj **haute classe** high-class **haute finance** high finance **haute saison** high season **haut de gamme** (product) up-market **de haut rang** high-ranking **hauts dirigeants** top management

**hebdomadaire** adj weekly adj

**héritage** nm inheritance n

**hériter** vb inherit vb

**heure** nf hour n **heure d'affluence** rush/peak hour **heure de fermeture** closing time **heure du méridien de Greenwich** GMT (Greenwich Mean Time) **heures de bureau** office hours **heures indues** unsocial hours **heures d'ouverture** opening times, office hours **heures ouvrables** business hours **heures de pointe** rush hour **heures régulières** fixed hours **heures supplémentaires** overtime **heures de travail** working hours

**hiérarchie** nf (corporate) hierarchy n **hiérarchie des données** data hierarchy

**homologue** nmf opposite number n

**honoraires** nmpl fee n

**honorifique** adj honorary adj

**horaire** nm **horaire flexible** flexitime n, flextime (US) **horaires normaux de travail** normal trading hours

**hors** prep apart from prep, except prep **hors intérêts** ex interest **hors-lieu** offshore **hors des limites** out of bounds **hors taxe** exclusive of tax **hors taxe** (goods) duty-free

**hôte** nmf host n

**hôtel** nm **hôtel cinq étoiles** five-star hotel

**huissier** nm bailiff n

**hydroélectricité** nf hydroelectricity n

**hygiène** nf **hygiène du travail** industrial health

**hyperinflation** nf hyperinflation n

**hypermarché** nm hypermarket n

**hypothèque** nf mortgage n

**hypothèse** nf hypothesis n

**île** nf island n **îles britanniques** British Isles

**illégal** adj illegal adj

**image** nf **image de marque** brand image **image de marque (de l'entreprise)** corporate image

**immatriculé** adj registered adj

**immobilier** nm real estate n

**immobilisations** nfpl fixed assets npl

**immobiliser** vb (capital) tie up vb

**impasse** nf stalemate n

**implication** nf implication n

**importateur** nm importer n

**importation** nf import n, importation n **importations invisibles** invisible imports

**importer** vb import vb

**imposer** vb tax vb **imposer des restrictions** impose restrictions

**imposition** nf taxation n **imposition sur les ventes au détail** retail sales tax

**impôt** nm tax n **après impôt** after tax **avant impôt** before tax **impôt sur les bénéfices exceptionnels** excess profit(s) tax **impôt sur le chiffre d'affaires** turnover tax **impôt sur les dépenses** expenditure tax **impôt direct** direct tax **impôt d'exportation** export tax **impôt foncier** land tax **impôt forfaitaire** flat-rate income tax **impôt sur la fortune** wealth tax **impôt indirect** indirect tax **impôt sur les plus-values** capital gains tax **impôt sur le revenu** income tax **impôt sur les sociétés** corporate taxation, corporation tax **impôt supplémentaire** surtax n

**imprudence** nf **imprudence de la part du sinistré** contributory negligence

**inattendu** adj unexpected adj

**incitation** nf incentive n **incitation financière** financial incentive

**incommode** adj inconvenient adj

**inconditionel** adj unconditional adj

**inconvénient** nm inconvenience n, disadvantage n

**incorporé** adj built-in adj

**indemniser** vb indemnify vb

**indemnité** nf indemnity n **indemnité de chômage** unemployment benefit **indemnité de départ** golden parachute **indemnité de licenciement** severance pay **indemnité de logement** accommodation allowance

**indépendant 1.** *adj* freelance *adj*, self-employed *adj* **2.** *nm* freelancer *n*
**indexé, -e** *adj* index linked *adj*
**indicatif** *nm* telephone code *n*
**indication** *nf* indication *n*
**indice** *nm* ratio *n*, index *n* **indice du côut de la vie** cost of living index **indice de croissance** growth index **indice Dow Jones** Dow Jones index, Dow-Jones average (US) **indice pondéré** weighted index **indice des prix** price index **indice des valeurs** share index
**indiquer** *vb* indicate *vb*
**indirect** *adj* indirect *adj*
**indisponible** *adj* not available *adj*
**industrie** *nf* industry *n* **les besoins de l'industrie** needs of industry **industrie aérospatiale** aerospace industry **industrie automobile** motor industry **industrie du bâtiment** construction industry **industrie chimique** chemical industry **industrie clé** key industry **industrie hôtelière** hotel industry/trade **industrie lourde** heavy industry **industrie minière** mining industry **industrie pétrolière** petroleum industry **industrie pharmaceutique** pharmaceutical industry **industrie plastique** plastics industry **industries agro-alimentaires** food industry **industrie textile** textile industry **industrie de transformation** processing industry
**industriel** *adj* industrial *adj*
**inefficace** *adj* inefficient *adj*
**inférieur** *adj* (goods) inferior *adj*
**infime** *adj* fractional *adj*
**inflation** *nf* inflation *n* **inflation galopante** galloping inflation
**inflationniste** *adj* inflationary *adj*
**infographie** *nf* computer graphics *npl*
**information** *nf* information *n* **les informations** *nfpl* news *n* **information sérieuse** hard news/information **informations financières** financial news
**informatique** *nf* computing *n*, information technology (IT) *n*, (electronic) data processing (EDP) *n* **qui connaît l'informatique** computer literate
**informer** *vb* inform *vb* **être trés bien informé sur qch** have a thorough knowledge of sth
**infraction** *nf* contravention *n*, breach *n*
**infrastructure** *nf* infrastructure *n* **infrastructure économique** economic infrastructure
**ingénierie** *nf* engineering *n*
**initié** *nm* insider *n*
**inscription** *nf* inscription *n*, registration *n* **inscription définitive** final entry **inscription au registre** ledger entry
**inscrit** *adj* registered *adj*
**INSEE (Institut national de la statistique et des études économiques)** *abbr* French national statistics agency
**insister sur** *vb* insist on *vb*
**insolvabilité** *nf* insolvency *n*

**insolvable** *adj* insolvent *adj*
**inspecter** *vb* inspect *vb*
**inspecteur** *nm* inspector *n* **inspecteur du travail** factory inspector
**instabilité** *nf* instability *n*
**installation** *nf* installation *n*, facility *n* **les installations** fixtures and fittings **installations portuaires** harbour facilities
**installer** *vb* install *vb*, instal (US) **installer des micros (dans une salle)** bug *vb*
**instituer** *vb* set up *vb* **instituer un fidéicommis** set up a trust
**institut** *nm* institute *n*
**institution** *nf* institution *n*
**instruction** *nf* instruction *n*
**insuffisance** *nf* deficiency *n*
**insuffisant** *adj* inadequate *adj*, deficient *adj*
**intégration** *nf* **intégration économique** economic integration **intégration horizontale** horizontal integration **intégration verticale** vertical integration
**intégré** *adj* built-in *adj*
**intendant** *nm* bursar *n*
**intensif** *adj* intensive *adj*
**intensifier (s')** *vb* escalate *vb*
**intenter** *vb* **intenter une action en justice** take legal action **intenter un procès** take legal action
**intéressant** *adj* advantageous *adj*
**intérêt** *nm* interest *n* **sans intérêt** interest-free **intérêt national** national interest **intérêt net** net(t) interest **intérêts bruts** gross interest **intérêts composés** compound interest **intérêts cumulés** accrued interest **intérêts personnels** vested interests
**interface** *nf* interface *n*
**intérieur** *adj* inland *adj*
**intermédiaire 1.** *adj* intermediary *adj* **2.** *nm* middleman *n*
**international** *adj* international *adj*
**intervenir** *vb* intervene *vb*
**intervention** *nf* intervention *n* **intervention de l'état** state intervention
**interviewer** *vb* interview *vb*
**introduire** *vb* (computer) key in *vb* (product) introduce *vb*
**invendable** *adj* unsaleable *adj*, unmarketable *adj*
**invendu** *adj* unsold *adj*
**inventaire** *nm* stocktaking *n*, inventory *n* **inventaire de fin d'année** year-end inventory
**investir** *vb* (money) invest *vb*
**investissement** *nm* investment *n* **investissement brut** gross investment **investissement étranger** foreign investment **investissement financier** financial investment **investissement net** net(t) investment **investissements des entreprises** corporate investment
**investisseur** *nm* investor *n*
**invitation** *nf* invitation *n*
**inviter** *vb* invite *vb* **inviter à un entretien** to

invite sb to an interview
**irrécouvrable** adj (loss) irrecoverable adj
**irrévocable** adj irrevocable adj, binding adj
**isoloir** nm (voting) booth n
**italique** adj **en italique** italic type
**itinéraire** nm itinerary n
**jaune** 1. adj yellow adj 2. nm strikebreaker n, scab* n
**jetable** adj disposable adj
**jeune** adj young adj **jeune économie** nf young economy
**joindre** vb enclose vb
**joint** adj joint adj
**joint-venture** nm joint venture n
**jour** nm day n **à jour** up to date **jour de congé** day off work **jour férié** bank holiday (GB) **jour ouvrable** working day, workday (US)
**journal** nm **journal d'entreprise** house journal/magazine **être à la une des journaux** hit the headlines
**journalisme** nm journalism n
**journée** nf **journée de travail** working day
**judiciaire** adj judicial adj
**jugement** nm judgement n **jugement qui fait jurisprudence** test case
**juré** nm juror n
**juridiction** nf jurisdiction n
**jury** nm jury n
**juste** adj fair adj **juste retour** fair rate of return
**justifier** vb rationalize vb
**kilométrage** nm mileage n
**kilowatt** nm kilowatt n
**krach** nm (stock market) collapse n, crash n
**label** nm **label de qualité** kite mark (GB)
**laisser** vb leave vb **laisser flotter** (currency) float
**lancement** nm (of product) launch n
**lancer** vb (product) launch vb (computer) boot vb **lancer un appel** appeal vb
**lancer (se)** vb **se lancer dans les affaires** set up in business vb
**langage** nm **langage de programmation** computer language
**langue** nf **langue de travail** working language
**large** adj broad adj
**laxisme** nm (laxity) slackness n
**lecteur** nm **lecteur de disques** disk drive
**légal** adj legal adj
**légiférer** vb introduce legislation vb, legislate vb
**législation** nf legislation n **législation du travail** labour law
**legs** nm legacy n, bequest n
**léguer** vb bequeath vb
**lettre** nf letter n **lettre recommandée** registered letter **lettre de canditature** letter of application **lettre de couverture** cover note **lettre de crédit** letter of credit **lettre de recommandation** letter of introduction
**liberté** nf **liberté de choix** freedom of choice
**libraire** nmf bookseller n

**librairie** nf bookshop n, bookstore (US)
**libre** adj **libre circulation des marchandises** free movement of goods **libre-échange** free trade nm **libre-service de gros** cash and carry
**licence** nf **licence d'exportation** export licence **licence d'importation** import licence
**licencié** 1. adj redundant adj 2. nm licensee n (of university) graduate n
**licenciement** nm redundancy n **licenciement abusif** unfair dismissal **licenciement arbitraire** wrongful dismissal
**licencier** vb (workers) lay off vb (employee) dismiss vb, sack vb, fire* (US)
**lieu** nm place n **lieu du colloque** conference venue **lieu commun** common place **lieu de travail** workplace
**ligne** nf **en ligne** (on phone) on hold **ligne ouverte 24 heures sur 24** hot line **ligne de produits** product line
**limitation** nf restriction n **limitation des salaires** wage restraint **limitation volontaire des salaires** voluntary wage restraint
**limite** nf limit n **limite de crédit** credit limit
**limité** adj limited adj
**limiter** vb **limiter les dégâts** minimise losses
**liquidateur, -trice** nm,f **liquidateur judiciaire** (bankruptcy) receiver n, administrator (US)
**liquidation** nf winding-up n, liquidation n, break-up n **liquidation des stocks** clearance sale
**liquide** adj liquid adj
**liquider** vb sell up vb, sell off vb, liquidate vb
**liquidité** nf liquidity n
**liste** nf **liste d'attente** waiting list
**litige** nm litigation n
**livraison** nf delivery n **livraison à domicile** home delivery **livraison gratuite** free delivery **livraison le lendemain** overnight delivery **livraison rapide** express delivery
**livre** nf (currency, weight) pound n (general) book n **les livres comptables** account books **livre sterling** pound sterling **livre verte** green pound
**livrer** vb (goods) deliver vb
**local** 1. adj local adj 2. nm room n **locaux commerciaux** business premises
**locataire** nmf tenant n, leaseholder n
**location** nf hire n **location de matériel** plant hire, leasing equipment **location-vente** hire purchase
**logement** nm accommodation n
**logiciel** nm software n, software package n
**logistique** nf logistics n
**loi** nf statute n, law n **loi de finances** Finance Act **loi des rendements décroissants** law of diminishing returns **loi qui réprime la publicité mensongère** Trade Descriptions Act **lois de succession** inheritance laws
**long** adj long adj **long terme** long term
**longueur** nm length n **longueur d'onde** wavelength

**lot** *nm* (auction) lot *n* (of goods) batch *n* **le gros lot** jackpot
**louche** *adj* (dealings) shady* *adj*
**louer** *vb* (house, office) rent *vb* (property) let *vb* (car) hire *vb*, rent out *vb* **à louer** for hire **louer à bail** lease *vb*
**loyer** *nm* rent *n*, rental *n*
**lucratif** *adj* lucrative *adj* **dans un but lucratif** profit-making
**machine** *nf* machine *n* **machine bien/mal conçue** a machine of good/bad design **machine à écrire** typewriter **machine de traitement de textes** word processor
**macroéconomie** *nf* macroeconomics *n*
**magasin** *nm* shop *n*, store (US) **magasin franchisé** franchise outlet **magasin à succursales multiples** chain store, multiple store
**magazine** *nm* magazine *n*
**magnat** *nm* tycoon *n*, magnate *n* **magnat de la presse** press baron
**magnétique** *adj* magnetic *adj*
**magnétoscope** *nm* video cassette recorder (VCR) *n*
**main d'oeuvre** *nf* labour *n*, manpower *n*, workforce *n* **main d'oeuvre contractuelle** labour contract
**maintenir (se)** *vb* **se maintenir au courant des événements** (events) keep up with *vb*
**mairie** *nf* town hall *n*
**maison** *nf* parent company *n* **maison de courtage** brokerage firm **maison d'édition** publishing house **maison mère** parent company **maison de vente par correspondance** mail-order house
**majeur** *adj* major *adj*
**majoration** *nf* markup *n*
**majorer** *vb* (price, interest rate) raise *vb*
**majoritaire** *adj* in the majority *adj*
**majorité** *nf* majority *n* **majorité suffisante** working majority
**maladie** *nf* **maladie professionnelle** occupational disease
**manager** *nm* manager *n*
**mandat** *nm* term of office *n*, money order *n*
**mandataire** *nm* authorized agent *n* **mandataire d'un actionnaire** nominee shareholder
**manier** *vb* handle *vb*
**mannequin** *nm* (fashion) model *n*
**manoeuvre** *nf* **manoeuvres dilatoires** delaying tactics
**manque** *nm* lack *n*, deficiency *n* **manque à gagner** shortfall **manque d'investissement** lack of investment
**manquer** *vb* (attempts) fail *vb*
**manuel** 1. *adj* manual *adj* 2. *nm* handbook *n* **manuel d'utilisation** instruction book
**manuscrit** *adj* handwritten *adj*
**manutentionner** *vb* (deal) handle *vb*
**marasme** *nm* slump *n*
**marchand** 1. *adj* mercantile *adj* 2. *nm* dealer *n*

**marchander** *vb* bargain *vb*
**marchandisage** *nm* merchandizing *n*
**marchandise** *nf* **marchandise non dédouanée** undeclared goods **marchandises** wares, goods **marchandises défectueues** faulty goods **marchandises délaissées** abandoned goods
**marchandiser** *vb* merchandise *vb*
**marchandiseur** *nm* merchandizer *n*
**marché** *nm* market *n*, deal *n* **marché acheteur** buyer's market **marché à la baisse** bear market **marché calme** quiet market **marché changeant** fluid market **marché des changes** foreign exchange market **Marché Commun** Common Market **marché au comptant** spot market **marché conclu!** it's a deal! **marché de détail** retail market **marché durement négocié** hard bargain **le marché s'est effondré** the bottom has fallen out of the market **marché des eurodevises** eurocurrency market **marché ferme** firm market, buoyant market **marché financier** capital market, financial market **marché de gros** wholesale market **marché immobilier** property market, real estate market (US) **marché intérieur** domestic market, home market **marché libre** open market **marché mondial** global market **marché monétaire** money market **marché noir** black market **marché à options** options market **marché secondaire** secondary market **marché à terme** terminal market **marché du travail** labour market **marché visé** target market **physionomie du marché** market trend
**marge** *nf* margin *n* **marge bénéficiaire** profit margin **marge brute** gross margin **marge commerciale** trading margin, return on sales **marge faible** narrow margin **marge de manoeuvre** room for manoeuvre
**marginal** *adj* marginal *adj*
**marine** *nf* marine *n*, navy *n* **marine marchande** merchant navy, merchant marine (US)
**maritime** *adj* marine *adj*
**Mark** *nm* Deutsche Mark deutschemark
**marketing** *nm* marketing *n* **marketing international** export marketing
**marque** *nf* brand *n* **marque déposée** registered trademark, proprietary brand **marque de fabrique** trademark, brand name
**masse** *nf* **masse monétaire** money supply **masse salariale** wages bill, (total pay) payroll
**matériau** *nm* material *n* **matériaux de construction** building materials
**matériel** *nm* (industrial) plant *n* (general) equipment *n* **matériel de bureau** office equipment **matériel informatique** computer hardware
**matière** *nf* **matières premières** *nfpl* raw materials *npl*
**matrice** *nf* matrix *n*
**mauvais** *adj* **mauvaise gestion** mismanagement **mauvaise nouvelle** bad

news **de mauvaise qualité** shoddy* *adj*
**maximiser** *vb* maximise *vb*
**MBA (marge brute d'autofinancement)**
**abbr** cash-flow
**mécanique 1.** *adj* mechanical *adj* **2.** *nf*
mechanical engineering **mécanique de précision** precision engineering
**mécanisme** *nm* **mécanisme du taux de
change** exchange rate mechanism (ERM) *n*
**média** *nm* media *n* **les médias** the media
**médian** *adj* median *adj*
**médiateur** *nm* mediator *n*, ombudsman *n*,
arbitrator *n*
**médiation** *nf* mediation *n*
**médical** *adj* medical *adj*
**mégaoctet** *nm* megabyte *n*
**meilleur** *adj* better *adj* **meilleur produit** *nm*
leading product
**membre** *nm* member *n* **membre à vie** life
member
**mémo** *nm* memo *n*
**mémoire** *nf* (DP) memory *n*
**mémorandum** *nm* memorandum *n*
**ménage** *nm* household *n*
**mener** *vb* **mener une campagne** wage a
campaign
**mensuel** *adj* monthly *adj*
**mention** *nf* reference *n*
**message** *nm* message *n*
**messager** *nm* messenger *n*
**messagerie** *nf* **service de messageries**
express carrier
**mesure** *nf* measure *n* **mesure financière**
financial measure **mesures anti-inflationnistes** anti-inflationary measures **mesures
d'économie** cost-cutting measures **mesure
de sécurité** safety measure **mesures fiscales**
fiscal measures
**mesurer** *vb* measure *vb*
**métal** *nm* metal *n*
**méthode** *nf* method *n* **méthode de classement** filing system **méthode empirique** hit-
or-miss **méthode de fabrication** production
method
**métier** *nm* trade *n* **de son métier** by trade
**être du métier** be in the business
**mètre** *nm* (measure of length) metre *n*, meter
(US) **mètre carré** square metre **mètre cube**
cubic metre
**métrique** *adj* metric *adj*
**métropole** *nf* metropolis *n*
**mettre** *vb* **mettre en boîte** box sth up **mettre
à l'épreuve** put sth to the test **mettre en
marche** (machine) turn on **se mettre à quai**
(ship) dock **mettre en vigueur** (policy)
enforce
**micro-économie** *nf* microeconomics *n*
**micro-ordinateur** *nm* microcomputer *n*
**microfiche** *nf* microfiche *n*
**microprocesseur** *nm* microprocessor *n*
**milieu** *nm* **milieux d'affaires** business circles
**milieux bancaires** banking circles

**million** *nm* million *n*
**millionnaire** *nm* millionaire *n*
**mine** *nf* mine *n* **mine de charbon** coal mine
**minérai** *nm* ore *n*
**mineur** *adj* minor *adj*
**minimal** *adj* minimal *adj*
**minimum** *nm* **minimum imposable** tax
threshold
**ministère** *nm* ministry *n*, government
department *n* **Ministère du Commerce**
Board of Trade (GB) **le Ministère des
Finances** the Treasury Department (US) *nm*
**Ministère de la Santé** Ministry of Health
**Ministère des Transports** Ministry of Transport
**ministre** *nm* minister *n* **Ministre des Finances** Chancellor of the Exchequer (GB)
**minorité** *nf* minority *n* **être en minorité** to be
in the minority
**mise** *nf* **mise en demeure** injunction **mise de
fonds** capital expenditure **mise de fonds
spéculative** venture capital **mise en oeuvre**
implementation **mise en vigueur** enforcement
**mission** *nf* assignment *n*
**mix** *nm* **mix des produits** product mix
**mobiliser** *vb* **mobiliser des capitaux** raise
capital
**modalité** *nf* mode *n*, method *n* **modalités**
terms and conditions
**mode** *nm* mode *n*, method *n* **mode de
paiement** method of payment
**modèle** *nm* (general) model *n* **modèle réduit**
small scale model
**modem** *nm* modem *n*
**modération** *nf* moderation *n*
**modéré** *adj* moderate *adj*
**modérer** *vb* moderate *vb*
**moderne** *adj* modern *adj*
**modernisation** *nf* modernization *n*
**moderniser** *vb* upgrade *vb*, modernize *vb*
**modification** *nf* amendment *n*
**modifier** *vb* amend *vb*
**module** *nm* module *n*
**moins** *adv* **moins-value** capital loss
**moitié** *nf* half *n* **(à) moité prix** half-price
**monde** *nm* world *n*
**mondial** *adj* global *adj*, worldwide *adj*
**mondialisation** *nf* globalization *n*
**monétaire** *adj* monetary *adj*
**monétarisme** *nm* monetarism *n*
**monnaie** *nf* currency *n* (coins) loose/small
change (from purchase) change *n* **monnaie
convertible** convertible currency **monnaie
de réserve** reserve currency **monnaie verte**
green currency
**monnayer** *vb* mint *vb*
**monopole** *nm* monopoly *n*
**montant** *nm* amount *n* **montant de l'adjudication** tender price **montant brut** gross
amount **montant de l'imposition** liability tax
**montant net** net(t) amount

**montée** nf (prices) escalation n **montée du chômage** rise in unemployment **montée du taux d'inflation** rise in inflation

**monter** vb rise vb **monter à bord** go aboard

**montrer** vb display vb

**mot** nm word n **mot-clé** (computer) keyword **mot pour mot** verbatim **mots à la minute** wpm (words per minute)

**motion** nf **motion de censure** vote of no confidence **motion de remerciements** vote of thanks

**mouvement** nm **mouvement de grève** strike action

**moyen, -enne** 1. adj medium adj, mean adj, average adj **moyen terme** medium term 2. nm means npl **je n'ai pas les moyens de l'acheter** I cannot afford it **nous avons les moyens de...** we have ways of... nf (average) mean n **moyenne arithmétique** arithmetical mean **moyenne pondérée** weighted average

**multilatéral** adj multilateral adj

**multinational** adj multinational adj

**multinationale** nf multinational company n

**multiplier (se)** vb multiply vb

**multipropriété** nf timeshare n

**mutuel, -elle** 1. adj mutual adj 2. nf **mutuelle** nf Friendly Society n

**mutuellement** adv mutually adv

**nantissement** nm collateral security n

**nation** nf nation n **nation commerçante** trading nation **Nations Unies** United Nations

**nationalisation** nf nationalization n

**nationaliser** vb nationalize vb

**nationalité** nf nationality n

**navette** nf shuttle n

**navire** nm **navire marchand** merchant ship

**nécessaire** adj necessary adj

**négatif** adj negative adj

**négligence** nf negligence n

**négligent** adj negligent adj

**négliger** vb overlook vb, neglect vb

**négociable** adj negotiable adj

**négociant** nm dealer n

**négociateur** nm negotiator n

**négociation** nf negotiation n, negotiating session n **négociations** (salaries etc) collective bargaining **négociations commerciales** trade talks **négociations salariales** wage negotiations

**négocier (pour)** vb negotiate vb

**net** adj net(t) adj

**neutre** adj neutral adj

**niveau** nm tier n, level n **à haut niveau** top-level **niveau d'emploi** level of employment **niveau d'inflation** level of inflation **niveau de vie** standard of living

**nom** nm name n **au nom de** in the name of **nom et prénom(s)** full name

**nombre** nm number n **nombre de chômeurs** unemployment figure

**nominal** adj nominal adj

**nomination** nf nomination n **nomination à un poste** (to a position) appointment

**nommer** vb nominate vb **nommer qn membre d'un conseil** nominate sb to a board/committee **nommer qn à un poste** appoint sb to a position

**non** pref **non assurable** uninsurable **non compensé** (cheque) uncleared **non confirmé** unconfirmed **non convertible** non-convertible **non discriminatoire** non-discriminatory **non entièrement souscrit** undersubscribed **non garanti** unsecured credit **non négociable** non-negotiable **non porteur d'intérêts** non-interest-bearing **non repris** non-returnable

**non-acceptation** nf non-acceptance n

**non-accomplissement** nm non-completion n

**non-cotisé** adj non-contributory adj

**non-essentiel** adj non-essential adj

**non-intervention** nf non-intervention n

**non-livraison** nf non-delivery n

**non-paiement** nm non-payment n

**normal** adj standard adj

**norme** nf norm n **norme de qualité** quality standard **normes comptables** accounting conventions **normes de conformité** trading standards

**notaire** nm solicitor n, notary n, lawyer (US)

**note** nf **note de frais** expense account

**notification** nf notification n

**nouveau, -elle** adj new adj **nouveau compte** new account **nouveaux clients** new business

**nouvelle** nf **bonne nouvelle** good news

**nouvellement** adj **nouvellement industrialisé** newly-industrialised **nouvellement nommé** newly-appointed

**nul** adj **nul et non avenu** null and void

**numéraire** nm cash n, specie n

**numérique** adj digital adj

**numéro** nm **numéro de commande** order number **numéro de compte** account number **numéro de référence** reference number **numéro de série** serial number **numéro de téléphone** telephone number

**objectif** nm objective n **objectif de production** production target **objectif de vente** sales target

**objection** nf objection n

**obligation** nf (stock exchange) bond n, obligation n, debenture n **obligation hautement spéculative** junk bond **obligation libellée en yen** yen bond **obligation nominative** registered bond **obligation au porteur** bearer bond **obligations fixes** fixed liabilities

**obligatoire** adj binding adj, obligatory adj **obligatoire irrévocable** legally binding

**observation** nf observation n

**observer** vb comply with legislation vb **observer les règles** observe the rules, comply with the rules

**obtenir** *vb* obtain *vb* **obtenir la communication avec qn** (phone) get through to sb **obtenir un crédit** obtain a credit **obtenir sa licence** graduate **obtenir une mise en demeure** take out an injunction

**occasion** *nf* bargain *n*, window of opportunity *n*, opportunity *n* **c'est une occasion** it's a bargain

**occupant** *nm* occupant *n*, occupier *n* **propriétaire-occupant** *nmf* owner-occupier *n*

**occupé** *adj* busy *adj*

**occuper** *vb* (premises) occupy *vb* **s'occuper d'un client** look after a customer *vb*

**octet** *nm* byte *n*

**offense** *nf* offence *n*, offense (US)

**officiel** *adj* official *n*

**offre** *nf* bid *n*, offer *n* **offre d'achat avec paiement comptant** cash offer **l'offre et la demande** supply and demand **offre écrite** offer in writing **offre d'emploi** job offer **offre d'essai** trial offer **offre ferme** firm offer **offre promotionnelle** bargain offer **offre provisoire** offer subject to confirmation **offre publique d'achat (OPA)** takeover bid **offre publique d'achat (OPA)** takeover bid **offre spéciale** bargain offer **offre supérieure** higher bid **offre valable jusqu'à...** offer valid until

**offrir** *vb* bid *vb*

**offshore** *adj* offshore *adj*

**oisif** *adj* idle *adj*

**oléoduc** *nm* oil pipeline *n*

**oligopole** *nm* oligopoly *n*

**omission** *nf* oversight *n*

**OPCVM (Organisme de placement collectif en valeurs mobilières)** *abbr* unit trust *n*

**OPEP (Organisation des pays exportateurs de pétrole)** *abbr* OPEP (organisation of petroleum exporting countries) *abbr*

**opérateur, -trice** *nm,f* dealer *n*, trader *n*, operator *n* **opérateur sur ordinateur** computer operator

**opération** *nf* (of business) operation *n* **opération au comptant** cash transaction **opérations bancaires à distance** telebanking **opérations de banque électroniques** electronic banking **opérations de change** foreign exchange dealings, foreign exchange tradings (US) **opération à terme** future commodity, forward transaction **opération de troc** barter transaction

**opérer** *vb* **opérer des coupes** (make cuts) axe* *vb*, ax (US)

**opposer** *vb* **opposer son veto à** *vb* veto *vb*

**option** *nf* option *n* **option d'achat** option to buy **option d'achat d'actions** share option, stock option (US) **option d'annulation** option to cancel

**optionnel** *adj* optional *adj*

**or** *nm* gold *n* **or en barre** gold bullion **or en lingots** ingot gold

**ordinaire** *adj* ordinary *adj*, regular *adj*

**ordinateur** *nm* computer *n* **ordinateur individuel** personal computer (PC) **ordinateur portable** portable computer

**ordonnance** *nf* **ordonnance de mise en liquidation** winding-up order **ordonnance de paiement** warrant for payment

**ordre** *nm* **ordre du jour** agenda **ordre de virement permanent** standing order

**organigramme** *nm* organization chart *n*

**organisation** *nf* organization *n* **organisation caritative** charity, charitable trust **organisation fonctionnelle** functional organization **organisation internationale** international organization

**organisé** *adj* organized *adj*

**organiser** *vb* organize *vb* **organiser un colloque** arrange a conference

**organisme** *nm* **organisme de crédit** credit institution

**orientation** *nf* **orientation des prix** price trend **orientation professionnelle** career(s) guidance

**origine** *nf* origin *n*

**oublier** *vb* overlook *vb*

**outre-mer** *adv* overseas *adv*

**ouvert** *adj* open *adj*

**ouverture** *nf* opening *n* **faire une ouverture** to make a tentative offer

**ouvrier, -ière** *nm,f* labourer *n*, worker *n* **ouvrier membre du conseil d'administration** worker-director **ouvrier qualifié** skilled worker **ouvrier spécialisé** unskilled worker

**ouvrir** *vb* **ouvrir un compte** open an account **ouvrir le marché** open up the market *vb*

**PAC (Politique Agricole Commune)** *abbr* CAP (Common Agricultural Policy) *abbr*

**paie** *nf* pay *n*, salary *n*, wages *npl*

**paiement** *nm* payment *n* **demander un paiement** to charge a fee **paiement d'avance** prepayment **paiement comptant** cash payment **paiement à la livraison** COD (cash on delivery), (collect on delivery) (US) **paiements échelonnés** staged payments **paiement symbolique** token payment

**palette** *nf* pallet *n*

**panier** *nm* **panier de devises** basket of currencies

**panne** *nf* breakdown *n*

**panneau** *nm* **panneau avertisseur** warning sign

**paperasserie** *nf* red tape *n*

**papier** *nm* **papier commercial** commercial paper **papier-monnaie** paper currency **papier de première classe** first-class paper

**paquet** *nm* block *n*, bundle *n*, pack *n*, packet *n*

**par** *prep* **par an** per annum, per year **par avion** by plane **par coursier** by courier service **par étapes** in stages **par heure de production** per hour output **par semaine** per week **par tête** per capita, per head **par transport routier** by road

**parenthèse** *nf* bracket *n*

**parité** *nf* parity *n*

**parlement** *nm* Parliament *n* **Parlement Européen** European Parliament

**parler** *vb* **parler affaires** talk business **parler boutique** (informal) talk shop

**parrainage** *nm* patronage *n*

**part** *nf* share *n* **part de marché** market share **part(s)** (share) equity

**partage** *nm* **partage des gains** gain sharing **partage du travail** work sharing

**partager** *vb* share *vb* **partager les responsabilités** share the responsibilities

**partenaire** *nm* **partenaire commercial** trading partner

**participation** *nf* profit-sharing scheme *n* (company) equity interest *n* **participation majoritaire/minoritaire** majority/minority holding

**participer** *vb* **participer aux bénéfices** to share in the profits

**partie** *nf* **partie prenante** stakeholder **partie d'un procès** litigant **parties contractantes** the contracting parties

**partiel** *adj* partial *adj*

**partir** *vb* leave *vb*

**passager** *nm* passenger *n* **passager en transit** (t.ansport) transit passenger

**passation** *nf* **passation par pertes et profits** write-off *n*

**passer** *vb* **passer une commande** place an order **passer en fraude** smuggle **passer par profits et pertes** (debts) write off **passer quelqu'un à** (call) transfer *vb* **passer en tête** take the lead

**passible** *adj* **passible de dommages-intérêts** liable for damages **passible de l'impôt** liable for tax

**patrimoine** *nm* **patrimoine géré par fedéicommis** trust estate **patrimoine national** national wealth

**patron** *nm* boss *n*

**pause** *nf* **faire une pause** take a break

**payable** *adj* **payable d'avance** payable in advance **payable à la commande** cash with order, cash before delivery **payable à la livraison** cash on delivery **payable à (la) réception** cash on receipt of goods

**payé** *adj* paid *adj*

**payer** *vb* pay *vb* **faire payer qch** charge for sth **payer l'addition** pay a bill **payer en argent liquide** pay in cash **payer d'avance** pay in advance **payer pa. carte bancaire** pay by credit card **payer par chèque** pay by cheque **payer comptant** pay in cash **payer en espèces** pay in cash **payer des honoraires** pay a fee **payer des intérêts** pay interest **payer à l'ordre de...** pay to the order of **payer un service** pay for a service

**pays** *nm* country *n* **pays d'acceuil** host country **pays avancé** advanced country **pays d'origine** country of origin **pays pétrolier** oil state **pays de résidence** home country **pays sous-développé** underdeveloped country **pays du Tiers Monde** third-world country **pays en voie de développement** developing country, developing economy

**péage** *nm* toll *n*

**pénétration** *nf* **pénétration du marché** market penetration

**pension** *nf* pension *n*

**pénurie** *nf* scarcity *n*, shortage *n*

**PEPS** *abbr* **premier entré premier sorti** FIFO (first in first out) *abbr*

**percée** *nf* **faire une percée** make a breakthrough

**percer** *vb* **percer sur un marché** to break into a market

**percevoir** *vb* **percevoir des impôts** levy taxes

**perdre** *vb* forfeit *vb* **perdre de la clientèle** (custom) lose **perdre la partie** go to the wall **perdre de la valeur** lose value

**péréquation** *nf* **péréquation des charges** equalization of burdens

**performance** *nf* **performance économique** economic performance

**périmé** *adj* out of date *adj*

**période** *nf* timescale *n*, period *n* **période d'essai** trial period **période d'exonération fiscale** tax holiday **période d'intérêt** interest period **période de pointe** peak period

**périphérique** *adj* peripheral *adj*

**périssable** *adj* perishable *adj*

**permis** *nm* licence *n*, permit *n* **permis de construire** building permit **permis de travail** work permit

**permission** *nf* leave *n*, authorization *n*

**personne** *nf* **personne nommée** nominee

**personnel** **1.** *adj* personal *adj* **2.** *nm* staff *n* **personnel de bureau** office staff **personnel compétent** qualified personnel **personnel d'encadrement** executive personnel

**perspective** *nf* prospect *n* **perspective économique** business outlook

**perte** *nf* forfeit *n*, forfeiture *n*, loss *n*, waste *n* **perte brute** gross loss **perte comptable** paper loss **perte en cours de route** lost in transit **perte d'emploi** loss of job **perte nette** net(t) loss **perte de revenus** loss of earnings **perte sèche** clear loss **pertes et profits** profit and loss **perte de temps** waste of time

**pertinent** *adj* relevant *adj*

**peser** *vb* **peser le pour et le contre** weigh up the pros and the cons

**peseta** *nf* peseta *n*

**petit** *adj* small *adj* **petit défaut** minor fault **petite annonce** classified advertisement, small ads **en petits caractères** in lower case

**pétrodollar** *nm* petrodollar *n*

**pétrolier** *nm* oil tanker *n* **pétrolier géant** supertanker

**peu** *adv* little *adv* **peu rentable** unprofitable **peu satisfaisant** unsatisfactory

**pharmaceutique** *adj* pharmaceutical *adj*
**photocopie** *nf* photocopy *n*
**photocopier** *vb* photocopy *vb*, xerox *vb*
**photocopieur** *nm* (machine) Xerox (R) *n*
**photocopieuse** *nf* photocopier *n*, copier *n*
**PIB (Produit Intérieur Brut)** *abbr* GDP (Gross Domestic Product) *abbr*
**pièce** *nf* (of a machine) part *n* **pièce jointe (p.j.)** enclosure **pièce d'or** gold coin **pièce de rechange** (for machine) spare part
**pipeline** *nm* pipeline *n*
**piquet** *nm* **piquet de grève** strike picket
**piratage** *nm* **piratage de logiciels** software piracy
**piraterie** *nf* (at sea) piracy *n*
**placard** *nm* broadsheet *n*
**plafond** *nm* (on prices) ceiling *n*
**plafonner** *vb* put a ceiling on sth *vb*, cap *vb* **plafonner le taux d'intérêt** cap the interest rate
**plaindre (se)** *vb* make a complaint *vb*
**plainte** *nf* complaint *n*
**plan** *nm* project *n* **plan de campagne** plan of campaign **plan pyramidal** pyramid scheme **plan de redressement** recovery scheme **plan de vente** sales plan
**planification** *nf* planning *n* **planification centralisée** central planning **planification financière** financial planning
**planifier** *vb* plan *vb*
**plein** *adj* **plein emploi** full employment
**plénier** *adj* (assembly, session) plenary *adj*
**plus-value** *nf* capital gain (in value) appreciation *n*
**PNB (Produit National Brut)** *abbr* GNP (Gross National Product) *abbr*
**poids** *nm* weight *n* **poids brut** gross weight **poids lourd** heavy goods vehicle **poids et mesures** weights and measures **poids net** net(t) weight
**poignée** *nf* **poignée de main** handshake *n*
**poinçon** *nm* hallmark *n*
**point** *nm* **point de vente** point of sale, retail outlet, sales outlet
**pointe** *nf* peak *n* **de pointe** hi-tech **technologie de pointe** advanced technology
**pointer** *vb* clock in *vb*
**police** *nf* policy *n* **police d'assurance** insurance contract, insurance policy
**politique** 1. *adj* political *adj* 2. *nf* politics *n*, policy *n* **Politique Agricole Commune** Common Agricultural Policy (CAP) **politique budgétaire** budgetary policy **politique de commerce loyal** fair-trade policy **politique de croissance** growth strategy **politique économique** economic policy **politique financière** financial policy **politique fiscale** fiscal policy **politique gouvernementale** government policy **politique monétaire** monetary policy **politique des prix** pricing policy **politique salariale** wage policy **politique de la société** company policy

**polyvalent** *adj* multipurpose *adj*
**pondéré** *adj* weighted *adj*
**population** *nf* **population active** working population
**port** *nm* port *n*, postage *n*, carriage *n*, harbour *n* **port dû** carriage forward **port d'entrée** port of entry **port payé** Freepost (R) (GB), carriage paid, carriage included
**portable** *nm* laptop computer *n*
**portatif** *adj* portable *adj*
**porte** *nf* **porte-à-porte** door-to-door selling
**porte-conteneurs** *nm* container ship *n*
**porte-parole** *nm* spokesperson *n*
**portefeuille** *nm* **portefeuille d'investissements** investment portfolio
**porter** *vb* **porter des intérêts** bear interest
**porteur** *nm* bearer *n* **porteur d'obligations** bondholder
**poser** *vb* **poser sa candidature à** apply for
**posséder** *vb* own *vb*
**possession** *nf* ownership *n*
**postal** *adj* postal *adj*
**postdater** *vb* postdate *vb*
**poste** *nm* (job) post *n* **poste vacant** vacancy *nf* (service) post *n* **poste aérienne** airmail **poste restante** poste restante, general delivery (US)
**poster** *vb* post *vb*
**pot-de-vin** *nm* bribe *n*, backhander *n*, sweetener* *n*, payola (US)
**potentiel** *nm* potential *n* **potentiel de ventes** sales potential
**pour** *prep* **pour et contre** for and against **pour cent** per cent **pour des raisons imprévues** due to unforeseen circumstances
**pourboire** *nm* gratuity *n*
**pourcentage** *nm* percentage *n* **pourcentage des bénéfices** percentage of profit
**pouvoir** *nm* power *n* (official) authority *n* **pouvoir d'achat** buying power, purchasing power
**pratique** 1. *adj* convenient *adj* 2. *nf* **pratique commerciale loyale** fair-trade practice **pratique malhonnête** sharp practice **pratiques commerciales restrictives** restrictive practices
**préavis** *nm* advance notice *n*
**précieux, -euse** *adj* valuable *adj*, precious *adj*
**précis** *adj* accurate *adj*
**préciser** *vb* specify *vb*, make oneself clear *vb*
**précision** *nf* accuracy *n*
**précité** *adj* above-mentioned *adj*
**préférence** *nf* **préférence communautaire** community preference
**préférentiel** *adj* preferential *adj*
**prélèvement** *nm* **prélèvement bancaire** direct debiting
**prélever** *vb* (tax) levy *vb* charge *vb* **prélever une commission** charge commission **prélever un intérêt** charge interest
**premier** *adj* **premier client** first customer **première classe** first class **de première main**

first hand **première qualité** high-grade
**prendre** *vb* **prendre congé (de qn)** take leave
of sb **prendre congé** take leave **prendre
contact (avec qn)** get in contact with sb
**prendre livraison** accept delivery **prendre
note** make a note of sth **prendre des notes**
take notes **prendre part (à)** take part in
**prendre rendez-vous (avec qn)** make an
appointment (with sb) **prendre la résolution
(de faire)** resolve to do sth **prendre la
responsabilité (de)** take responsibility for sth
**prendre sa retraite** retire **prendre son temps**
take one's time **prendre de la valeur** (rise in
value) appreciate
**préretraite** *nf* early retirement *n*
**présentation** *nf* (of goods) display *n*
**présenter** *vb* (motion, paper) table *vb*,
introduce *vb*
**présenter (se)** *vb* **se présenter à l'enregistrement** (airport) check in *vb*
**président** *nm* **président-directeur général
(PDG)** (of company) president *n*
**présider** *vb* take the chair *vb* **présider une
réunion** chair a meeting
**prestation** *nf* allowance *n*, benefit *n* **prestations de maladie** sickness benefit
**prêt 1.** *adj* ready *adj* **prêt à expédier** ready
for despatch **2.** *nm* loan *n*, financial loan
**prêt bancaire** bank loan **prêt conditionnel**
tied loan **prêt garanti** secured loan **prêt
hypothécaire** mortgage loan **prêt immobilier** home loan **prêt personnel** personal loan
**prétendre** *vb* (profess) claim *vb*
**prêter** *vb* lend *vb*
**prêteur, -euse** *nm,f* lender *n*
**prévenir** *vb* give notice of sth *vb*, warn *vb*
**prévision** *nf* forecast *n*, forcasting *n* **prévisions des ventes** sales forecast
**prévoir** *vb* forecast *vb*
**prime** *nf* premium *n*, bonus *n*, giveaway *n*,
insurance premium *n* **prime de départ**
golden handshake, terminal bonus **prime
d'engagement** golden hello **prime de rendement** merit payment, performance-related
bonus
**principal** *adj* main *adj*
**priorité** *nf* priority *n* **priorité absolue** top
priority
**prise** *nf* **prise de contrôle** takeover
**privatisation** *nf* privatization *n*
**privatiser** *vb* privatize *vb*
**prix** *nm* charge *n*, price *n* **faire grimper les
prix** (prices) bump up **prix d'achat** buying
price, purchase price **prix avantageux**
favourable price **prix (de) catalogue** list
price **prix ferme** firm price **prix fixe** fixed
price **prix flexible** flexible price **prix de gros**
trade price, wholesale price **prix de liquidation** clearance offer **prix de marché** market
price **prix maximum** maximum price **prix
maximums** top prices **prix net** net(t) price
**prix réduit** cut price **prix de référence** bench

mark price **prix de revient** cost price **prix de
seuil** threshold price **prix de transfert**
transfer price **prix unitaire** unit price **prix
usine** factory price **prix de vente au détail**
retail price
**procédé** *nm* process **procédé de fabrication**
manufacturing method
**procédure** *nf* **procédure de réclamation**
claims procedure
**procès** *nm* lawsuit *n*
**procès-verbal** *nm* (meeting) the minutes *npl*
**processus** *nm* process *n* **fabrication par
processus continu** continuous process
manufacturing
**procuration** *nf* (power) proxy *n* power of
attorney *nf*
**procurer** *vb* **procurer de l'argent** raise money
**producteur** *nm* producer *n*
**productif** *adj* productive *adj*
**production** *nf* output *n*, production *n* **production brute** gross output **production à la
chaîne** flow line production, flow production
**productivité** *nf* productivity *n*
**produire** *vb* yield *vb*, produce *vb*
**produit** *nm* product *n*, proceeds *npl* **produit
de base** basic commodity, primary product
**produit leader** brand leader **produit national
brut** gross national product (GNP) **produit
net** net(t) proceeds **produit(s) agricole(s)**
produce **produits chimiques** chemical
products **produits finis** final products, finished goods, finished stock
**profession** *nf* occupation *n*, profession *n*
**professionnel** *adj* occupational *adj*,
vocational *adj*
**profit** *nm* profit **profit comptable** book profit
**profiter** *vb* benefit *vb*
**programmateur** *nm* computer programmer *n*
**programmation** *nf* (DP) programming *n*
**programme** *nm* broadcast *n*, schedule *n*,
programme *n* **programme d'aide extérieure**
foreign aid programme **programme d'investissements** investment programme,
investment program (US) **programme informatique** computer program **programme
de travaux publics** public works programme
(GB)
**programmer** *vb* schedule *vb*
**programmeur** *nm* (DP) programmer *n*
**progrès** *nm* progress *n*
**progresser** *vb* (research, project) progress *vb*
make headway *vb*
**projet** *nm* project *n* **faire des projets** make
plans **projet de contrat** draft contract **projet
de loi de finances** finance bill **projet pilote**
pilot scheme
**prolongation** *nf* (of contract) extension *n*
**prolonger** *vb* **prolonger un contrat** extend a
contract **prolonger un crédit** extend credit
**promoteur** *nm* developer *n* **promoteur immobilier** property developer
**promotion** *nf* (of product, person)

promotion *n* **promotion agressive** hard sell
**promotionnel** *adj* promotional *adj*
**promouvoir qn** *vb* (person) promote *vb*
**propager** *vb* (document) circulate *vb*
**propriétaire** *nm* landlord *n*, proprietor *n*,
owner *n* **propriétaire absentéiste** absentee
landlord **propriétaire foncier** landowner
**propriétaire de maison** home owner
**propriété** *nf* property *n* **propriété privée**
private property
**prorata** *nm* proportional share *n* **au prorata**
in proportion to
**prospectus** *nm* prospectus *n*
**prospère** *adj* prosperous *adj*
**prospérer** *vb* thrive *vb*
**protectionnisme** *nm* protectionism *n*
**protectionniste** *adj* protectionist *adj*
**provision** *nf* supply *n* (for contract)
consideration *n*
**provisoire** *adj* interim *adj*
**public** *adj* public *adj*
**publication** *nf* publication *n*, publishing *n*
**publication assistée par ordinateur** desk-top
publishing
**publicité** *nf* advertising *n*, publicity *n* **faire de
la publicité pour un produit** to promote a
product
**publipostage** *nm* mailshot *n*, (mass)
mailing *n*
**puce** *nf* microchip *n*
**pyramide** *nf* pyramid *n*
**quai** *nm* quay *n* **à prendre à quai** ex-quay
**qualification** *nf* qualification *n* **qualification
professionnelle** professional qualification
**qualitatif** *adj* qualitative *adj*
**qualité** *nf* quality *n*
**quant (à)** *prep phrase* regarding *prep*
**quantitatif** *adj* quantitative *adj*
**quantité** *nf* quantity *n*
**quelque chose** *pron* something *pron*
**quelque chose d'urgent** a matter of urgency
**querelle** *nf* dispute *n*
**questionnaire** *nm* questionnaire *n* **questionnaire d'etude de marché** market
research questionnaire
**queue** *nf* queue *n*
**quitter** *vb* (resign from) leave *vb* **"ne quittez
pas!"** (phone) "hold the line!"
**quorum** *nm* quorum *n* **quorum de créanciers**
quorum of creditors
**quota** *nm* quota **quota d'importation** import
quota **quota de vente** sales quota
**quote-part** *nf* share *n*, portion *n*
**quotidien** *adj* daily *adj*
**rabais** *nm* markdown *n*, rebate *n*, discount *n*
**raccrocher** *vb* (telephone) hang up *vb*
**rachat** *nm* LBO (leveraged buy-out) *abbr*
repurchase *n*, buyout *n*, takeover *n*
**racheter** *vb* (company) take over *vb* buy
out *vb*
**racket** *nm* racket *n*, racketeering *n*
**racketteur** *nm* racketeer *n*

**raison** *nf* reason *nf* **raison sociale** registered
trade name
**raisonnable** *adj* (price) reasonable *adj*
**raisonnement** *nm* argument *n*
**ralentir** *vb* slow down *vb*
**ralentissement** *nm* slowdown *n* **ralentissement économique** economic slowdown
**ramasser** *vb* collect *vb*
**rapatriement** *nm* repatriation *n*
**rapide** *adj* prompt *adj*
**rappel** *nm* reminder *n* **rappel de salaire** back
pay
**rappeler** *vb* (on phone) call back *vb*
**rapport** *nm* report *n* **rapport annuel** annual
report **rapport financier** financial report
**rapport de qualité** quality report
**rapporter** *vb* **rapporter un intérêt** bear interest
**ratification** *nf* ratification *n*
**ratifier** *vb* ratify *vb*
**ratio** *nm* **ratio chiffres d'affaires-immobilisations** turnover ratio
**rationalisation** *nf* rationalization *n*
**rationaliser** *vb* rationalise *vb*, make
efficient *vb*
**réaffectation** *nf* (of funds) reallocation *n*
**réalisable** *adj* workable *adj*
**réalisation** *nf* accomplishment *n*,
achievement *n* **réalisation d'actifs** realization of assets
**réaliser** *vb* achieve *vb* **réaliser des bénéfices**
to make a profit
**réalité** *nf* actuality *n*
**réaménagement** *nm* **réaménagement des
zones urbaines** urban renewal
**réassurance** *nf* reinsurance *n*
**réassurer** *vb* reinsure *vb*
**réattribuer** *vb* (funds) reallocate *vb*
**recensé** *adj* registered *adj*
**récent** *adj* up-to-date *adj*
**récession** *nf* recession *n*
**recette** *nf* takings *npl*, proceeds *npl* **recettes
fiscales** tax revenue **recettes publicitaires**
advertising revenue
**recevoir** *vb* receive *vb* **recevoir un client**
entertain a client
**recherche** *nf* research *n* **recherche et développement** research and development (R&D)
**recherche documentaire** document retrieval
**réciproque** *adj* reciprocal *adj*
**réclamant** *nm* claimant *n*
**réclamation** *nf* complaint **faire une réclamation** lodge/make a complaint
**réclame** *nf* advertisement *n*
**réclamer** *vb* demand *vb* claim *vb* **réclamer un
dédommagement** claim compensation **réclamer des dommages et intérêts** claim for
damages
**recommandation** *nf* recommendation *n*
**recommander** *vb* advocate *vb*,
recommend *vb*
**récompense** *nf* recompense *n*, reward *n*

**reconductible** *adj* renewable *adj*
**reconduire** *vb* (policy, contract) renew *vb*
**reconnaissance** *nf* **reconnaissance de dette** acknowledgement of debt
**reconversion** *nf* retraining *n*
**reconvertir** *vb* retrain *vb*
**recours** *nm* recourse **avoir recours à** have recourse to
**recouvrement** *nm* **recouvrement de dette** debt collection
**recouvrer** *vb* (debt) collect *vb*, recover money from sb *vb*
**recrue** *nf* recruit *vb*
**recrutement** *nm* recruitment *n*
**reçu** *nm* receipt *n* **faire un reçu** make out a receipt
**récupérer** *vb* salvage *vb*
**recyclable** *adj* recyclable *adj*
**recyclage** *nm* retraining *n*
**recycler** *vb* recycle *vb*
**redevance** *nf* licence fee *n*
**rédiger** *vb* **rédiger un contrat** draw up a contract **rédiger un rapport** draw up a report
**redressement** *nm* (company) turn round *n*, turn around (US) (economic) recovery *n*
**réduction** *nf* abatement *n*, depletion *n*, discount *n*, reduction *n* **réduction d'impôt** tax cut **réduction sur quantité** volume discount
**réduire** *vb* shrink *vb*, abate *vb* (reduce) cut *vb* **réduire les dépenses** axe* expenditure **réduire de moitié** halve
**réduit** *adj* reduced *adj*
**rééchelonner** *vb* (debt) reschedule *vb*
**réel** *adj* actual *adj*, real *adj*
**réélection** *nf* re-election *n*
**réélire** *vb* re-elect *vb*
**réévaluation** *nf* (of currency) revaluation *n*
**réévaluer** *vb* (currency) revalue *vb*
**réexpédier** *vb* (mail) redirect *vb*
**référence** *nf* box number **références (attestation)** reference **références bancaires** credit reference
**référendum** *nm* referendum *n*
**refiler** *vb* **refiler la responsabilité à qn d'autre** pass the buck*
**réforme** *nf* reform *n* **réforme agraire** land reform **réforme des tarifs douaniers** tariff reform
**refrain** *nm* **refrain publicitaire** advertising jingle
**refus** *nm* refusal *n*
**refuser** *vb* (offer) turn down *vb* (contract) repudiate *vb* **refuser un chèque** bounce* a cheque **refuser de communiquer une pièce** withhold a document **refuser des marchandises** refuse goods **refuser un règlement** refuse payment
**régime** *nm* **régime de retraite** pension scheme **régime de retraite proportionnelle** earnings-related pension
**région** *nf* **région industrielle** industrial region

**régional** *adj* regional *adj*
**registre** *nm* ledger *n*, record *n*, register *n* **registre du personnel** payroll
**réglage** *nm* adjustment *n*
**règlement** *nm* regulation *n* **règlement définitif** final settlement **règlement partiel** part payment **règlements douaniers** customs regulations
**réglementation** *nf* regulation *n*, control *n* **réglementation des changes** exchange restrictions
**régler** *vb* (dispute, account) settle *vb* pay an invoice **régler un compte** settle an account **régler une dette** pay off a debt **régler une facture** settle an invoice **régler sa note** (hotel) check out **régler un sinistre** adjust a claim, settle a claim
**régulier** *adj* aboveboard *adj*, regular *adj*
**réimplantation** *nf* relocation *n*
**réimplanter** *vb* relocate *vb*
**réimplanter (se)** *vb* relocate *vb*
**réimportation** *nf* reimportation *n*
**réimporter** *vb* reimport *vb*
**réinvestir** *vb* (profits) plough back *vb*, plow back (US)
**rejeter** *vb* (contract) repudiate *vb* (offer) turn down *vb*, negative (US) **rejeter une réclamation** refuse a claim
**relance** *nf* boost *n*, reflation *n*
**relancer** *vb* **relancer la demande** boost demand **relancer la production** boost production **relancer les ventes** boost sales
**relation** *nf* **relation d'affaires** business acquaintance **relations d'affaires** business connections, business contacts, business relations **relations avec la clientèle** customer relations **relations humaines** human relations **relations publiques** public relations **relations sociales** labour relations **relations du travail** industrial relations
**relevé** *nm* **relevé de compte** bank statement, statement of account
**relever** *vb* **relever les droits de douane** raise tariffs
**remarquable** *adj* noteworthy *adj*
**remarquer** *vb* notice *n*
**remboursable** *adj* refundable *adj*
**remboursement** *nm* (of loan) repayment *n* rebate *n*, redemption *n*, refund *n*, reimbursement *n* **remboursement intégral** full payment
**rembourser** *vb* repay *vb*, amortize *vb*, reimburse *vb*, refund *vb* redeem *vb*
**remettre** *vb* handover *vb*, adjourn *vb*, postpone *vb*
**remise** *nf* remittance *n*, discount *n* **remise quantitative** quantity discount
**remonter** *vb* **remonter le moral** boost morale
**remplaçant, -ante** *nm,f* (person) replacement *n*
**remplacer** *vb* replace *vb*
**remplir** *vb* fill in *vb* **remplir une fiche d'hôtel**

fill in a hotel check-in form

**rémunération** *nf* remuneration *n* **rémunération des cadres** executive compensation

**rémunéré, -e** *adj* paid *adj* **bien rémunéré** well paid

**rémunérer** *vb* remunerate *vb*

**rencontrer** *vb* meet *vb*

**rendement** *nm* output *n*, yield *n* **rendement des capitaux investis** return on capital **rendement des fonds propres** return on equity **rendements décroissants** diminishing returns

**rendez-vous** *nm* (meeting) appointment *n*, engagement *n*

**rendre** *vb* **rendre compte (de)** *vb* account for *vb* **rendre un service à qn** do sb a favour **rendre visite à** visit sb

**renomination** *nf* reappointment *n*

**renommer** *nf* reappoint *vb*

**renouvelable** *adj* renewable *adj*

**renouveler** *vb* (policy, contract) renew *vb*

**rénovation** *nf* refurbishment *n*

**rénover** *vb* refurbish *vb*

**renseignement** *nm* information *n* **renseignements secrets** classified information

**renseigner** *vb* **se renseigner** enquire

**rentabilité** *nf* earning power *n*, profitability *n*

**rentable** *adj* (profitable) moneymaking *adj*

**rente** *nf* annuity *n*, unearned income *n*

**rentrée** *nf* **rentrée d'argent** flow of income

**renverser** *vb* reverse *vb*

**renvoyer** *vb* send back *vb* (dismiss) fire* *vb* **renvoyer un chèque à l'émetteur** refer a cheque to drawer

**réparation** *nf* repairing *n* **le coût des réparations** costs of repair

**réparer** *vb* repair *vb*

**répondeur** *nm* **répondeur téléphonique** answering machine

**répondre** *vb* answer *vb* **répondre à un appel d'offres** tender for a contract

**réponse** *nf* answer *n* **en réponse à** in response to... **en réponse à votre lettre du...** in response to your letter dated the...

**reportage** *nm* report *n*, news coverage *n*

**reporter** *vb* adjourn *vb*, bring forward *vb*, carry forward *vb* **reporter au mois prochain** (to next month) carry over

**reprendre** *vb* (company) take over *vb* **reprendre possession de** repossess

**représentant** *nm* **représentant de commerce** sales representative, commercial traveller **représentant régional** area representative

**reprise** *nf* upswing *n*, upturn *n* **reprise de possession** repossession

**réputation** *nf* reputation *n*

**RES** *nm* **rachat d'entreprise par ses salariés** management buy-out

**réseau** *nm* network *n* **réseau bancaire** banking network **réseau de communication** communication network **réseau de distribution** distribution network **réseau infor-matique** computer network

**réservation** *nf* reservation *n* **faire une réservation** make a reservation

**réserve** *nf* reserve *n*, stock *n* **réseau en devise** currency reserve **réserves excédentaires** excess reserves **réserves d'or** gold reserves

**réserver** *vb* book *vb*, reserve *vb* **réserver d'avance** book in advance **réserver une chambre d'hôtel** book a hotel room **réserver un vol** book a flight

**résiduel** *adj* residual *adj*

**résiliation** *nf* termination *n* **résiliation du contrat de travail** termination of employment

**résilier** *vb* rescind *vb* **résilier un contrat** cancel a contract

**résister (à)** *vb* withstand *vb*, stand the test *vb*

**résolution** *nf* resolution *n*, solution *n*

**résorber** *vb* reduce *vb* **résorber des surplus** absorb surplus stock

**résoudre** *vb* (problem) resolve *vb*

**respecter** *vb* respect *vb*, observe *vb* **respecter les formalités** observe formalities

**responsabilité** *nf* accountability *n*, liability *n* **responsabilité conjointe** joint obligation, joint responsibility **responsabilité illimitée** unlimited liability **responsabilité limitée** limited liability **responsabilité pleine et entière** full liability **responsabilités contractuelles** contractual obligations

**responsable** 1. *adj* accountable *adj*, liable *adj*, responsible *adj* 2. *nmf* (person) executive *n* **responsable du marketing** marketing director **responsable de la sécurité** safety officer

**resserer** *vb* tighten *vb*, squeeze *vb*

**resserrement** *nm* tightening *n* **resserrement du crédit** credit squeeze

**ressource** *nf* resource *n* **ressources de l'Etat** government resources **ressources financières** financial resources **ressources humaines** human resources **ressources naturelles** natural resources

**restant** *adj* residual *adj*

**restreindre** *vb* restrict *vb*

**restrictif** *adj* restrictive *adj*

**restriction** *nf* restriction *n* **restrictions à l'importation** import restrictions

**restructurer** *vb* restructure *vb*

**résultat** *nm* outcome *n* **résultat d'exploitation** operating profit **résultat net** net(t) result

**résumé** *nm* abstract *n*, summary *n*

**rétablissement** *nm* (economic) recovery *n*

**retard** *nm* delay *n*, holdup *n* **en retard** overdue *adj* **en retard dans ses paiements** late in his/her payments

**retarder** *vb* (delay) hold up *vb*

**retenir** *vb* (money) keep back *vb* (not release) hold back *vb*

**retirer** *vb* withdraw *vb* **retirer une offre** withdraw an offer

**retombée** *nf* spin-off *n*

**retour** *nm* return *n* **retour sur investissements** return on investment

**retourner** *vb* reverse *vb*

**retrait** *nm* withdrawal *n* **retrait de fonds** withdrawal of funds

**retraite** *nf* retirement *n* **pension de retraite** retirement pension **retraite anticipée** early retirement

**retraité** *nm* pensioner *n*

**rétroactif** *adj* retroactive *adj*, backdated *adj*

**rétrograder** *vb* (employee) demote *vb*

**réunion** *nf* meeting *n*, committee meeting *n* **réunion d'affaires** business meeting **réunion du conseil d'administration** board meeting **réunion à huis clos** closed session/meeting **réunion de vendeurs** sales conference

**revendication** *nf* claim *n*, demand *n* **revendications salariales** wage claims, pay claims

**revendiquer** *vb* (demand) claim *vb*

**revenir (à)** *vb* revert to *vb*, come back *vb*, amount to *vb* **ça revient au même** it amounts to the same thing

**revente** *nf* resale *n*

**revenu** *nm* income *n*, revenue *n* **revenu annuel** yearly income **revenu brut** gross income **revenu du capital** unearned income **revenu direct** basic income **revenu disponible** disposable income **revenus personnels** private income **revenu fixe** fixed income **revenu imposable** taxable income **revenu marginal** marginal revenue **Revenu minimum d'insertion (RMI)** income support **revenu national** national income **revenu net** net(t) income **revenu non imposable** franked income

**réviser** *vb* revise *vb*

**révoquer** *vb* (licence) revoke *vb*

**revue** *nf* journal *n*

**richesse** *nf* wealth *n*

**risque** *nm* hazard *n*, risk *n* **à haut risque** high-risk **au risque du client** at the customer's risk **risque financier** financial exposure, financial risk **risque professionnel** occupational hazard **risque pour la santé** health hazard

**ristourne** *nf* rebate *n*

**rompre** *vb* break *vb* **rompre un accord** break an agreement

**rompu** *nm* fractional share *n*

**rotation** *nf* turnover *n*, rotation *n* **rotation du capital** capital turnover **rotation des postes** job rotation

**rouge** *adj* red *adj* **être dans le rouge** be in the red

**RSVP (répondez s'il vous plaît)** *abbr* RSVP (reply requested) *abbr*

**rudiments** *nmpl* working knowledge *n*

**ruiner** *vb* wreck *vb*

**rupture** *nf* breach *n*, breakdown *n* **rupture de contrat** breach of contract

**rythme** *nm* rate *n* **rythme d'accumulation** rate of accrual **rythme annuel** annual rate

**sain** *adj* (finances) healthy *adj*

**saisie** *nf* foreclosure *n* **saisie de données** data capture

**saisir** *vb* impound *vb* **saisir un bien hypothéqué** foreclose **saisir l'occasion** seize an opportunity

**saison** *nf* season *n*

**saisonnier** *adj* seasonal *adj*

**salaire** *nm* pay *n*, salary *n*, wage *n* **salaire de départ** starting wage **salaire hebdomadaire** weekly wages **salaire honnête** fair wage **salaire minimum** minimum wage **salaire minimum interprofessionnel de croissance (SMIC)** index-linked minimum wage **salaire moyen** average wage **salaire net** net(t) wage **salaire réel** real wage

**salarié, -e** *nm,f* wage earner *n*

**salle** *nf* room *n* **salle du conseil** board room **salle d'exposition** showroom **salle de transit** (transport) transfer lounge

**salon** *nm* **salon professionnel** trade fair

**sanction** *nf* sanction *n*, penalty *n* **sanctions commerciales** trade sanctions **sanctions économiques** economic sanctions

**sans** *prep* without *prep* **sans arrêt** non-stop **sans but lucratif** non-profitmaking **sans délai** without delay **sans emploi** jobless, unemployed **sans prévenir** without warning **sans valeur marchande** no commercial value

**santé** *nf* health *n* **le secteur de la santé** health care industry

**satisfaction** *nf* satisfaction *n* **satisfaction des consommateurs** consumer satisfaction **satisfaction professionnelle** job satisfaction

**savoir-faire** *nm* know-how *n*

**sceau** *nm* seal *n*

**sceller** *vb* seal *vb*

**science** *nf* science *n* **science économique** economics

**scission** *nf* split division *n*

**secondaire** *adj* secondary *adj*

**secret** *nm* **secret commercial** trade secret

**secrétaire** *nmf* secretary *n* **secrétaire de direction** executive secretary **secrétaire général** company secretary

**secteur** *nm* sector *n* **secteur primaire** primary sector **secteur privé** private sector **secteur public** public sector **secteur secondaire** secondary sector **le secteur secondaire** secondary industry **secteur tertiaire** service industry, tertiary sector

**sécurité** *nf* security *n* **Sécurité sociale** National Health Service (GB), Social Security

**segmentation** *nf* **segmentation du marché** market segmentation

**sellette** *nf* **être sur la sellette** be in the hot seat

**selon** *prep* **selon les conditions contractuelles** under the terms of the contract **selon le ministre** according to the minister **selon vos besoins** in accordance with your requirements

**semaine** *nf* week *n* **semaine de travail** working week, workweek (US)

**semestre** *nm* half-year *n*

**semestriel** *adj* biannual *adj*, twice a year *adj*

**sens** *nm* **sens des affaires** business acumen **sens du commandement** leadership

**serré** *adj* tight *adj*

**serrer** *vb* (spending) squeeze *vb*

**service** *nm* department *n*, favour *n* **service après-vente** after-sales service **service compris** service included **service de dépannage** breakdown service **service de la dette** debt service **service export** export department **service d'importation** import department **service du marketing** marketing department **service ministériel** government body **service du personnel** personnel department **service public** public utility **service des réclamations** claims department, complaints department **services postaux** postal services **service vingt-quatre heures sur vingt-quatre** twenty-four-hour service

**servir** *vb* serve *vb* **servir comme intermédiaire** mediate

**seuil** *nm* threshold *n* **seuil de rentabilité** break-even point

**SICAV (société d'investissement à capital variable)** *abbr* mutual fund *n*

**sidérurgie** *nf* steel industry *n*

**siège** *nm* HO (head office) *abbr* **siège social** head office, main office, registered office

**signaler** *vb* notify *vb*

**signataire** *nmf* signatory *n*

**signature** *nf* signature *n*

**signer** *vb* sign *vb* **signer un chèque** sign a cheque **signer un contrat** sign a contract

**simulateur** *nm* malingerer *n*

**situation** *nf* **situation financière** financial status, financial situation

**slogan** *nm* slogan *n*

**SMIC (salaire minimum interprofessionnel de croissance)** *abbr* index-linked minimum wage *n*

**société** *nf* company *n*, society *n* **société d'abondance** affluent society **société par actions** joint-stock company **société anonyme** public company, public limited company **société d'assurances** insurance company **société bidon** phoney* company **société en commandite simple** limited partnership **société de consommation** consumer society **société de construction** building firm **société cotée en bourse** quoted company **société holding** holding company **société immobilière** property company **Société inscrite au registre du commerce** registered company **société d'investissement** investment trust, trust company **société d'investissement à capital variable (SICAV)** unit trust **société d'investissement et de crédit immobiliers** building society **société mère** parent company **so-**

ciété multinationale multinational corporation **société de premier ordre** blue-chip company **société à responsabilité limitée (S.A.R.L.)** limited company, private limited company **société soeur** sister company

**solde** *nm* balance *n* **solde en banque** bank balance **solde commercial** trade balance **solde créditeur** balance in hand **solde débiteur** debit balance **solde non acquitté** unpaid balance **soldes de fermeture** closing-down sale, closing-out sale (US) **soldes de marchandises** sales

**solliciter** *vb* (loan) request *vb*

**solvabilité** *nf* creditworthiness *n*, solvency *n*

**solvable** *adj* creditworthy *adj*, in credit *adj*, solvent *adj*

**somme** *nf* sum total *n*, amount *n* **le restant de la somme** outstanding amount **somme forfaitaire** lump sum settlement

**sommet** *nm* peak *n*

**sondage** *nm* survey *n*, poll *n* **sondage économique** economic survey **sondage par quota** quota sampling

**sonder** *vb* sample *vb*

**sortir** *vb* (product) bring out *vb*

**soumettre** *vb* (report) submit *vb*

**soumission** *nf* tender *n*, bid *n*

**soumissionnaire** *nmf* tenderer *n*

**souplesse** *nf* (of prices) flexibility *n*

**source** *nf* source *n*

**sous** *prep* under *prep* **sous-assuré** underinsured **sous-capitalisé** undercapitalized **sous-directeur** *nm* assistant manager **sous douane** in bond **sous-employé** underemployed **sous-estimer** undervalue **sous garantie** under warranty **sous la main** to hand **sous-payer** underpay **sous-produit** by-product **sous-traitant** subcontractor **sous-traiter** farm out, subcontract

**souscription** *nf* takeup *n*

**souscrire** *vb* subscribe *vb*

**soutien** *nm* support *n*, backing *n* **soutien financier** financial backing

**spécialisé** *adj* semi-skilled *adj*, unskilled *adj*

**spécialiser (se)** *vb* specialize *vb*

**spécialiste** *nm* specialist *n*

**spécialité** *nf* speciality *n*

**spécification** *nf* specification *n*

**spectateur, -trice** *nm,f* viewer *n*

**spéculateur, -trice** *nm,f* speculator *n* **spéculateur à la baisse** (stock exchange) bear *n* **spéculateur à la hausse** (stock exchange) bull *n*

**spéculer** *vb* speculate *vb*, play the market *vb* **spéculer à la hausse** (stock exchange) bull *vb*

**spirale** *nf* **spirale inflationniste** inflationary spiral

**sponsor** *nm* sponsor *n*

**sponsorisation** *nf* sponsorship *n*

**spot** *nm* **spot publicitaire** advertisement *n*

**stabiliser** vb (prices) peg vb
**stabilité** nf **stabilité financière** financial stability
**stable** adj (economy) stable adj
**stage** nm training course n, internship (US) **stage de formation** training course, work experience **stage de perfectionnement** advanced training course **stage de reconversion** retraining programme, retraining program (US)
**stagiaire** nmf trainee n
**stagnation** nf stagnation n
**standard** 1. adj standard adj 2. nm switchboard n
**standardisation** nf standardization n
**standardiser** vb standardize vb
**standardiste** nmf switchboard operator n
**statistiques** nfpl statistics n
**statu quo** nm status quo n
**stipulation** nf provision n, stipulation n
**stock** nm stock n, inventory (US) **en stock** in stock **stock de réserve** reserve stock
**stockage** nm stocking n, storage n **stockage de l'information** information storage
**stocker** vb (stock) carry vb
**stratégie** nf strategy n **stratégie d'exportation** export strategy **stratégie financière** financial strategy
**stratégique** adj strategic adj
**stress** nm stress n **stress des cadres** executive stress
**structure** nf structure n **structure financière** financial structure
**structurel** adj structural adj
**subordonné, -e** 1. adj junior adj 2. nm,f subordinate n
**subornation** nf bribery n
**suborner** vb bribe vb
**subvention** nf subsidy n **subvention de l'état** state subsidy **subvention du gouvernement** government subsidy **subventions agricoles** farming subsidies **subventions à l'exportation** export subsidies
**subventionner** vb subsidize vb
**succursale** nf branch n, branch company n, branch office n
**suite (à)** prep phrase with reference to, further to
**suivre** vb follow vb **suivre les instructions** follow instructions
**supermarché** nm supermarket n
**superpuissance** nf superpower n **superpuissance économique** economic superpower
**supplément** nm additional charge n, extra cost n
**supplémentaire** adj extra adj, supplementary adj
**support** nm medium n **support publicitaire** advertising medium
**suppression** nf abolition n
**supprimer** vb abolish vb, cancel vb
**sûr** adj safe adj, secure adj

**surapprovisionner** vb oversupply vb
**surcharge** nf overload vb
**surchauffe** nf (of economy) overheating n
**surcote** nf premium n
**sureffectifs** nmpl surplus staff n
**suréquipé** adj overmanned adj
**suréquiper** vb overequip vb
**surévaluer** vb overvalue vb
**surgénérateur** nm fast breeder reactor n
**surmené** adj overworked adj
**surpaye** nf overpayment n
**surpayer** vb overpay vb
**surplus** nm surplus n
**surpopulation** nf overpopulation n
**surproduction** nf overproduction n
**surproduire** vb overproduce vb
**sursouscrit** adj oversubscribed adj
**surtaxe** nf supertax n
**surveillant** nm supervisor n
**survendre** vb oversell vb
**survendu** adj oversold adj
**suspension** nf adjournment n
**symbolique** adj nominal adj
**syndicat** nm industrial union, trade union, labor union (US) **la confédération des syndicats britanniques** Trades Union Congress **syndicat patronal** employer's federation
**syndiqué, -e** nm,f union member n
**synergie** nf synergy n
**synthèse** nf synthesis n
**synthétique** adj man-made adj, synthetic adj
**système** nm system n **système de contingentment** quota system **système économique** economy **système expert** expert system **Système Monétaire Européen** European Monetary System (EMS) **systèmes informatiques** information systems
**tableau** nm spreadsheet n **tableau d'affichage** bulletin board
**tâche** nf task n
**tacite** adj tacit adj
**tactique** nf tactic n **tactiques de vente** selling tactics
**taille** nf size n
**talent** nm talent n **talents de négociateur** negotiating skills n
**talon** nm counterfoil n
**taper** vb type vb
**tarif** nm tariff n **tarif uniforme** flat-rate tariff
**taux** nm rate n **taux d'accroissement naturel** natural rate of increase **taux de base** base rate, basic rate, prime lending rate **taux de change** rate of exchange **taux de chômage** rate of unemployment **taux de croissance** growth rate, rate of growth **taux d'endettement** debt-equity ratio **taux d'escompte** bank rate, discount rate **taux d'expansion** rate of expansion **taux flottant** floating rate interest **taux horaire** hourly rate **taux d'inflation** rate of inflation **taux d'intérêt** interest rate, rate of interest **taux**

**d'investissement** rate of investment **taux Lombard** Lombard Rate **taux de rendement** rate of return **taux variable** variable rate **à taux variable** (at) variable rate **taux zéro** zero rate/rating

**taxe** *nf* tax *n* **taxe à l'importation** import duty **taxes locales** local taxes **taxe à la valeur ajoutée (TVA)** value-added tax (VAT), sales tax (US)

**technicien, -ne** *nm,f* technician *n*

**technique** *nf* skill *n* **technique de vente** sales technique

**technologie** *nf* technology *n* **technologie de pointe** advanced technology

**téléachats** *nmpl* home shopping *n*

**télécommunications** *nfpl* telecommunications *npl*

**télécopie** *nf* facsimile *n*, fax *n*

**télécopier** *vb* fax *vb*

**télécopieur** *nm* telecopier *n*, telefax *n*

**téléinformatique** *nf* teleprocessing *n*

**téléphone** *nm* telephone *n*

**télétraitement** *nm* teleprocessing *n*

**télétravail** *nm* teleworking *n*

**télévente** *nf* telesales *npl*

**télévirement** *nm* EFT (electronic funds transfer) *abbr*

**téléviser** *vb* televise *vb*

**télex** *nm* telex *n*

**témoin** *nm* witness *n* **être témoin de** witness *vb*

**temporaire** *adj* temporary *adj*

**temps** *nm* time *n* **qui prend du temps** time-consuming *adj* **à temps partiel** part-time **à temps plein** full-time **temps réel** real time

**tendance** *nf* tendency *n*, trend *n* **la tendance actuelle** current trend **tendance économique** economic trend **tendances de la consommation** consumer trends

**tenir** *vb* hold *vb* **tenir bon** hold up **tenir compte de qch** take sth into account **tenir debout** (argument) hang together **tenir qn responsable de** hold sb responsible **tenir une réunion** call a meeting, hold a meeting **tenir ses engagements** meet one's obligations

**terme** *nm* term **à court terme** in the short term **à long terme** in the long term **termes de l'échange** terms of trade

**terminal** 1. *adj* terminal *adj* 2. *nm* **terminal des conteneurs** container terminal **terminal d'ordinateur** computer terminal

**terminer** *vb* complete *vb*, end *vb* **se terminer** come to an end

**territoire** *nm* territory *n*, area *n* **territoire d'outre-mer** overseas territory

**testament** *nm* will *n*

**tête** *nf* head *n* **être à la tête de** be head of

**textile** *nm* textile *n*

**textuellement** *adv* verbatim *adv*

**thésauriser** *vb* hoard *vb*

**tiers** *adj* third *adj* **tierce personne** third party, third person **Tiers Monde** Third World

**tirage** *nm* drawing *n*, draft *n* **tirage au sort** random selection

**tire** *nm* **tire-au-flanc** shirker* *n*

**tirer** *vb* (chèque) draw *vb*

**titre** *nm* heading *n*, qualification *n*, clearance certificate *n* **titre d'action** share certificate, stock certificate (US) **titre de propriété** certificate of ownership, title deed **titres** securities **titres cotés en Bourse** listed securities **titres d'état** gilt-edged securities

**titulaire** *nmf* holder *n* **titulaire d'une maîtrise en gestion** MBA (Master of Business Administration) *abbr* **titulaire de permis** licence holder **titulaire de poste** office holder

**tonalité** *nf* (phone) dialling tone, dial tone (US) **tonalité occupée** engaged tone, busy signal (US)

**tonnage** *nm* tonnage *n* **tonnage brut** gross tonnage **tonnage net** net(t) tonnage

**tonne** *nf* ton *n* **tonne métrique** metric ton

**torchon** *nm* rag *n*

**total** 1. *adj* total *adj* 2. *nm* total *n* **le total des ventes** total sales

**touché** *adj* affected *adj* **être durement touché** be badly hit

**toucher** *vb* (be of importance to) concern *vb* **toucher un chèque** cash a cheque

**tourisme** *nm* tourism *n* **l'industrie du tourisme** the tourist trade

**touriste** *nmf* tourist *n*

**tourner** *vb* run *vb*, turn over *vb* **tourner à plein rendement** work to full capacity **tourner au ralenti** tick over

**trace** *nf* track *n*

**trafic** *nm* traffic *n*, dealings *npl* **trafic aérien** air traffic **trafic ferroviaire** rail traffic **trafic maritime** sea traffic

**train** *nm* train *n* **en train de** in the process of **par train** by train **train de marchandises** goods train, freight train (US) **train de voyageurs** passenger train

**traite** *nf* (financial) draft *n* (invoice) bill *n* **traite à vue** sight draft

**traité** *nm* treaty *n* **traité commercial** commercial treaty **Traité de Rome** Treaty of Rome

**traitement** *nm* treatment *n*, handling *n*, processing *n* **traitement des données** data handling, data processing **traitement de l'information** information processing **traitement de texte** word processing

**traiter** *vb* process *vb* (deal) handle *vb*

**tranche** *nf* part *n*, section *n* **tranche d'imposition** tax bracket

**transaction** *nf* transaction *n* **transaction commerciale** business transaction

**transbordé** *adj* ex ship *adj*

**transborder** *vb* transship *vb*

**transcrire** *vb* transcribe *vb*

**transfert** *nm* transfer *n* **transfert de devises**

currency transfer **transfert électronique de fonds** EFT (electronic funds transfer) *abbr* **transfert de technologie** technology transfer

**transformer** *vb* process *vb*

**transit** *nm* transit *n* **en transit** in transit

**transitaire** *nm* forwarding agent *n*, transport agent *n*

**transmettre** *vb* transmit *vb*

**transmissible** *adj* transferable *adj*

**transmission** *nf* handing over *n*, transfer *n* **transmission de capital** capital transfer

**transnational** *adj* transnational *adj*

**transport** *nm* transport *n*, transportation *n* **transport aérien** air transport, air freight **transport sur courte distance** short-haul **transport ferroriaire** rail transport **transport sur longue distance** long-haul **transport maritime** sea transportation **transport par route** road transport **transport routier** road transport, road haulage, road freight (US) **transports en commun** public transport

**transporteur** *nm* carrier *n*, freighter *n*, shipper *n* **transporteur de vrac** bulk carrier

**travail** *nm* work *n* **travail de bureau** clerical work, office work **travail de conseil** consultancy work, consulting (US) **travail défectueux** faulty workmanship **travail à domicile** home industry **travail par équipes** shift work **travail à forfait** contract work **travail payé à l'heure** hourly-paid work **travail à la pièce** piecework **travail posté** shift **travail temporaire** casual work, temporary employment **travail sur le terrain** field work **travail d'urgence** rush job **travail d'usine** factory work **travaux de conférence** conference proceedings **travaux publics** civil engineering, building works

**travailler** *vb* work *vb* **travailler en dehors des horaires normaux** work unsocial hours **travailler au noir** moonlight*

**travailleur, -euse** *nm,f* worker *n* **travailleur immigré** guest worker, migrant worker **travailleur manuel** manual worker **travailleur temporaire** casual worker **travailleur à temps plein** full-time worker

**travaillistique** *adj* labour-intensive *adj*

**trésor** *nm* **le Trésor (public)** *nm* the Treasury *n*

**trésorerie** *nf* cash flow *n* **trésorerie négative** negative cash flow

**tribunal** *nm* criminal court *n*, tribunal *n* **devant un tribunal** in court

**trimestre** *nm* (of year) quarter *n*

**trimestriel** *adj* quarterly *adj*

**troc** *nm* barter *n*, swap *n*

**troquer** *vb* barter *vb*, swap *vb*

**trouver** *vb* find *vb* **trouver à redire à qch** find fault with sth

**TTC (toutes taxes comprises)** *abbr* including tax

**tuyau** *nm* (suggestion) tip *n* **tuyau sur le marché** market tip

**TVA (Taxe sur la valeur ajoutée)** *abbr* VAT

(value added tax) *abbr* **assujetti à la TVA** subject to VAT

**type** *nm* kind *n*, type *n*

**unanime** *adj* unanimous *adj*

**unification** *nf* unification *n*

**unilatéral** *adj* (contract) unilateral *adj*

**union** *nf* union *n* **union douanière** customs union **union économique** economic union **Union européenne** European Union **Union de l'Europe Occidentale** WEU (Western European Union) **Union Monétaire Européenne** European Monetary Union (EMU)

**unité** *nf* unit *n* **unité de compte européenne** European Unit of Account (EVA) **unité de production** unit of production

**urbanisme** *nm* town planning *n*

**urgence** *nf* emergency *n* **de toute urgence** very urgently

**urgent** *adj* urgent *adj*

**usine** *nf* factory *n* **usine pilote** pilot plant

**usiner** *vb* machine *vb*

**usure** *nf* usury *n*, wear and tear *n*

**utilisateur, -trice** *nm,f* user *n*, utilizer *n* **utilisateur final** end consumer, end user

**utilisation** *nf* utilization *n* **utilisation intensive** intensive usage

**utiliser** *vb* utilize *vb*

**utilité** *nf* utility *n* **utilité marginale** marginal utility

**vacance** *nf* holiday *n*, vacation (US) **en vacances** on holiday, on vacation (US)

**vague** *nf* (of mergers, takeovers) wave *n*

**valable** *adj* valid *adj*

**valeur** *nf* value *n* **valeur actualisée nette** discounted cash flow (DCF) **valeur comptable** book value **valeur cotée en bourse** quoted share, quoted stocks (US) **valeur de liquidation** liquidation value **valeur marchande** market value **valeur nominale** face value, nominal value **valeurs du marché hors-cote** unlisted securities **valeurs mobilières** stocks and shares **valeurs de premier ordre** gilts, blue-chip securities

**validation** *nf* probate *n*

**valide** *adj* valid *adj*

**valider** *vb* validate *vb*

**validité** *nf* validity *n*

**valoir** *vb* be worth *vb*

**variable** *adj* variable *adj*

**véhicule** *nm* vehicle *n* **véhicule utilitaire** commercial vehicle

**vendable** *adj* marketable *adj*

**vendeur, -euse** *nm,f* salesperson *n*, seller *n*, vendor *n* **vendeurs associés** joint vendor

**vendre** *vb* sell *vb* **à vendre** for sale **vendre qch à crédit** sell sth on credit **vendre qch au détail** sell sth retail **vendre qch aux enchères** sell sth at auction **vendre qch en gros** sell sth wholesale **vendre en vrac** sell sth in bulk

**venir** *vb* come *vb* **venir à l'esprit** come to mind **venir à un rendez-vous** keep an appointment

**vente** *nf* sale *n*  **vente agressive** hard sell
**vente au comptant** cash sale  **vente par
correspondance (VPC)** mail order  **vente
discrète** soft sell  **vente aux enchères** auction
**vente immobilière** house sale  **ventes à
l'exportation** export sales  **ventes sur le
marché intérieur** home sales  **ventes nettes**
net(t) sales  **vente par soumission** sale by
tender  **vente à terme** future delivery
**ventilation** *nf* (of figures) breakdown *n*
**vérification** *nf* examination *n*, inspection *n*
  **vérification des comptes** audit
**vérifier** *vb* check *vb*
**vers** *prep* toward(s) *prep*  **vers le bas** downward
**versement** *nm* deposit *n*, instalment *n*,
remittance *n*, installment (US)  **premier versement** down payment  **versement au
clearing** clearing payment  **versements
échelonnés** instalments
**verser** *vb* deposit *vb*
**veto** *nm* veto *n*
**viabilité** *nf* viability *n*
**vieillissement** *nm* obsolescence *n*  **vieillissement programmé** built-in obsolescence,
planned obsolescence
**vif** *adj* (competition) keen *adj*
**ville** *nf* town *n*
**violer** *vb* contravene *vb*
**virement** *nm* transfer *n*, payment *n*  **virement
bancaire** bank transfer, banker's order  **virement de crédit** credit transfer
**visa** *nm* visa *n*, entry visa *n*
**visible** *adj* visible *adj*
**visiophone** *nm* visual telephone *n*
**visite** *nf* visit *n*
**visiter** *vb* visit *vb*
**visiteur** *nm* visitor *n*

**vitesse** *nf* speed *n*  **à deux vitesses** two speed
  **vitesse de rotation** turnover rate
**vivre** *vb* live *vb*  **vivre au-dessus de ses
moyens** live beyond one's means
**voie** *nf* track *n*, path *n*  **être sur la bonne voie**
be on the right track  **voie ferrée** railway
**vol** *nm* (aviation) flight *n*  **vol charter** charter
flight
**volteface** *nf* turnabout *n*
**volume** *nm* bulk *n*  **volume des transactions**
trading volume
**vote** *nm* vote *nm*  **vote pour ou contre la
grève** strike ballot
**voter** *vb* vote *vb*
**voyage** *nm* journey *n*, trip *n*  **voyage d'affaires**
business trip  **voyage aller et retour** round
trip  **voyage organisé** package tour  **voyages
à l'étranger** foreign travel
**voyageur, -euse** *nm,f* traveller *n*, traveler
(US)
**vrac** *nm* bulk *n*  **en vrac** in bulk, loose
**VRP (voyageur-représentant)** *abbr* commercial traveller, commercial traveler (US)
**zénith** *nm* zenith *n*
**zéro** *nm* nil *n*, zero *n*  **zéro défaut** zero defect
**zonage** *nm* zoning *n*  **zonage fiscal** fiscal
zoning
**zone** *nf* area *n*, zone *n*  **zone d'activité**
business park  **zone d'attente** hold area
**zone de chalandise** trading area  **zone d'entreprise** enterprise zone  **zone d'exclusion**
exclusion zone  **zone industrielle** trading
estate  **zone de libre-échange** free trade area
**zone monétaire** currency zone  **zone postale**
postal zone  **zone sterling** sterling area  **zone
de travail** working area
**ZUP (zone à urbaniser en priorité)** *abbr*
urban development area *n*

# English–French

**a.s.a.p. (as soon as possible)** *abbr* dès que possible

**abandon** *vb* abandonner *vb*

**abandoned** *adj* **abandoned goods** marchandises délaissées *nfpl*

**abate** *vb* réduire *vb*, annuler *vb*

**abatement** *n* réduction *nf*, annulation *nf*

**abbreviate** *vb* abréger *vb*

**abbreviated** *adj* abrégé *adj*

**abbreviation** *n* abréviation *nf*

**abeyance** *n* **to fall into abeyance** tomber en désuétude

**ability** *n* compétence *nf*, aptitude *nf* **ability to pay** solvabilité *nf*

**aboard** *adv* **to go aboard** monter à bord *vb*

**abolish** *vb* supprimer *vb*, abolir *vb*

**abolition** *n* suppression *nf*, abolition *nf*

**above-mentioned** *adj* précité *adj*

**aboveboard** *adj* régulier *adj*

**abroad** *adv* **to go abroad** aller à l'étranger

**absence** *n* **in the absence of information** faute de renseignements

**absent** *adj* absent *adj*

**absentee** *adj* absentéiste *adj* **absentee landlord** propriétaire absentéiste *nm*

**absenteeism** *n* absentéisme *nm*

**absolute** *adj* absolu *adj*

**absorb** *vb* absorber *vb*, amortir *vb* **to absorb surplus stock** résorber des surplus

**abstract** *n* résumé *nm*

**abundance** *n* abondance *nf*

**abuse 1.** *n* **abuse of power/trust** abus de pouvoir/confiance *nm* **2.** *vb* abuser *vb*

**accelerate** *vb* accélérer *vb*

**acceleration** *n* accélération *nf*

**accept** *vb* **accept delivery** prendre livraison (de)

**acceptance** *n* **consumer acceptance** acceptation par les consommateurs **acceptance house** banque d'acceptation **market acceptance** acceptation du produit par le marché

**access 1.** *n* accès *nm* **2.** *vb* accéder (à) *vb*

**accessibility** *n* accessibilité *nf*

**accident** *n* accident *nm* **industrial accident** accident du travail

**accidental** *adj* **accidental damage** dommages *nmpl*, avaries *nfpl*

**accommodation** *n* logement *nm* **accommodation allowance** indemnité de logement **accommodation bill** billet de complaisance **to come to an accommodation** arriver à un compromis

**accomplish** *vb* accomplir *vb*

**accomplishment** *n* exécution *nf*, réalisation *nf*

**accordance** *n* **in accordance with** conformément à

**according to** *prep* **according to plan** comme prévu **according to the minister** selon le ministre

**account** *n* **bank account** compte en banque *nm* **Account Day** (stock exchange) jour de liquidation *nm* **expense account** note de frais *nm* **payment on account** acompte *nm*, arrhes *nfpl* **profit and loss account** compte de profits et pertes *nm* **savings account** compte d'épargne *nm* **accounts receivable** comptes clients *nmpl*, créances *nfpl* **statement of account** relevé de compte *nm* **to open an account** ouvrir un compte *vb* **to overdraw on an account** mettre un compte à découvert *vb* **to settle an account** régler un compte *vb* **to take sth into account** tenir compte de qch *vb* **trading account** compte d'exploitation *nm*

**account for** *vb* rendre compte (de) *vb*

**accountability** *n* responsabilité *nf*

**accountable** *adj* responsable *adj*

**accountancy** *n* comptabilité *nf*

**accountant** *n* comptable *nm* **chartered accountant** expert comptable *nm*

**accounting** *n* **accounting conventions** normes comptables *nfpl* **financial accounting** comptabilité générale *nf* **management accounting** comptabilité analytique *nf* **accounting period** exercice comptable *nm*

**accredit** *vb* accréditer *vb*, garantir *vb*

**accrual** *n* accumulation *nf* **rate of accrual** rythme d'accumulation *nm*

**accrued** *adj* **accrued interest** intérêts cumulés *nmpl*

**accumulate** *vb* accumuler *vb*

**accumulated** *adj* cumulé *adj*

**accuracy** *n* exactitude *nf*, précision *nf*

**accurate** *adj* exact *adj*, précis *adj*

**achieve** *vb* accomplir *vb*, réaliser *vb*

**achievement** *n* réalisation *nf*, réussite *nf*

**acknowledge** *vb* **to acknowledge receipt of sth** accuser réception de qch

**acknowledgement** *n* **acknowledgement of debt** reconnaissance de dette *nf*

**acquaintance** *n* **business acquaintance** relation d'affaires *nf* **to make the acquaintance**

**of sb** faire la connaissance de qn
**acquire** *vb* acquérir *vb*
**acquisition** *n* acquisition *nf*
**acquisitive** *adj* avide *adj*, acquisitif *adj*
**action** *n* **industrial action** grève *nf* **legal action** action en justice *nf* **out of action** en panne
**actual** *adj* réel *adj*
**actuality** *n* réalité *nf*
**actuary** *n* actuaire *nmf*
**acumen** *n* **business acumen** sens des affaires *nm*
**additional** *adj* **additional charge** supplément *nm*
**address 1.** *n* **home address** adresse personnelle *nf* **registered address** (adresse du) siège social *nm* **to change address** changer d'adresse **2.** *vb* adresser *vb*
**addressee** *n* destinataire *nmf*
**adjourn** *vb* ajourner *vb*, remettre *vb*, reporter *vb* lever (une séance) *vb*
**adjournment** *n* ajournement *nm*, suspension *nf*
**adjust** *vb* ajuster *vb* **to adjust a claim** régler un sinistre **to adjust the figures** corriger les statistiques
**adjustment** *n* ajustement *nm*, réglage *nm*
**administer** *vb* gérer *vb*, administrer *vb*
**administration** *n* administration *nf*
**administrative** *adj* **administrative costs** frais administratifs *nmpl*
**administrator** *n* administrateur *nm*
**advance 1.** *adj* **advance notice** préavis *nm* **payable in advance** payable d'avance *adj* **advance payment** acompte *nm*, avance *nf*, arrhes *nfpl* **2.** *n* (on salary) avance *nf* **cash advance** avance *nf*, arrhes *nfpl* **3.** *vb* (salary) avancer *vb*
**advanced** *adj* **advanced country** pays avancé *nm* **advanced technology** technologie de pointe *nf*
**advantage** *n* avantage *nm* **comparative advantage** avantage comparatif *nm* **competitive advantage** avantage concurrentiel *nm*
**advantageous** *adj* avantageux *adj*, intéressant *adj*
**adverse** *adj* **adverse balance of trade** balance commerciale défavorable *nf*
**advertise** *vb* faire de la publicité (pour) *vb*
**advertisement** *n* annonce *nf*, réclame *nf*, spot (publicitaire) *nm*
**advertising** *adj* **advertising agency** agence publicitaire *nf* **advertising budget** budget de publicité *nm* **advertising campaign** campagne de publicité *nf* **advertising medium** support publicitaire *nm* **advertising revenue** recettes publicitaires *nfpl*
**advice** *n* conseil *nm*
**advise** *vb* conseiller *vb* **to advise sb about sth** conseiller qn sur qch *vb*
**adviser/advisor** *n* conseiller *nm*

**advisory** *adj* consultatif *adj*
**advocate** *vb* recommander *vb*
**aerospace** *adj* **aerospace industry** industrie aérospatiale *nf*
**affidavit** *n* déclaration sous serment *nf*
**affiliated** *adj* **affiliated company** filiale *nf*
**affluent** *adj* **affluent society** société d'abondance *nf*
**afford** *vb* **I can't afford (to buy a new printer)** je n'ai pas les moyens (d'acheter une nouvelle imprimante) **we cannot afford (to take) the risk** nous ne pouvons pas nous permettre de courir le risque
**after-sales service** *n* service après-vente *nm*
**agency** *n* **advertising agency** agence de publicité *nf* **employment agency** agence de recrutement *nm* **travel agency** agence de voyages *nf*
**agenda** *n* ordre du jour *nm*
**agent** *n* agent *nm*
**AGM (Annual General Meeting)** *abbr* assemblée générale annuelle *nf*
**agrarian** *adj* agraire *adj*
**agree** *vb* consentir *vb*, accepter *vb*, être d'accord *vb*
**agreed** *adj* convenu *adj*
**agreement** *n* accord *nm* **by mutual agreement** d'un commun accord **verbal agreement** accord verbal **wage agreement** accord salarial
**agribusiness** *n* industries agro-alimentaires *nfpl*
**agriculture** *n* agriculture *nf*
**agronomist** *n* agronome *nm*
**aid** *n* **financial aid** aide financière *nf*
**air** *n* **by air** par avion **air freight** transport aérien *nm* **air traffic controller** aiguilleur du ciel *nm*
**air-conditioned** *adj* climatisé *adj*
**airline** *n* compagnie d'aviation *nf*
**airmail** *n* poste aérienne *nf*
**airport** *n* aéroport *nm*
**allocate** *vb* allouer *vb*
**allowance** *n* allocation *nf* **family allowance** allocation familiale *nf*
**amalgamate** *vb* fusionner *vb*
**amalgamation** *n* fusion *nf*
**amend** *vb* amender *vb*, modifier *vb*
**amendment** *n* modification *nf*
**amends** *npl* **to make amends** faire amende honorable
**amenities** *npl* aménagements *nmpl*, équipements *nmpl*
**amortization** *n* amortissement *nm*
**amortize** *vb* amortir *vb*, rembourser *vb*
**amount** *n* montant *nm*
**amount to** *vb* monter à *vb*, s'élever à *vb*
**analysis** *n* **cost-benefit analysis** analyse coûts-rendements *nf* **systems analysis** analyse des systèmes *nf*
**analyze** *vb* analyser *vb*
**annual** *adj* **annual general meeting (AGM)**

assemblée générale (annuelle) nf **annual report** rapport annuel nm
**annuity** n rente nf
**annulment** n annulation nf
**Ansaphone (R)** n répondeur (téléphonique) nm
**answer 1.** n réponse nf **2.** vb répondre vb
**answering** adj **answering machine** répondeur (téléphonique) nm
**anti-inflationary** adj **anti-inflationary measures** mesures anti-inflationnistes nfpl
**antitrust** adj **antitrust laws** lois antitrust nfpl
**appeal 1.** n appel nm **2.** vb faire appel, lancer un appel
**application** n **application form** dossier de candidature nm **letter of application** lettre de candidature nf
**apply for** vb faire une demande, poser sa candidature (à)
**appoint** vb **to appoint sb to a position** nommer qn à un poste
**appointment** n (to meet) rendez-vous nm (to a position) nomination à un poste nf **to make an appointment** prendre rendez-vous (avec qn)
**appraisal** n évaluation nf
**appreciate** vb (rise in value) prendre de la valeur
**appreciation** n (in value) accroissement de la valeur nm, plus-value nf
**apprentice** n apprenti, -e nm,f
**apprenticeship** n apprentissage nm
**appropriation** n affectation nf, dotation nf
**approval** n approbation nf **on approval** à l'essai
**approve** vb approuver vb
**approximate** adj approximatif adj
**approximately** adv approximativement adv
**arbitrage** n arbitrage nm
**arbitrary** adj arbitraire adj
**arbitrate** vb arbitrer vb
**arbitration** n arbitrage nm
**arbitrator** n arbitre nm, médiateur nm
**area** n **area manager** directeur régional nm
**arithmetic** n arithmétique nf
**arithmetical** adj **arithmetical mean** moyenne arithmétique nf
**arms** npl **arms trade** commerce des armes nm
**arrangement** n (agreement) arrangement nm, accord nm
**arrears** npl arriéré nm **in arrears** en retard dans ses paiements **to fall/get into arrears** s'arriérer
**articulated** adj **articulated lorry** semi-remorque nm
**asking** adj **asking price** prix demandé au départ nm
**assembly** n **assembly line** chaîne de montage nf
**assess** vb calculer vb, évaluer vb
**assessment** n calcul nm, évaluation nf

**asset** n élément d'actif nm **capital assets** actifs immobiliers nmpl **asset stripping** dégraissage d'actif nm
**assign** vb assigner vb, attribuer vb
**assignee** n cessionnaire nmf
**assignment** n mission nf, cession nf
**assistant** adj **assistant manager** sous-directeur nm, directeur adjoint nm
**associate 1.** adj **associate director** directeur adjoint nm **2.** n associé, -e nm,f
**attestation** n attestation nf
**attorney** n **power of attorney** procuration nf
**auction 1.** n vente aux enchères nf **2.** vb vendre aux enchères vb
**auctioneer** n commissaire-priseur nm
**audit** n audit nm, vérification des comptes nf
**auditor** n commissaire aux comptes nm
**authority** n (official) autorités nfpl, pouvoir nm
**authorize** vb autoriser vb
**authorized** adj **authorized dealer** concessionnaire nmf
**automatic** adj automatique adj **automatic cash dispenser** distributeur automatique de billets nm
**automation** n automatisation nf
**automobile** adj **automobile industry** industrie automobile nf
**autonomous** adj autonome adj
**auxiliary** adj auxiliaire adj
**average** adj moyen adj **average unit** unité moyenne nf
**avoid** vb éviter vb
**avoidance** n **tax avoidance** évasion fiscale nf
**axe, ax** (US) vb opérer des coupes vb, réduire vb **to axe expenditure** réduire les dépenses vb
**back** vb **to back a venture** financer un projet vb
**back pay** n rappel de salaire nm
**backdate** vb **to backdate a cheque** antidater un chèque vb
**backer** n bailleur de fonds nm, commanditaire nm
**backhander\*** n pot-de-vin nm
**backing** n soutien financier nm
**backlog** n arriéré nm
**bad** adj **bad cheque** chèque sans provision nm **bad debt** créance irrécouvrable nf
**bail** n caution nf
**bailiff** n huissier nm
**balance 1.** n (financial) balance nf, équilibre nm, solde nm **bank balance** solde en banque nm **final balance** solde final nm **balance in hand** solde créditeur nm **balance of payments** balance des paiements nf **balance of payments deficit** balance commerciale déficitaire nf **balance of payments surplus** balance commerciale excédentaire nf **balance of trade** balance commerciale nf **balance sheet** bilan nm

**trade balance** balance commerciale *nf* **2.** *vb* équilibrer *vb* **to balance the books** arrêter les comptes *vb* **to balance the budget** établir le solde *vb*

**bank** **1.** *n* banque *nf* **bank account** compte en banque *nm* **bank balance** solde en banque *nm* **bank card** carte bancaire *nf* **bank charges** frais bancaires *nmpl* **bank clerk** employé de banque *nm* **bank draft** chèque de banque *nm* **bank holiday** jour férié *nm* **bank loan** prêt bancaire *nm* **bank manager** directeur de banque *nm* **bank overdraft** découvert *nm* **bank rate** taux d'escompte *nm* **bank statement** relevé de compte *nm* **2.** *vb* **to bank a cheque** déposer un chèque à la banque

**banker** *n* banquier *nm* **banker's order** virement bancaire *nm*

**banking** *adj* **banking circles** les milieux bancaires *nmpl* **banking hours** heures d'ouverture (de la banque) *nfpl*

**banknote** *n* billet de banque *nm*

**bankrupt** *adj* en faillite *adj phr* **to be bankrupt** être en faillite *vb*

**bankruptcy** *n* faillite *nf*

**bar code** *n* code (à) barres *nm*

**bargain** **1.** *adj* **bargain offer** offre spéciale *nf*, offre promotionnelle *nf* **bargain price** prix exceptionnel *nm* **2.** *n* occasion *nf* **it's a bargain** c'est une occasion **3.** *vb* marchander *vb*

**barrier** *n* barrière *nf* **trade barrier** barrière douanière *nf*

**barrister, lawyer** (US) *n* avocat *nm*

**barter** **1.** *adj* **barter agreement** accord de troc *nm* **barter transaction** opération de troc *nf* **2.** *n* troc *nm* **3.** *vb* échanger *vb*, troquer *vb*

**base** *adj* **base lending rate** taux de base *nm*

**basic** *adj* **basic commodity** produit de base *nm* **basic income** revenu direct *nm* **basic rate** taux de base *nm* **basic training** formation élémentaire *nf*

**basis** *n* **basis of assessment** assiette *nf*, base d'imposition *nf*

**basket** *n* **basket of currencies** panier de devises *nm*

**batch** *n* (of goods) lot *nm*, paquet *nm* **batch processing** (DP) traitement par lots *nm*

**bear** **1.** *n* (stock exchange) spéculateur à la baisse *nm* **bear market** marché à la baisse *nm* **2.** *vb* **to bear interest** rapporter un intérêt

**bearer** *n* porteur *nm* **bearer bond** obligation au porteur *nm* **bearer cheque** chèque au porteur *nm* **bearer share** action au porteur *nm*

**bench** *n* **bench mark price** prix de référence *nm*

**benefactor** *n* bienfaiteur *nm*

**benefit** **1.** *n* (social security) avantage *nm*, allocation *nf* **2.** *vb* profiter *vb*, bénéficier

(à) *vb*

**bequeath** *vb* léguer *vb*

**bequest** *n* legs *nm*

**best** *adj* **best-before date** date de fraîcheur *nf*

**best seller** bestseller *nm*, (livre à) succès de librairie *nm*

**biannual** *adj* (twice a year) semestriel *adj*, (every two years) biennal *adj*

**bid** **1.** *n* offre *nf*, (auction) enchère *nf* **2.** *vb* (auction) offrir *vb*, faire une enchère *vb*

**biennial** *adj* biennal *adj*

**bilateral** *adj* **bilateral trade** commerce bilatéral *nm*

**bill** **1.** *n* (invoice) facture *nf*, effet *nm*, traite *nf* **bill of exchange** effet de commerce *nm*, traite *nf* **bill of lading** connaissement *nm* **bill of sale** acte de vente *nm* **bills discounted** effets escomptés *nmpl* **to pay a bill** payer l'addition *vb* **2.** *vb* (invoice) facturer *vb*

**bimonthly** *adj* (twice a month) bimensuel *adj*, (every two months) bimestriel *adj*

**binding** *adj* obligatoire *adj*, irrévocable *adj* **legally binding** obligatoire *adj*, irrévocable *adj*

**biweekly** *adj* (twice in a week) bihebdomadaire *adj* (fortnightly) bimensuel *adj*

**black** *adj* **black economy** économie parallèle *nf* **black market** marché noir *nm* **to be in the black** avoir un solde créditeur *vb*

**blank** *adj* **blank cheque** chèque en blanc *nm*

**block** **1.** *n* bloc *nm*, paquet *nm* **2.** *vb* bloquer *vb*, entraver *vb*

**blockade** **1.** *n* blocus *nm* **2.** *vb* bloquer *vb*

**blocked** *adj* **blocked account** compte bloqué *nm*

**blue** *adj* **blue-chip company** société de premier ordre *nf* **blue-collar worker** col bleu *nm* **blue-chip securities** valeurs de premier ordre *nfpl*

**board** *n* conseil *nm*, comité *nm*, commission *nf* **Board of Trade** Ministère du Commerce *nm* **board meeting** réunion du conseil d'administration *nf* **board of directors** (GB) conseil d'administration *nm* **board room** salle du conseil *nf*

**bona fide** *adj* de bonne foi *adj*

**bond** *n* obligation *nf*, engagement *nm* **bond certificate** certificat d'obligation *nm* **government bond** bon du Trésor *nm* **in bond** sous douane *adj*

**bonded** *adj* **bonded warehouse** entrepôt sous douane *nm*

**bondholder** *n* porteur d'obligations *nm*

**bonus** *n* prime *nf*

**book** **1.** *n* **cheque book** carnet de chèques *nm* **book profit** profit comptable *nm* **the books** les livres comptables *nmpl* **book value** valeur comptable *nf* **2.** *vb* **to book a hotel room** réserver une chambre d'hôtel *vb* **to book in advance** réserver d'avance *vb*

**booking** *n* (reservation) réservation *nf*
**bookkeeper** *n* comptable *nmf*
**bookkeeping** *n* comptabilité *nf*
**bookseller** *n* libraire *nmf*
**bookshop, bookstore** (US) *n* librairie *nf*
**boom** 1. *n* **economic boom** essor économique *nm* **boom in demand** la demande est en plein essor 2. *vb* être en plein essor *vb*
**booming** *adj* en plein essor, en pleine expansion
**boost** 1. *n* relance *nf*, coup de pouce *nm* 2. *vb* **to boost demand** relancer la demande *vb* **to boost morale** remonter le moral *vb* **to boost production** relancer la production *vb* **to boost sales** relancer les ventes *vb*
**boot** *vb* (computer) amorcer *vb*, lancer *vb*
**booth** *n* (voting) cabine *nf*, isoloir *nm*
**borrow** *vb* emprunter *vb*
**borrowing** *n* emprunt *nm*
**boss** *n* patron *nm*
**bottleneck** *n* goulot *nm* **bottleneck inflation** inflation par la demande *nf*
**bottom** 1. *adj* **bottom price** le prix le plus bas *nm* 2. *n* **at the bottom** au bas 3. *vb* **to bottom out** toucher le fond *vb*
**bought** *adj* **bought ledger** grand livre des achats *nm*
**bounce*** *vb* (cheque) un chèque qui est refusé *nm*, un chèque sans provision *nm*
**bound** *n* **out of bounds** hors les limites
**box** 1. *n* **box number** référence *nf* **box office** bureau de location *nm* **PO box** B.P./boîte postale *nf* 2. *vb* **to box sth up** mettre en boîte *vb*
**boycott** 1. *n* boycottage *nm* 2. *vb* boycotter *vb*
**bracket** *n* tranche *nf*, fourchette *nf*, parenthèse *nf* **tax bracket** tranche d'imposition *nf*
**branch** *n* succursale *nf*, agence *nf*, filiale *nf* **branch company** succursale *nf* **branch manager** directeur de succursale *nm* **branch office** succursale *nf*, agence *nf*
**brand** *n* marque *nf* **brand image** image de marque *nf* **brand leader** produit leader *nm*
**breach** *n* infraction *nf*, rupture *nf* **breach of contract** rupture de contrat *nf*
**break** 1. **to take a break** faire une pause *vb*, prendre un congé *vb* 2. *vb* rompre *vb* **to break an agreement** rompre un accord *vb*
**break even** *vb* rentrer dans ses frais *vb*
**break up** *vb* se terminer *vb*, prendre fin *vb*
**break-even** *adj* **break-even point** seuil de rentabilité *nm*
**breakdown** *n* panne *nf*, rupture *nf* (of figures) ventilation *nf*, décomposition *nf* **breakdown service** service de dépannage *nm*
**breakthrough** *n* percée *nf* **to make a breakthrough** faire une percée *vb*
**breakup** *n* liquidation *nf*

**bribe** 1. *n* pot-de-vin *nm* 2. *vb* acheter *vb*, suborner *vb*
**bribery** *n* corruption *nf*, subornation *nf*
**bridging** *adj* **bridging loan, bridge loan** (US) crédit relais *nm*
**brief** 1. *n* dossier *nm* 2. *vb* donner des instructions (à qn) *vb*
**briefing** *n* briefing *nm*
**bring down** *vb* (prices) baisser les prix *vb*
**bring forward** *vb* reporter *vb*
**bring out** *vb* (product) sortir *vb*
**brinkmanship** *n* stratégie du bord de l'abîme *nf*
**Britain** *n* Grande-Bretagne *nf*
**British** *adj* britannique *adj* **British Council** British Council *nm* **British Isles** Iles Britanniques *nfpl*
**broad** *adj* large *adj* **broad market** marché vaste/large *nm*
**broadcast** 1. *n* programme *nm*, émission *nf* 2. *vb* diffuser *vb*, émettre *vb*
**broadsheet** *n* (advertising) placard publicitaire *nm*, (newspaper) journal de grand format *nm*
**brochure** *n* brochure *nf*
**broker** *n* courtier *nm*, agent de change *nm*
**brokerage** *n* courtage *nm* **brokerage firm** maison de courtage *nf*
**buck*** (US) *n* dollar *nm* **to pass the buck*** refiler la responsabilité à quelqu'un d'autre *vb*
**budget** *n* budget *nm* **to draw up a budget** établir un budget *vb*
**budget for** *vb* établir un budget pour qch *vb*
**budgetary** *adj* **budgetary deficit** déficit budgétaire *nm* **budgetary policy** politique budgétaire *nf*
**bug** 1. *n* (listening device) bogue *nf*, défaut *nm* 2. *vb* installer des micros (dans une salle) *vb* **to bug a call** écouter (clandestinement) un appel téléphonique *vb*
**build** *vb* **to build a reputation** bâtir une réputation *vb*
**builder** *n* constructeur *nm*
**building** *adj* **building contractor** entrepreneur en bâtiment *nm* **building firm** société de construction *nf* **building industry/trade** industrie du bâtiment *nf* **building permit** permis de construire *nm* **building site** chantier de construction *nm* **building society** société d'investissement et de crédit immobiliers *nf*
**built-in** *adj* incorporé *adj*, intégré *adj*
**built-up** *adj* **built-up area** agglomération (urbaine) *nf*
**bulk** *n* volume *nm*, vrac *nm* **the bulk of** la plus grosse partie *nf* **to buy in bulk** acheter en gros *vb*
**bull** 1. *n* (stock exchange) spéculateur à la hausse *nm* **bull market** marché haussier *nm* 2. *vb* (stock exchange) spéculer à la hausse *vb*

**bulletin** n bulletin nm **bulletin board** tableau d'affichage nm
**bullion** n or en barre nm
**bump up** vb (prices) faire grimper les prix vb
**bundle** n paquet nm
**bundle up** vb grouper vb
**buoyant** adj **buoyant market** marché ferme nm
**bureau** n bureau de change bureau de change nm **Federal Bureau (US)** Bureau Fédéral nm
**bureaucracy** n bureaucratie nf
**bureaucrat** n bureaucrate nmf
**bureaucratic** adj bureaucratique adj
**bursar** n intendant nm, économe nm
**bus** n autobus nm, bus nm **bus station** gare routière nf
**business** 1. adj **business address** adresse commerciale nf **business associate** associé nm **business consultant** conseiller en gestion nm **business expenses** frais professionnels nmpl **business hours** heures ouvrables nmpl **business premises** locaux commerciaux nmpl **business studies** études de gestion nfpl **business suit** costume sobre nm **business transaction** transaction commerciale nf **business trip** voyage d'affaires nm 2. n affaires nfpl **to go out of business** fermer boutique vb **big business** les grands milieux d'affaires nmpl **family business** entreprise familiale nf **to set up in business** se lancer dans les affaires vb
**businesslike** adj efficace adj
**busy** adj occupé adj **busy signal (US)** tonalité occupé nf
**buy** 1. n **a good buy** une bonne affaire nf 2. vb acheter vb **to buy sth at a high price** acheter à prix fort vb **to buy sth on credit** acheter qch à crédit vb **to buy sth second hand** acheter qch d'occasion vb **to buy sth wholesale** acheter qch en gros vb
**buy out** vb racheter vb
**buy-out** n rachat nm
**buyer** n acheteur nm **buyer's market** marché acheteur nm
**buying** n **buying and selling** achats et ventes nmpl & nfpl **buying power** pouvoir d'achat nm **buying price** prix d'achat nm **buying rate** cours acheteur nm
**by-product** n sous-produit nm
**bypass** 1. n **bypass** (operation) pontage nm 2. vb contourner vb
**byte** n octet nm
**c.i.f. (cost, insurance and freight)** abbr CAF (coût, assurance, fret) abbr
**CAD (computer-aided or assisted design)** abbr CAO (conception assistée par ordinateur) nf
**calculate** vb calculer vb
**calculation** n calcul nm
**calculator** n calculatrice nf
**call** 1. n **call money** emprunt remboursable sur demande nm **person-to-person call** appel avec préavis nm **reverse-charge call, collect call (US)** communication en PCV nf 2. vb **to call a meeting** tenir une réunion vb **to call it a deal** considérer l'affaire comme conclue vb
**call back** vb (on phone) rappeler vb
**call for** vb faire un appel (de) vb, appeler vb
**call in** vb (demand the repayment of a loan) exiger le remboursement d'un prêt vb
**campaign** n campagne nf **advertising campaign** campagne publicitaire nf **publicity campaign** campagne publicitaire nf **sales campaign** campagne de vente nf **to run a campaign** faire campagne vb
**cancel** vb annuler vb, supprimer vb **cancel a contract** résilier un contrat vb **cancel an appointment** annuler un rendez-vous vb
**cancellation** n annulation nf **cancellation charge** frais d'annulation nm
**candidate** n (for job) candidat nm
**cap** vb plafonner vb **to cap the interest rate** plafonner le taux d'intérêt vb
**CAP (Common Agricultural Policy)** abbr PAC ( politique agricole commune) nf
**capacity** n capacité nf **earning capacity** capacité bénéficiaire nf **industrial capacity** capacité industrielle nf **in my capacity as chairman** en tant que Président **manufacturing capacity** capacité de production nf **storage capacity** capacité de stockage nf **to expand capacity** capacité d'expansion nf **to work to full capacity** tourner à plein rendement vb
**capital** n capital nm **capital assets** actif immobilisé nm **capital budget** budget d'investissement nm **capital cost** coût d'immobilisation nm **capital expenditure** mise de fonds nf **capital exports** flux de capitaux vers l'extérieur nm **fixed capital** capital fixe nm **capital funds** fonds propres nmpl **capital gains** plus-value nf **capital gains tax** impôt sur les plus-values nm **capital goods** biens d'équipement nmpl **initial capital** capital de départ nm **invested capital** capital engagé nm **capital loss** moins-value nf **capital market** marché financier nm **to raise capital** mobiliser des capitaux vb **capital turnover** rotation du capital nf **venture capital** mise de fonds spéculatif nf **working capital** fonds de roulement nmpl
**capitalism** n capitalisme nm
**capitalist** 1. adj capitaliste adj 2. n capitaliste nmf
**capitalize** vb capitaliser vb
**card** n **bank card** carte bancaire nf **business card** carte de visite nf **chargecard** carte de crédit nf **cheque card** carte bancaire nf **credit card** carte de crédit nf **identity card** carte d'identité nf **smart card** carte à mémoire nf

**career** *n* carrière *nf* **careers advice** orientation professionnelle *nf*

**cargo** *n* cargaison *nf* **bulk cargo** cargaison en vrac *nf* **cargo ship** cargo *nm*

**carriage** *n* **carriage charge** frais de port *nm* **carriage costs** frais de port *nmpl* **carriage forward** port dû **carriage included** port payé **carriage paid** port payé

**carrier** *n* transporteur *nm* **bulk carrier** transporteur de vrac *nm* **express carrier** messageries *nfpl*

**carry** *vb* (stock) stocker *vb*

**carry forward** *vb* reporter *vb*

**carry out** *vb* exécuter *vb*

**carry over** *vb* (to next month) reporter au mois prochain *vb*

**carrying** *adj* **carrying cost** frais de possession *nm*, frais financier *nm*

**cartel** *n* cartel *nm*

**cash** **1.** *n* espèces *nfpl*, argent liquide *nm* **cash and carry** libre-service de gros *nm* **cash before delivery** payable à la commande *adj* **cash crop** récolte destinée à la vente *nf* **cash desk** caisse *nf* **cash discount** escompte de caisse *nm* **cash flow** cash-flow *nm* **for cash** contre espèces **cash machine/dispenser** distributeur de billets *nm* **cash offer** offre d'achat avec paiement comptant *nf* **cash on delivery (COD)** paiement à la livraison *nm* **cash on receipt of goods** payable à (la) réception *adj* **cash payment** paiement comptant *nm* **cash sale** vente au comptant *nf* **to pay in cash** payer comptant *vb*, payer en espèces *vb*, payer en argent liquide *vb* **cash transaction** opération au comptant *nf* **cash with order** payable à la commande *adj* **2.** *vb* encaisser *vb* **to cash a cheque** encaisser un chèque *vb*

**cash up** *vb* faire la caisse *vb*

**cashier** *n* caissier *nm*

**caution** *cpd* **caution money** caution *nf*

**ceiling** *n* (on prices) plafond *nm* **to put a ceiling on sth** plafonner *vb*

**central** *adj* **central bank** banque centrale *nf* **central planned economy** planification centralisée *nf* **central planning** planification centralisée *nf* **central processing unit (CPU)** (DP) centre de traitement *nm*

**centralization** *n* centralisation *nf*

**centralize** *vb* centraliser *vb*

**centre** *n* **business centre** centre commercial *nm* **Jobcentre** Agence nationale pour l'emploi *nf*

**certificate** **1.** *n* certificat *nm* **clearance certificate** congé de navigation *nm*, titre *nm*, certificat *nm* **marriage certificate** certicat de mariage *nm* **certificate of employment** certificat d'emploi *nm* **certificate of origin** certificat d'origine *nm* **certificate of ownership** titre de propriété *nm* **share certificate, stock certificate** (US) titre d'action *nm* **2.** *vb* certifier *vb*

**certified** *adj* **certified cheque** chèque certifié *nm*

**certify** *vb* certifier *vb*

**chain** *n* **chain of shops** chaîne de magasins *nf* **retail chain** chaîne de magasins *nf* **chain store** grand magasin à succursales multiples *nm*

**chair** *vb* présider *vb* **to chair a meeting** présider une réunion *vb*

**chamber** *n* **Chamber of Commerce** chambre de commerce *nf*

**chancellor** *n* **chancellor of the exchequer (GB)** Chancelier de l'Echiquier *nm*, Ministre des finances *nm*

**change** *n* (from purchase) monnaie *nf* **bureau de change** bureau de change *nm* **loose/ small change** (coins) monnaie *nf*

**charge** **1.** *n* prix *nm*, frais *nm* **charge account** compte clients *nm* **bank charges** frais de banque *nmpl* **delivery charges** frais de port *nmpl* **handling charges** frais de manutention *nmpl* **legal charge** frais de contentieux *nmpl*, frais judiciaires *nmpl* **to be in charge** être responsable (de) *vb* **2.** *vb* **charge a price** demander un prix *vb*, prélever *vb*, mettre qch sur le compte de qn *vb* **to charge commission** prélever une commission *vb* **to charge for sth** faire payer qch *vb* **to charge sth to an account** débiter un compte (pour qch) *vb* **to take charge of sth** assumer la responsabilité (de qch) *vb* **to charge sb with sth** accuser (qn de qch) *vb*

**chargeable** *adj* à payer

**charitable** *adj* **charitable trust** organisation caritative *nf*

**charity** *n* organisation caritative *nf*

**chart** *n* **bar chart** graphique en barres *nm* **flow chart** diagramme de circulation *nm* **pie chart** graphique circulaire *nm*, "camembert" *nm*

**charter** *n* **charter flight** vol charter *nm*

**chartered** *adj* **chartered accountant** expert-comptable *nm* **chartered bank** banque à charte *nf* **chartered surveyor** expert immobilier *nm*

**chattels** *npl* biens *nmpl*

**check** **1.** *n* **customs check** contrôle douanier *nm* **to make a check on sth** contrôler qch *vb*, vérifier qch *vb* **2.** *vb* contrôler *vb*, vérifier *vb*

**check in** *vb* (at airport) se présenter à l'enregistrement *vb* (register in an hotel) remplir une fiche (d'hôtel) *vb*

**check out** *vb* (pay the hotel bill) régler sa note *vb*

**checkbook (US)** *n* carnet de chèques *nm*

**chemical** *adj* chimique *adj* **chemical industry** industrie chimique *nf* **chemical products** produits chimiques *nmpl*

**cheque, check** (US) *n* chèque *nm* **return a cheque to drawer** renvoyer un chèque à l'émetteur *vb* **blank cheque** chèque en

blanc *nm* **cheque book** carnet de
chèques *nm* **crossed cheque** chèque
barré *nm* **dud cheque** chèque sans
provision *nm*, chèque en bois *nm* **a cheque
for the amount of £100** un chèque pour la
somme de £100 *nm* **to bounce a cheque**
refuser un chèque *vb* **to cash a cheque**
toucher un chèque *vb*, encaisser un
chèque *vb* **to make out a cheque to** faire un
chèque à l'ordre de *vb* **to pay by cheque**
payer par chèque *vb* **to sign a cheque** signer
un chèque *vb* **to stop a cheque** bloquer un
chèque *vb* **traveller's cheque, traveler's
cheque** (US) chèque de voyage *nm*
**chief** *adj* **chief accountant** chef comptable *nm*
**chief cashier** caissier principal *nm* **chief
executive** président-directeur général
(PDG) *nm* **chief financial officer** directeur
financier *nm*
**circular** *n* (letter) circulaire *nf*
**circulate** *vb* (document) propager *vb*,
circuler *vb*
**circulation** *n* **in circulation** en circulation
**circumstance** *n* circonstance *nf* **circumstances beyond our control** circonstances
indépendantes de notre volonté **due to
unforeseen circumstances** pour des raisons
imprévues **under no circumstances** en
aucun cas
**civil** *adj* **civil engineering** génie civil *nm* **civil
servant** fonctionnaire *nmf* **civil service**
fonction publique *nf*
**claim** 1. *n* **claim form** fomulaire de
déclaration de sinistre *nm* **claims department** service des réclamations *nm* **claims
procedure** procédure de réclamation *nf* **to
put in a claim** faire une réclamation *vb* **to
settle a claim** régler un sinistre *vb* **wage
claim** revendication salariale *nf* 2. *vb*
(demand) réclamer *vb*, revendiquer *vb*, prétendre (profess) *vb* **to claim for damages**
réclamer des dommages et intérêts *vb*
**claimant** *n* réclamant *nm*, demandeur *nm*
**class** *n* **business class** (plane) classe
affaires *nf* **first class** (plane) première
classe *nf*
**classified** *adj* **classified advertisement** petite
annonce *nf* **classified information** renseignements secrets *nmpl*
**clause** *n* (in contract) clause *nf* **escape clause**
clause résolutoire *nf* **option clause** disposition facultative *nf*
**clear** 1. *adj* clair *adj* **clear loss** perte sèche *nf*
**to make oneself clear** préciser *vb* 2. *vb* (a
cheque) compenser (un chèque) *vb* **to clear
sth through customs** dédouaner *vb*
**clearance** *n* **clearance offer** prix de
liquidation *nm* **clearance sale** liquidation
des stocks *nf*
**clearing** *adj* **clearing bank** banque de dépôt *nf*
**clearing house** chambre de compensation *nf*
**clearing payment** versement au clearing *nm*

**clerical** *adj* **clerical error** erreur d'écriture *nf*
**clerical work** travail de bureau *nm*
**clerk** *n* employé (de bureau) *nm*
**client** *n* client *nm*
**clientele** *n* clientèle *nf*
**clinch** *vb* conclure *vb* **clinch a deal** conclure
un marché *vb*
**clock in** *vb* pointer *vb*
**clock out** *vb* pointer (à la sortie) *vb*
**close** *vb* **to close a business** fermer une
entreprise *vb* **to close a deal** conclure une
transaction *vb* **to close a meeting** clôturer
une réunion *vb* **to close an account** fermer
un compte *vb*
**closed** *adj* fermé *adj* **closed session/meeting**
réunion à huis clos *nf* **closed shop** entreprise à monopole syndical *nf*
**closing** *adj* **closing bid** dernière enchère/
offre *nf* **closing price** cours de clôture *nm*
**closing time** heure de fermeture *nf*
**closure** *n* fermeture *nf* **closure of a company**
fermeture d'une entreprise *nf*
**COD (cash on delivery), (collect on delivery)**
(US) *abbr* paiement à la livraison *nm*
**code** *n* **bar code** code à barres *nm* **professional code of practice** code de bonne
conduite *nm*, déontologie *nf* **post code, zip
code** (US) code postal *nm* **telephone code**
indicatif *nm* **tax code** code des impôts *nm*
**collaborate** *vb* collaborer *vb*
**collaborative** *adj* **collaborative venture**
entreprise jointe *nf*
**collapse** *n* (of company, economy)
effondrement *nm* (on stock market) krach *nm*
**collateral** *adj* collatéral *adj* **collateral security**
nantissement *nm*
**colleague** *n* collègue *nmf*
**collect** *vb* recouvrer *vb*, collecter *vb*,
ramasser *vb* **to collect a debt** recouvrer une
dette *vb*
**collecting** *adj* **collecting agency** banque de
recouvrement
**collection** *n* recouvrement *nm*, collection *nf*
**debt collection** recouvrement (de dette) *nm*
**collective** 1. *adj* **collective agreement**
convention collective *nf* **collective bargaining** négociations (salariales etc) *nfpl* 2. *n*
**workers' collective** collectif des
travailleurs *nm*
**colloquium** *n* colloque *nm*
**comment** *n* commentaire *nm*
**commerce** *n* commerce *nm*
**commercial** *adj* commercial *adj* **commercial
bank** banque de dépôt *nf* **commercial
traveller, commercial traveler** (US) représentant de commerce *nm*, VRP (voyageur-
représentant) *abbr*, *nm* **commercial vehicle**
véhicule utilitaire *nm*
**commission** *n* commission *nf* **commission
agent** agent *nm* **commission broker**
courtier *nm* **commission fee** commission *nf*
**to charge commission** prélever une

commission *vb*
commit *vb* engager *vb*
commitment *n* engagement *nm*
committee *n* comité *nm*, commission *nf*
advisory committee commission
consultative *nf* committee meeting
réunion *nf*
common *adj* commun, -e *adj* Common
Agricultural Policy (CAP) Politique Agricole
Commune *nf* Common Market Marché
Commun *nm* common law droit
coutumier *nm*
communication *n* communication *nf* communication network réseau de
communication *nm*
company *n* compagnie *nf*, société *nf*,
entreprise *nf* holding company société
holding *nf* incorporated company (US)
société enregistrée *nf* joint-stock company
société par actions *nf* company law droit
des sociétés *nm* limited company société à
responsabilité limitée *nf*, société anonyme *nf*
parent company maison/société mère *nf/nf*
company policy politique de la société *nf*
private limited company société à responsabilité limitée (S.A.R.L.) *nf* public limited
company société anonyme *nf* registered
company société inscrite au registre du
commerce *nf* company secretary secrétaire
général(e) *nmf* sister company société
soeur *nf* subsidiary company filiale *nf*
comparative *adj* comparatif *adj*
compatible *adj* compatible *adj*
compensate for *vb* compenser *vb*
compensation *n* compensation *nf*,
dédommagement *nm* to claim compensation réclamer un dédommagement *vb* to
pay compensation dédommager *vb*
compete *vb* faire concurrence *vb* to compete
with a rival faire concurrence à *vb*
competing *adj* competing company compagnie en concurrence *nf*
competition *n* concurrence *nf* cut-throat
competition concurrence acharnée *nf* market competition concurrence au marché *nf*
unfair competition concurrence déloyale *nf*
competitive *adj* compétitif *adj*,
concurrentiel *adj*
competitiveness *n* compétitivité *nf*
competitor *n* concurrent *nm*
complain *vb* to complain about sth se
plaindre de qch *vb*
complaint *n* plainte *nf* to make a complaint
se plaindre *vb*, faire une réclamation *vb* + *nf*
complaints department service des
réclamations *nm*
complete *vb* achever *vb*, terminer *vb*,
compléter *vb*
complex 1. *adj* complexe *adj* 2. *n*
complexe *nm*, ensemble *nm* housing
complex grand ensemble *nm*
complimentary *adj* gracieux *adj*, gratuit *adj*

comply *vb* to comply with legislation
observer *vb* to comply with the rules
observer les règles *vb*
compound *adj* compound interest intérêts
composés *nmpl*
comprehensive *adj* détaillé *adj*, complet *adj*
comprehensive insurance policy assurance
tous risques *nf*
compromise *n* compromis *nm* to reach a
compromise aboutir à un compromis *vb*
computer *n* ordinateur *nm* computer-aided
design (CAD) conception assistée par ordinateur (CAO) *nf* computer-aided learning
(CAL) enseignement assisté par
ordinateur *nm* computer-aided manufacture (CAM) fabrication assistée par
ordinateur *nf* computer centre, center (US)
centre informatique *nm* computer file
fichier informatique *nm* computer language
langage de programmation *nm* laptop
computer portable *nm* computer literate
qui connaît l'informatique  mainframe
computer gros ordinateur *nm* computer
operator opérateur sur ordinateur *nm* personal computer (PC) ordinateur
individuel *nm* portable computer ordinateur
portable *nm* computer program programme informatique *nm* computer programmer programmeur *nm* computer
terminal terminal *nm*
concern 1. *n* going concern une affaire qui
marche *nf* 2. *vb* (be of importance to)
concerner *vb*, toucher *vb*
concur *vb* être d'accord (avec qn) *vb*, être
d'accord (sur qch) *vb*
condition *n* living conditions conditions de
vie *nfpl* conditions of purchase conditions
de vente *nfpl* conditions of sale conditions
de vente *nfpl* working conditions conditions
de travail *nfpl*
conference *n* colloque *nm*, conférence *nf*
conference proceedings travaux de
conférence *nmpl* to arrange a conference
organiser un colloque *vb* conference venue
lieu du colloque *nm*
confidence *n* in strictest confidence
confidentiellement *adv*
confidential *adj* confidentiel *adj*
confirm *vb* to confirm receipt of sth confirmer réception de qch *vb*
confirmation *n* confirmation *nf*
conglomerate *n* conglomérat *nm*
congress *n* congrès *nm*
connect *vb* could you connect me to...
(telephone) pourriez-vous me mettre en
communication avec
connection *n* business connections relations
d'affaires *nfpl*
consent 1. *n* consentement *nm* 2. *vb*
consentir *vb*
consequence *n* conséquence *nf*
consideration *n* (for contract) provision *nf*

**consignee** *n* consignataire *nmf*
**consigner/or** *n* consignateur *nm*
**consignment** *n* expédition *nf*
**consolidate** *vb* consolider *vb*
**consolidated** *adj* **consolidated figures** chiffres consolidés *nmpl*
**consortium** *n* consortium *nm*
**construction** *n* **construction industry** industrie du bâtiment *nf*
**consul** *n* consul *nm*
**consulate** *n* consulat *nm*
**consult** *vb* consulter *vb* **to consult with sb** consulter qn
**consultancy, consulting** (US) *cpd* **consultancy fees** frais d'expertise *nmpl* **consultancy firm** cabinet de conseil *nm* **consultancy work** travail de conseil *nm*
**consultant** *n* consultant *nm*, conseil *nm*
**consumer** *n* consommateur, -trice *nm,f* **consumer credit** crédit à la consommation *nm* **consumer demand** demande des consommateurs *nf* **consumer habits** habitudes de consommation *nfpl* **consumer research** étude de consommation *nf* **consumer satisfaction** satisfaction des consommateurs *nf* **consumer survey** étude de consommation *nf* **consumer trends** tendances de la consommation *nfpl*
**consumerism** *n* consumérisme *nm*
**contact** 1. *n* **business contacts** relations d'affaires *nfpl* **to get in contact with sb** prendre contact avec qqn 2. *vb* contacter *vb*
**container** *n* conteneur *nm* **container depot** entrepôt-conteneurs *nm* **container ship** porte-conteneurs *nm* **container terminal** terminal de conteneurs *nm*
**contract** *n* contrat *nm* **breach of contract** rupture de contrat *nf* **draft contract** projet de contrat *nm* **contract labour** main d'oeuvre contractuelle *nf* **law of contract** droit contractuel *nm* **the terms of the contract** conditions contractuelles *nfpl* **the signatories to the contract** les signataires du contrat *nmpl* **to cancel a contract** annuler/résilier un contrat *vb* **to draw up a contract** rédiger un contrat *vb* **to sign a contract** signer un contrat *vb* **to tender for a contract** faire une soumission, répondre à un appel d'offres **under the terms of the contract** selon les conditions contractuelles **contract work** travail à forfait *nm*
**contracting** *adj* **the contracting parties** parties contractantes *nfpl*
**contractor** *n* entrepreneur *nm* **building contractor** entrepreneur en bâtiment *nm* **haulage contractor** entrepreneur de transports *nm*
**contractual** *adj* **contractual obligations** responsabilités contractuelles *nfpl*
**contravene** *vb* violer *vb*, enfreindre *vb*
**contravention** *n* infraction *nf*
**contribute** *vb* contribuer *vb*

**contribution** *n* **social security contributions** cotisation à la Sécurité Sociale *nf*
**control** *n* **financial control** contrôle financier *nm* **production control** contrôle de la production *nm* **quality control** contrôle de qualité *nm* **stock control** gestion des stocks *nf*
**convene** *vb* **to convene a meeting** convoquer une assemblée *vb*
**convenience** *n* **at your earliest convenience** dans les meilleurs délais
**convenient** *adj* commode *adj*, pratique *adj*
**convertible** *adj* **convertible currency** monnaie convertible *nf*, devise convertible *nf*
**copier** *n* (photocopier) photocopieuse *nf*
**copy** 1. *n* copie *nf*, photocopie *nf* 2. *vb* (photocopy) photocopier *vb*
**copyright** *n* droits d'auteurs *nm*, copyright *nm* **copyright law** droits de copyright *nm*
**corporate** *adj* de société *adj*, d'entreprise *adj* **corporate image** image de marque (de l'entreprise) *nf* **corporate investment** investissements des entreprises *nmpl*
**corporation** *n* société commerciale *nf* **corporation tax** impôt sur les sociétés *nm*
**correspondence** *n* correspondance *nf*
**corruption** *n* corruption *nf*
**cosignatory** *n* cosignataire *nmf*
**cost** 1. *n* coût *nm* **cost breakdown** analyse des coûts *nf* **cost centre** centre de coût *nm* **cost-cutting** mesures d'économie *nfpl* **cost of living** coût de la vie *nm* **operating cost** frais d'exploitation *nmpl* **cost price** prix de revient *nm* **running cost** frais d'exploitation *nmpl* 2. *vb* **to cost a job** calculer le coût d'un travail *vb*
**counterfeit** 1. *n* faux *nm*, contrefaçon *nf* 2. *vb* contrefaire *vb*
**counterfoil** *n* talon *nm*
**countersign** *vb* contresigner *vb*
**country** *n* **developing country** pays en voie de développement *nm* **third-world country** pays du Tiers Monde *nm*
**coupon** *n* coupon *nm*
**courier** 1. *n* coursier *nm* **by courier service** par coursier 2. *vb* **send by courier** *vb* envoyer par coursier *vb*
**court** *n* **Court of Appeal, Court of Appeals** (US) cour d'appel *nf* **criminal court** tribunal *nm* **in court** devant un tribunal
**covenant** *n* convention *nf*
**covenantee** *n* créancier *nm*
**covenantor** *n* débiteur *nm*
**cover** *n* **insurance cover** couverture *nf* **cover note** lettre de couverture *nf*
**credit** 1. *n* crédit *nm* **credit agency** établissement de crédit *nm* **to buy sth on credit** acheter qch à crédit *vb* **credit card** carte de crédit *nf* **credit company** compagnie de crédit *nf* **credit control** encadrement du crédit *nm* **credit enquiry** enquête de

solvabilité *nf* **in credit** solvable *adj* **letter of credit** lettre de crédit *nf* **long credit** crédit à long terme *nm* **credit note** avis de crédit *nm* **credit rating** degré de solvabilité *nm*, rating **credit terms** conditions de paiement *nfpl* 2. *vb* **to credit sth to an account** créditer un compte *vb*

**creditor** *n* créancier *nm*

**creditworthiness** *n* solvabilité *nf*

**creditworthy** *adj* solvable *adj*, digne de confiance *adj*

**crossed** *adj* **crossed cheque** chèque barré *nm*

**currency** *n* monnaie *nf* **convertible currency** monnaie convertible *nf* **foreign currency** devise *nf*, monnaie étrangère *nf* **hard currency** devise forte *nf* **legal currency** monnaie légale *nf* **paper currency** papier-monnaie *nm* **soft currency** devise faible *nf* **currency transfer** transfert de devises *nm*

**current** *adj* **current account** compte courant *nm*

**curriculum vitae (CV), résumé** (US) *n* curriculum vitae (CV) *nm*

**customer** *n* client *nm* **customer loyalty** fidélité du client *nf* **regular customer** client régulier *nm* **customer relations** relations avec la clientèle *nfpl*

**customs** *npl* douane *nf* **customs charges** frais de douane *nmpl* **customs clearance** dédouanement *nm* **customs declaration** déclaration en douane *nf* **customs office** bureaux de douane *nmpl* **customs officer** douanier *nm* **customs regulations** règlements douaniers *nmpl* **to clear sth through customs** dédouaner *vb* **customs union** union douanière *nf* **customs warehouse** entrepôt de douane *nm*

**cut** 1. *n* **tax cut** réduction d'impôt *nf* 2. *vb* (reduce) réduire *vb*

**damage** 1. *n* dommages *nmpl* **to cause extensive damage** causer des dommages/dégâts importants *vb* **to claim damages** (legal) réclamer des dommages-intérêts *vb* **damage to goods in transit** avaries de route *nfpl* **damage to property** dommages matériels *nmpl* 2. *vb* endommager *vb*

**data** *npl* données *nfpl* **data bank** banque de données *nf* **database** base de données *nf* **data capture** saisie de données *nf* **data processing** informatique *nf*, traitement de données *nm*

**date** *n* **delivery date** date de livraison *nf* **out of date** périmé *adj*, démodé *adj* **up to date** à jour

**deal** *n* affaire *nf*, marché *nm* **it's a deal!** marché conclu! *nm*

**dealer** *n* négociant *nm*, marchand *nm*, concessionnaire *nm* **foreign exchange dealer** cambiste *nmf*

**dealing, trading** (US) *n* transactions *nfpl*, opérations *nfpl* **foreign exchange dealings** opérations de change *nfpl* **insider dealing**

délit d'initié *nm*

**debenture** *n* obligation *nf* **debenture bond** obligation *nf* **debenture capital, debenture stock** (US) capital-obligations *nm* **debenture loan** emprunt obligataire *nm*

**debit** 1. *n* débit *nm* **debit balance** solde débiteur *nm* 2. *vb* (account) débiter *vb*

**debiting** *n* **direct debiting** prélèvement bancaire *nm*

**debt** *n* dette *nf* **corporate debt** endettement des entreprises *nm* **to get into debt** s'endetter *vb* **to pay off a debt** régler une dette *vb* **to reschedule a debt** rééchelonner une dette *vb* **debt service** service de la dette *nm*

**debtor** *n* débiteur *nm*

**decline** *n* (economic) déclin *nm*

**decrease** 1. *n* diminution *nf* 2. *vb* diminuer *vb*

**deduct** *vb* déduire *vb*

**deductible** *adj* déductible *adj*

**deduction** *n* déduction *nf*

**deed** *n* (law) acte *nm* **deed of sale** acte de vente *nm* **deed of transfer** acte translatif de propriété *nm*

**default** 1. *n* défaut *nm* 2. *vb* faire défaut *vb*

**defect** *n* défaut *nm*, défectuosité *nf*

**defective** *adj* défectueux *adj*

**defer** *vb* (postpone) ajourner *vb*, différer *vb*

**deferment** *n* ajournement *nm*

**deferred** *adj* (tax) différé *adj*

**deficiency** *n* insuffisance *nf*, manque *nm*

**deficient** *adj* insuffisant *adj*

**deficit** *n* déficit *nm* **deficit financing** financement déficitaire *nm*

**deflation** *n* déflation *nf*

**deflationary** *adj* déflationniste *adj*

**defraud** *vb* frauder *vb*

**del credere** *adj* ducroire *adj* **del credere agent** ducroire *nm*

**delay** 1. *n* retard *nm* **without delay** sans délai 2. *vb* retarder *vb*

**delegate** 1. *n* délégué *nm* 2. *vb* déléguer *vb*

**delegation** *n* délégation *nf*

**deliver** *vb* (goods) livrer *vb*

**delivery** *n* livraison *nf* **cash on delivery** payable à la livraison *adj* **delivery date** date de livraison *nf* **free delivery** livraison gratuite *nf* **general delivery (US)** poste restante *nf* **recorded delivery** envoi recommandé *nm* **delivery time** délai de livraison *nm*

**demand** 1. *n* demande *nf* **supply and demand** offre et demande *nf* 2. *vb* exiger *vb*, réclamer *vb*

**demography** *n* démographie *nf*

**demote** *vb* (employee) rétrograder *vb*

**denationalize** *vb* dénationaliser *vb*

**department** *n* département *nm*, ministère *nm*, service *nm* **government department** ministère *nm* **personnel department** service du personnel *nm*

**department store** grand magasin *nm*
**depletion** *n* réduction *nf*, épuisement *nm*
**deposit** 1. *n* versement *nm* **deposit account** compte sur livret *nm* 2. *vb* verser *vb*
**depository** *n* dépôt *nm*
**depreciate** *vb* se dévaloriser *vb*
**depreciation** *n* dévalorisation *nf*, amortissement *nm*
**depression** *n* (economic) dépression *nf*
**deputy** 1. *adj* adjoint *adj* **deputy director** directeur adjoint *nm* 2. *n* adjoint *nm*
**design** 1. *n* conception *nf* **a machine of good/bad design** machine bien/mal conçue *nf* 2. *vb* concevoir *vb*
**designer** *n* (commercial) dessinateur *nm*, concepteur *nm*, designer *nm*
**Deutschmark** *n* Deutsche Mark *nm*
**devaluation** *n* dévaluation *nf*
**developer** *n* promoteur *nm*
**digital** *adj* numérique *adj*
**diminishing** *adj* **diminishing returns** rendements décroissants *nmpl*
**director** *n* directeur *nm* **board of directors** conseil d'administration *nm* **managing director** président-directeur général (PDG) *nm*
**disburse** *vb* débourser *vb*
**discount** *n* réduction *nf*, rabais *nm*, remise *nf* **at a discount** au rabais **discount rate** taux d'escompte *nm*
**discounted** *adj* **discounted cash flow (DCF)** valeur actualisée nette *nf*
**disk** *n* disque *nm*, disquette *nf* **disk drive** lecteur de disques *nm* **floppy disk** disque souple *nm* **hard disk** disque dur *nm* **magnetic disk** disque magnétique *nm*
**dismiss** *vb* (employee) licencier *vb*
**dispatch** 1. *n* expédition *nf*, envoi *nm* **date of dispatch** date d'expédition *nf* 2. *vb* (goods) expédier *vb*
**dispatcher** *n* expéditeur *nm*
**display** 1. *n* (of goods) étalage *nm*, présentation *nf* 2. *vb* montrer *vb*
**disposable** *adj* (not for reuse) jetable *adj* **disposable income** revenu disponible *nm*
**dispute** *n* conflit *nm*, querelle *nf* **industrial dispute** conflit du travail *nm*
**distribution** *n* distribution *nf*
**distributor** *n* distributeur *nm*
**diversification** *n* diversification *nf*
**diversify** *vb* se diversifier *vb*
**dividend** *n* dividende *nm*
**division** *n* (of company) division *nf* **division of labour** division du travail *nf*
**dock** 1. *n* (for berthing) dock *nm* 2. *vb* (ship) entrer aux docks *vb*, se mettre à quai *vb*
**dockyard** *n* chantier naval *nm*
**document** *n* document *nm* **document retrieval** recherche documentaire *nf*
**domestic** *adj* **domestic policy** politique intérieure *nf*
**door** *n* **door-to-door selling** vendre en porte-à-porte *nm*
**double** *adj* **double-entry** (bookkeeping) comptabilité en partie double *nf*
**Dow-Jones average (US)** *n* indice Dow Jones *nm*
**down** *adj* **down payment** acompte *nm*
**downturn** *n* (economic) ralentissement *nm*
**downward** 1. *adj* vers le bas *adj* 2. *adv* à la baisse
**draft** *n* (financial) traite *nf*
**draw** *vb* (cheque) tirer (un chèque) *vb*
**dry** *adj* **dry goods** produits secs *nmpl*
**dumping** *n* dumping *nm*
**durable** *adj* **durable goods** biens (de consommation) durables *nmpl*
**duty** *n* (customs) droits (de douane) *nmpl* **duty-free** (goods) hors taxe, exempté de droits de douane
**dynamic** *adj* dynamique *adj*
**dynamics** *npl* dynamique *nf*
**early** *adj* tôt *adj* **early retirement** préretraite *nf*
**earn** *vb* gagner *vb*
**earned** *adj* **earned income** revenus salariaux *nmpl* **earned surplus** bénéfices non distribués *nmpl*
**earnest** *adj* **earnest money** arrhes *nfpl*
**earning** 1. *adj* **earning capacity** capacité de gain *nf* **earning power** rentabilité *nf* 2. *npl* **earnings** *npl* (person) salaire *nm*, (business) bénéfices *nmpl* **earnings drift** dérapage sur les bénéfices *nm* **loss of earnings** perte de revenus *nf* **earnings-related pension** régime de retraite proportionnelle *nm* **earnings yield** bénéfices *nmpl*
**easy** *adj* **easy-money policy** politique de l'argent facile *nf*
**EC (European Community)** *abbr* Communauté Européenne *nf*
**econometrics** *n* économétrie *nf*
**economic** *adj* **economic adviser** conseiller économique *nm* **economic analysis** analyse économique *nf* **economic crisis** crise économique *nf* **economic cycle** cycle économique *nm* **economic decline** déclin économique *nm* **economic development** développement économique *nm* **Economic and Monetary Union** Union économique et monétaire *nf* **economic expansion** expansion économique *nf* **economic forecast** prévision économique *nf* **economic geography** géographie économique *nf* **economic growth** croissance économique *nf* **economic infrastructure** infrastructure économique *nf* **economic integration** intégration économique *nf* **economic objective** objectif économique *nm* **economic performance** performance économique *nf* **economic planning** planification *nf* **economic policy** politique économique *nf* **economic sanction** sanctions économiques *nfpl* **economic slowdown** ralentissement économique *nm* **economic strategy** straté-

gie économique *nf* **economic superpower**
superpuissance économique *nf* **economic
survey** sondage économique *nm* **economic
trend** tendance économique *nf* **economic
union** union économique *nf*
**economical** *adj* économe *adj*
**economics** *n* science économique *nf*,
économie *nf*
**economist** *n* économiste *nmf*
**economy** *n* (system) système économique *nm*
**advanced economy** économie avancée *nf*
**developing economy** pays en voie de
développement *nm* **free market economy**
économie de marché *nf* **global economy**
économie mondiale *nf* **economies of scale**
économies d'échelle *nfpl* **national economy**
économie nationale *nf* **planned economy**
économie planifiée *nf* **underdeveloped economy** économie sous-développée *nf*
**ECSC (European Coal and Steel
Community)** *abbr* CECA (Communauté
européenne du charbon et de l'acier) *nf*
**ECU (European Currency Unit)** *abbr* écu *nm*
**edge** *n* **competitive edge** avantage
concurrentiel *nm*
**effect** *n* effet *nm* **financial effects** effets
financiers *nmpl*
**efficiency** *n* efficacité *nf*, bonne
performance *nf*
**efficient** *adj* efficace *adj*
**EFT (electronic funds transfer)** *abbr* transfert électronique de fonds *nm*,
télévirement *nm*
**EFTA (European Free Trade
Association)** *abbr* AELE (Association européenne de libre échange) *nf*
**elasticity** *n* élasticité *nf* **income elasticity**
élasticité-revenu *nf* **elasticity of demand**
élasticité de la demande *nf* **elasticity of
production** élasticité de la production *nf*
**election** *n* élection *nf* **general election** élections législatives *nfpl* **local election** élections municipales *nfpl*
**electronic** *adj* électronique *adj* **electronic
banking** opérations de banque
électroniques *nfpl* **electronic data processing** informatique *nf* **electronic mail** courrier
électronique *nm*
**elimination** *n* **elimination of tariffs** élimination des tarifs *nf*
**email** *n* courrier électronique *nm*
**embargo** *n* embargo *nm* **to impose an
embargo** mettre l'embargo sur *vb* **to lift an
embargo** lever un embargo *vb* **trade
embargo** embargo *nm*
**embassy** *n* ambassade *nf*
**embezzle** *vb* détourner *vb*
**embezzlement** *n* détournement de fonds *nm*
**embezzler** *n* escroc *nm*
**emergency** *n* urgence *nf* **emergency fund**
caisse de secours *nf*
**emigration** *n* émigration *nf*

**employ** *vb* employer *vb*
**employee** *n* employé, -e *nm,f* **employee
recruitment** recrutement/embauche de
personnel *nm/nf* **employee training**
formation *nf*
**employer** *n* employeur *nm* **employer's federation** syndicat patronal *nm* **employers'
liability insurance** assurance responsabilité
civile de l'employeur *nf*
**employment** *n* emploi *nm* **employment
agency** bureau de placement *nm*, Agence
nationale pour l'emploi (ANPE) *nf* **employment contract** contrat de travail *nm* **full
employment** plein emploi *nm* **employment
law** droit du travail *nm*
**encashment** *n* encaissement *nm*
**enclose** *vb* joindre qch à une lettre *vb*
**enclosure** *n* pièce jointe (p.j.) *nf*
**end** *n* **end consumer/user** utilisateur final *nm*
**endorse** *vb* (cheque) endosser *vb*
**endorsement** *n* endossement *nm*
**endowment** *n* dotation *nf* **endowment insurance** assurance à capital différé *nf* **endowment policy** assurance à capital différé *nf*
**enforce** *vb* (policy) mettre en vigueur *vb*, faire
observer *vb*
**enforcement** *n* mise en vigueur *nf*,
coercition *nf*
**engagement** *n* (meeting) rendez-vous *nm*
**engineering** *n* ingénierie *nf* **civil engineering**
génie civil *nm* **electrical engineering**
électrotechnique *nf* **mechanical engineering**
mécanique *nf* **precision engineering** mécanique de précision *nf*
**enhance** *vb* (value) augmenter *vb*,
améliorer *vb*
**enlarge** *vb* agrandir *vb*
**enquire** *vb* se renseigner *vb*
**enquiry** *n* demande (de renseignements) *nf*
**enterprise** *n* (project) entreprise *nf* **private
enterprise** entreprise privée *nf*
**entertain** *vb* **to entertain a client** recevoir un
client *vb*, (inviter un client à déjeuner etc) *vb*
**entrepôt** *n* entrepôt *nm*
**entrepreneur** *n* entrepreneur *nm*
**entrepreneurial** *adj* d'entrepreneur *adj*
**entry** *n* **entry for free goods** admission en
franchise **entry into force** mise en
application *nf* **port of entry** port d'entrée *nm*
**entry visa** visa *nm*
**equalization** *n* **equalization of burdens** péréquation des charges *nf*
**equalize** *vb* égaliser *vb*
**equilibrium** *n* équilibre *nm*
**equip** *vb* équiper *vb*
**equipment** *n* équipement *nm*, matériel *nm*
**equipment leasing** location de matériel *nf*
**equity** *n* équité *nf*, part(s) **equity capital**
capitaux propres *nmpl* **equity financing**
financement par capitaux propres *nm*
**equity interests** participation (dans une
société) *nf* **equity share** action ordinaire *nf*

equity trading financement par émission d'actions *nm*
ergonomics *n* ergonomie *nf*
escalate *vb* s'intensifier *vb*
escalation *n* (prices) escalade *nf*, montée *nf*
escalator *n* escalier roulant *nm*
escudo *n* escudo *nm*
establish *vb* établir *vb*
establishment *n* établissement *nm*
estate *n* estate agency, real estate agency (US) agence immobière *nf* estate agent, real estate agent (US) agent immobilier *nm*
estimate 1. *n* évaluation *nf* estimate of costs devis *nm*, coût estimatif *nm* 2. *vb* évaluer *vb*
eurobond *n* euro-obligation *nf*
eurocapital *n* euro-capital *nm*
eurocheque *n* eurochèque *nm*
eurocracy *n* eurocratie *nf*
eurocrat *n* eurocrate *nm*
eurocredit *n* crédit en eurodevises *nm*
eurocurrency *n* eurodevises *nfpl* eurocurrency market marché des eurodevises *nm*
eurodollar *n* eurodollar *nm*
eurofunds *npl* crédits européens *nmpl*
euromarket *n* euromarché *nm*
euromerger *n* fusion d'entreprises européennes *nf*
euromoney *n* eurodevises *nfpl*, crédits européens *nmpl*
Europe *n* Council of Europe Conseil de l'Europe *nm*
European *adj* européen *adj* European Advisory Committee comité consultatif européen *nm* European Commission Commission Européenne *nf* European Community (EC) Communauté Européenne *nf*, (Union Européenne) European Council Conseil Européen *nm* European Court of Justice (ECJ) Cour de Justice Européenne *nf* European Development Fund (EDF) Fonds de Développement Européen *nm* European Investment Bank (EIB) Banque Européenne d'Investissement *nf* European Monetary Agreement (EMA) Accord Monétaire Européen *nm* European Monetary Cooperation Fund (EMCF) Fonds Européen de Coopération Monétaire *nm* European Monetary System (EMS) Système Monétaire Européen *nm* European Monetary Union (EMU) Union Monétaire Européenne *nf* European Parliament Parlement Européen *nm* European Recovery Plan Plan Européen de Redressement *nm* European Regional Development Fund (ERDF) Fonds Européen de Développement Régional *nm* European Social Fund (ESF) Fonds Social Européen *nm* European Union (EU) Union Européenne *nf* European Unit of Account (EUA) unité de compte européenne *nf*
eurosceptic *n* euro-sceptique *nmf*

evade *vb* éviter *vb*
evasion *n* tax evasion évasion fiscale *nf*
eviction *n* expulsion *nf*
ex *prep* ex factory/works départ usine ex gratia payment versement d'une indemnité non prévue *nm* ex interest hors intérêts ex quay franco à quai ex repayment hors remboursement *nm* ex ship transbordé *adj* ex stock départ magasin ex store/warehouse départ entrepôt ex wharf à prendre à quai
examination *n* examen *nm*
examine *vb* examiner *vb*
exceed *vb* dépasser *vb*
excess *adj* excess capacity capacité excédentaire *nf* excess demand inflation inflation par la demande *nf* excess profit(s) tax impôt sur les bénéfices exceptionnels *nm* excess reserves réserves excédentaires *nfpl*
exchange *n* exchange broker cambiste *nmf* exchange cheque un chèque de change *nm* exchange clearing agreement accord de clearing *nm* exchange control contrôle des changes *nm* foreign exchange change *nm* exchange market marché des changes *nm* exchange rate taux de change *nm*, cours *nm* exchange rate mechanism (ERM) mécanisme du taux de change *nm* exchange restrictions réglementation des changes *nf* exchange risk risque de change *nm* Stock Exchange Bourse *nf*
excise *n* excise duty droit d'accise *nm* the Board of Customs and Excise administration des douanes et accises *nf*
exclude *vb* exclure *vb*
exclusion *n* exclusion clause clause d'exclusion *nf* exclusion zone zone d'exclusion *nf*
executive 1. *adj* executive committee comité exécutif *nm* executive compensation rémunération des cadres *nf* executive duties fonctions de cadre *nfpl* executive hierarchy organigramme *nm*, hierarchie de l'entreprise *nf* executive personnel personnel d'encadrement *nm* 2. *n* exécutif *nm*, responsable *nmf*, cadre *nm*
exempt *adj* exempt *adj* tax-exempt exonoré d'impôt *adj*
exemption *n* exemption *nf*
exhaust *vb* (reserves) épuiser les réserves *vb*
exhibit *vb* exposer *vb*
exhibition *n* exposition *nf*
exorbitant *adj* exorbitant *adj*
expand *vb* augmenter *vb*, accroître *vb*
expansion *n* expansion *nf* expansion of capital expansion du capital *nf* expansion of trade expansion des échanges *nf*
expectation *n* attente *nf* consumer expectations attente du consommateur *nf*
expedite *vb* accélérer *vb*
expenditure *n* dépense *nf* expenditure rate taux des dépenses *nm* state expenditure

dépenses publiques *nfpl* **expenditure taxes** impôt sur les dépenses *nm*

**expense** *n* dépense *nf* **expense account** note de frais *nf* **expense control** contrôle des dépenses *nm* **entertainment expenses** frais de représentation *nmpl* **travelling expenses, travel expenses** (US) frais de transport *nmpl*

**experience 1.** *n* **experience curve** courbe d'expérience *nf* **2.** *vb* éprouver *vb*

**experienced** *adj* expérimenté *adj*

**expert 1.** *adj* expert *adj* **2.** *n* expert *nm*

**expertise** *n* compétence *nf*

**expiration** *n* expiration *nf*

**expire** *vb* expirer *vb*

**expiry, expiration** (US) *n* expiration *nf* **expiry date** date d'expiration *nf*

**export 1.** *n* exportation *nf* **export bill of lading** connaissement *nm* **export credit** crédit à l'exportation *nm* **export credit insurance** assurance pour le commerce extérieur *nf* **export department** service export *nm* **export-led growth** croissance entraînée par les exportations *nf* **export licence** licence d'exportation *nf* **export marketing** marketing international *nm* **export of capital** exportations invisibles *nfpl* **export operations** exportation *nf* **export strategy** stratégie d'exportation *nf* **export subsidies** subventions à l'exportation *nfpl* **export surplus** excédent d'exportation *nm* **export tax** impôt d'exportation *nm* **export trade** commerce international *nm* **2.** *vb* exporter *vb*

**exporter** *n* exportateur *nm*

**express** *adj* **express agency** agence de messageries *nf* **express delivery** livraison rapide *nf* **express service** courrier exprès *nm*

**expropriate** *vb* exproprier *vb*

**expropriation** *n* expropriation *nf*

**extend** *vb* **to extend a contract** prolonger un contrat *vb* **to extend credit** prolonger un crédit *vb* **to extend the range** accroître la gamme *vb*

**extension** *n* (of contract) prolongation *nf*

**extent** *n* **extent of cover** étendue de la garantie *nf*

**external** *adj* extérieur *adj* **external audit** audit externe *nm*

**extortion** *n* extorsion *nf*

**extra** *adj* supplémentaire *adj* **extra cost** supplément *nm* **extra profit** bénéfice supplémentaire *nm*

**extraordinary** *adj* **extraordinary meeting** assemblée extraordinaire *nf* **extraordinary value** valeur extraordinaire *nf*

**facility** *n* équipement *nm*, installation *nf* **facility planning** planification des équipements *nf*

**facsimile (fax)** *n* télécopie *nf*, fax *nm*

**factor 1.** *n* (buyer of debts) facteur *nm* **factor income** revenu factoriel *nm* **limiting factor** facteur de limitation *nm* **factor market**

marché de l'affacturage *nm* **factor of production** facteur de production *nm* **factor price** prix de facteur *nm* **2.** *vb* (debts) affacturer *vb*

**factoring** *n* (of debts) affacturage des dettes *nm*

**factory** *n* usine *nf* **factory board** conseil d'administration *nm* **factory costs** coûts de production *nmpl* **factory inspector** inspecteur du travail *nm* **factory ledger** grand livre de l'usine *nm* **factory overheads** frais généraux de fabrication *nmpl* **factory price** prix usine *nm*

**fail** *vb* (negotiations) échouer *vb* (attempts) échouer à *vb*, manquer *vb*

**failure** *n* échec *nm*

**fair** *adj* juste *adj* **fair competition** concurrence loyale *nf* **fair market value** prix honnête *nm* **fair rate of return** juste retour *nm* **fair-trade agreement** accord commercial réciproque *nm* **fair-trade policy** politique de commerce loyal *nf* **fair-trade practice** pratique commerciale loyale *nf* **fair trading** commerce loyal *nm* **fair wage** salaire honnête *nm*

**fall due** *vb* venir à échéance *vb*

**falling** *adj* **falling prices** prix en baisse *nmpl* **falling rate of profit** bénéfices en diminution *nmpl*

**false** *adj* **false representation** fausse déclaration *nf*

**falsification** *n* falsification *nf* **falsification of accounts** falsification des comptes *nf*

**family** *n* **family allowance** allocation familiale *nf* **family branding** élaboration d'une marque familiale *nf* **family corporation** entreprise familiale *nf* **family income** revenu familial *nm* **family industry** entreprise familiale *nf*

**farm out** *vb* sous-traiter *vb*

**farming** *n* agriculture *nf* **farming of taxes** attribution du droit de perception des impôts *nm* **farming subsidies** subventions agricoles *nfpl*

**FAS (free alongside ship)** *abbr* FLB (franco le long du bord) *abbr*

**fast** *adj* rapide *adj* **fast food** nourriture de fast food *nf*, prêt-à-manger *nm* **fast-selling goods** articles à forte rotation *nmpl* **fast track** destiné à promotion rapide

**fault** *n* défaut *nm* **minor fault** petit défaut *nm* **serious fault** défaut grave *nm* **to find fault with** trouver à redire (à qch/qn) *vb*, critiquer *vb*

**faulty** *adj* **faulty goods** marchandises défectueuses *nfpl* **faulty workmanship** travail défectueux *nm*

**favour** *n* service *nm* **to do sb a favour** rendre un service à qn

**favourable** *adj* **favourable balance of payments** balance des paiements excédentaire *nf* **favourable balance of trade** balance commerciale excédentaire *nf*

**favourable exchange** échange avantageux *nm* **favourable price** prix avantageux *nm* **favourable terms** conditions avantageuses *nfpl*
**fax** 1. *n* télécopie *nf*, fax *nm* 2. *vb* télécopier *vb*
**feasibility** *n* faisabilité *nf* **feasibility study** étude de faisabilité *nf*
**feasible** *adj* faisable *adj*, possible *adj*, réalisable *adj*
**federal** *adj* fédéral *adj*
**federation** *n* fédération *nf*
**fee** *n* honoraires *nmpl* **to charge a fee** demander un paiement *vb* **to pay a fee** payer un prix *vb*, payer des honoraires *vb*
**feedback** *n* rétroaction *nf*
**fiat** *n* **fiat money** monnaie fiduciaire *nf*
**fictitious** *adj* fictif *adj* **fictitious assets** avoirs fictifs *nmpl* **fictitious purchase** achat fictif *nm* **fictitious sale** vente fictive *nf*
**fidelity** *n* fidélité *nf* **fidelity bond** assurance détournement et vol *nf* **fidelity insurance** assurance détournement et vol *nf*
**fiduciary** *adj* **fiduciary bond** caution fiduciaire *nf* **fiduciary issue** émission fiduciaire *nf*
**field** *n* **field investigation** enquête sur le terrain *nf* **field manager** directeur (des ventes) *nm* **field personnel** personnel de terrain *nm* **field research** étude sur le terrain *nf* **field test** essai sur le terrain *nm* **field work** travail sur le terrain *nm*
**FIFO (first in first out)** *abbr* PEPS (premier entré premier sorti) *abbr*
**file** 1. *n* dossier *nm*, (computer) fichier *nm* 2. *vb* classer *vb*
**filing** *adj* **filing cabinet** classeur *nm* **filing system** méthode de classement *nf*
**final** *adj* **final accounts** comptes définitifs *nmpl* **final demand** dernier rappel *nm* **final entry** inscription définitive *nf* **final invoice** dernière facture *nf* **final offer** dernière offre *nf* **final products** produits finis *nmpl* **final settlement** règlement définitif *nm* **final utility** utilité finale *nf*
**finance** 1. *n* finance/finances *nf/nfpl* **finance bill** projet de loi de finances *nm* **finance company** compagnie financière *nf* **Finance Act** loi de finances *nf* 2. *vb* financer *vb*
**financial** *adj* financier *adj* **financial accounting** comptabilité financière *nf* **financial assets** actifs financiers *nmpl* **financial balance** bilan financier *nm* **financial company** compagnie financière *nf* **financial consultancy** conseil financier *nm* **financial consultant** conseiller financier *nm* **financial control** contrôle financier *nm* **financial crisis** crise monétaire *nf* **financial difficulty** difficulté financière *nf* **financial exposure** risque financier *nm* **financial incentive** incitation financière *nf* **financial institution** établissement financier *nm* **financial investment**

investissement financier *nm* **financial loan** prêt *nm* **financial management** gestion financière *nf* **financial market** marché financier *nm* **financial measures** mesures financières *nfpl* **financial operation** opération financière *nf* **financial planning** planification financière *nf* **financial policy** politique financière *nf* **financial report** rapport financier *nm* **financial resources** ressources financières *nfpl* **financial risk** risque financier *nm* **financial situation** situation financière *nf* **financial stability** stabilité financière *nf* **financial statement** bilan *nm*, état financier *nm* **financial strategy** stratégie financière *nf* **financial structure** structure financière *nf* **financial year** exercice financier *nm*, exercice comptable *nm*
**financier** *n* financier *nm*
**financing** *n* financement *nm* **financing surplus** financement excédentaire *nm*
**fine** *adj* **fine rate of interest** taux d'intérêt privilégié *nm*
**finished** *adj* **finished goods** produits finis *nmpl* **finished stock** produits finis *nmpl* **finished turnover** rotation des produits finis *nf*
**fire\*** *vb* vider *vb*, renvoyer *vb*
**firm** *adj* **firm offer** offre ferme *nf* **firm price** prix ferme *nm*
**first** *adj* **first bill of exchange** première de change *nf* **first class** première classe *nf* **first-class paper** papier de première classe *nm* **first customer** premier client *nm* **first-hand** de première main *adj* **first mortgage** obligation de première hypothèque *nf* **first-rate** (investment) investissement de premier ordre *nm*
**fiscal** *adj* **fiscal agent** agent financier *nm* **fiscal balance** solde fiscal *nm* **fiscal charges** frais fiscaux *nmpl* **fiscal measures** mesures fiscales *nfpl* **fiscal policy** politique fiscale *nf* **fiscal receipt** recettes fiscales *nfpl* **fiscal year** exercice comptable *nm* **fiscal year end (fye)** fin d'exercice comptable **fiscal zoning** zonage fiscal *nm*
**fix** *vb* **to fix the price** fixer un prix *vb*
**fixed** *adj* **fixed assets** capitaux fixes *nmpl* **fixed asset turnover** rotation des capitaux fixes *nf* **fixed budget** budget fixe *nm* **fixed charges** charges fixes *nfpl* **fixed costs** coûts fixes *nmpl* **fixed credit** crédit fixe *nm* **fixed income** revenu fixe *nm* **fixed interest** taux d'intérêt fixe *nm* **fixed liabilities** obligations fixes *nfpl* **fixed price** prix fixe *nm*
**fixture** *n* **fixtures and fittings** les installations *nfpl*
**flat** *adj* **flat bond** une obligation sans intérêt couru *nf* **flat market** marché inactif *nm* **flat rate** à forfait *adj*, forfaitaire *adj* **flat-rate income tax** impôt forfaitaire *nm* **flat-rate tariff** tarif uniforme *nm*
**flexibility** *n* (of prices) souplesse *nf*,

élasticité *nf*
**flexible** *adj* **flexible budget** budget
flexible *nm* **flexible exchange rate** taux de
change flexible *nm* **flexible price** prix
flexible *nm*
**flexitime, flextime** (US) *n* horaire flexible *nm*
**flight** *n* (in plane) vol *nm* **flight capital** fuite
de capitaux *nf* **to book a flight** réserver un
vol *vb*
**float** *vb* (currency) laisser flotter *vb*
**floating** *adj* **floating assets** capitaux
mobiles *nmpl* **floating exchange rate** taux
flottant *nm* **floating rate interest** taux
flottant *nm*
**floor** *n* **floor broker** courtier *nm* **shopfloor** les
ateliers *nmpl*
**flotation** *n* émission *nf*
**flow** *n* **cash flow** trésorerie *nf* **flow chart**
diagramme de circulation *nm* **flow line
production** production à la chaîne *nf* **flow of
income** rentrée d'argent *nf* **flow production**
production à la chaîne *nf*
**fluctuate** *vb* fluctuer *vb*
**fluctuation** *n* fluctuation *nf* **fluctuation in
sales** fluctuation des ventes *nf*
**fluid** *adj* fluide *adj* **fluid market** marché
changeant *nm*
**FOB (free on board)** *abbr* FAB (franco à
bord) *abbr*
**for** *prep* **for sale** à vendre *adj*
**forced** *adj* **forced currency** cours forcé *nm*
**forecast** 1. *n* prévision *nf* 2. *vb* prévoir *vb*
**forecasting** *n* prévision *nf*
**foreclose** *vb* saisir (un bien hypothéqué) *vb*
**foreclosure** *n* saisie *nf*
**foreign** *adj* étranger *adj* **foreign aid** aide
extérieure *nf* **foreign aid programme** programme d'aide extérieure *nm* **foreign bank**
banque étrangère *nf* **foreign company**
compagnie étrangère *nf* **foreign competition** concurrence étrangère *nf* **foreign currency** devises étrangères *nfpl* **foreign
exchange** devise *nf*, change *nm* **foreign
exchange dealer** cambiste *nmf* **foreign
exchange market** marché des changes *nm*
**foreign currency holdings** avoirs en
devises *nmpl* **foreign investment** investissement étranger *nm* **foreign loan** emprunt
extérieur *nm* **foreign travel** voyages à
l'étranger *nmpl*
**foreman** *n* contremaître *nm*
**forestall** *vb* devancer *vb*
**forfeit** 1. *n* dédit *nm* (shares) perte *nf* 2. *vb*
perdre *vb*
**forfeiture** *n* perte *nf*
**forgery** *n* contrefaçon *nf*
**form** *n* (document) formulaire *nm*
**formal** *adj* formel *adj* **formal agreement**
accord formel *nm* **formal contract** contrat
en bonne et due forme *nm*
**formality** *n* **customs formalities** formalités
douanières *nfpl* **to observe formalities** res-

pecter les formalités *vb*
**formation** *n* (of company) fondation *nf* **capital formation** formation de capital *nf*
**forward** 1. *adj* **forward contract** contrat à
terme *nm* **forward cover** couverture à
terme *nf* **forward market** marché à terme *nm*
**forward transaction** opération à terme *nf*
2. *vb* expédier *vb*
**forwarder** *n* expéditeur *nm*
**forwarding** *n* expédition *nf* **forwarding
agency** bureau de transitaires *nm* **forwarding agent** transitaire *nm* **forwarding charges**
frais d'expédition *nmpl* **forwarding note**
connaissement de transitaire *nm*
**found** *vb* **to found a company** fonder une
société *vb*
**founder** *n* fondateur *nm*
**fraction** *n* fraction *nf*
**fractional** *adj* infime *adj* **fractional currency**
monnaie divisionnaire *nf* **fractional shares**
rompus *nmpl*
**franc** *n* **Belgian franc** franc belge *nm* **French
franc** franc français *nm* **Swiss franc** franc
suisse *nm*
**franchise** 1. *n* concession *nf* **franchise outlet**
magasin franchisé *nm* 2. *vb* franchiser *vb*
**franchisee** *n* franchisé *nm*
**franchising** *n* franchisage *nm*
**franchisor** *n* franchiseur *nm*
**franco** *adv* franco *adv* **franco domicile** franco
domicile **franco frontier** franco frontière
**frank** *vb* affranchir *vb*
**franked** *adj* **franked income** revenu non
imposable *nm*
**franking** *n* **franking machine** machine à
affranchir *nf*
**fraud** *n* fraude *nf*
**fraudulent** *adj* frauduleux *adj*
**free** *adj* **free agent** agent libre *nm* **free
alongside ship (FAS)** franco le long du bord
(FAS) **free competition** concurrence libre *nf*
**free delivery** livraison gratuite *nf* **duty free**
hors taxe *adj* **free economy** économie
libérale *nf* **free entry** entrée libre *nf* **free
goods** marchandises libres *nfpl* **free market**
économie libérale *nf* **free movement of
goods** libre circulation des marchandises *nf*
**free of charge** gratuit *adj* **free of freight**
franco de fret *adj* **free of tax** hors taxe *adj*
**free on board (FOB)** franco à bord **free on
quay** franco à quai *adj* **free port** port
franc *nm* **free trade** libre-échange *nm* **free
trade area** zone de libre-échange *nf*
**freedom** *n* **freedom of choice** liberté de
choix *nf*
**Freefone (R) (GB)** *n* appel gratuit *nm*
**freelance** 1. *adj* indépendant *adj* 2. *n*
indépendant *nm*
**freelancer** *n* travailleur indépendant *nm*
**Freepost (R) (GB)** *n* port payé *nm*
**freeze** 1. *n* (prices, wages) gel *nm* 2. *vb*
(prices, wages) geler *vb*

**freight** n fret nm **freight forwarder** expéditeur nm **freight traffic** circulation de marchandises nf

**freighter** n transporteur nm

**frequency** n fréquence nf

**friendly** adj amical adj **Friendly Society** mutuelle nf

**fringe** adj **fringe benefits** avantages divers nmpl, avantages en nature nmpl, avantages supplémentaires nmpl **fringe market** marché de frange nm

**frontier** n frontière nf

**fronting** n confrontation nf

**frozen** adj **frozen assets** avoirs gelés nmpl **frozen credits** crédits gelés nmpl

**FT Index (Financial Times Index)** n indice FT nm

**full** adj **full cost** prix de revient complet nm **full liability** responsabilité pleine et entière nf **full payment** remboursement intégral nm **full-time** à plein temps

**function** n (role) fonction nf

**functional** adj **functional analysis** analyse fonctionnelle nf **functional organization** organisation fonctionnelle nf

**fund** 1. n fonds nm **funds flow** flux des capitaux nm **funds surplus** capitaux en surplus nmpl 2. vb financer vb

**funded** adj financé adj **funded debt** dette consolidée nf

**funding** n financement nm **funding bonds** bons de provisionnement nmpl

**furlough (US)** 1. n chômage temporaire/technique nm 2. vb mettre en chômage temporaire/technique vb

**future** adj **future commodity** opération à terme nf **future delivery** achat à terme nm, vente à terme nf **future goods** marchandises à terme nfpl

**futures** npl opérations à terme nfpl **futures contract** contrat à terme nm **futures exchange** marché à terme nm **futures market** marché à terme nm **futures marketing** opérations à terme nfpl **futures price** cours à terme nm **futures trading** opérations à terme nfpl

**fye (fiscal year end)** abbr fin de l'année budgétaire nf, fin de l'exercice comptable nf

**gain** 1. n gain nm **capital gain** plus-value nf **capital gains tax** impôt sur les plus-values nm **gain in value** accroissement de valeur nm **gain sharing** partage des gains nm 2. vb gagner vb

**gainful** adj lucratif adj **gainful employment** activité lucrative nf

**galloping** adj galopant adj **galloping inflation** inflation galopante nf

**Gallup poll (R)** sondage Gallup

**gap** n **population gap** déficit demographique nm **trade gap** déficit commercial nm

**gas** n **natural gas** gaz naturel nm

**GATT (General Agreement on Tariffs and Trade)** abbr GATT nm

**gazump** vb (annuler une promesse de vente pour accepter une offre plus avantageuse)

**GDP (Gross Domestic Product)** abbr PIB (Produit Interieur Brut) nm

**general** adj **general accounting** comptabilité générale nf **general agencies (US)** services des administrations publiques nmpl **general agent** agent général nm **general average** avarie commune nf **general election** élection législative nf **general management** direction générale nf **general manager** directeur général nm **general partner** associé nm **general partnership** association nf **general strike** grève générale nf

**generate** vb **to generate income** générer des revenus vb

**generation** n **income generation** génération de revenus nf

**generosity** n générosité nf

**gentleman** n **gentleman's agreement** gentlemen's agreement nm, (accord reposant sur l'honneur)

**gilt-edged** adj **gilt-edged market** marché des valeurs de premier ordre nm **gilt-edged security** titres d'état nmpl

**gilts** npl valeurs de premier ordre nfpl

**giveaway** n prime nf

**global** adj global adj, mondial adj **global economy** économie mondiale nf **global market** marché mondial nm **global marketing** marketing mondial nm

**globalization** n mondialisation nf

**GMT (Greenwich Mean Time)** abbr heure du méridien de Greenwich nf

**gnome** n **the Gnomes of Zurich** les banquiers suisses nmpl

**GNP (Gross National Product)** abbr PNB (Produit National Brut) nm

**go-slow** n (strike) grève du zèle nf

**going** adj courant adj **going concern** une affaire prospère nf

**gold** n or nm **gold bullion** or en lingots nm **gold coin** pièce d'or nf **gold market** marché de l'or nm **gold reserves** réserves d'or nfpl **gold standard** étalon or nm

**golden** adj **golden handshake** prime de départ nf **golden hello** prime d'engagement nf **golden parachute** indemnité de départ nf

**goods** npl marchandises nfpl **bulk goods** marchandises en vrac nfpl **domestic goods** biens domestiques nmpl **export goods** biens d'exportation nmpl **import goods** biens importés nmpl **goods on approval** biens à l'essai nmpl **goods in process** biens en cours nmpl **goods in progress** biens en cours nmpl **goods on consignment** biens en consignation nmpl **goods transport** transport de marchandises nm

**goodwill** n bonne volonté nf
**govern** vb gouverner vb
**government** n gouvernement nm **government body** service ministériel nm **government bond** bon du Trésor nm **government enterprise** entreprise gouvernementale nf **government loan** emprunt d'état nm **government policy** politique gouvernementale nf **government sector** secteur gouvernemental nm **government security** titre d'état nm **government subsidy** subvention du gouvernement nf
**graduate** 1. n (of university) diplômé nm, licencié nm 2. vb obtenir sa licence vb
**grant** 1. n (of money) aide nf (of a patent) délivrance d'un brevet nf 2. vb allouer vb
**graphics** npl **computer graphics** infographie nf
**gratuity** n pourboire nm, gratification nf
**green** adj **green card** carte de séjour nf **green currency** monnaie verte nf **green pound** livre verte nf
**Greenwich** n **Greenwich Mean Time (GMT)** heure GMT nf
**grievance** n grief nm
**gross** adj brut adj **gross amount** montant brut nm **gross domestic product (GDP)** produit intérieur brut (PIB) nm **gross interest** intérêts bruts nmpl **gross investment** investissement brut nm **gross loss** perte brute nf **gross margin** marge brute nf **gross national product (GNP)** produit national brut (PNB) nm **gross negligence** faute grave nf **gross output** production brute nf **gross sales** chiffre d'affaires brut nm **gross weight** poids brut nm
**group** n **group insurance** assurance collective nf **group of countries** groupe de pays nm **group travel** voyages organisés nmpl
**growth** n croissance nf **annual growth rate** taux de croissance annuel nm **economic growth** croissance économique nf **export-led growth** croissance entraînée par les exportations nf **market growth** croissance du marché nf **growth rate** taux de croissance nm **sales growth** augmentation des ventes nf **growth strategy** politique de croissance nf
**guarantee** n garantie nf **quality guarantee** garantie de qualité nf
**guarantor** n garant nm
**guest** n **guest worker** travailleur immigré nm
**guild** n corporation nf
**guilder** n florin nm
**h** abbr (hour) h (heure) abbr
**half** n moitié nf **half-an-hour** une demi-heure nf **half-board** demi-pension nf **half-pay** demi-salaire nm **half-price** moitié prix nm **to reduce sth by half** réduire qqch de moitié vb **half-year** semestre nm
**hall** n **exhibition hall** hall d'exposition nm

**hallmark** n poinçon nm
**halt** vb (inflation) arrêter vb
**halve** vb réduire de moitié vb
**hand** n **in hand** disponible adj **to hand** sous la main adj
**hand over** vb remettre vb
**handbook** n manuel nm
**handle** vb (deal) s'occuper de vb, traiter vb, manutentionner, vb (money) gérer, vb manier vb **handle with care** fragile adj
**handling** n **handling charges** frais de manutention nmpl **data handling** traitement de données nm
**handmade** adj fait main adj
**handshake** n poignée de main nf
**handwritten** adj manuscrit adj
**handy** adj commode adj
**hang on** vb (wait) attendre vb (on telephone) ne quittez pas!
**hang together** vb (argument) tenir debout vb
**hang up** vb (telephone) raccrocher vb
**harbour** n port nm **harbour authorities** autorités portuaires nfpl **harbour dues** droits de port nmpl **harbour facilities** installations portuaires nfpl **harbour fees** droits de port nmpl
**hard** adj **hard bargain** un marché durement négocié nm **hard cash** espèces nfpl **hard currency** devise forte nf **hard disk** disque dur nm **hard-earned** durement gagné adj **hard-hit** durement touché adj **hard-line** ligne dure nf **hard loan** prêt à des conditions rigoureuses nm **hard news/information** information sérieuse nf **hard price** cours ferme nm **hard sell** promotion agressive nf **the hard facts** la réalité brutale nf **hard-working** travailleur nm
**hardware** n quincaillerie nf **computer hardware** matériel informatique nm
**haul** n **long-haul** transport sur longue distance nm **short-haul** transport sur courte distance nm
**haulage, freight (US)** n **road haulage** transport routier nm **haulage company** entreprise de transports routiers nf
**haulier** n entrepreneur de transports routiers nm
**hazard** n risque nm **natural hazard** risque naturel nm **occupational hazard** risque du métier nm
**hazardous** adj hasardeux adj
**head** 1. adj **head accountant** chef comptable nm **head office** siège social nm 2. n **at the head of** à la tête de **head of department** chef de service nm **head of government** chef de gouvernement nm **per head** par tête **to be head of** être à la tête de vb 3. vb (department) diriger vb
**head for** vb se diriger vers vb
**headed** adj **headed notepaper** papier en-tête nm
**heading** n titre nm

**headquarters** n siège (social) nm
**headway** i; **to make headway** progresser vb
**health** n santé nf **health benefits** prestations
maladie nfpl **health care industry** les
industries de santé nfpl, le secteur de la
santé nm **health hazard** risque pour la
santé nm **industrial health** hygiène du
travail nf **health insurance** assurance
maladie nf **Ministry of Health** Ministère de
la Santé nm
**healthy** adj (finances) sain adj
**heavy** adj **heavy-duty** à usage industriel adj
**heavy goods vehicle** poids lourd nm **heavy
industry** industrie lourde nf **heavy trading**
un niveau élevé de transactions nm **heavy
user** gros utilisateur nm
**hedge** n **hedge against inflation** une couverture contre l'inflation nf **hedge clause (US)**
clause de sauvegarde nf
**hidden** adj **hidden assets** actifs cachés nmpl
**hidden defect** défaut caché nm
**hierarchy** n (corporate) hiérarchie nf **data
hierarchy** hiérarchie des données nf **hierarchy of needs** hiérarchie des besoins nf
**high** adj **high-class** haute classe nf **high
finance** haute finance nf **high-grade** première qualité nf **high-income** à revenu
élevé adj **high-level** à haut niveau adj **high-
powered** énergique adj **high-priced** cher adj
**high-ranking** de haut rang adj **high-risk** à
haut risque adj **high season** haute saison nf
**hi-tech** de pointe adj
**higher** adj supérieur adj **higher bid** offre
supérieure nf
**hire** 1. n location nf **hire charges** frais de
location nmpl **hire contract** contrat de
location nm **for hire** à louer adj **hire
purchase** location-vente nf 2. vb (person)
embaucher vb
**history** n **employment/work history** expérience professionnelle nf
**hit** vb **hit-or-miss** méthode empirique nf **to
hit the headlines** être à la une des
journaux vb **to hit the market** arriver sur le
marché vb **to be hard hit by** être durement
touché par vb
**HO (head office)** abbr siège social nm
**hoard** vb thésauriser vb
**hold** 1. n **hold area** zone d'attente nf **on hold**
(on phone) en attente, en ligne **hold queue,
hold line (US)** (computer) file de travaux en
attente nf 2. vb tenir vb, détenir vb **to hold a
meeting** tenir une réunion vb **to hold sth as
security** détenir qch en garantie vb **to hold
sb liable** tenir qn pour responsable vb **hold
the line** (on phone) ne quittez pas **to hold sb
responsible** tenir qn responsable de vb
**hold back** vb (not release) retenir vb
**hold on** vb (on phone) attendre vb
**hold over** vb (to next period) remettre vb,
reporter vb
**hold up** vb (delay) retarder vb (withstand

scrutiny) tenir bon vb
**holder** n détenteur nm **joint holder**
codétenteur nm **licence holder** titulaire de
permis nm **office holder** titulaire de
poste nm **policy holder** assuré nm
**holding** 1. adj **holding company** société
holding nf 2. n participations nfpl **foreign
exchange holdings** avoirs en devises nmpl
**majority/minority holding** participation
majoritaire/minoritaire nf **to have holdings**
avoir des participations vb
**holdup** n retard nm
**holiday, vacation** (US) n vacances nfpl **bank
holiday (GB)** jour férié nm **on holiday** en
vacances adj **paid holiday** congés payés **tax
holiday** période d'exonération fiscale nf
**home** n **home address** adresse personnelle nf
**home buying** accession à la propriété **home
country** pays de résidence nm **home delivery** livraison à domicile nf **home industry**
travail à domicile nm **home loan** prêt
immobilier nm **home market** marché
intérieur nm **home owner** propriétaire de sa
maison nm **home sales** ventes sur le marché intérieur nfpl **home service** service de
vente à domicile nm **home shopping**
téléachats nmpl
**honorarium** n honoraires nmpl
**honorary** adj honorifique adj
**horizontal** adj **horizontal analysis** analyse
horizontale nf **horizontal integration** intégration horizontale nf
**host** n hôte nm **host country** pays
d'accueil nm
**hot** adj chaud adj **hot line** ligne ouverte 24
heures sur 24 nf **hot money** capitaux
spéculatifs nmpl **to be in the hot seat** être
sur la sellette vb **to be in hot demand** être
en très forte demande vb
**hotel** n hôtel nm **hotel accommodation**
chambre d'hôtel nf **hotel chain** chaîne
hôtelière nf **five-star hotel** hôtel cinq
étoiles nm **hotel industry/trade** industrie
hôtelière nf **hotel management** gestion
hôtelière nf **to run a hotel** diriger un hôtel vb
**hour** n **after hours** après l'heure de fermeture
**business hours** heures ouvrables nfpl **busy
hours (US)** heures d'affluence nfpl **fixed
hours** heures régulières nfpl **office hours**
heures de bureau nfpl **per hour** de l'heure
**per hour output** par heure de production
**hourly** adj **hourly-paid work** travail payé à
l'heure nm **hourly rate** taux horaire nm
**hourly workers** ouvriers payés à
l'heure nmpl
**house** n **clearing house** comptoir de
liquidation nm **house duty (US)** taxe
d'habitation nf **house journal/magazine**
journal d'entreprise nm **mail-order house**
maison de vente par correspondance nf
**packing house (US)** conserverie nf **house
prices** prix immobiliers nmpl **publishing**

**house** maison d'édition *nf* **house sale** vente immobilière *nf* **house telephone** téléphone intérieur *nm*

**household** *n* ménage *nm* **household expenditure** dépenses des ménages *nfpl* **household goods** biens ménagers *nmpl* **household survey** enquête sur les ménages *nf*

**householder** *n* chef de famille *nm*

**housewares (US)** *npl* biens d'équipement ménager *nmpl*

**housing** *n* **housing estate, tenement (US)** cité *nf* **housing industry** le bâtiment *nm* **housing project** cité *nf* **housing scheme** cité *nf*

**hull** *n* coque *nf* **hull insurance** assurance sur corps *nf*

**human** *adj* humain *adj* **human relations** relations humaines *nfpl* **human resource management (HRM)** gestion des ressources humaines *nf* **human resources** ressources humaines *nfpl* **human rights** droits de l'homme *nmpl*

**hundred** *adj* **one hundred per cent** cent pour cent *adj*

**hydroelectricity** *n* hydroélectricité *nf*

**hype** *n* battage publicitaire *nm*

**hyperinflation** *n* hyperinflation *nf*

**hypermarket** *n* hypermarché *nm*

**hypothesis** *n* hypothèse *nf*

**idle** *adj* oisif *adj* **idle capacity** capacité inutilisée *nf*

**illegal** *adj* illégal *adj*

**implication** *n* implication *nf* **this will have implications for our sales** cela aura des conséquences sur nos ventes

**import imports** importations *nfpl* importation *nf* **import agent** commissionnaire importateur *nm* **import barrier** barrière à l'importation *nf* **import control** contrôle des importations *nm* **import department** service d'importation *nm* **import duty** taxe à l'importation *nf* **import licence** licence d'importation *nf* **import office** bureau d'importation *nm* **import quota** contingent d'importation *nm* **import restrictions** restrictions à l'importation *nfpl* **import surplus** excédent d'importation *nm* **1.** *vb* importer *vb*

**importation** *n* importation *nf*

**importer** *n* importateur *nm*

**importing** *adj* **importing country** pays importateur *nm*

**impose** *vb* **to impose a tax** imposer *vb* **to impose restrictions** imposer des restrictions *vb*

**imposition** *n* (of tax) impôt *nm*

**impound** *vb* saisir *vb*

**imprint** *n* **to take an imprint** (credit card) faire une empreinte *vb*

**improve** *vb* améliorer *vb*, s'améliorer *vb* **we must improve our performance** il faut améliorer nos performances

**inadequate** *adj* insuffisant *adj*

**incentive** *n* incitation *nf*

**incidental** *adj* **incidental expenses** faux frais *nmpl*

**include** *vb* **our price includes delivery** notre prix comprend les frais de livraison **taxes are included** toutes taxes comprises (ttc)

**inclusive** *adj* compris *adj* **inclusive of tax and delivery costs** taxes et livraison comprises

**income** *n* revenu *nm* **gross income** revenu brut *nm* **net(t) income** revenu net *nm* **private income** revenus personnels *nmpl* **income tax** impôt sur le revenu *nm*

**inconvenience** *n* inconvénient *nm*

**inconvenient** *adj* incommode *adj*

**increase 1.** *n* augmentation *nf* **increase in the cost of living** augmentation du coût de la vie **price increase** augmentation de prix **wage increase** augmentation du salaire **2.** *vb* (prices, taxes) augmenter *vb*

**incur** *vb* (expenses) encourir des dépenses *vb*, encourir des frais *vb*

**indebted** *adj* endetté *adj*

**indemnify** *vb* indemniser *vb*

**indemnity** *n* indemnité *nf* **indemnity insurance** assurance *nf*

**index** *n* indice *nm* **cost of living index** indice du coût de la vie *nm* **growth index** indice de croissance *nm* **price index** indice des prix *nm* **share index** indice des valeurs *nm*

**indicate** *vb* indiquer *vb*

**indication** *n* indication *nf*

**indirect** *adj* indirect *adj* **indirect cost** charges indirectes *nfpl* **indirect expenses** frais indirects *nmpl* **indirect tax** impôt indirect *nm*

**industrial** *adj* industriel *adj* **industrial accident** accident du travail *nm* **industrial arbitration** arbitrage *nm* **industrial democracy** démocratie industrielle *nf* **industrial dispute** conflit du travail *nm* **industrial expansion** expansion industrielle *nf* **industrial region** région industrielle *nf* **industrial relations** relations du travail *nfpl* **industrial tribunal** conseil de prud'hommes *nm* **industrial union** syndicat *nm*

**industry** *n* industrie *nf*

**inefficient** *adj* inefficace *adj*

**inferior** *adj* (goods) inférieur *adj*

**inflation** *n* inflation *nf* **rate of inflation** taux d'inflation *nm*

**inflationary** *adj* inflationniste *adj* **inflationary gap** écart d'inflation *nm* **inflationary spiral** spirale inflationniste *nf*

**inform** *vb* informer *vb*

**information** *n* informations *nfpl*, renseignements *nmpl* **information desk** l'accueil *nm* **information management** gestion de l'information *nf* **information office** bureau de reseignements *nm* **information processing** traitement de l'information *nm* **information retrieval** collecte des données *nf*

**information storage** stockage de l'information *nm* **information systems** systèmes informatiques *nmpl* **information technology (IT)** informatique *nf*
**infrastructure** *n* infrastructure *nf*
**inherit** *vb* hériter *vb*
**inheritance** *n* héritage *nm* **inheritance laws** lois de succession *nfpl*
**inhouse** *adj* interne *adj* **inhouse training** formation interne
**injunction** *n* mise en demeure *nf* **to take out an injunction** obtenir une mise en demeure *vb*
**inland** *adj* intérieur *adj* **the Inland Revenue, The Internal Revenue Service (IRS)** (US) le fisc *nm*
**insider** *n* initié *nm* **insider dealing, insider trading** (US) délit d'initiés *nm*
**insist on** *vb* insister sur *vb*
**insolvency** *n* insolvabilité *nf*
**insolvent** *adj* insolvable *adj*
**inspect** *vb* inspecter *vb*
**inspection** *n* (customs) contrôle douanier *nm*
**inspector** *n* inspecteur *nm* **customs inspector** douanier *nm*
**instability** *n* instabilité *nf*
**instal(l)** *vb* installer *vb*
**installation** *n* installation *nf*
**instalment, installment** (US) *n* versement *nm*, traite *nf*
**institute** *n* institut *nm*
**institution** *n* institution *nf* **credit institution** organisme de crédit *nm*
**instruction** *n* instruction *nf* **instruction book** manuel d'utilisation *nm* **instruction sheet** feuille d'instructions *nf* **to follow instructions** suivre les instructions *vb*
**insurable** *adj* **insurable risk** risque assurable
**insurance** *n* assurance *nf* **insurance agent** agent d'assurances *nm* **insurance broker** courtier d'assurances *nm* **car insurance** assurance automobile *nf* **insurance certificate** certificat d'assurance *nm* **insurance company** société d'assurances *nf* **comprehensive insurance** assurance tous risques *nf* **insurance contract** police d'assurance *nf* **fire insurance** assurance contre incendie *nf* **insurance fund** fonds d'assurance *nm* **National Insurance (GB)** Sécurité Sociale *nf* **insurance policy** police d'assurance *nf* **insurance premium** prime d'assurance *nf*, cotisation d'assurance *nf* **insurance salesperson** agent d'assurances *nm* **third party insurance** assurance au tiers *nf* **to take out insurance** contracter une assurance *vb* **insurance underwriter** assureur *nm* **unemployment insurance** assurance chômage *nf*
**insure** *vb* assurer *vb*, faire assurer *vb*
**intangible** *adj* **intangible asset** actifs incorporels *nmpl*
**intensive** *adj* intensif *adj* **capital-intensive** capitalistique *adj* **labour-intensive**

travaillistique *adj*
**interest** *n* intérêt(s) *nm(pl)* **interest-bearing** productif d'intérêts *adj* **interest-free** sans intérêt *adj* **interest period** période d'intérêt *nf* **interest rate** taux d'intérêt *nm* **to bear interest** porter des intérêts *vb* **to charge interest** prélever des intérêts *vb* **to pay interest** payer des intérêts *vb*
**interface** *n* interface *nf*
**interim** *adj* provisoire *adj*
**intermediary** *adj* intermédiaire *adj*
**internal** *adj* **internal audit** audit interne *adj* **internal auditor** auditeur interne *nm* **the Internal Revenue Service (IRS) (US)** le fisc *nm*
**international** *adj* international *adj* **international agreement** accord international *nm* **international competition** concurrence internationale *nf* **International Date Line** ligne de changement de date *nf* **international organization** organisation internationale *nf* **international trade** commerce international *nm*
**intervene** *vb* intervenir *vb*
**intervention** *n* intervention *nf* **state intervention** intervention de l'état *nf*
**interview** 1. *n* entrevue *nf*, entretien *nm* **to attend for interview** passer un entretien *vb* **to hold an interview** avoir un entretien *vb* **to invite sb to interview** inviter qn à un entretien *vb* 2. *vb* interviewer *vb*
**introduce** *vb* (product) introduire *vb*
**inventory** *n* inventaire *nm* **inventory control** contrôle des stocks *nm*
**invest** *vb* (money) investir *vb*
**investment** *n* investissement *nm* **investment adviser** courtier de placement *nm* **investment portfolio** portefeuille d'investissements *nm* **investment programme, investment program** (US) programme d'investissements *nm* **investment strategy** stratégie d'investissement *nf*
**investor** *n* investisseur *nm*
**invisible** *adj* **invisible exports** exportations invisibles *nfpl* **invisible imports** importations invisibles *nfpl*
**invitation** *n* invitation *nf*
**invite** *vb* inviter *vb*
**invoice** *n* facture *nf* **duplicate invoice** double de la facture *nm* **to issue an invoice** facturer *vb* **to settle an invoice** régler une facture *vb*
**irrecoverable** *adj* (loss) irrécouvrable *adj*
**irrevocable** *adj* irrévocable *adj* **irrevocable letter of credit** lettre de crédit irrévocable *nf*
**issue** 1. *n* **bank of issue** banque de placement *nf* **share issue, stock issue** (US) émission de titres *nf* 2. *vb* (cheques, shares, notes) émettre *vb* (policy, tickets) délivrer *vb* **to issue sb with sth** fournir qch à qn *vb*
**issuing** *adj* **issuing bank** banque d'émission *nf*

**item** n article nm
**itemize** vb détailler vb, spécifier vb
**itemized** adj **itemized account** facture
détaillée
**itinerary** n itinéraire nm
**jackpot** n le gros lot nm
**jingle** n **advertising jingle** refrain
publicitaire nm
**job** n **job analysis** analyse des tâches nf **job creation** création d'emplois nf **job description** description du poste nf **job offer** offre d'emploi nf **job rotation** rotation des postes nf **job satisfaction** satisfaction professionnelle nf **job shop** atelier travaillant sur commande nm
**jobber** n jobber nm
**Jobcentre (GB)** n agence pour l'emploi nf
**jobless** adj sans emploi adj **the jobless** chômeurs nmpl
**joint** adj joint adj **joint account** compte joint nm **joint obligation/responsibility** responsabilité conjointe nf **joint ownership** copropriété nf **joint-stock company** société par actions nf **joint venture** joint venture nm
**jointly** adv en commun adv
**journal** n revue nf
**journalism** n journalisme nm
**judicial** adj judiciaire adj
**junior** adj cadet adj, subordonné adj
**junk** n bric-à-brac nm **junk bond** obligation hautement spéculative nf
**jurisdiction** n juridiction nf
**juror** n juré nm
**jury** n jury nm
**K** abbr (1000) il gagne 30KF (30 000 francs) abbr
**keen** adj (competition) vif adj (price) bon adj
**keep** vb (goods) conserver vb **to keep an appointment** venir à un rendez-vous vb **to keep the books** tenir les livres vb **to keep the business running** continuer l'activité vb
**keep back** vb (money) retenir vb
**keep down** vb (prices) maintenir les prix bas vb
**keep up with** vb (events) se maintenir au courant des évènements vb
**key** adj **key currency** monnaie clé nf **key industry** industrie clé nf **key person** homme-clé nm, femme-clé nf **key question** question-clé nf
**key in** vb introduire vb
**keyboard** n clavier nm
**keynote** adj **keynote speech** discours-programme nm
**keyword** n (computer) mot-clé nm
**kill** vb **to kill a project** enterrer un projet vb
**kind** 1. adj bon adj, aimable adj **would you be so kind as to...** voulez-vous avoir la bonté de... 2. n type nm
**king-size(d)** adj très grand adj, géant adj
**kiosk** n (phone) cabine nf
**kit** n (equipment) matériel nm,

équipement nm
**kite** n **kite mark (GB)** label de qualité nm
**km, kilometer (US)** abbr km abbr,
kilomètre nm
**knock** vb (disparage) critiquer vb
**knock down** vb (price) baisser vb
**knock off*** vb (finish work) cesser le travail vb
**knock-for-knock** adj à torts partagés **knock-for-knock agreement** (insurance) accord entre compagnies dans lequel chacune rembourse ses propres clients
**knock-on** adj **knock-on effect** réaction en chaîne
**knockdown** adj **knockdown price** à prix réduit adj
**know-how** n savoir-faire nm
**knowledge** n connaissances nfpl **knowledge base** base de connaissances nf **it is common knowledge** c'est un lieu commun **to have a thorough knowledge of sth** être très bien informé sur qch **to have a working knowledge of sth** avoir des connaissances de qch **to my knowledge** à ma connaissance
**knowledgeable** adj bien informé adj
**known** adj **known facts** les faits connus nmpl
**krona** n (Swedish) couronne nf
**krone** n (Danish, Norwegian) couronne nf
**kudos** n gloire nf
**kWh** abbr kWh (kilowatt heure) abbr
**label** 1. n étiquette nf 2. vb étiqueter vb
**labour, labor (US)** n main-d'oeuvre nf **labour costs** coûts de la main-d'oeuvre nmpl **labour dispute** conflit social nm **labour-intensive** travaillistique adj **labour law** législation du travail nf **labour market** marché du travail nm **labour relations** relations sociales nfpl
**labourer** n ouvrier nm
**lack** n manque nm **lack of investment** manque d'investissement nm
**land** n **land purchase** achat de terrain nm **land reform** réforme agraire nf **land register** cadastre nm **land tax** impôt foncier nm
**landlord** n propriétaire nm
**landowner** n propriétaire foncier nm
**language** n langue nf **language specialist** spécialiste des langues nm
**large** adj grand adj **large-scale** à grande échelle adj
**launch** 1. n **product launch** lancement d'un produit nm 2. vb (product) lancer vb
**law** n loi nf **business law** droit des sociétés nm **civil law** droit civil nm **criminal law** droit pénal nm **international law** droit international nm **law of diminishing returns** loi des rendements décroissants nf **public law** droit public nm
**lawsuit** n procès nm
**lay off** vb (workers) licencier vb
**LBO (leveraged buy-out)** abbr rachat d'entreprise financé par l'endettement nm

**leader** *n* **market leader** entreprise leader *nf*
**leadership** *n* sens du commandement *nm*
**leading** *adj* **leading product** meilleur produit *nm*
**lease** *vb* louer *vb*
**leasehold** *n* loué à bail *adj*
**leaseholder** *n* locataire *nm*
**leave** 1. *n* permission *nf* **leave of absence** congé *nm* **sick leave** congé de maladie *nm* 2. *vb* partir *vb* (resign from) quitter *vb* **to take leave** prendre congé *vb* **to take leave of sb** prendre congé de qn *vb*
**ledger** *n* registre *nm* **bought ledger** grand livre des achats *nm* **ledger entry** inscription au registre *nf*
**left** *adj* **left luggage** consigne *nf* **left-luggage locker** casier de consigne *nm* **left-luggage office** consigne *nf*
**legacy** *n* legs *nm*
**legal** *adj* légal *adj* **legal tender** cours légal *nm* **to take legal action** intenter une action en justice *vb*
**legislate** *vb* légiférer *vb*
**legislation** *n* législation *nf* **to introduce legislation** légiférer *vb*
**lend** *vb* prêter *vb*
**lender** *n* prêteur *nm*
**lessee** *n* locataire (à bail) *nm*
**lessor** *n* bailleur *nm*
**let** *vb* (property) louer *vb*
**letter** *n* **letter of application** lettre de candidature *nf* **letter of credit** lettre de crédit *nf* **letter of introduction** lettre de recommandation *nf*
**letterhead** *n* en-tête *nm*
**level** *n* **level of employment** niveau d'emploi *nm* **level of inflation** niveau d'inflation *nm* **level of prices** niveau des prix *nm*
**levy** 1. *n* prélèvement *nm* 2. *vb* (tax) prélever *vb*
**liability** *n* responsabilté *nf* **current liabilities** dettes à court terme *nfpl* **fixed liability** passif exigible à long terme *nm* **limited liability** responsabilité limitée *nf*
**liable** *adj* responsable *adj* **liable for damages** passible de dommages-intérêts *adj* **liable for tax** passible de l'impôt *adj*
**libel** *n* diffamation *nf*
**licence** *n* permis *nm* **licence fee** redevance *nf*
**license** *vb* autoriser *vb*
**licensee** *n* licencié *nm*
**licensor** *n* bailleur de licence *nm*
**life** *n* **life assurance/insurance** assurance vie *nf* **life member** membre à vie *nm*
**LIFO (last in first out)** *abbr* DEPS (dernier arrivé premier sorti) *nm*
**limit** *n* limite *nf* **credit limit** limite de crédit *nf*
**limited** *adj* limité *adj* **limited capital** capital limité *nm* **limited company** compagnie à responsabilité limitée *nf* **limited liability** responsabilité limitée *nf* **limited partnership**

société en commandite simple *nf*
**line** *n* **above the line** (bookkeeping) au dessus de la ligne **assembly line** chaîne de montage *nf* **below the line** (bookkeeping) au dessous de la ligne **line management** ligne hiérarchique *nf* **line manager** responsable opérationnel *nm* **line of business** branche *nf* **product line** ligne de produits *nf*, gamme *nf*
**liquid** *adj* liquide *adj* **liquid assets** actifs disponibles *nmpl* **liquid capital** liquidités *nfpl*
**liquidate** *vb* liquider *vb*
**liquidation** *n* liquidation *nf* **liquidation value** valeur de liquidation *nf*
**liquidity** *n* liquidité *nf*
**list** 1. *n* liste *nf* **list price** prix de catalogue *nm* 2. *vb* (computer) lister *vb*, faire une liste *vb*
**listed** *adj* **listed share, listed stock** (US) valeur cotée *nf*
**litigant** *n* partie d'un procès *nf*
**litigate** *vb* intenter un procès *vb*
**litigation** *n* litige *nm*
**load** 1. *n* charge *nf* 2. *vb* charger *vb*
**loan** *n* prêt *nm* **loan agreement** contrat de prêt *nm* **bank loan** prêt bancaire *nm* **bridging loan, bridge loan** (US) crédit-relais *nm* **personal loan** prêt personnel *nm* **to grant a loan** accorder un prêt *vb* **to request a loan** solliciter un prêt *vb*
**local** *adj* local *adj* **local taxes** taxes locales *nfpl*
**location** *n* emplacement *nm*
**lockout** *n* (of strikers) lock-out *nm*
**logistics** *n* logistique *nf*
**Lombard Rate** *n* taux Lombard *nm*
**long** *adj* **long capital** capital à long terme *nm* **long credit** crédit à longue échéance *nm* **long deposit** dépôt à long terme *nm* **long-distance** longue distance *nf* **long-range** à long terme *adj* **long-term** long terme *nm* **long-term planning** planification à long terme *nf*
**lose** *vb* (custom) perdre de la clientèle *vb*
**loss** *n* perte *nf* **financial loss** perte financière *nf* **gross loss** perte brute *nf* **loss leader** article d'appel *nm* **net(t) loss** perte nette *nf* **loss of earnings** perte de revenus *nf* **loss of job** perte d'emploi *nf* **to minimise losses** limiter les dégâts *vb*
**lost-property** *adj* **lost-property office** bureau des objets trouvés *nm*
**lot** *n* (at auction) lot *nm*
**low** *adj* (price) bas *adj*
**lower** *vb* (price, interest rate) baisser *vb*
**lucrative** *adj* lucratif *adj*
**luggage** *n* **excess luggage** excédent de bagages *nm* **luggage insurance** assurance bagages *nf*
**lump** *n* **lump sum settlement** somme forfaitaire *nf*
**luxury** *adj* **luxury goods** articles de luxe *nmpl* **luxury tax** impôt sur les produits de luxe *nm*

**machine 1.** *n* machine *nf* **2.** *vb* usiner *vb*
**machinery** *n* machines *nfpl* **machinery of government** la machine administrative *nf*
**macroeconomics** *n* macroéconomie *nf*
**made** *adj* **made in France** fabriqué en France *adj*
**magazine** *n* (journal) magazine *nm*
**magnate** *n* magnat *nm*
**magnetic** *adj* magnétique *adj* **magnetic tape** (DP) bande magnétique *nf*
**mail order** *n* vente par correspondance (VPC) *nf*
**mailing** *n* **mailing list** fichier d'adresses *nm*
**main** *adj* principal *adj* **main office** siège social *nm* **main supplier** fournisseur principal *nm*
**mainframe** *n* (DP) gros ordinateur *nm*
**maintenance** *n* entretien *nm* **maintenance costs** frais d'entretien *nmpl*
**major** *adj* majeur *adj*
**majority** *n* majorité *nf* **majority holding** participation majoritaire *nf* **in the majority** majoritaire *adj*
**make** *vb* **to make a fortune** faire fortune *vb* **to make a living** gagner sa vie *vb* **to make money** gagner de l'argent *vb*
**malingerer** *n* simulateur *nm*
**mall** *n* **shopping mall** centre commercial *nm*
**malpractice** *n* faute professionnelle *nf*
**man-made** *adj* synthétique *adj*
**manage** *vb* gérer *vb*
**management** *n* gestion *nf* **business management** gestion d'entreprise *nf* **management buy-out** rachat d'une entreprise par ses salariés (RES) *nm* **management by objectives** direction par objectifs *nf* **management consultant** conseiller en gestion *nm* **financial management** gestion financière *nf* **middle management** cadres moyens *nmpl* **personnel management** gestion du personnel *nf* **top management** cadres supérieurs *nmpl* **management training** formation des cadres *nf*
**manager** *n* directeur *nm*, manager *nm*
**manpower** *n* main d'oeuvre *nf*
**manual** *adj* manuel *adj* **manual worker** travailleur manuel *nm*
**manufacture 1.** *n* fabrication *nf* **2.** *vb* fabriquer *vb*
**manufacturer** *n* fabricant *nm*
**margin** *n* marge *nf* **profit margin** marge bénéficiaire *nf*
**marginal** *adj* marginal *adj* **marginal cost** coût marginal *nm* **marginal revenue** revenu marginal *nm*
**marine 1.** *adj* maritime *adj* **marine engineering** génie maritime *nm* **marine insurance** assurance maritime *nf* **2.** *n* **merchant marine** marine marchande *nf*
**mark down** *vb* (price) baisser *vb*
**mark up** *vb* augmenter (le prix) *vb*
**markdown** *n* rabais *nm*

**market 1.** *n* marché *nm* **market analysis** analyse du marché *nf* **bear market** marché orienté à la baisse *nm* **black market** marché noir *nm* **bond market** marché obligataire *nm* **bull market** marché orienté à la hausse *nm* **buyer's market** marché acheteur *nm* **capital market** marché financier *nm* **Common Market** Marché Commun *nm* **domestic market** marché intérieur *nm* **down-market** (product) bas de gamme *adj* **market economy** économie de marché *nf* **falling market** marché en baisse *nm* **firm market** marché ferme *nm* **market forces** forces du marché *nfpl* **foreign market** marché extérieur *nm* **futures market** marché à terme *nm* **labour market** marché du travail *nm* **market leader** entreprise leader *nf* **money market** marché monétaire *nm* **market opportunity** débouché *nm*, créneau *nm* **market price** prix du marché *nm* **property market (GB) / real estate market (US)** marché immobilier *nm* **market research** étude de marché *nf* **retail market** marché de détail *nm* **market segmentation** segmentation du marché *nf* **seller's market** marché vendeur *nm* **market share** part de marché *nf* **stock market** bourse des valeurs *nf* **the bottom has fallen out of the market** le marché s'est effondré **to play the market** spéculer *vb* **up-market** (product) haut de gamme *adj* **market value** valeur marchande *nf* **wholesale market** marché de gros *nm* **2.** *vb* commercialiser *vb*
**marketable** *adj* vendable *adj*
**marketing** *n* marketing *nm* **marketing consultant** conseil en marketing *nm* **marketing department** service du marketing *nm* **marketing director** responsable du marketing *nm*
**markup** *n* majoration *nf*
**mart** *n* centre commercial *nm*
**mass** *adj* **mass marketing** commercialisation de masse *nf* **mass media** médias *nmpl* **mass production** fabrication en série *nf* **mass unemployment** chômage généralisé *nm*
**material** *adj* **material needs** besoins matériels *nmpl*
**materials** *npl* matériaux *nmpl* **building materials** matériaux de construction *nmpl* **raw materials** matières premières *nfpl*
**maternity** *n* **maternity leave** congé de maternité *nm*
**matrix** *n* matrice *nf*
**mature** *vb* (business, economy) venir à échéance *vb*
**maximise** *vb* maximiser *vb*
**maximum** *adj* **maximum price** prix maximum *nm*
**MBA (Master of Business Administration)** *abbr* titulaire d'une maîtrise en gestion *nm*

**mean 1.** *adj* (average) moyen, -enne *adj* **2.** *n* (average) moyenne *nf*

**means** *npl* moyens *nmpl* **financial means** moyens (financiers) *nmpl* **to live beyond one's means** vivre au-dessus de ses moyens *vb* **we do not have the means to...** nous n'avons pas les moyens de...

**measure 1.** *n* mesure *nf* **financial measure** mesure financière *nf* **safety measure** mesure de sécurité *nf* **2.** *vb* mesurer *vb*

**mechanical** *adj* mécanique *adj* **mechanical engineering** mécanique *nf*

**media** *npl* médias *nmpl*

**median** *adj* médian *adj*

**mediate** *vb* servir comme intermédiaire *vb*

**mediation** *n* médiation *nf*

**mediator** *n* médiateur *nm*

**medical** *adj* médical *adj* **medical insurance** assurance maladie *nf*

**medium 1.** *adj* moyen *adj* **medium-sized firm** entreprise moyenne *nf* **medium term** moyen terme *nm* **2.** *n* **advertising medium** support publicitaire *nm*

**meet** *vb* rencontrer *vb*

**meeting** *n* réunion *nf* **board meeting** réunion du conseil d'administration *nf* **business meeting** réunion d'affaires *nf* **to hold a meeting** tenir une réunion *vb*

**megabyte** *n* mégaoctet *nm*

**member** *n* membre *nm* **Member of Parliament (MP) (GB)** député *nm* **Member of the European Parliament (MEP)** député européen *nm*

**memo** *n* mémo *nm*

**memorandum** *n* mémorandum *nm*

**memory** *n* (DP) mémoire *nf* **memory capacity** capacité de mémoire *nf*

**mercantile** *adj* marchand *adj*

**merchandise** *vb* marchandiser *vb*

**merchandizer** *n* marchandiseur *nm*

**merchandizing** *n* marchandisage *nm*

**merchant** *n* commerçant *nm* **merchant bank** banque d'affaires *nf* **merchant navy, merchant marine** (US) marine marchande *nf* **merchant ship** navire marchand *nm*

**merge** *vb* fusionner *vb*

**merger** *n* fusion *nf*

**merit** *n* **merit payment** prime de rendement *nf*

**message** *n* message *nm*

**messenger** *n* messager *nm*

**metal** *n* métal *nm*

**meter** *n* compteur *nm*

**method** *n* **method of payment** mode de paiement *nm* **production method** méthode de fabrication *nf*

**metre, meter** (US) *n* mètre *nm* **cubic metre** mètre cube *nm* **square metre** mètre carré *nm*

**metric** *adj* métrique *adj*

**metrication** *n* conversion au système métrique *nf*

**metropolis** *n* métropole *nf*

**microchip** *n* puce *nf*

**microcomputer** *n* micro-ordinateur *nm*

**microeconomics** *n* micro-économie *nf*

**microfiche** *n* microfiche *nf*

**microprocessor** *n* microprocesseur *nm*

**middle** *adj* **middle management** cadres moyens *nmpl* **middle manager** cadre moyen *nm*

**middleman** *n* intermédiaire *nm*

**migrant** *n* **migrant worker** travailleur immigré *nm*

**mile** *n* mile *nm*, mille *nm* **nautical mile** mille nautique *nm*

**mileage** *n* kilométrage *nm*

**million** *n* million *nm*

**millionaire** *n* millionnaire *nm*

**mine** *n* mine *nf* **coal mine** mine de charbon *nf*

**mineral** *n* minérai *nm*, minéral *nm*

**minimal** *adj* minimal *adj*

**minimum** *adj* **index-linked minimum wage** SMIC *nm*, salaire minimum interprofessionnel de croissance *nm* **minimum lending rate** taux de base bancaire *nm*

**mining** *n* exploitation minière *nf* **mining industry** industrie minière *nf*

**minister** *n* ministre *nm*

**ministry** *n* ministère *nm* **Ministry of Transport** Ministère des Transports *nm*

**minor** *adj* mineur *adj*

**minority** *n* minorité *nf* **minority holding** participation minoritaire *nf* **to be in the minority** être en minorité *nf*

**mint 1.** *n* la Monnaie *nf* **2.** *vb* monnayer *vb* **he/she mints money** il/elle fait des affaires d'or

**minutes** *npl* **the minutes (of the meeting)** procès-verbal *nm*, compte-rendu *nm*

**misappropriation** *n* détournement *nm*

**miscalculation** *n* erreur de calcul *nf*

**misconduct** *n* (bad management) mauvaise administration *nf*

**mishandling** *n* mauvaise approche (du problème) *nf*

**mismanagement** *n* mauvaise gestion *nf*

**mistake** *n* erreur *nf* **to make a mistake** faire une erreur *vb*

**mix** *n* **marketing mix** plan de marchéage *nm* **product mix** mix de produits *nm*

**mixed** *adj* **mixed economy** économie mixte *nf*

**mode** *n* (method) mode *nm*

**model** *n* (person) modèle *nm*, mannequin *nm*

**modem** *n* modem *nm*

**moderate 1.** *adj* modéré *adj* **2.** *vb* modérer *vb*

**moderation** *n* modération *nf*

**modern** *adj* moderne *adj*

**modernization** *n* modernisation *nf*

**modernize** *vb* moderniser *vb*

**module** *n* module *nm*

**monetarism** *n* monétarisme *nm*

**monetary** *adj* monétaire *adj* **European**

**Monetary System (EMS)** Système Monétaire Européen *nm* **International Monetary Fund (IMF)** Fonds Monétaire International *nm* **monetary policy** politique monétaire *nf* **money** *n* **dear money** argent cher *nm* **money market** marché monétaire *nm* **money order** mandat *nm* **public money** fonds publics *nmpl*, deniers publics *nmpl* **money supply** masse monétaire *nf* **to raise money** se procurer de l'argent *vb* **money trader** cambiste *nmf*

**moneymaking** *adj* (profitable) rentable *adj*

**monopoly** *n* monopole *nm* **Monopolies and Mergers Commission** Commission de la concurrence *nf*

**monthly** *adj* mensuel *adj*

**moonlight\*** *vb* travailler au noir *vb*

**moor** *vb* amarrer *vb*

**mooring** *n* **mooring rights** droits d'amarrage *nmpl*

**mortgage** *n* hypothèque *nf* **mortgage deed** contrat d'hypothèque *nm* **mortgage loan** prêt hypothécaire *nm*

**mortgagee** *n* créancier hypothécaire *nm*

**mortgagor** *n* débiteur hypothécaire *nm*

**motor** *n* **motor industry** industrie automobile *nf*

**multilateral** *adj* multilatéral *adj*

**multinational** *adj* multinational *adj* **multinational corporation** (société) multinationale *nf*

**multiple** *adj* **multiple store** magasin à succursales multiples *nm*

**multiply** *vb* se multiplier *vb*

**multipurpose** *adj* polyvalent *adj*

**municipal** *adj* **municipal bonds** obligations municipales *nfpl*

**mutual** *adj* mutuel *adj* **mutual fund (US)** fonds commun de placement *nm*, SICAV (société d'investissement à capital variable) *nf*

**mutually** *adv* mutuellement *adv*

**N/A (not applicable)** *abbr* ne s'applique pas

**name** 1. *n* **brand name** marque de fabrique *nf* **by name** par nom **full name** nom et prénom(s) *nmpl* **in the name of** au nom de **registered trade name** raison sociale *nf* 2. *vb* nommer *vb*

**named** *adj* **named person** personne nommée *nf*

**narrow** *adj* étroit *adj* **narrow margin** marge faible *nf* **narrow market** marché étroit *nm*

**nation** *n* nation *nf* **the United Nations** les Nations Unies *nfpl*

**national** *adj* **national debt** dette publique *nf* **national income** revenu national *nm* **national insurance (NI)(GB)** assurances sociales *nfpl*, assurance nationale *nf* **national interest** intérêt national *nm* **National Bureau of Economic Research (US)** bureau national des recherches économiques *nm*

**nationality** *n* nationalité *nf*

**nationalization** *n* nationalisation *nf*

**nationalize** *vb* nationaliser *vb*

**nationalized** *adj* **nationalized industry** industrie nationalisée *nf*

**nationwide** *adj* à l'échelon national *adj*

**natural** *adj* naturel *adj* **natural rate of increase** taux d'accroissement naturel *nm* **natural resources** ressources naturelles *nfpl*

**necessary** *adj* nécessaire *adj* **necessary qualifications** les capacités requises *nfpl*

**necessity** *n* (goods) choses nécessaires *nfpl*

**need** *n* **needs assessment** évaluation des besoins *nf* **needs of industry** les besoins de l'industrie *nmpl* **to be in need** avoir besoin (de) *vb*

**negative** *adj* négatif *adj* **negative cash flow** trésorerie négative *nf* **negative feedback** contre-réaction *nf*

**negative (US)** *vb* rejeter *vb*

**neglect** *n* **neglect clause** clause de négligence *nf*

**negligence** *n* négligence *nf* **negligence clause** clause de négligence *nf* **contributory negligence** imprudence de la part du sinistré *nf* **gross negligence** faute grave *nf*

**negligent** *adj* négligent *adj*

**negotiable** *adj* négociable *adj* **negotiable bill** effet négociable *nm* **negotiable cheque** chèque négociable *nm*

**negotiate** *vb* négocier (pour) *vb*, traiter (pour) *vb*

**negotiated** *adj* **negotiated price** prix négocié *nm*

**negotiating** *n* **negotiating session** négociation *nf* **negotiating skills** talents de négociateur *nmpl*

**negotiation** *n* négociation *nf* **by negotiation** par négociation **to begin negotiations** entamer des pourparlers *vb* **under negotiation** en cours de négociation **wage negotiations** négociations salariales *nfpl*

**negotiator** *n* négociateur *nm*

**net, nett** 1. *adj* net, nette *adj* **net amount** montant net *nm* **net assets** actif net *nm* **net cost** prix de revient net *nm* **net earnings** bénéfice net *nm* **net interest** intérêt net *nm* **net investment** investissement net *nm* **net loss** perte sèche *nf* **net, nett price** prix net *nm* **net proceeds** produit net *nm* **net profit** bénéfice net *nm* **net result** résultat net *nm* **net sales** ventes nettes *nfpl* **net saving** épargne nette *nf* **terms strictly net** prix nets *nmpl* **net wage** salaire net *nm* **net weight** poids net *nm* 2. *vb* gagner *vb*

**network** 1. *n* **banking network** réseau bancaire *nm* **computer network** réseau informatique *nm* **distribution network** réseau de distribution *nm* 2. *vb* connecter en réseau *vb*

**neutral** *adj* neutre *adj*

**new** *adj* **new account** nouveau compte *nm*

**new business** nouveaux clients *nmpl* **new product** produit nouveau *nm* **new technology** technologie de pointe *nf*

**newly** *adv* **newly-appointed** nouvellement nommé **newly-industrialised** nouvellement industrialisé

**news** *n* informations *nfpl* **news agency** agence de presse *nf* **bad news** mauvaises nouvelles *nf* **news bulletin** bulletin d'informations *nm* **news coverage** reportage *nm* **financial news** informations financières *nfpl* **good news** bonnes nouvelles *nf*

**newsagent, newsdealer** (US) *n* marchand, -e de journaux *nm,f*

**newsletter** *n* bulletin *nm*

**newspaper** *n* journal *nm* **newspaper advertisement** annonce dans la presse *nf* **daily newspaper** (journal) quotidien *nm* **newspaper report** reportage *nm*

**nil** *n* zéro *nm*, rien *nm* **nil profit** bénéfice nul *nm*

**no** *det* **no agents wanted** intermédiaires s'abstenir **no-claims bonus** bonification pour non-sinistre *nf* **no commercial value** sans valeur marchande

**nominal** *adj* nominal *adj*, symbolique *adj* **nominal amount** montant symbolique *nm* **nominal assets** actif fictif *nm* **nominal damages** franc symbolique *nm* **nominal inflation** taux d'inflation nominal *nm* **nominal price** prix nominal *nm* **nominal value** valeur nominale *nf*

**nominate** *vb* nommer *vb* **nominate sb to a board/committee** nommer qn membre d'un conseil

**nomination** *n* nomination *nf*

**nominee** *n* personne nommée *nf* **nominee shareholder** mandataire d'un actionnaire *nm*

**non-acceptance** *n* non-acceptation *nf*

**non-attendance** *n* absence *nf*

**non-completion** *n* non-accomplissement *nm*

**non-contributory** *adj* non-cotisé *adj*

**non-convertible** *adj* non convertible *adj*

**non-delivery** *n* non-livraison *nf*

**non-discriminatory** *adj* non discriminatoire *adj*

**non-essential** *adj* non-essentiel *adj*

**non-interest-bearing** *adj* non porteur d'intérêts *adj*

**non-intervention** *n* non-intervention *nf*

**non-negotiable** *adj* non négociable *adj*

**non-payment** *n* non-paiement *nm*

**non-profitmaking** *adj* sans but lucratif

**non-returnable** *adj* non repris *adj*

**non-stop** *adj* sans arrêt

**non-transferable** *adj* (stocks) obligations nominatives *nfpl*

**norm** *n* norme *nf*

**normal** *adj* **normal trading hours** horaires normaux de travail *nmpl*

**not** *adv* **not applicable** ne s'applique pas **not**

**available** indisponible *adj* **not dated** non daté *adj*

**notary** *n* notaire *nm*

**note** *n* **advice note** bon de livraison *nm* **cover note** lettre de couverture *nf* **credit note** avis de crédit *nm* **debit note** avis de débit *nm* **delivery note** bon de livraison *nm* **dispatch note** bordereau d'expédition *nm* **open note (US)** emprunt à découvert *nm* **to compare notes** échanger ses impressions *vb* **to make a note of sth** prendre note de qch *vb*

**noteworthy** *adj* remarquable *adj*

**notice 1.** *n* **advance notice** préavis *nm* **at short notice** à court terme **final notice** dernier avertissement *nm* **notice period** délai de préavis *nm* **term of notice** délai de préavis *nm* **to come to the notice of sb** venir à la connaissance de qn **to give notice of sth** prévenir qn de qch **to take notice** tenir compte **until further notice** jusqu'à nouvel ordre **2.** *vb* remarquer *vb*

**notification** *n* notification *nf*

**notify** *vb* signaler *vb*

**null** *adj* **null and void** nul et non avenu *adj*

**number** *n* **account number** numéro de compte *nm* **opposite number** homologue *nmf* **order number** numéro de commande *nm* **serial number** numéro de série *nm* **telephone number** numéro de téléphone *nm* **wrong number** (phone) faux numéro *nm*

**numeracy** *n* capacités en calcul *nfpl*

**numerate** *adj* fort en calcul *adj*

**numeric** *adj* **numeric-alphabetic** alpha-numérique *adj* **numeric character** caractère numérique *nm*

**numerical** *adj* **numerical analysis** analyse numérique *nf*

**NYSE (New York Stock Exchange)** *abbr* Bourse de New York *nf*

**object** *vb* élever une objection (contre) *vb*

**objection** *n* objection *nf* **to make/raise an objection** élever une objection

**objective** *n* objectif *nm* **to reach an objective** atteindre un objectif

**obligation** *n* obligation *nf* **to meet one's obligations** tenir ses engagements

**obligatory** *adj* obligatoire *adj*

**oblige** *vb* **to be obliged to do sth** être obligé de faire qch

**observation** *n* observation *nf* **under observation** à l'étude

**observe** *vb* **observe the rules** observer les règles

**obsolescence** *n* vieillissement *nm* **built-in obsolescence** vieillissement programmé *nm*

**obsolete** *adj* dépassé *adj*

**obtain** *vb* obtenir *vb* **to obtain credit** obtenir un crédit *vb*

**occupant** *n* occupant *nm*

**occupation** *n* profession *nf*

**occupational** *adj* professionnel *adj* **occupa-**

**tional disease** maladie professionnelle *nf*
**occupational hazard** risque professionnel *nm*
**occupier** *n* occupant *nm*
**occupy** *vb* (premises) occuper *vb*
**off-the-job** *adj* **off-the-job training** stages de formations à l'extérieur de l'entreprise
**offence, offense** (US) *n* offense *nf*
**offer** *n* **firm offer** offre ferme *nf* **offer in writing** offre écrite *nf* **offer subject to confirmation** offre provisoire *nf* **offer valid until...** offre valable jusqu'à... *nf*
**offeree** *n* destinataire d'une offre *nm*
**offeror** *n* auteur d'une offre *nm*
**office** *n* bureau *nm* **office equipment** matériel de bureau *nm* **office hours** heures d'ouverture *nfpl* **office management** gestion de bureau *nf* **office staff** personnel de bureau *nm* **to hold office** avoir des fonctions **to resign from office** se démettre de ses fonctions
**official** *n* officiel *adj* **official strike** grève légale *nf*
**offshore** *adj* offshore *adj*, hors-lieu *adj* **offshore company** filiale offshore *nf*
**oil** *n* **oil industry** industrie pétrolière *nf* **oil state** pays pétrolier *nm*
**oilfield** *n* gisement de pétrole *nm*
**oligopoly** *n* oligopole *nm*
**ombudsman** *n* médiateur *nm*
**on-line** *adj* connecté *adj*, direct *adj*, en ligne *adj*
**on-the-job** *adj* **on-the-job training** formation sur le lieu de travail
**onus** *n* **the onus is on us to...** nous avons la responsabilité de...
**open** 1. *adj* ouvert *adj* **open cheque** chèque non barré *nm* **open credit** crédit libre *nm* **open market** marché libre *nm* **open shop** atelier ouvert aux non syndiqués *nm* 2. *vb* **to open an account** ouvrir un compte *vb*
**open up** *vb* (market) ouvrir (le marché) *vb*
**opening** *adj* **opening price** cours d'ouverture *nm* **opening times** heures d'ouverture *nfpl*
**operate** *vb* **to operate a business** gérer une affaire *vb*
**operating** *n* **operating expenditure** dépenses d'exploitation *nfpl* **operating expenses** frais d'exploitation *nmpl* **operating income** bénéfices d'exploitation *nmpl* **operating profit** bénéfices d'exploitation *nmpl* **operating statement** compte d'exploitation *nm*
**operation** *n* (of business) opération *nf*, activité *nf*, exploitation *nf*, gestion *nf* (of machine) fonctionnement *nm*, opération *nf*
**operator** *n* opérateur *nm*
**opportunity** *n* occasion *nf* **market opportunities** créneaux sur un marché *nmpl* **to seize an opportunity** saisir l'occasion *vb*
**option** *n* option *nf* **share option, stock option** (US) option d'achat d'actions *nf* **options market** marché à options *nm* **option to buy** option d'achat *nf* **option to cancel** option d'annulation *nf*
**optional** *adj* optionnel *adj*
**order** *n* **order book** carnet de commandes *nm* **order form** bon de commande *nm* **order number** numéro de commande *nm* **pay to the order of...** payer à l'ordre de... **to cancel an order** annuler une commande *vb* **to place an order** passer une commande *vb*
**ordinary** *adj* ordinaire *adj* **ordinary general meeting** assemblée générale ordinaire *nf* **ordinary share, ordinary stock** (US) action ordinaire *nf*
**organization** *n* organisation *nf*
**organize** *vb* organiser *vb*
**organized** *adj* organisé *adj* **organized labour** (trade unions) les syndicats *nmpl*
**origin** *n* (of a product) origine *nf* **country of origin** pays d'origine *nm* **statement of origin** certificat d'origine *nm*
**original** *adj* **original cost** coût initial *nm*
**outbid** *vb* enchérir sur *vb*
**outcome** *n* résultat *nm*
**outgoings** *npl* dépenses *nfpl*
**outlay** *n* **capital outlay** dépenses d'investissement *nfpl*
**outlet** *n* **market outlet** débouché *nm* **sales outlet** point de vente *nm*
**outlook** *n* **business outlook** perspective économique *nf*
**output** *n* production *nm*, rendement *nm* **to increase output** augmenter la production *vb*
**outstanding** *adj* **outstanding amount** le restant de la somme *nm* **outstanding debt** dette *nf* **outstanding stock** actions en circulation *nfpl*
**overcharge** *vb* vendre trop cher *vb*, faire trop payer *vb*
**overdraft** *n* découvert *nm* **to request an overdraft** demander un découvert
**overdraw** *vb* mettre à découvert *vb*
**overdrawn** *adj* à découvert *adj* **overdrawn account** compte à découvert *nm*
**overdue** *adj* en retard *adj*
**overhead** *adj* **overhead costs** frais généraux *nmpl*
**overheads** *npl* frais généraux *nmpl*
**overheating** *n* (of economy) surchauffe *nf*
**overload** *vb* surcharge *nf*
**overlook** *vb* négliger *vb*, oublier *vb*
**overman** *vb* suréquiper en personnel *vb*
**overmanned** *adj* suréquipé *adj*
**overmanning** *n* (excess staff) les sureffectifs *nmpl*
**overnight** *adj* **overnight delivery** livraison le lendemain *nf*
**overpay** *vb* surpayer *vb*
**overpayment** *n* surpaye *nf*, rémunération excessive
**overpopulation** *n* surpopulation *nf*
**overproduce** *vb* surproduire *vb*
**overproduction** *n* surproduction *nf*

**overseas** adj d'outre-mer adj **overseas market** marché extérieur nm **overseas territory** territoire d'outre-mer nm **overseas trade** commerce extérieur nm
**oversell** vb survendre vb
**oversight** n omission nf, erreur nf **due to an oversight** à cause d'une erreur
**oversold** adj survendu adj
**oversubscribed** adj sursouscrit adj
**oversupply** vb surapprovisionner vb
**overtime** n heures supplémentaires nfpl
**overvalue** vb surévaluer vb
**overworked** adj surmené adj
**owe** vb devoir vb
**own** vb posséder vb
**owner** n propriétaire nm
**owner-occupier** n occupant-propriétaire nm
**ownership** n possession nf
**pack** vb paquet nm
**package** n colis nm **package deal** accord global nm **package tour** voyage organisé nm
**packaging** n emballage nm, conditionnement nm
**packet** n paquet nm
**paid** adj payé adj **paid holiday** congé payé nm
**paid-up** adj **paid-up capital** capital versé nm
**pallet** n palette nf
**palletized** adj **palletized freight** fret chargé sur palette
**paper** n **commercial paper** papier commercial nm **paper loss** perte comptable nf **paper profit** plus-value non-matérialisée nf
**paperwork** n documents nmpl
**par** n **above par** au-dessus du pair prep **below par** au-dessous du pair prep
**parent** n **parent company** société mère nf
**parity** n parité nf
**part** n (of a machine) pièce nf **part payment** règlement partiel nm **part shipment** expédition partielle nf **spare part** (for machine) pièce de rechange nf
**part-time** adj à temps partiel
**participation** n **worker participation** participation nf
**partner** n associé nm **sleeping partner** commanditaire nm
**partnership** n association nf **trading partnership** association commerciale nf
**passenger** n passager nm
**patent** n brevet nm
**patented** adj breveté adj
**patronage** n parrainage nm
**pattern** n **spending patterns** habitudes d'achat nfpl
**pay 1.** n (salary, wages) paye nf, paie nf, salaire nm **equal pay** égalité des salaires nf **pay rise** augmentation de salaire nf **severance pay** indemnités de licenciement nf **unemployment pay** chômage nf **2.** vb **to pay an invoice** payer vb, régler vb **to pay by credit card**

payer par carte bancaire **to pay for a service** payer un service **to pay in advance** payer d'avance **to pay in cash** payer en espèces
**payable** adj **accounts payable** comptes fournisseurs nmpl
**payee** n bénéficiaire nm
**payer** n payeur nm **prompt payer** bon payeur nm **slow payer** mauvais payeur nm
**payload** n (of vehicle) charge utile nf
**payment** n paiement nm **down payment** acompte nm
**payola (US)** n pot-de-vin nm
**payroll** n masse salariale nf, effectifs nmpl, registre du personnel nm **to be on the payroll** être employé par une entreprise
**peak** n sommet nm **peak demand** demande maximale nf **peak period** période de pointe nf
**pecuniary** adj **for pecuniary gain** dans un but lucratif
**peddle** vb colporter vb
**peg** vb (prices) stabiliser vb **the HK dollar is pegged to the US dollar** le dollar de HK est indexé sur le dollar américain
**penetration** n **market penetration** pénétration du marché nf
**pension** n pension nf **pension fund** fonds de retraite nm **retirement pension** (pension de) retraite nf **pension scheme** régime de retraite nm
**per** prep **per annum** par an **per capita** par tête **per cent** pour cent
**percentage** n pourcentage nm **percentage of profit** pourcentage des bénéfices nm
**performance** n (behaviour) comportement nm **performance appraisal** évaluation des performances nf **performance-related bonus** prime de rendement nf
**period** n **cooling-off period** délai de réflexion nm **period of grace** délai de grâce nm
**peripheral** adj périphérique adj
**perishable** adj périssable adj **perishable goods** denrées périssables nfpl
**perk** n (informal) avantages en nature nmpl
**permanent** adj **permanent employment** emploi permanent nm
**permit** n permis nm **building permit** permis de construire nm
**perquisite** n (formal) avantages en nature nmpl
**person** n **third person** tierce personne nf
**personal** adj personnel adj
**personnel** n **personnel department** service du personnel nm **personnel management** gestion du personnel nf
**peseta** n peseta nf
**petrodollar** n pétrodollar nm
**petroleum** n **petroleum industry** industrie pétrolière nf
**pharmaceutical** adj pharmaceutique adj **pharmaceutical industry** industrie

pharmaceutique *nf*

**phoney\*** *adj* **phoney\* company** une société bidon *nf*

**photocopier** *n* photocopieuse *nf*

**photocopy** 1. *n* photocopie *nf* 2. *vb* photocopier *vb*

**pick up** *vb* (improve) s'améliorer *vb*

**picket** *n* (strike) piquet de grève *nm*

**piecework** *n* travail à la pièce *nm*

**pig iron** *n* fonte brute *nf*

**pilferage** *n* chapardage *nm*

**pilot** *n* **pilot plant** usine pilote *nf* **pilot scheme** projet pilote *nm*

**pipeline** *n* pipeline *nm*

**piracy** *n* (at sea) piraterie *nf* **software piracy** piratage de logiciels *nm*

**place** *vb* **to place an order** passer une commande *vb*

**plan** 1. *n* **economic plan** plan économique *nm* **plan of campaign** plan de campagne *nm* **to make plans** faire des projets 2. *vb* planifier *vb* faire des projets *vb*

**planned** *adj* **planned economy** économie planifiee *nf* **planned obsolescence** vieillissement programmé *nm*

**planning** *n* planification *nf* **regional planning** aménagement du territoire *nm*

**plant** *n* (machinery) matériel *nm* **plant hire** location de matériel *nf* **plant manager** directeur d'usine *nm*

**plastics** *npl* **plastics industry** industrie plastique *nf*

**pledge** *n* gage *nm*

**plenary** *adj* (assembly, session) plénier *adj*

**plough back, plow back, to** (US) *vb* (profits) réinvestir *vb*

**point** *n* **point of sale** point de vente *nm*

**policy** *n* **insurance policy** police d'assurance *nf* **pricing policy** politique des prix *nf*

**political** *adj* politique *adj*

**politics** *n* politique *nf*

**port** *n* port *nm*

**portable** *adj* portatif *adj*

**portfolio** *n* **investment portfolio** portefeuille d'investissements *nm*

**post** 1. *n* (job) poste *nm* 2. *vb* poster *vb*

**post office** bureau de poste *nm*

**postal** *adj* postal *adj* **postal services** services postaux *nmpl*

**postdate** *vb* postdater *vb*

**poste restante** *n* poste restante *nf*

**poster** *n* (advertising) affiche *nf*

**postpone (until)** *vb* remettre à *vb*

**potential** *n* potentiel *nm* **sales potential** potentiel de ventes *nm*

**pound** *n* (weight) livre *nf* **pound sterling** livre *nf*

**power** *n* pouvoir *nm* **power of attorney** procuration *nf*

**preference** *n* **community preference** préférence communautaire *nf*

**preferential** *adj* préférentiel *adj*

**premises** *npl* locaux *nmpl* **office premises** bureaux *nmpl*

**premium** *n* prime *nf* **at a premium** au-dessus du pair

**prepayment** *n* paiement d'avance *nm*

**president** *n* (of company) président-directeur général (PDG) *nm*

**press** *n* **press baron** magnat de la presse *nm* **press conference** conférence de presse *nf*

**price** *n* prix *nm* **market price** prix de marché *nm* **stock exchange prices** cours *nmpl* **threshold price** prix de seuil *nm*

**pricing** *adj* **pricing policy** politique des prix *nf*

**primary** *adj* **primary industry** industrie primaire *nf*

**prime** *adj* **prime lending rate** taux de base *nm*

**priority** *n* priorité *nf*

**private** *adj* **private sector** le secteur privé *nm*

**privatization** *n* privatisation *nf*

**privatize** *vb* privatiser *vb*

**pro** 1. *n* **pros and cons** le pour et le contre 2. *prep* pro- *pref* **pro rata** au prorata *adv*

**probate** *n* validation *nf*, homologation *nf*

**proceeds** *npl* produit *nm*

**process** 1. *n* processus *nm*, procédé *nm*, méthode *nf* 2. *vb* traiter *vb*, transformer *vb*

**produce** 1. *n* produit(s) agricole(s) *nmpl* 2. *vb* produire *vb*, fabriquer *vb*

**producer** *n* producteur *nm*

**product** *n* produit *nm* **primary product** produit de base *nm*

**production** *n* production *nf* **production line** chaîne de fabrication *nf*

**productive** *adj* productif *adj*

**productivity** *n* productivité *nf* **productivity gains** gains de productivité *mpl*

**profession** *n* profession *nf* **the professions** les professions *nfpl*

**profit** *n* bénéfice *nm*, profit *nm* **profit and loss** pertes et profits *nfpl,nmpl* **profit margin** marge bénéficiaire **net(t) profit** bénéfice net **operating profit** résultat d'exploitation **profit-sharing scheme** participation *nf* **to make a profit** faire des bénéfices

**profitability** *n* rentabilité *nf*

**profiteer** *vb* faire des bénéfices excessifs *vb*

**program** *n* (DP) programme *nm*

**programmer** *n* (DP) programmeur *nm*

**programming** *n* (DP) programmation *nf*

**progress** 1. *n* progrès *nm*, avancement *nm* 2. *vb* (research, project) progresser *vb*, avancer *vb*

**project** *n* projet *nm*, plan *nm*

**promissory** *adj* **promissory note** billet à ordre *nm*

**promote** *vb* (person) promouvoir (qn) *vb* (product) faire de la publicité (pour un produit) *vb*

**promotion** *n* (of product) promotion *nf* (of person) promotion *nf*, avancement *nm*

**promotional** *adj* promotionnel *adj*,

publicitaire *adj* **promotional budget** budget publicitaire *nm*

**prompt** *adj* rapide *adj*

**property** *n* biens *nmpl*, possessions *nfpl*, propriété *nf* **property company** société immobilière *nf* **property developer** promoteur immobilier *nm* **private property** propriété privée *nf*

**proprietary** *adj* de marque déposée *adj* **proprietary brand** marque déposée *nf*

**proprietor** *n* propriétaire *nm*

**prospect** *n* perspective *nf* **future prospects** les perspectives d'avenir

**prospectus** *n* prospectus *nm*

**prosperous** *adj* prospère *adj*

**protectionism** *n* protectionnisme *nm*

**protectionist** *adj* protectionniste *adj*

**provide** *vb* (supply) approvisionner *vb*, fournir *vb*

**provision** *n* (stipulation) provision *nf*, disposition *nf*, stipulation *nf*

**proxy** *n* (power) procuration *nf*, mandat *nm*

**public** *adj* public *adj*, nationalisé *adj*, étatisé *adj* **public company** société anonyme *nf* **public funds** fonds publics *nmpl* **public relations** relations publiques *nfpl* **public sector** secteur public *nm* **public service** la fonction publique *nf*

**publicity** *n* publicité *nf*

**publishing** *n* édition *nf*, publication *nf* **desktop publishing** publication assistée par ordinateur

**purchase 1.** *n* achat *nm* **purchase price** prix d'achat *nm* **2.** *vb* acheter *vb*

**purchasing** *n* achat *nm*, approvisionnement *nm* **purchasing power** pouvoir d'achat

**pyramid** *n* pyramide *nf* **pyramid scheme** plan pyramidal *nm* **pyramid selling** plan pyramidale

**qualification** *n* compétence *nf*, aptitude *nf* **academic qualification** diplômes *nmpl*, titres *nmpl* **educational qualification** formation *nf* **professional qualification** qualifications professionnelles *nfpl*

**qualified** *adj* diplômé *adj*, ayant les titres requis **qualified acceptance** conditionnel *adj* **qualified personnel** personnel compétent *nm*

**qualitative** *adj* qualitatif *adj*

**quality** *n* qualité *nf* **quality control** contrôle de qualité *nm* **quality report** rapport de qualité **quality standard** norme de qualité *nf*

**quantitative** *adj* quantitatif *adj*

**quantity** *n* quantité *nf* **quantity discount** remise quantitative **quantity theory of money** théorie quantitative

**quarter** *n* (of year) trimestre *nm*

**quarterly** *adj* trimestriel *adj* **quarterly interest** intérêts trimestriels *nmpl* **quarterly trade accounts** comptes d'exploitation trimestriels *nmpl*

**quasi-contract** *n* quasi-contrat *nm*

**quasi-income** *n* quasi-revenu *nm*

**quay** *n* quai *nm*

**quayage** *n* droit de quai *nm*

**questionnaire** *n* questionnaire *nm* **market research questionnaire** questionnaire d'étude de marché *nm*

**queue** *n* queue *nf*, file d'attente *nf*

**quick** *adj* **quick assets** actif disponible à court terme *nm*

**quiet** *adj* **quiet market** marché calme *nm*

**quit** *vb* (resign) démissionner *vb*

**quittance** *n* quittance *nf*

**quorate** *adj* (meeting) (une réunion) où le quorum est atteint

**quorum** *n* quorum *nm* **quorum of creditors** quorum de créanciers *nm*

**quota** *n* quota *nm*, contingent *nm* **quota agreement** accord contingentaire *nm* **quota buying** quota d'achat *nm* **import quota** quota d'importation *nm* **sales quota** quota de vente *nm* **quota sampling** sondage par quota *nm* **quota system** système de contingentement *nm*

**quotation** *n* (price) devis *nm*

**quoted** *adj* **quoted company** société cotée en bourse *nf* **quoted investment** investissement coté en bourse *nm* **quoted share, quoted stock** (US) valeur cotée en bourse *nf*

**racket** *n* racket *nm*, escroquerie *nf*

**racketeer** *n* racketteur *nm*

**racketeering** *n* racket *nm*

**rag** *n* torchon *nm* **the rag trade** (informal) la confection *nm*

**rail** *n* **by rail** en train

**railway, railroad** (US) *n* chemin de fer *nm*, réseau ferroviaire *nm*

**raise** *vb* (price, interest rate) augmenter *vb*, majorer *vb* (capital, loan) se procurer (des fonds) *vb*, émettre (un emprunt) *vb*

**RAM (random access memory)** *abbr* (DP) RAM *abbr nf*

**random 1.** *adj* **random selection** tirage au sort *nm* **2.** *n* **at random** au hasard

**range** *n* (of products) gamme de produits *nf*

**rate** *n* **base rate** taux de base **rate of exchange** taux de change *nm* **rate of expansion** taux d'expansion *nm* **rate of growth** taux de croissance *nm* **rate of inflation** taux d'inflation *nm* **rate of interest** taux d'intérêt *nm* **rate of investment** taux d'investissement *nm* **rate of return** taux de rendement *nm* **rates** (tax) taxe foncière *nf*, impôts locaux *nmpl*

**ratification** *n* ratification *nf*

**ratify** *vb* ratifier *vb*

**ratio** *n* ratio *nm*, coefficient *nm*, indice *nm*

**rationale** *n* raisonnement *nm*, exposé raisonné *nm*

**rationalization** *n* rationalisation *nf*

**rationalize** *vb* justifier *vb*, rationaliser *vb*

**raw** *adj* (inexperienced) inexpérimenté *adj* (unprocessed) brut *adj*

**re** *prep* re
**re-elect** *vb* réélire *vb*
**re-election** *n* réélection *nf*
**ready** *adj* prêt *adj* **ready for despatch** prêt à expédier
**real** *adj* réel *adj* **real estate** immobilier *nm* **real price** prix réel *nm* **real time** temps réel *nm* **real value** valeur effective *nf* **real wages** salaire réel *nm*
**realization** *n* **realization of assets** réalisation d'actifs *nf*
**realize** *vb* (profit) réaliser (des bénéfices) *vb*
**reallocate** *vb* (funds) réattribuer *vb*
**reallocation** *n* (of funds) réaffectation *nf*
**realtor (US)** *n* agent immobilier *nm*
**reappoint** *vb* renommer *nf*
**reappointment** *n* renomination *nf*
**reasonable** *adj* (price) raisonnable *adj*
**rebate** *n* rabais *nm*, remboursement *nm* **to grant a rebate** accorder un rabais, faire une ristourne
**receipt** *n* **to acknowledge receipt** accuser réception de **to issue a receipt** faire un reçu
**receive** *vb* recevoir *vb*
**receiver, administrator** (US) *n* (bankruptcy) liquidateur judiciaire *nm*
**recession** *n* récession *nf*
**recipient** *n* destinataire *nm*, bénéficiaire *nm*
**reciprocal** *adj* réciproque *adj*
**reclaimable** *adj* (materials) qui peut être réclamé, qui peut être récupéré
**recommend** *vb* recommander *vb*
**recommendation** *n* recommandation *nf*
**recompense** *n* récompense *nf*, dédommagement *nm*
**record** *n* rapport *nm*, registre *nm* **according to our records** d'après votre dossier *nm*
**recover** *vb* **to recover money from sb** se faire rembourser *vb*
**recovery** *n* (of debt) recouvrement *nm* (economic) redressement *nm*, rétablissement *nm*
**recruit** *vb* recruter *vb*
**recruitment** *n* recrutement *nm*, embauche *nf* **recruitment campaign** une campagne de recrutement
**recyclable** *adj* recyclable *adj*
**recycle** *vb* recycler *vb*, récupérer *vb*
**red** *adj* rouge *adj* **red tape** paperasserie *nf* **to be in the red** être à découvert, être dans le rouge
**redeem** *vb* rembourser *vb*, amortir *vb*
**redeemable** *adj* rachetable *adj*, amortissable *adj* **redeemable bond** une obligation remboursable.
**redemption** *n* amortissement *nm*, remboursement *nm* **redemption fund** caisse d'amortissement *nf*
**redirect** *vb* (mail) faire suivre *vb*, réexpédier *vb*
**reduce** *vb* (prices) baisser (les prix) (taxes) diminuer (les impôts)
**reduced** *adj* réduit *adj* **at a greatly reduced price** à un prix vraiment réduit
**reduction** *n* réduction *nf*
**redundancy** *n* licenciement *nm*
**redundant** *adj* licencié *adj*, au chômage *adj* **to make sb redundant** licencier qn
**refer** *vb* **we refer to our letter of...** Suite à notre lettre du... **we refer you to our head office** Nous vous prions de vous adresser à notre siège social
**referee** *n* personne qui fournit des références *nf* **to act as referee** fournir des références
**reference** *n* mention *nf*, références *nfpl* **credit reference** références bancaires *nfpl* **reference number** numéro de référence *nm* **to take up a reference** prendre des renseignements sur quelqu'un **with reference to** suite à
**referendum** *n* référendum *nm*
**reflation** *n* relance *nf*
**reflationary** *adj* de relance *adj*
**reform** *n* réforme *nf* **currency reform** une réforme monétaire
**refund 1.** *n* remboursement *nm* **2.** *vb* rembourser *vb*
**refundable** *adj* remboursable *adj*
**refurbish** *vb* rénover *vb*
**refurbishment** *n* rénovation *nf*
**refusal** *n* refus *nm*
**refuse** *vb* **to refuse a claim** rejeter une réclamation *vb* **to refuse goods** refuser des marchandises *vb* **to refuse payment** refuser un règlement
**regard** *n* **with regard to...** en ce qui concerne
**regarding** *prep* en ce qui concerne, quant à
**regional** *adj* régional *adj* **regional office** bureau local, agence locale
**register** *n* liste *nf*, registre *nm*
**registered** *adj* inscrit *adj*, immatriculé *adj*, recensé **registered bond** contrat nominatif *nm*, obligation nominative *nf* **registered capital** capital social *nm* **registered company** Société inscrite au registre du commerce *nf* **registered letter** lettre recommandée *nf* **registered mail** courrier recommandé *nm* **registered office** siège social *nm* **registered share** action nominale *nf* **registered trademark** marque déposée *nf*
**regret** *vb* **we regret to inform you that...** nous avons le regret de vous informer que
**regular** *adj* régulier *adj*, ordinaire *adj* **regular customer** client fidèle *nm*
**regulation** *n* règlement *nm*, arrêté *nm* **according to the regulations** si l'on considère les règlements
**reimburse** *vb* rembourser *vb*
**reimbursement** *n* remboursement *nm*
**reimport** *vb* réimporter *vb*
**reimportation** *n* réimportation *nf*
**reinsurance** *n* réassurance *nf*
**reinsure** *vb* réassurer *vb*

**reject** vb (goods) refuser des marchandises vb

**relations** npl **business relations** relations d'affaires nfpl **industrial relations** relations patronat-syndicats nfpl

**relationship** n **working relationship** relations professionnelles nfpl

**relax** vb (restrictions) assouplir vb, alléger vb

**relevant** adj pertinent adj

**reliability** n fiabilité nf

**reliable** adj fiable adj, digne de confiance adj

**relocate** vb réimplanter vb, se réimplanter vb

**relocation** n réimplantation nf

**remaining** adj (sum) restant adj, qui reste

**reminder** n rappel nm, avertissement nm

**remittance** n remise nf, versement nm **remittance advice** avis de versement nm

**remunerate** vb rémunérer vb

**remuneration** n rémunération nf

**renew** vb (policy, contract) renouveler vb, reconduire vb

**renewable** adj renouvelable adj, reconductible adj

**rent** 1. n loyer nm, location nf 2. vb (house, office) louer vb, prendre en location vb

**rental** n loyer nm, prix de location nm

**repair** 1. n **costs of repair** le coût des réparations 2. vb réparer vb

**reparation** n réparation nf

**repatriation** n rapatriement nm

**repay** vb rembourser vb

**repayment** n (of loan) remboursement nm

**repeat** adj **repeat order** commande renouvelée nf

**replace** vb remplacer vb

**replacement** n (person) remplaçant(e) nm(f)

**reply** n **in reply to your letter of...** en réponse à votre lettre du...

**report** n rapport nm, compte-rendu nm **annual report** rapport annuel nm **to draw up a report** rédiger un rapport **to submit/ present a report** soumettre/présenter un rapport

**repossess** vb reprendre possession de vb

**repossession** n reprise de possession nf

**representative** n représentant nm **area representative** représentant régional **sales representative** représentant de commerce

**repudiate** vb (contract) rejeter vb, refuser vb

**reputation** n réputation nf **to enjoy a good reputation** avoir une bonne réputation

**request** n demande nf **request for payment** demander un règlement

**requirement** n besoin nm, exigence nf **in accordance with your requirements** selon vos besoins **it is a requirement of the contract that...** il est stipulé dans le contrat que...

**resale** n revente nf

**rescind** vb annuler vb, abroger vb, résilier vb

**research** n recherche nf **research and development (R&D)** recherche et développement **market research** étude de marché nf

**reservation** n restriction nf, réservation nf **to make a reservation** faire une réservation

**reserve** 1. adj **reserve currency** monnaie de réserve **reserve stock** stock de réserve 2. n **currency reserve** réserve en devises nf **to hold sth in reserve** garder qch en réserve 3. vb réserver vb

**residual** adj restant adj, résiduel adj

**resign** vb démissioner vb

**resignation** n démission nf **to hand in one's resignation** donner sa démission

**resolution** n (decision) résolution nf **to make a resolution** prendre une résolution

**resolve** vb (sort out) résoudre (un problème) vb **to resolve to do sth** prendre la résolution de faire qch

**resort to** vb (have recourse) avoir recours à vb

**resources** npl ressources nfpl

**respect** n **in respect of...** à l'égard de

**response** n **in response to...** en réponse à

**responsibility** n **to take responsibility for sth** prendre la responsabilité de

**responsible** adj responsable adj

**restrict** vb restreindre vb, limiter vb

**restriction** n restriction nf, limitation nf **to impose restrictions on** imposer des restrictions à

**restrictive** adj restrictif adj **restrictive practices** pratiques commerciales restrictives nfpl

**restructure** vb restructurer vb

**retail** adj **retail outlet** point de vente nm **retail price** prix de vente au détail nm **retail sales tax** imposition sur les ventes au détail nf **retail trade** commerce de détail nm

**retailer** n détaillant, -e nm,f

**retain** vb garder vb, conserver vb

**retention** n conservation nf, maintien nm **retention of title** réserve de propriété

**retire** vb prendre sa retraite vb

**retirement** n retraite nf, remboursement nm **to take early retirement** retraite anticipée nf, pré-retraite nf

**retrain** vb reconvertir vb

**retraining** n recyclage nm, reconversion nf **retraining programme, retraining program** (US) stage de reconversion

**return** n retour nm **in return** en échange **return on capital** rendement des capitaux investis **return on equity** rendement des fonds propres **return on investment** retour sur investissements **return on sales** marge commerciale

**returnable** adj (deposit) consigné adj

**revaluation** n (of currency) réévaluation nf

**revalue** vb (currency) réévaluer vb

**revenue** n revenu nm

**reverse** vb renverser vb, retourner vb

**revert** vb revenir (à) vb

**revert to** vb revenir à vb

**revise** vb revoir vb, modifier vb, réviser vb

**revocable** adj **revocable letter of credit** lettre de crédit révocable

**revoke** *vb* (offer) annuler *vb* (licence) révoquer *vb*

**right** *n* droit *nm* **right of recourse** droit de recours *nm* **right of way** droit de passage *nm*, priorité *nf* **the right to do sth** le droit de faire qch *nm* **the right to sth** droit à qch *nm*

**rights** *npl* **rights issue** émission de droits de souscription *nf* **sole rights** droits exclusifs *nmpl*

**rise, raise** (US) **1.** *n* (earnings, sales, prices) augmentation *nf*, hausse *nf*, progression *nf* (bank rate) relèvement *nm* (unemployment) montée (du chômage) *nf* **2.** *vb* monter *vb*

**risk** *n* risque *nm* **all-risks insurance** assurance tous risques *nf* **risk analysis** analyse des risques *nf* **risk assessment** évaluation des risques *nf* **at the buyer's risk** au risque du client **risk capital** capital risque *nm* **risk management** gestion des risques *nf* **the policy covers the following risks...** cette assurance couvre les risques suivants

**road** *n* **by road** par transport routier **road haulage** transports routiers *nmpl* **road haulage company** compagnie de transports routiers *nf* **road traffic** circulation routière *nf* **road transport** transport routier *nm*

**ROM (read only memory)** *n* ROM

**Rome** *n* **the Treaty of Rome** le Traité de Rome *nm*

**room** *n* **room for manoeuvre** marge de manoeuvre *nf*

**royal** *adj* **the Royal Mint (GB)** la Monnaie Royale *nf*

**RSVP (répondez s'il vous plaît)** *abbr* RSVP (répondez s'il vous plaît)

**run** *vb* (manage) diriger *vb* **to run low** (stocks) s'épuiser *vb*

**run down** *vb* (stocks) épuiser *vb*

**running** *n* **running costs** frais de fonctionnement *nmpl*

**rush** *adj* **rush hour** heures de pointe *nfpl* **rush job** travail d'urgence *nm* **rush order** commande urgente *nf*

**sack\*, fire\*** (US) *vb* licencier *nm*

**safe** *adj* sûr *adj*

**safety** *n* sécurité *nf* **safety officer** responsable de la sécurité *nm*

**salary** *n* salaire *nm* **salary scale** échelle des salaires *nf*

**sale** *n* vente *nf* **closing-down sale, closing-out sale** (US) soldes de fermeture *nmpl* **sales campaign** campagne de vente *nf* **sales conference** réunion de vendeurs *nf* **sales department** service commercial *nm*, service des ventes *nm* **export sales** ventes à l'exportation *nfpl* **sales figures** chiffre des ventes *nmpl* **sales forecast** prévisions des ventes *nfpl* **home sales** ventes sur le marché intérieur *nfpl* **sales ledger** grand livre des ventes *nm* **sales management** direction commerciale *nf*

**salesperson** *n* vendeur, -euse *nm,f*

**salvage** *vb* récupérer *vb*

**sample 1.** *n* échantillon *nm* **2.** *vb* sonder *vb*

**sampling** *n* échantillonnage *nm*

**sanction** *n* **trade sanctions** sanctions commerciales *nfpl*

**savings** *npl* économies *nfpl*, épargne *nf* **savings bank** caisse d'épargne *nf*

**scab\*** *n* jaune *nm*

**scale** *n* échelle *nf*

**scarcity** *n* pénurie *nf*

**schedule 1.** *n* programme *nm* **2.** *vb* programmer *vb*

**scheme** *n* **pension scheme** régime de retraite *nm* **recovery scheme** plan de redressement *nm*

**scrap** *n* (metal) ferraille *nf*

**scrip** *n* certificat d'obligation *nm*

**SDRs (special drawing rights)** *abbr* DTS (droits de tirage spéciaux) *nmpl*

**sea** *n* mer *nf* **by sea** par bateau, par mer **sea freight** transport maritime

**seal 1.** *n* sceau *nm* **2.** *vb* sceller *vb*

**sealed** *adj* **sealed bid** soumission cachetée *nf*

**season** *n* saison *nf* **high season** haute saison *nf* **low season** basse saison *nf*

**seasonal** *adj* saisonnier *adj*

**SEC (Securities and Exchange Commission) (GB)** *abbr* Commission des opérations de Bourse (COB) *nf*

**secondary** *adj* secondaire *adj* **secondary industry** le secteur secondaire *nm* **secondary market** marché secondaire *nm*

**secondment** *n* détachement *nm*

**secretary** *n* secrétaire *nmf* **executive secretary** secrétaire de direction *nmf*

**sector** *n* secteur *nm* **primary sector** secteur primaire *nm* **secondary sector** secteur secondaire *nm* **tertiary sector** secteur tertiaire *nm*

**secure** *adj* sûr *adj*

**secured** *adj* garanti *adj* **secured loan** prêt garanti *nm*

**securities** *npl* titres *nmpl* **gilt-edged securities** titres d'état *nmpl* **listed securities** titres cotés en Bourse *nmpl* **unlisted securities** valeurs du marché hors-cote *nfpl*

**security** *n* sécurité *nf* **Social Security (GB)** Sécurité sociale *nf*

**self-assessment** *n* auto-évaluation *nf*

**self-employed** *adj* (travailleur) indépendant *adj*

**self-financing** *adj* autofinancé *adj*

**self-management** *n* autogestion *nf*

**self-sufficient** *adj* autosuffisant *adj*

**sell 1.** *n* **hard sell** vente agressive *nf* **soft sell** vente discrète *nf* **2.** *vb* vendre *vb* **to sell sth at auction** vendre qch aux enchères *vb* **to sell sth in bulk** vendre en vrac *vb* **to sell sth on credit** vendre qch à crédit *vb* **to sell sth retail** vendre qch au détail *vb* **this article sells well** cet article se vend bien **to sell sth**

**wholesale** vendre qch en gros *vb*
**sell off** *vb* liquider *vb*, brader *vb*
**sell up** *vb* liquider *vb*
**seller** *n* vendeur, -euse *nm,f*
**semi-skilled** *adj* spécialisé *adj* **semi-skilled worker** ouvrier, -ère spécialisé, -e *nm,f*
**send** *vb* envoyer *vb*
**send back** *vb* renvoyer *vb*
**sendee** *n* destinataire *nm*
**sender** *n* expéditeur *nm*
**senior** *adj* aîné *adj* **senior management** les cadres supérieurs *nmpl*
**seniority** *n* ancienneté *nf*
**service** *n* **after-sales service** service après-vente *nm* **civil service** la fonction publique *nf* **service included** service compris *nm* **service industry** secteur tertiaire *nm* **National Health Service (GB)** la Sécurité Sociale *nf*
**set up** *vb* (company) établir *vb*
**settle** *vb* (dispute, account) régler *vb*
**severance** *n* **severance pay** indemnité de licenciement *nf*
**shady*** *adj* (dealings) louche *adj*, douteux *adj*
**share** 1. *n* part *nf*, action *nf* **a share in the profits** participer aux bénéfices *vb* **market share** part de marché *nf* **ordinary share** action ordinaire *nf* 2. *vb* partager *vb* **to share the responsibilities** partager les responsabilités *vb*
**shareholder** *n* actionnaire *nm*
**shark*** *n* escroc *nm*
**sharp** *adj* **sharp practice** pratique malhonnête *nf*
**shiftwork** *n* travail posté *nm*, travail par équipes *nm* **the three-shift system** les trois huit *nmpl*
**shipbuilding** *n* construction navale *nf*
**shipment** *n* (consignment) expédition *nf*
**shipper** *n* expéditeur *nm*, affréteur *nm*, transporteur *nm*
**shipping** *n* transport maritime *nm* **shipping agent** agent maritime *nm* **shipping broker** courtier maritime *nm* **shipping line** compagnie de navigation *nf*
**shipyard** *n* chantier naval *nm*
**shirker*** *n* tire-au-flanc *nm*, fainéant *nm*
**shoddy*** *adj* de mauvaise qualité
**shop** *n* **shop assistant** employé de magasin *nm* **closed shop** entreprise avec un monopole syndical de l'embauche *nf* **shop steward** délégué d'atelier *nm* **to shut up shop** (informal) fermer boutique *vb* **to talk shop** (informal) parler boutique
**shopping** *n* **shopping centre** centre commercial *nm*
**short** *adj* court *adj* **short delivery** livraison partielle *nf* **to be on short time** être en chômage partiel
**shortage** *n* pénurie *nf*
**show** *n* (exhibition) exposition *nf*
**showroom** *n* salle d'exposition *nf*
**shredder** *n* broyeur *nm*

**shrink** *vb* réduire *vb*
**shrinkage** *n* diminution *nf* **stock shrinkage** freinte de stock *nf*
**shutdown** *n* fermeture *nf*
**shuttle** *n* navette *nf*
**SIB (Securities and Investment Board) (GB)** *abbr* COB (commission des opérations de bourse) *nf*
**sick** *adj* **sick leave** congé de maladie *nm*
**sickness** *n* **sickness benefit** allocation de maladie *nf*
**sight** *n* **sight draft** traite à vue *nf*
**sign** *vb* signer *vb*
**signatory** *n* signataire *nm*
**signature** *n* signature *nf*
**silent** *adj* **silent partner** commanditaire *nm*
**sinking** *adj* **sinking fund** fonds d'amortissement *nm*
**sit-in** *n* (strike) grève sur le tas *nf*
**size** *n* taille *nf*
**skill** *n* technique *nf*
**skilled** *n* (worker) ouvrier, -ère qualifié, -e *nm,f*
**slackness** *n* (laxity) laxisme *nm*
**sliding** *adj* **sliding scale** échelle mobile *nf*
**slogan** *n* slogan *nm*
**slow down** *vb* ralentir *vb*
**slowdown** *n* ralentissement *nm*
**slump** 1. *n* marasme *nm* 2. *vb* s'effondrer *vb*
**slush** *adj* **slush fund** caisse noire *nf*
**small** *adj* petit *adj* **small ads** petites annonces *nfpl* **on a small scale** sur une petite échelle
**smuggle** *vb* passer en fraude *vb*
**society** *n* société *nf* **building society** société d'investissement et de crédit immobilier *nf* **consumer society** société de consommation *nf*
**socio-economic** *adj* socio-économique *adj* **socio-economic categories** catégories socio-professionnelles *nfpl*
**software** *n* logiciel *nm* **software package** logiciel *nm*
**sole** *adj* exclusif *adj* **sole agent** représentant exclusif *nm*, dépositaire exclusif *nm*
**solicitor, lawyer (US)** *n* avocat *nm*, notaire *nm*
**solvency** *n* solvabilité *nf*
**solvent** *adj* solvable *adj*
**source** *n* source *nf*
**sourcing** *n* approvisionnement *nm*
**specialist** *n* specialiste *nm*
**speciality** *n* spécialité *nf*
**specialize** *vb* se spécialiser *vb*
**specification** *n* spécification *nf*
**specify** *vb* préciser *vb*
**speculate** *vb* spéculer *vb*
**speculator** *n* spéculateur *nm*
**spend** *vb* dépenser *vb*
**spending** *n* dépenses *nfpl*
**spendthrift** *adj* dépensier *adj*
**sphere** *n* sphère *nf* **sphere of activity** domaine d'activité *nm*
**spin-off** *n* retombée *nf*

**split 1.** *n* scission *nf* **2.** *vb* diviser *vb*, se diviser *vb*
**spoilage** *n* déchet *nm*
**spoils** *npl* butin *nm*
**spokesperson** *n* porte-parole *nm*
**sponsor** *n* sponsor *nm*
**sponsorship** *n* sponsorisation *nf*
**spot** *adj* **spot cash** argent comptant *nm* **spot market** marché au comptant *nm* **spot price** prix sur place *nm* **spot rate** cours du comptant *nm*
**spread** *vb* (payments) étaler *vb*, échelonner (les paiements) *vb*
**spreadsheet** *n* tableau *nm*
**squander** *vb* dilapider *vb*
**squeeze 1.** *n* **credit squeeze** resserrement du crédit *nm* **2.** *vb* (spending) serrer *vb*
**stable** *adj* (economy) stable *adj*
**staff** *n* personnel *nm*
**staffing** *n* embauche de personnel *nf*
**stage** *n* **in stages** par étapes
**staged** *adj* **staged payments** paiements échelonnés *nmpl*
**stagger** *vb* (holidays) étaler *vb*
**stagnation** *n* stagnation *nf*
**stake** *n* enjeu *nm*
**stakeholder** *n* partie prenante *nf*
**stalemate** *n* impasse *nf*
**standard 1.** *adj* standard *adj*, normal *adj* **standard agreement** contrat type *nm* **2.** *n* **gold standard** étalon or *nm* **standard of living** niveau de vie *nm*
**standardization** *n* standardisation *nf*
**standardize** *vb* standardiser *vb*
**standing** *adj* **standing charges** frais fixes *nmpl* **standing order** ordre de virement permanent *nm*
**staple** *adj* **staple commodities** denrées de base *nfpl*
**start-up** *n* démarrage *nm* **start-up capital** capital initial *nm*
**state** *n* **state-owned enterprise** entreprise publique *nf*
**statement** *n* déclaration *nf* **bank statement** relevé de compte *nm*
**statistics** *n* statistiques *nfpl*
**status** *n* **financial status** situation financière *nf* **status quo** statu quo *nm*
**statute** *n* loi *nf*
**steel** *n* acier *nm* **steel industry** sidérurgie *nf*
**sterling** *n* livre sterling *nf* **sterling area** zone sterling *nf* **sterling balance** balance sterling *nf* **pound sterling** livre sterling *nf*
**stock, inventory** (US) *n* (goods) stock *nm* **stock control** gestion des stocks *nf* **stock exchange** Bourse *nf* **in stock** en stock **stock market** Bourse des valeurs *nf* **out of stock** épuisé *adj* **stocks and shares** valeurs mobilières *nfpl*
**stockbroker** *n* agent de change *nm*
**stockholder** *n* actionnaire *nm*
**stocktaking** *n* inventaire *nm*

**stoppage** *n* (strike) arrêt (de travail) *nm*
**storage** *n* **storage capacity** capacité de stockage *nf* **cold storage plant** entrepôt frigorifique *nm*
**store** *n* (shop) magasin *nm* **chain store** magasin à succursales multiples *nm* **department store** grand magasin *nm*
**stowage** *n* arrimage *nm*
**strategic** *adj* stratégique *adj*
**strategy** *n* stratégie *nf*
**stress** *n* **executive stress** le stress des cadres *nm*
**strike 1.** *n* grève *nf* **strike action** mouvement de grève *nm* **strike ballot** vote pour ou contre la grève *nm* **wildcat strike** grève sauvage *nf* **2.** *vb* faire grève *vb*
**strikebreaker** *n* briseur de grève *nm*, jaune *nm*
**striker** *n* gréviste *nm*
**subcontract** *vb* sous-traiter *vb*
**subcontractor** *n* sous-traitant *nm*
**subordinate** *n* subordonné *nm*
**subscribe** *vb* souscrire *vb*
**subsidiary** *n* filiale *nf*
**subsidize** *vb* subventionner *vb*
**subsidy** *n* subvention *nf* **state subsidy** subvention de l'état *nf*
**suburbs** *npl* la banlieue *nf* **outer suburbs** la grande banlieue *nf*
**supermarket** *n* supermarché *nm*
**supertanker** *n* pétrolier géant *nm*
**supertax** *n* surtaxe *nf*
**supervisor** *n* surveillant *nm*, contremaître *nm*
**supervisory** *adj* **supervisory board** conseil de surveillance *nm*
**supplementary** *adj* supplémentaire *adj*
**supplier** *n* fournisseur *nm*
**supply 1.** *n* provision *nf* **supply and demand** l'offre et la demande *nf* **2.** *vb* approvisionner *vb*, fournir *vb*
**surface** *n* **surface mail** courrier ordinaire *nm*
**surplus** *n* surplus *nm*, excédent *nm* **budget surplus** excédent budgétaire *nm* **trade surplus** excédent commercial *nm*
**surtax** *n* impôt supplémentaire *nm*
**survey** *n* **market research survey** étude de marché *nf*
**swap 1.** *n* troc *nm* **2.** *vb* troquer *vb*
**sweetener\*** *n* (bribe) pot-de-vin *nm*, dessous-de-table *nm*
**swindle\*** *n* escroquerie *nf*
**swindler\*** *n* escroc *nm*
**switchboard** *n* standard *nm* **switchboard operator** standardiste *nmf*
**syndicate** *n* consortium *nm*
**synergy** *n* synergie *nf*
**synthesis** *n* synthèse *nf*
**synthetic** *adj* synthétique *adj*
**system** *n* système *nm* **expert system** système expert *nm* **systems analyst** analyste-programmeur *nm*
**table** *vb* (motion, paper) présenter *vb*

**tabulate** *vb* (data) disposer (des données) en tableau *vb*

**tabulated** *adj* **tabulated data** données disposées en tableau *nfpl*

**tacit** *adj* tacite *adj* **by tacit agreement** par accord tacite

**tactic** *n* tactique *nf* **delaying tactics** manoeuvres dilatoires *nfpl* **selling tactics** tactiques de vente *nfpl*

**tailor** *vb* (adapt) façonner *vb*, adapter *vb*

**take** *vb* prendre *vb* **to take legal action** intenter un procès **to take notes** prendre des notes **to take part in** prendre part à **to take the chair** présider **to take the lead** passer en tête **to take one's time** prendre son temps

**take over** *vb* (company) reprendre *vb*, racheter *vb*

**takeover** *n* rachat *nm*, prise de contrôle *nf*

**takeup** *n* souscription *nf*

**takings** *npl* recettes *nfpl*

**talk 1.** *n* **sales talk** arguments de vente *nmpl*, *baratin *nm* **2.** *vb* **to talk business** parler affaires

**tally 1.** *n* comptage *nm* **2.** *vb* correspondre *vb*

**tally up** *vb* faire le compte *vb*

**tally with** *vb* correspondre à *vb*

**tangible** *adj* **tangible asset** bien corporel *nm*

**tap** *vb* percer *vb* **to tap a market** exploiter un marché *vb*

**target** *n* cible *nf*, objectif *nm* **target date** date prévue *nf*, date limite *nf* **target market** marché visé *nm* **production target** objectif de production *nm* **sales target** objectif de vente *nm* **to set a target** fixer un objectif *vb*

**targeted** *pp* **targeted campaign** une campagne ciblée *nf*

**tariff** *n* tarif *nm*, barème *nm* **tariff barrier** barrière douanière *nf* **tariff negotiations** négociations tarifaires *nfpl* **tariff quota** contingent tarifaire *nm* **tariff reform** réforme des tarifs douaniers *nf* **to raise tariffs** relever les droits de douane *vb*

**task** *n* tâche *nf* **task management** gestion des tâches *nf*

**tax** *n* taxe *nf*, impôt *nm* **after tax** après impôt **tax allowance** abattement fiscal *nm* **before tax** avant impôt **capital gains tax** impôt sur les plus-values *nm* **tax claim** créance fiscale *nf* **tax-deductible** déductible des impôts *adj* **direct tax** impôt direct *nm* **tax-free** exonéré d'impôts *adj* **income tax** impôt sur le revenu *nf* **indirect tax** impôt indirect *nm* **tax liability** montant de l'imposition *nm* **tax rate** taux d'imposition *nm* **to levy taxes** percevoir des impôts *vb* **value-added tax (VAT), sales tax** (US) taxe à la valeur ajoutée (TVA) *nf* **tax year** exercice fiscal *nm*

**taxable** *adj* **taxable income** revenu imposable *nm*

**taxation** *n* imposition *nf* **corporate taxation** impôt sur les sociétés *nm*

**taxpayer** *n* contribuable *nm*

**team** *n* équipe *nf* **research team** équipe de chercheurs *nf*

**technical** *adj* **technical director** directeur technique *nm*

**technician** *n* technicien,-ne *nm,f*

**technique** *n* **sales technique** technique de vente *nf*

**technology** *n* technologie *nf* **information technology** informatique *nf* **technology transfer** transfert de technologie *nm*

**telebanking** *n* opérations bancaires à distance *nfpl*

**telecommunications** *npl* télécommunications *nfpl*

**telecopier** *n* télécopieur *nm*

**telefax** *n* télécopieur *nm*

**telephone** *n* téléphone *nm* **telephone box, telephone booth** (US) cabine téléphonique *nf* **telephone call** appel téléphonique *nm* **telephone directory** annuaire téléphonique *nm* **telephone number** numéro de téléphone *nm*

**teleprocessing** *n* télétraitement *nm*, téléinformatique *nf*

**telesales** *npl* télévente *nf*

**televise** *vb* téléviser *vb*

**teleworking** *n* télétravail *nm*

**telex 1.** *n* télex *nm* **2.** *vb* envoyer un message par télex *vb*

**teller** *n* caissier,-ière *nm,f*, guichetier,-ière *nm,f*

**temporary** *adj* temporaire *adj*, provisoire *adj* **temporary employment** travail temporaire *nm*

**tenant** *n* locataire *nmf*

**tend** *vb* avoir tendance à *vb* **to tend toward** être orienté envers *vb*

**tendency** *n* tendance *nf*, orientation *nf* **market tendencies** évolutions du marché *nfpl*

**tender** *n* soumission *nf* **call for tenders** appel d'offres *nm* **tender offer** offre publique *nf* **tender price** montant de l'adjudication *nm* **sale by tender** vente par soumission *nf* **to lodge a tender** adresser une soumission *vb* **to put sth out for tender** faire un appel d'offre *vb*

**tenderer** *n* soumissionnaire *nm*

**tentative** *adj* **to make a tentative offer** faire une ouverture *vb* **tentative plan** avant-projet *nm*

**tenure** *n* durée *nf*, pèriode *nf* **to have tenure** être titulaire *vb*

**term** *n* **at term** à terme **long term** long terme **medium term** moyen terme **term of office** mandat *nm* **terms and conditions** modalités *nfpl* **short term** court terme **terms of reference** attributions *nfpl* **terms of trade** termes de l'échange *nmpl*

**terminal 1.** *adj* terminal *nm* **terminal bonus** prime de départ *nf* **terminal market** marché à terme *nm* **2.** *n* **air terminal** aérogare *nm*

**computer terminal** terminal d'ordinateur *nm*
**termination** *n* résiliation *nf*, résolution *nf*
  **termination date** date de licenciement *nf*
  **termination of employment** résiliation du contrat de travail *nf*
**tertiary** *adj* **tertiary industry** le secteur tertiaire *nm*
**test** *n* examen *nm*, contrôle *nm* **test case** jugement qui fait jurisprudence *nm* **test data** données d'essai *nfpl* **to put sth to the test** mettre qch à l'épreuve *vb* **to stand the test** résister à *vb*
**test-market** *vb* marché témoin *nm*
**testimonial** *n* certificat *nm*, attestation *nf*
**textile** *n* textile *nm* **textile industry** l'industrie textile *nf*
**theory** *n* **in theory** en théorie
**third** *adj* troisième *adj* **third party** tierce personne *nf* **third-party insurance** assurance au tiers *nf* **the Third World** le Tiers Monde *nm*
**thirty** *adj* trente *adj* **Thirty-Share Index (GB)** indice des principales valeurs industrielles
**thrash out** *vb* (agreement, policy) élaborer *vb*
**three** *adj* trois *adj* **three-way split** division en trois *nf*
**threshold** *n* seuil *nm* **tax threshold** minimum imposable *nm*
**thrive** *vb* prospérer *vb*
**through** *prep* à travers *prep* **to get through to sb** (phone) obtenir la communication avec quelqu'un **to put sb through (to sb)** (phone) passer *vb*
**tick over** *vb* tourner au ralenti *vb*
**ticket** *n* billet *nm* **ticket agency** agence de voyages *nf* **ticket office** guichet de vente des billets *nm* **price ticket** prix du billet *nm* **return ticket, round-trip ticket** (US) billet aller et retour *nm* **season ticket** carte d'abonnement *nf* **single/one-way ticket** (rail/flight) aller simple *nm*
**tide over** *vb* dépanner qn *vb*
**tie up** *vb* (capital) immobiliser *vb*
**tied** *adj* **tied loan** prêt conditionnel *nm*
**tier** *n* niveau *nm*, étage *nm* **two-tier system** structure à deux niveaux *nf*
**tight** *adj* serré *adj* **to be on a tight budget** avoir un budget serré
**time** *n* temps *nm* **time and a half** heures supplementaires payées à 150 pour cent *nfpl* **double time** heures supplémentaires *nfpl* **time frame** durée *nf* **lead time** délai de réapprovisionnement *nm* **time limit** délai *nm* **time management** gestion du temps de travail *nf*
**time-consuming** *adj* qui prend du temps
**time-saving** *adj* qui fait gagner du temps
**timescale** *n* pèriode *nf*, laps de temps *nm*
**timeshare** *n* multipropriété *nf*
**timetable** *n* emploi du temps *nm*
**timing** *n* chronométrage *nm*
**tip** *n* (suggestion) tuyau *nm*,

renseignement *nm* **market tip** tuyau sur le marché *nm*
**title** *n* (to goods) droit de propriété *nm* **title deed** titre de propriété *nm*
**token** *n* jeton *nm*, bon *nm*, coupon *nm* **token payment** paiement symbolique *nm* **token strike** grève symbolique *nf*, grève d'avertissement *nf*
**toll** *n* péage *nm*
**ton** *n* tonne *nf* **metric ton** tonne métrique *nf*
**tone** *n* **dialling tone, dial tone** (US) (phone) tonalité *nf*
**tonnage** *n* tonnage *nm* **bill of tonnage** certificat de tonnage *nm* **gross tonnage** tonnage brut *nm* **net(t) tonnage** tonnage net *nm*
**top** *adj* **top management** hauts dirigeants *nmpl* **top prices** prix maximums *nmpl* **top priority** priorité absolue *nf*
**top-level** *adj* au plus haut niveau
**top-of-the-range** *adj* haut de gamme
**total** 1. *adj* total *adj* **total sales** le total des ventes *nm* 2. *n* somme *nf*, total *nm* **the grand total** la somme totale *nf*
**tough** *adj* dur *adj* **tough competition** forte concurrence *nf*
**tour** *n* **tour of duty** période de service *nf*
**tourism** *n* tourisme *nm*
**tourist** *n* touriste *nmf* **the tourist trade** le tourisme *nm*, l'industrie du tourisme *nf*
**town** *n* ville *nf* **town centre** centre-ville *nm* **town council** conseil municipal *nm* **town hall** mairie *nf* **town planning** urbanisme *nm*
**TQM (Total Quality Management)** *abbr* Contrôle général de la qualité *nm*
**track** *n* trace *nf* **track record** expérience professionnelle *nf* **to be on the right track** être sur la bonne voie
**trade** 1. *adj* **trade agreement** accord commercial *nm* **trade balance** balance commerciale *nf* **trade barrier** barrière douanière *nf* **trade cycle** cycle économique *nm* **trade directory** annuaire du commerce *nm* **trade fair** foire-exposition *nf*, salon professionnel *nm* **trade figures** chiffre d'affaires *nm*, résultats *nmpl* **trade name** raison sociale *nf*, nom de marque *nm* **trade price** prix de gros *nm* **trade restrictions** barrières douanières *nfpl* **trade secret** secret commercial *nm* **trade talks** négociations commerciales *nfpl* **Trade Descriptions Act** Loi qui réprime la publicité mensongère **Trades Union Congress** la confédération des syndicats britanniques **trade union** syndicat *nm* 2. *n* commerce *nm* **balance of trade** le solde commercial *nm* **by trade** de son métier **fair trade** commerce loyale *nm* **foreign trade** commerce extérieur *nm* **retail trade** commerce de détail *nm* **to be in the trade** (informal) être dans la branche **wholesale trade** commerce

de gros *nm* **3.** *vb* avoir des relations commerciales **to trade as** (name) exercer (sous le nom de) *vb* **to trade with sb** avoir des relations commerciales avec qn

**trademark** *n* marque de fabrique *nf* **registered trademark** marque déposée *nf*

**trader** *n* commerçant(e) *nm(f)*

**trading** *adj* **trading area** zone de chalandise *nf* **trading capital** capital de roulement *nm* **trading company** entreprise commerciale *nf* **trading estate** zone industrielle *nf* **trading loss** perte d'exploitation *nf* **trading margin** marge commerciale *nf* **trading nation** nation commerçante *nf* **trading partner** partenaire commercial *nm* **trading standards** normes de conformité *nfpl* **Trading Standards Office (US)** Direction de la concurrence et des prix *nf* **trading year** exercice *nm*

**traffic** *n* **air traffic** trafic aérien *nm* **rail traffic** trafic ferroviaire *nm* **road traffic** circulation routière *nf* **sea traffic** trafic maritime *nm*

**train 1.** *n* **goods train, freight train** (US) train de marchandises *nm* **passenger train** train de voyageurs *nm* **2.** *vb* (staff) former *vb*

**trainee** *n* stagiaire *nmf* **trainee manager** cadre en formation *nm*

**training** *n* formation *nf* **advanced training** stage de perfectionnement *nm* **training centre** centre de formation *nm* **training course** stage de formation *nm*

**transaction** *n* transaction *nf*, négociation *nf* **cash transaction** opération au comptant *nf* **transaction management** gestion transactionnelle *nf*

**transcribe** *vb* transcrire *vb*

**transfer 1.** *adj* **transfer desk** (transport) bureau de transit *nm* **transfer duty** droits de transfert *nmpl* **transfer lounge** (transport) salle de transit *nf* **transfer payments** virements *nmpl* **transfer price** prix de transfert *nm* **transfer tax** droits de mutation *nmpl* **transfer technology** transfert de technologie *nm* **2.** *n* transfert *nm* (ownership) cession de propriété *nf* **bank transfer** virement bancaire *nm* **capital transfer** transmission de capital *nf* **credit transfer** virement *nm* **3.** *vb* (telephone) passer quelqu'un à *vb* (transport) changer d'avion/de train *vb*

**transferable** *adj* transmissible *adj*, cessible *adj*

**transit** *n* transit *nm* **transit goods** transit de marchandises *nm* **in transit** en transit **lost in transit** perte en cours de route *nf* **transit lounge** (transport) salle de correspondance *nf* **transit passenger** (transport) passager en transit *nm*

**transmit** *vb* transmettre *vb*

**transnational** *adj* transnational *adj*

**transport** *n* **transport agent** transitaire *nm* **air transport** transport aérien *nm* **transport**

**company** compagnie de transport *nf* **public transport** transports en commun *nmpl* **rail transport** transport ferroviaire *nm* **road transport** transport routier *nm*

**transportation** *n* transport *nm*

**transship** *vb* transborder *vb*

**travel** *n* **travel agency** agence de voyages *nf* **air travel** les voyages en avion *nmpl* **business travel** voyages d'affaires *nmpl* **travel insurance** assurance voyage *nf*

**traveller, traveler** (US) *n* voyageur *nm* **traveller's cheque, traveler's check** (US) chèque de voyage *nm*

**travelling, traveling** (US) *n* voyages *nmpl*, déplacements *nmpl* **travelling expenses, travel expenses** (US) frais de déplacement *nmpl*

**treasurer** *n* **treasurer check (US)** chèque bancaire *nm* **company treasurer** directeur financier *nm*

**treasury** *n* **Treasury bill** bon du Trésor *nm* **the Treasury** le Trésor *nm* **the Treasury Department (US)** le Ministère des Finances *nm*

**treaty** *n* traité *nm* **commercial treaty** traité commercial *nm* **to make a treaty** conclure un traité *vb*

**trend** *n* tendance *nf*, orientation *nf*, mode *nf* **trend analysis** analyse de la tendance *nf* **current trend** la tendance actuelle *nf* **economic trend** conjoncture *nf* **market trend** physionomie du marché *nf* **price trend** orientation des prix *nf* **to buck a trend** agir à contre-courant *vb* **to set a trend** créer une mode *vb*

**trial** *n* **trial and error** approche par tâtonnements *nf* **trial offer** offre d'essai *nf* **trial period** période d'essai *nf* **to carry out trials** mettre à l'essai *vb*

**tribunal** *n* tribunal *nm* **industrial tribunal** Conseil des prud'hommes *nm*

**trim** *vb* (investment) tailler *vb*, faire des coupes *vb* (workforce) faire des compressions de personnel *vb*

**trimming** *n* compression *nf*, réduction *nf*, dégraissage *nm* **cost trimming** réduction des coûts *nf*

**trip** *n* **business trip** voyage d'affaires *nm* **round trip** voyage aller et retour *nm*

**triplicate** *n* triplicata *nm* **in triplicate** en trois exemplaires

**trust** *n* confiance *nf* **trust agreement** convention de fiducie *nf* **trust company** société d'investissement *nf* **trust estate** patrimoine géré par fidéicommis *nm* **trust fund** fonds en fidéicommis *nmpl* **investment trust** société d'investissement *nf* **to hold sth in trust** administrer par fidéicommis *vb* **to set up a trust** instituer un fidéicommis *vb* **to supply sth on trust** fournir à crédit *vb* **unit trust** société d'investissement à capital variable (SICAV) *nf*

**trustee** *n* fiduciaire *nm* **trustee department** (bank) le service fiduciaire de la banque *nm*
**trusteeship** *n* fidéicommis *nm*
**try out** *vb* essayer *vb*
**turn** *n* **turn of the market** (Stock Exchange) écart entre le cours vendeur et le cours acheteur *nm*
**turn down** *vb* (offer) refuser *vb*, rejeter *vb*
**turn on** *vb* (machine) mettre en marche *vb*, faire démarrer *vb*
**turn out** *vb* (end) s'avérer *vb*, se révéler *vb*
**turn over** *vb* réaliser un chiffre d'affaires *vb*
**turn round, turn around** (US) *vb* (company) redresser *vb*, rétablir *vb*
**turnabout** *n* volteface *nf*
**turning** *adj* **turning point** tournant *nm*, point critique *nm*
**turnover** *n* chiffre d'affaires *nm* **capital turnover** rotation du capital *nf* **turnover rate** vitesse de rotation *nf* **turnover ratio** ratio chiffre d'affaires-immobilisations *nm* **turnover tax** impôt sur le chiffre d'affaires *nm*
**twenty-four** *adj* **twenty-four-hour service** service vingt-quatre heures sur vingt-quatre *nm*
**two** *adj* deux *adj* **two-speed** à deux vitesses **two-tier** à deux étages **two-way** à double sens
**tycoon** *n* magnat *nm*, brasseur d'affaires *nm*
**type 1.** *n* type *nm* **bold type** en caractères gras **italic type** en italique **large type** en gros caractères **small type** en petits caractères **2.** *vb* taper *vb*, dactylographier *vb*
**typewriter** *n* machine à écrire *nf*
**typing** *n* dactylographie *nf* **typing error** faute de frappe *nf*
**typist** *n* dactylographe *nmf*
**ultimo** *adj* du mois dernier *adv*
**unanimous** *adj* unanime *adj*
**uncleared** *adj* (customs) non dédouané *adj* (cheque) non compensé *adj*
**unconditional** *adj* sans condition, sans réserve
**unconfirmed** *adj* non confirmé *adj*
**undeclared** *adj* (goods) non dédouané *adj*, non déclaré *adj*
**undercapitalized** *adj* sous-capitalisé *adj*
**undercharge** *vb* ne pas faire payer assez à qn *vb*
**undercut** *vb* vendre moins cher que *vb*
**underdeveloped** *adj* **underdeveloped country** pays sous-développé *nm*, pays en voie de développement *nm*
**underemployed** *adj* sous-employé *adj*, sous-exploité *adj*
**underinsured** *adj* sous-assuré *adj*
**underpay** *vb* sous-payer *vb*
**underpayment** *n* sous-paiement *nm*
**undersell** *vb* vendre moins cher que *vb*
**understanding** *n* accord *nm*, entente *nf*
**undersubscribed** *adj* non entièrement souscrit *adj*

**undertake** *vb* entreprendre *vb*, se charger de *vb*
**undertaking** *n* engagement *nm*, promesse *nf*
**undervalue** *vb* sous-estimer *vb*, sous évaluer *vb*
**underwrite** *vb* (risk) garantir *vb*, assurer *vb*
**underwriter** *n* garant *nm*, réassureur *nm*
**undischarged** *adj* (bankrupt) non réhabilité *adj*
**unearned** *adj* **unearned income** revenu du capital *nm*, rente *nf*
**unemployed** *adj* sans emploi *adj*, au chômage *adj*
**unemployment** *n* chômage *nm* **unemployment benefit** indemnité de chômage *nf* **unemployment insurance** assurance chômage *nf* **level of unemployment** nombre de chômeurs *nm* **rate of unemployment** taux de chômage *nm*
**unexpected** *adj* inattendu *adj*, inopiné *adj*
**unfair** *adj* **unfair dismissal** licenciement abusif *nm*
**unforeseen** *adj* **unforeseen circumstances** circonstances imprévues *nfpl*
**unification** *n* unification *nf*
**unilateral** *adj* (contract) unilatéral *adj*
**uninsurable** *adj* non assurable *adj*
**union** *n* syndicat *nm* **union member** syndiqué, -e *nm,f* **union representative** délégué syndical *nm* **trade union, labor union** (US) syndicat *nm*
**unit** *n* **unit cost** prix de revient unitaire *nm* **unit of production** unité de production *nf* **unit price** prix unitaire *nm* **unit trust** société d'investissement à capital variable (SICAV) *nf*
**united** *adj* uni *adj* **United Nations** Nations Unies *nfpl*
**unlimited** *adj* **unlimited company** société à responsabilité illimitée *nf* **unlimited credit** crédit illimité *nm* **unlimited liability** responsabilité illimitée *nf*
**unload** *vb* décharger *vb*
**unmarketable** *adj* invendable *adj*
**unofficial** *adj* **unofficial strike** grève sauvage *nf*
**unpack** *vb* déballer *vb*
**unpaid** *adj* **unpaid balance** solde non acquitté *nm* **unpaid bill** facture impayée *nf* **unpaid cheque** chèque non débité *nm*
**unprofessional** *adj* contraire au code de conduite de la profession
**unprofitable** *adj* peu rentable *adj*
**unsaleable** *adj* invendable *adj*
**unsatisfactory** *adj* peu satisfaisant *adj*
**unsecured** *adj* **unsecured bond** obligation non garantie *nf* **unsecured credit** non garanti *adj*
**unskilled** *adj* **unskilled worker** ouvrier, -ère non qualifié, -e *nm,f*
**unsold** *adj* invendu *adj*
**unsolicited** *adj* **unsolicited offer** offre spontanée *nf*

**up-to-date** *adj* récent *adj*, à jour *adj* **to bring sth up-to-date** actualiser *vb*, mettre à jour *vb*

**update** *vb* (records) actualiser *vb*

**upgrade** *vb* améliorer *vb*, moderniser *vb*

**upswing** *n* redressement *nm*, reprise *nf*

**upturn** *n* reprise *nf*, amélioration *nf*

**upward** *adj*, *adv* à la hausse *adj*, *adv*

**urban** *adj* **urban renewal** réaménagement des zones urbaines *nm* **urban sprawl** extension urbaine *nf*

**urgency** *n* **a matter of urgency** quelque chose d'urgent

**urgent** *adj* urgent *adj*

**urgently** *adv* sans délai *adv*, de toute urgence *adv*

**usage** *n* **intensive usage** utilisation intensive *nf*

**use** *n* emploi *nm*, utilisation *nf* **to make use of sth** utiliser quelque chose *vb*

**user-friendly** *adj* convivial *adj*, facile à utiliser *adj*

**usury** *n* usure *nf*

**utility** *n* utilité *nf* **marginal utility** utilité marginale *nf* **public utility** service public *nm*

**utilization** *n* utilisation *nf*, exploitation *nf*

**utilize** *vb* utiliser *vb*

**vacancy** *n* vacance *nf*, poste vacant *nm*

**vacant** *adj* vacant *adj*, libre *adj*, à pourvoir *adj*

**valid** *adj* valide *adj*, valable *adj*

**validate** *vb* valider *vb*

**validity** *n* validité *nf*

**valuable** *adj* de valeur *adj*, précieux *adj*

**valuation** *n* évaluation *nf*, estimation *nf*

**value** *n* valeur *nf*, prix *nm* **face value** valeur nominale *nf* **market value** valeur marchande *nf* **to gain value** prendre de la valeur *vb* **to get value for one's money** en avoir pour son argent **to lose value** perdre de la valeur *vb*

**variable** *adj* variable *adj* **variable costs** coûts variables *nmpl* **variable rate** taux variable *nm*

**variance** *n* écart *nm* **budget variance** écart budgétaire *nm*

**VAT (value added tax)** *abbr* T.V.A. (Taxe sur la valeur ajoutée) *nf*

**vendee** *n* acheteur *nm*, acquéreur *nm*

**vending machine** *n* distributeur automatique *nm*

**vendor** *n* vendeur(-euse) *nm(f)* **vendor capital** capital vendeur *nm* **joint vendor** vendeurs associés *nmpl*

**verbatim** *adv* textuellement *adv*, mot pour mot *adv*

**vertical** *n* **vertical integration** intégration verticale *nf*

**vested** *adj* **vested interests** intérêts personnels *nmpl* **vested rights** droits acquis *nmpl*

**veto** 1. *n* veto *nm* 2. *vb* opposer son veto à *vb*

**viability** *n* viabilité *nf*

**video** *n* magnétoscope *nm* **video facilities** équipement vidéo *m*

**viewer** *n* spectateur(trice) *nm(f)*

**VIP (very important person)** *n* VIP *m*, personnage de marque *nm*

**visa** *n* visa *nm*

**visible** *adj* visible *adj* **visible exports** exportations visibles *nfpl*

**visit** 1. *n* visite *nf*, séjour *nm* 2. *vb* rendre visite *vb*, inspecter *vb*, visiter *vb*

**visitor** *n* visiteur, -euse *nm,f*

**visual** *adj* **visual display unit (VDU)** écran de visualisation *nm* **visual telephone** visiophone *nm*

**vocational** *adj* professionnel *adj*

**volatile** *adj* (prices) erratique *adj*

**volume** *n* **volume discount** réduction sur quantité *nf* **trading volume** volume des transactions *nm*

**voluntary** *adj* **to go into voluntary liquidation** déposer son bilan *vb* **voluntary wage restraint** limitation volontaire des salaires *nf*

**vote** 1. *n* (single vote) voix *nf* (action) vote *nm* **vote of no confidence** motion de censure *nf* **vote of thanks** motion de remerciements *nf* 2. *vb* voter *vb*

**voting** *adj* **voting right** droit de vote *nm*

**voucher** *n* bon *nm*

**wage** 1. *adj* **wage demand** revendication salariale *nf* **wage earner** salarié(e) *nm(f)* **wage increase** augmentation de salaire *nf* **wage negotiations** négociations salariales *nfpl* **wage packet, salary package** (US) enveloppe de paye *nf* **wage policy** politique salariale *nf* **wage restraint** limitation des salaires *nf* **wage rise** augmentation de salaire *nf* **wage(s) agreement** convention salariale *nf* **wage(s) bill** masse salariale *nf* **wage scale** grille des salaires *nf* **wage(s) claim** revendication salariale *nf* **wage(s) freeze** blocage des salaires *nm* **wage(s) settlement** accord salarial *nm* 2. *n* salaire *nm*, paie *nf*, paye *nf* **average wage** salaire moyen *nm* **minimum wage** salaire minimum *nm* **net(t) wage** salaire net *nm* **real wage** salaire réel *nm* **starting wage** salaire de départ *nm* 3. *vb* **to wage a campaign** mener une campagne *vb*

**waiting** *n* attente *nf* **waiting list** liste d'attente *nf*

**waive** *vb* renoncer à *vb*, abandonner *vb*

**waiver** *n* abandon *nm*, renonciation *nf* **waiver clause** clause d'abandon *nf*

**wall** *n* mur *nm* **tariff wall** barrière tarifaire *nf* **to go to the wall** perdre la partie *vb* **Wall Street (US)** Wall Street, la Bourse de New-York

**war** *n* guerre *nf* **price war** guerre des prix *nf* **trade war** guerre commerciale *nf*

**warehouse** *n* entrepôt *nm* **bonded warehouse** entrepôt en douane *nm*

**warehousing** *n* entreposage *nm*,

emmagasinage *nm*
**wares** *npl* marchandises *nfpl*
**warn** *vb* prévenir *vb*, avertir *vb* **to warn sb against doing sth** déconseiller à quelqu'un de faire quelque chose
**warning** *n* **due warning** délai prévu *nm*
**warning sign** panneau avertisseur *nm*
**without warning** sans prévenir, à l'impro- viste
**warrant 1.** *n* mandat *nm*, bon de souscription *nm* **warrant for payment** ordonnance de paiement *nf* **2.** *vb* garantir *vb*, légitimer *vb*
**warranty** *n* garantie *nf* **under warranty** sous garantie
**wastage** *n* gaspillage *nm* **wastage rate** taux de pertes *nm*
**waste 1.** *adj* **waste products** déchets de fabrication *nmpl* **2.** *n* gaspillage *nm*, perte *nf* **industrial waste** déchets industriels *nmpl* **waste of time** perte de temps *nf* **to go to waste** être gaspillé **3.** *vb* gaspiller *vb*
**wasting** *adj* **wasting asset** actif défectible *nm*, actif consommable *nm*
**watch** *vb* regarder *vb*, consulter *vb* **to watch developments** suivre de près les dévelop- pements
**watchdog** *n* (fig.) gardien *nm* **watchdog committee** comité de vigilance *nm*
**water down** *vb* édulcorer *vb*, atténuer *vb*
**watered** *adj* gonflé *adj*, dilué *adj* **watered capital** capital dilué *nm* **watered stock** actions gonflées *nfpl*
**watertight** *adj* (fig.) étanche *adj*
**wave** *n* (of mergers, takeovers) vague *nf*
**wavelength** *n* longueur d'onde *nf* **to be on the same wavelength** être sur la même longueur d'onde
**weaken** *vb* (market) fléchir *vb*
**wealth** *n* richesse *nf* **national wealth** patri- moine national *nm* **wealth tax** impôt sur la fortune *m*
**week** *n* semaine *nf* **twice a week** deux fois par semaine **working week** semaine de travail *nf*
**weekly** *adj* hebdomadaire *adj* **weekly wages** salaire hebdomadaire *nm*
**weigh** *vb* **to weigh the pros and cons** peser le pour et le contre
**weight** *n* poids *nm* **dead weight** poids mort *nm* **excess weight** excédent de poids *nm* **gross weight** poids brut *nm* **net weight** poids net *nm* **weights and measures** poids et mesures *nmpl & nfpl*
**weighted** *adj* pondéré *adj* **weighted average** moyenne pondérée *nf* **weighted index** indice pondéré *nm*
**weighting** *n* indemnité *nf*, allocation *nf*
**weighty** *adj* pesant *adj*, lourd *adj*
**welfare 1.** *adj* **welfare benefits** avantages sociaux *nmpl* **welfare state** l'état providence *nm* **2.** *n* (well-being) bien-

être *nm*
**well-advised** *adj* **you would be well-advised to** vous auriez tout intérêt à
**well-informed** *adj* bien informé *adj*, bien renseigné *adj*
**well-known** *adj* bien connu *adj*
**well-made** *adj* bien fait *adj*
**well-paid** *adj* bien payé *adj*, bien rémunéré *adj*
**well-tried** *adj* qui a fait ses preuves *adj*, éprouvé *adj*
**WEU (Western European Union)** *abbr* l'Union de l'Europe Occidentale *nf*
**white** *adj* blanc *adj* **white-collar worker** employé de bureau *nm*, col blanc *nm*
**wholesale** *n* **at/by wholesale** en gros *adj* **wholesale price** prix de gros *nm* **wholesale trade** commerce de gros *nm*
**wholesaler** *n* grossiste *nm*
**wholly** *adv* **wholly-owned subsidiary** filiale à cent pour cent *nf*
**wide-ranging** *adj* de grande envergure *adj*
**will** *n* (last will and testament) testament *nm* volonté *nf*
**win** *vb* **win customers** se faire une clientèle **to win support** gagner du soutien *vb*
**wind up** *vb* clôturer *vb*, terminer *vb*
**windfall** *n* aubaine *nf* **windfall profit** bénéfi- ces exceptionnels *nmpl*
**winding-up** *n* clôture *nf*, liquidation *nf* **winding-up arrangements** concordat *nm* **winding-up order** ordonnance de mise en liquidation *nf*
**window** *n* fenêtre *nf*, vitrine *nf* **window of opportunity** occasion *nf*, possibilité *nf*
**withdraw** *vb* **to withdraw an offer** retirer une offre *vb*
**withdrawal** *n* retrait *nm* **withdrawal of funds** retrait de fonds *nm*
**withhold** *vb* (payment, decision) différer *vb*, remettre *vb* **to withhold a document** refuser de communiquer une pièce *vb*
**withstand** *vb* résister *vb*
**witness 1.** *n* témoin *nm* **2.** *vb* être témoin de **to witness a signature** contresigner *vb*
**word** *n* mot *nm* **word processing** traitement de texte *nm* **word processor** machine de traitement de texte *nf* **to give one's word** donner sa parole *vb* **to keep one's word** garder sa parole *vb*
**wording** *n* formulation *nf*, rédaction *nf*
**work 1.** *adj* **work experience** stage de formation *nm* **work permit** permis de travail *nm* **work schedule** emploi du temps *nm* **work sharing** partage du travail *nm* **work study** étude des méthodes de travail *nf* **2.** *n* travail *nm* **casual work** travail temporaire *nm* **day off work** jour de congé *nm* **day's work** une journée de travail *nf* **factory work** travail d'usine *nm* **office work** travail de bureau *nm* **to be in work** avoir du travail *vb* **to be out of work**

être sans emploi *vb*, être au chômage *vb* **to look for work** chercher du travail *vb* **3.** *vb* travailler *vb* **to work to rule** faire la grève du zèle *vb* **to work unsocial hours** travailler en dehors des horaires normaux *vb*, travailler à des heures indues *vb*

**workable** *adj* réalisable *adj*

**workaholic** *n* bourreau de travail *nm*

**workday (US)** *n* jour ouvrable *nm*

**worker** *n* ouvrier, -ère *nm,f*, travailleur, euse *nm,f* **casual worker** travailleur temporaire *nm* **clerical worker** employé de bureau *nm* **worker-director** ouvrier membre du conseil d'administration *nm* **manual worker** travailleur manuel *nm* **worker participation** participation des travailleurs à la gestion de l'entreprise *nf* **skilled worker** ouvrier qualifié *nm*, professionnel *nm* **unskilled worker** ouvrier spécialisé *nm*

**workforce** *n* main-d'oeuvre *nf*, effectif *nm*

**working** *adj* **working agreement** entente *nf*, convention *nf* **working area** zone de travail *nf* **working capital** fonds de roulement *nmpl* **working conditions** conditions de travail *nfpl* **working environment** conditions de travail *nfpl*, environnement de travail *nm* **working hours** heures de travail *nfpl* **working knowledge** rudiments *nmpl* **working language** langue de travail *nf* **working life** vie active *nf* **working majority** majorité suffisante *nf* **working model** modèle réduit *nm*, maquette *nf* **working paper** document de travail *nm* **working party** groupe de travail *nm* **working population** population active *nf* **working week (GB)** semaine de travail *nf*

**workload** *n* charge de travail *nf*

**workmate** *n* camarade de travail *nmf*

**workplace** *n* lieu de travail *nm*

**works** *n* usine *nf* **public works programme (GB)** programme de travaux publics **works committee** comité d'entreprise *nm* **works council** comité d'entreprise *nm* **works manager** directeur d'usine *nm*

**workshop** *n* atelier *nm*

**workweek (US)** *n* semaine de travail *nf*

**world** *n* monde *nm* **the commercial world** le monde du commerce *nm* **world consumption** consommation mondiale *nf* **world exports** exportations mondiales *nfpl* **world fair** exposition universelle *nf* **World Bank** la Banque Mondiale *nf* **World Court** la Cour

internationale de justice *nf*

**worldwide** *adj* mondial *adj*, global *adj*

**worth** *adj* **to be worth** valoir *vb*

**wpm (words per minute)** *abbr* mots à la minute *nmpl*

**wreck 1.** *n* épave *nf* **2.** *vb* briser *vb*, ruiner *vb*, anéantir *vb*

**writ** *n* acte judiciaire *nm* **to issue a writ** assigner quelqu'un (en justice) *vb*

**write down** *vb* (depreciation) amortir *vb*

**write off 1.** *vb* (debts) passer par profits et pertes *vb* (vehicle) être irréparable *vb*, être bon pour la ferraille *vb*

**write-off 1.** *n* passation par pertes et profits *nf*

**wrongful** *adj* **wrongful dismissal** licenciement arbitraire *nm*

**xerox** *vb* photocopier *vb*, faire une photocopie de *vb*

**Xerox (R)** *n* (machine) photocopieur *nm*

**year** *n* **year-end dividend** dividende de fin d'exercice *nm* **year-end inventory** inventaire de fin d'année *nm* **financial year** exercice financier *nm* **fiscal year** année budgétaire *nf* **tax year** exercice fiscal *nm*

**yearly** *adj* **yearly income** revenu annuel *nm*

**yellow** *adj* jaune *adj* **the Yellow pages (R) (GB)** les pages jaunes (de l'annuaire) *nfpl*

**yen** *n* (currency) yen *nm* **yen bond** obligation libellée en yen *nf*

**yield 1.** *n* rendement *nm* **yield curve** courbe de rendement *nf* **yield on shares** rendement des actions *nm* **2.** *vb* produire *vb*, rapporter *vb*

**young** *adj* jeune *adj* **young economy** jeune économie *nf*

**zenith** *n* zénith *nm*, apogée *nf*

**zero** *n* zéro *nm* **zero address** sans adresse **below zero** en dessous de zéro **zero defect** zéro défaut *nm* **zero growth** croissance zéro *nf* **zero hour** le moment critique *nm*, le moment décisif *nm* **zero rate/rating** taux zéro *nm* **zero-rate taxation** fiscalité à taux zéro *nf* **to be zero-rated for VAT** ne pas être assujetti à la TVA

**zip code (US)** *n* code postal *nm*

**zone 1.** *n* **currency zone** zone monétaire *nf* **enterprise zone** zone d'entreprise *nf* **postal zone** zone postale *nf* **time zone** fuseau horaire *nm* **wage zone** zone de salaire *nf* **2.** *vb* diviser en zones *vb*

**zoning** *n* zonage *nm*

# Index

# Index

# Business Correspondence

# Business Practice

# Belgium

# Grammar

# Glossary